DATE DUE

APR 11			
FEB 2 5			

Demco, Inc. 38-293

Literacy, Law, and Social Order

. . .

Literacy, Law, and Social Order

. . .

Edward W. Stevens, Jr.

Northern Illinois University Press

DeKalb, Illinois / 1988

Library of Congress Cataloging-in-Publication Data

Stevens, Edward, 1938-
Literacy, law, and social order / Edward W. Stevens, Jr., p. cm.
Bibliography: p.
Includes index.
ISBN 0-87580-131-5: $28.50
1. Law—United States. 2. Literacy—United States.
3. Sociological jurisprudence. I. Title.
KF380.S74 1987
340' .115—dc 19   87-16016 CIP

To My Parents
Margaret and Edward Stevens

Contents

. . .

Preface

. . .

Within the last decade the number of historical studies of literacy has increased rapidly. Historians have identified and explained trends in levels of literacy and, more recently, attempted to explore more fully the ideological and functional relationships among literacy, education, and broader political and economic ideals. One of the tasks of this work is to analyze the ideological and functional links between literacy and fundamental political/economic ideals as they have been expressed in the American legal system.

The study focuses on the contractual ideal in Anglo-American law, political thought, and economic behavior. In turn, the legal, political, and economic systems become important reference points for understanding the meaning and problems of illiteracy in constitutional democracies. Illiteracy strained both the institutions and persons it affected. I believe these two sides of the coin are analogous to the recurring concern with how individual and society are linked in the liberal ideal. I have attempted to treat both sides so as not to diminish the importance of the basic tension inherent in the liberal ideal. If I have favored one or the other of the symbolic faces, it is probably that of the individual.

The study uses the resources of legal theory and case law to gain a better understanding of the meanings of literacy in specific behavioral contexts. Literacy skills, their levels, and the consequences of their absence are analyzed for individuals as they deal with a broad range of economic and political relationships, for example, contracting, will-making, signing deeds, banking and checking, serving on jury duty, applying for workman's compensation, and voting. It has been possible, using such cases, to assess the function of literacy within specific contexts of behavior, and to observe the responses of judicial and legal authorities to the condition of the illiterate person. Except for cases in which illiteracy was a factor in jury selection, criminal cases are not included. Though large numbers of these are available, they present different legal issues. Most, as far as literacy is concerned, involve the rights to know how one is charged and to have an attorney.

Judicial decisions are first in order of importance as sources. These constitute a significant departure from the usual data used to investigate the meaning and significance of literacy in specific historical contexts. Statute law and administrative rulings cited in court decisions are also used. In some instances, statutes and administrative rulings not cited by the courts are helpful in understanding the decisions themselves. Both recent and period studies of jurisprudence and the sociology of law provide important frameworks for considering the theoretical links among law, literacy, and social ideals.

We know very little about the extent to which courts affected people's daily lives. They heard disputes that parties had brought to litigation and that they agreed to hear. Obviously these were a very small part of all disputes, potential and actual. The facts of a case were particular, but courts attempted to bring them within the confines of precedents and rules of law. Where this was not possible, they made common (judge-made) law. Their judgments were generalized in published and unpublished opinions. Thus courts were always in the background as potential arbitrators of controversy: "Their dispute-resolution function created pressure on the contending parties on both the civil and criminal sides of the docket to adjust their relations by their own immediate bargaining. The judges made themselves felt more by their readiness and their availability in the background than by the direct impact of their activity in deciding cases."[1]

In looking at the problem of illiteracy through the lens of political and legal systems, I am mindful of the division between theory and immediate practicality that is characteristic of the business of these institutions. James Willard Hurst reminds us that "people generally have used law in a narrowly practical way." As a result we should realize that "the values that people wrote into law and more or less implemented through law did not add up to a neatly balanced, conceptually complete pattern of human interests."[2] Because the process of law encompasses a broad range of values that affect social relations, however, it is a valuable tool to understand the situation of the illiterate person and the responses of the system to the problem of illiteracy.

There is no question that the legal system was required to respond to deviance just as the educational system aimed to prevent it. And illiteracy was deviance. In viewing the problem of illiteracy through the legal and political system we learn as much about the limitations and potential of the systems as about illiteracy as a personal attribute. When judges were dealing with illiterate persons they were dealing with the less-than-ideal. In one sense, all the provisions for dealing with illiteracy were exceptions to the rule or at least situations that had to be adjusted to the rules. This was especially true if law was conceived of as a science. The situation of illiteracy never could be interpreted in a fixed way. Illiterate persons forced judges back to the particular, the person, and the thousand shades of content, consent, and rationality found in the less-than-ideal. Judges seem to have been unavoidably trapped between a unitary conception of how the system should work and the imperfections of nonliterate people functioning in a documentary system.

In the judicial and statutory systems, we are looking at institutional responses to illiteracy. Though the underlying concerns, emanating as they do from certain social values, may be similar, this is quite different from an educational response that attempts to intervene in the developmental process to prevent an undesirable result. Courts had to distinguish between the people (citizens) and the anomalous attribute—illiteracy. Thus the responses to illiterate persons had to place them within the same contexts as literate persons, yet deal with the disturbing attribute of illiteracy. This, in essence, is what made it so difficult for courts and legislators to deal with the problem objectively. The community norm, the common expectation of rationality, was compromised.

A historical study of the political and economic contexts for functional literacy shows the problem to be greater than a mere technical solution would suggest. The different expectations, the great variations in context, and the plurality of uses to which literacy has been put suggest that the problem of functional literacy must be reconceptualized before it is solved. It suggests, moreover, that policy in one sector of a society cannot be divorced from policy in another, nor can ethical uses be divorced from issues of utility. The so-called problem of illiteracy is misrepresented if it is reduced to either a problem of individual attributes or one of social structure. It is both, of course, because it is fundamentally a problem of language and the representation of social and individual reality.

Acknowledgments

. . .

The research for this study was made possible by a grant from the National Institute of Education. I express special thanks to the librarians at the Library of Congress and the Ohio State University Law Library. My gratitude also goes to those who assisted me with archival research at the Delaware State Archives and Historical Society, the United States Army Archives, and the Washington County Court House in Marietta, Ohio. My thanks go to my colleagues in the history of literacy, especially Harvey Graff and Daniel Resnick. In the typing and processing of the manuscript I was fortunate to have had the able assistance of Sue Ann Bolin, Lillian Sands, and Carleen Woodruff. I thank my family for their patience.

Literacy, Law, and Social Order

• • •

1

Theoretical and Historical Perspectives on Literacy

· · · · · · ·

Context and Definition

Recent historical research on literacy, much of which has been quantitative in methodology, has helped to clarify the extent, level, and context for literacy in certain historical periods. The research of Gilmore, Graff, Lockridge, Vinovskis, Kaestle, and Soltow and Stevens, to varying degrees, has placed the study of literacy within larger social contexts, including religion, education, political ideology, criminality, economic growth, and technological advance. This has also been true for literacy studies of Great Britain, France, and Sweden, where the work of Cressey, Schofield, Stone, Furet and Ozouf, and Johannson has contributed greatly to our understanding of literacy in a comparative context.

Other studies such as that of Resnick and Resnick, Goody, and Clanchy have explored the changing paradigms for the meaning of literacy, and that of Scribner and Cole has contributed to our understanding of the relationships among literacy, culture, and cognitive development. Collectively, these studies have made it evident that the definitions and meanings of literacy are better understood by placing them within specific social, economic, and political contexts.[1] They remind us, moreover, that the problems of defining literacy, historically and currently, cannot be solved by treating literacy as an "essence" "that can be captured through some Aristotelian-like enterprise."[2]

Carl Kaestle has recently pointed out that the "categories 'literate' and 'illiterate' are neither precise nor mutually exclusive. . . . Some individuals learned to read but then forgot how. Some were literate but rarely read. Some perceived themselves to be literate but were perceived by others as illiterate, or vice versa."[3] Literate people have a "wide range of abilities," Kaestle reminds us. From a historical standpoint, our knowledge about the levels of literacy needed in selected populations to understand specified types of information is uncertain at best. We have found, observes Clifford, the meaning of literacy to be "uncertain," "unstable," and "ambiguous" when we attempt to "locate literacy and its place in past times."[4]

For both the historian and the researcher of current literacy problems, part of the dilemma in defining literacy is that its nature is both individual and social. An atomistic conception treats literacy as an individual attribute. This it clearly is, but only in part. Scribner reminds us that "the single most compelling fact about literacy is that it is a *social* achievement; individuals in societies without writing systems do not become literate."[5] Of course, it would make little sense to label them *illiterate*, unless there were some reason to compare their skills with those of others from a literate culture. Even when considering the problem of definition only within literate cultures, however, what counts for literacy will always depend on its expected function. This will vary greatly over time and space and will, no doubt, reflect certain dominant (or at least well-publicized) social, political, and economic relations in the population among whom literacy is distributed.[6]

Olson reminds us that even at the level of decoding and literal comprehension, reading something meaningfully and with anticipated future application is a complex act. It requires the ability "to bring the appropriate background knowledge to bear on the text and [the] ability to imagine a state of affairs of which that text would be taken as a true description."[7] Thus it is important to realize that contextualization is related to both new knowledge acquisition and higher order cognitive functioning.[8]

Goodman, Dillon, Klare, and others have shown us that the search for meanings in text is guided by the relevant experience and concepts brought to the text.[9] Language is situated. The meaning of a text in its broadest sense is "social, expressive, communicative, and . . . representational."[10] Seen in this light, success in becoming literate is linked to the particular situations in which the need for and interest in literacy are established and for which the application of literacy skills is anticipated. "There is no clear-cut scientific foundation for defining literacy," says Seitz, and the warning is well heeded.[11] We may speak of literacy at the very basic level of signing one's name or "decoding" a few words. Other measures may be number of years of schooling or reading and writing at a level considered to be functional in a particular social context. Large disparities have been observed between educational measures of literacy and assessments having a functional reference. In a study of Chicago's Woodlawn area, Harman found, for example, that "95.4% of the subjects were 'literate' in that they had completed grade 5; but on the basis of a reading achievement text, 50.7% were 'functionally' illiterate."[12]

Such differences suggest that we ought to speak in terms of stages of literacy. These, in turn, might be specified in terms of skills actually involved in becoming literate and the relation of these skills to specific behaviors. Bormuth has offered a taxonomy of reading skills, which includes decoding, literal comprehension, inference, critical reading, aesthetic appreciation, reading flexibility, and study.[13] Though Bormuth does not pursue the point, his taxonomy obviously assumes a hierarchy of cognitive development and understanding. Such a hierarchy is not unreasonable, but there are dangers present in making such an assumption for a definition of literacy. It is, for instance, only a short step to equating level of literacy with level of intelligence. This would not be unprecedented, as students of intelligent quotient (IQ) testing will recognize; it would, however, be unwise in view of the evidence that many illiterates have devised ingenious schemes for coping with their debility.

The difficulty in equating level of literacy with level of intelligence may be illustrated by example. Asbel talks of the "native cleverness" of illiterates and points to the case of Andrew Timmons (pseudonym). Timmons is able to make his way around downtown Chicago because he can read the numbers on buses. His other day-to-day matters, however, are not so easy. He must shop at a grocery store where one asks for a product rather than selecting it himself. This is more expensive. Timmons cannot read such signs as "Poison" or "Help Wanted" or "Keep off the Grass." He is clever, however, at disguising his illiteracy. He carries a newspaper tucked under his arm so people won't suspect he is illiterate. When he is asked to complete a job application, he uses the ploy of saying, "I just got my hands dirty. Could you put this in your typewriter, and I'll tell you the answers."[14]

The same "native cleverness" can be found in other examples. In their work on common schooling and literacy, Soltow and Stevens cite three interviewees—a miner, a mold maker, and a welder—who had learned to deal with their illiteracy in social situations. The welder delegated the responsibility for most of his legal and economic dealings to a banker and a lawyer. The miner relied upon a trusted friend for the same. The mold maker was forced to shop only where he could trust the salespeople to give him accurate information. Yet all of these illiterate persons were quite successful by middle-class standards. They were dependent upon friends and relatives, yet they kept abreast of their work: mining laws for the miner, for instance, and blueprints for the welder. The mold maker was secretary of his church and managed, with the help of his wife and the pastor, to keep his illiteracy a secret.[15]

Defining literacy by function is manifestly a valid approach to the problem of definition. It is, moreover, not incompatible with a skills approach. To speak in terms of literacy as helping an individual to cope or adjust better to his/her society seems to be reasonable. Yet it is not without difficulty. To say, as Gray did, that a literate person is one who "has acquired the knowledge and skills in reading and writing which enable him to engage effectively in all those activities in which literacy is normally assumed in his culture or group" only refers us further to specific standards of reference.[16] Similarly, literacy defined as "the ability to read, write and compute with the functional competence needed for meeting the requirements of adult living" or as the reading, writing and arithmetic skills that "make it possible [for a person] to continue to use these skills towards his own and the community's development and for active participation in the life of his country" tells us that literacy must have social and political utility.[17] It does not indicate any particular stage of literacy nor any specificity of the types of skill needed.

It is the same with other definitions. Hillerick's proves to be somewhat the exception in emphasizing independent thinking and social mobility: "Literacy is that demonstrated competence in communication skills which enables the individual to function, appropriate to his age, independently in his society and with a potential for movement in that society."[18] This last definition does allow for potentiality, and this suggests that the concept and fact of literacy cannot be fixed, even at the level of the individual.

Those in positions of authority (those significant others) help to define whether or not a person is illiterate. The skills of literal comprehension are important indeed, but it is the skills associated with critical reading, drawing of inferences, and reading flexibility that give the individual the potential to understand the expectations behind legal documents. This potential will be tested by those who determine the correct meaning of a document. In this study, *literacy* is defined by the demands made upon persons in political and legal settings and by the expectations of those having authority. The functional demands placed upon participants filing documents, appearing in court and acting in other civic roles constitute the standard of reference for the literacy/illiteracy dichotomy. There is no single, external defining group. The situation is everything, and it is important to be cognizant of Scribner and Cole's observation that "the representation of literacy as a fixed inventory of skills that can be assessed outside of their context" is not possible.[19]

Function and Meaning

Collectively and individually, the "stimuli to literacy vary widely."[20] Thus, for example, the achievement of literacy may be a response to the lofty ideals of nationalism, social justice, or religious conversion. Economic development and the utility of everyday concerns, such as child care and the reading of danger signs, might also be cited. The causes associated with literacy have been numerous and have included political stability, prevention of crime, eradication of poverty, and campaigns against moral turpitude in one form or another.

In an essay on literacy and social justice, Adiseshiah has spoken of the functionality of literacy in the struggle of Third World countries to achieve an "equitable and just social and political order":

> Above all the functionality of literacy relates to the fight of the poor, illiterate, exploited and disinherited man who forms the 60 percent majority in the Third World countries, to organize himself and his fellow sufferers and fight against the existing power centres and decision-making processes, against the growing poverty he is living in, and for an equitable and just social and political order.[21]

In this case literacy is clearly perceived as a source of autonomous behavior, and illiteracy is presumed to contribute to powerlessness; literacy is mind-expanding and a source of freedom; illiteracy is a cause of enslavement. As a social condition literacy is associated with empowerment, social justice, and greater opportunity for free, informed decision making.

Marshall McLuhan's observation that print is the architect of nationalism is readily seen in the developing nations of the Third World and Latin America.[22] The assumption has been similar to what Harold Innis has argued: that "written language provides a basis for the unification of diverse linguistic communities," that it gives these communities a shared language and, just as importantly, "an agreed-upon symbol of authority, whether through a written constitution, written laws or the like."[23] "The inability to read," Brown suggests, "may be seen as an obstacle to participation in the life of the political community."[24] A UNESCO report on *Literacy as a Factor in Development* (1965) saw illiteracy as an impediment both to national development in general and to participation in a "national community" specifically. The assumption of the political marginality of illiterates was clearly evident:

> Illiteracy among adults implies the nonparticipation of entire sections of the population in the life of the national community. . . . Illiteracy is simply the manifestation at the educational level of a complex series of . . . factors which has prevented entire groups of human beings from participating in the process of development going on around them.[25]

Literacy for national development and political awareness became an important feature of programs in French- and English-speaking African territories in the 1960s. Far earlier in the twentieth century, however, Lenin had expressed the relationship of literacy to politicalization and national transformation. In helping to launch the campaign "to make Russia literate," he had announced: "an illiterate man is non-political; first he must be taught how to read." Individual transformation became an important element in national transformation. The individual as a "passive object" of history subject to political manipulation became, instead, an autonomous subject and an agent of change. Literacy was not a neutral technology. As a tool for individual and social transformation it was always governed by purpose. For conserving established power elites, literacy was a powerful technology to reinforce ideology and channel individual imagination.[26]

One of the best known and frequently cited cases of the link between literacy and national development has been that of revolutionary Cuba. The campaign against illiteracy in Cuba that followed from the successes of the revolution had for its long-range goals the promotion of economic and cultural development and the indoctrination of Cuba's people in the ideology of the new revolutionary government. The year 1961 was declared the "Year of Education." The national Literacy Commission oversaw the direction of the campaign and produced 1.5 million copies of a "specially designed illustrated primer comprising fifteen lessons and entitled *Venceremos* (We Shall Conquer)." Teaching manuals were prepared that included twenty-four revolutionary themes.[27]

The campaign against illiteracy in Cuba was notable for both its short duration and the large numbers of instructional personnel involved. After approximately one year, using about one-quarter million volunteers and teachers, Cuba was declared to be free from illiteracy: "707,000 persons had been taught to read and write." The achievement of basic literacy was reinforced with subsequent programs conducted by the Worker–Farmer Educational National Office. These included adult education courses and home reading circles. The ideological and practical bent of instruction continued.[28]

The experience of revolutionary Cuba is a poignant reminder that the concept of literacy is not an abstraction; nor should it be defined in an arbitrary way. Literacy in Cuba was specifically tied to broader political goals, and the effectiveness of the campaign can, in part, be attributed to the sense of urgency and immediacy surrounding the effort. Both the type and level of literacy in Cuba probably differed substantially from those in other social contexts. Moreover, the value of literacy in terms of utility and personal satisfaction probably was specific to the situation.

A Historical Perspective on Illiteracy in the United States

Recently, reports of commissions on educational reform have stressed the need for higher levels of literacy as part of a national agenda for technological and economic progress. Many of these reports take the fears of foreign competition and economic crisis as their starting points. These fears are then translated into the issue of educational quality by using evidence of declining scores on nationally normed, standardized tests.

It is common to hear complaints of functional illiteracy. The National Assessment of Educational Progress shows 13 percent of seventeen year olds to be illiterate. Adult illiteracy figures range from one-sixth to one-third of the United States population.[29] In general, education and its basic output—literacy—are seen to be in a state of crisis. The productive capacity of the nation is at risk, to use the rhetoric of the highly publicized report *(A Nation at Risk)*.

The crisis mentality of current reports and exhortations to take up arms against illiteracy is deeply rooted in the evangelical style characteristic of, but not limited to, Anglo-American educational reform. Literacy used in support of religious and social ideals conjointly has been conspicuous since the Protestant Reformation. The teaching of Bible literacy to aid in spiritual salvation was common. That same literacy, moreover, was an efficient means of social control that brought spiritual values and social norms closer together in a vision of a more perfect social order.

In Great Britain, the work of Griffith Jones, Hannah More, and the Reverend Andrew Bell, though differing in method and emphasis, sought to convey the fixed moral precepts associated with religious indoctrination. In colonial America, the efforts of the New England Puritans to train their young through Bible literacy was predicated on the assumption that ignorance of the Bible was the way to damnation. Hornbook and primer provided carefully censored reading and an introduction to the spiritual lessons afforded by studying the Bible. Later, the Sunday School movement and the "tract" tradition served religious spokesmen well in their aim to preserve Christian morality and to keep a young nation on the righteous path of Protestantism.

By the midnineteenth century the pan-Protestantism of the common school had wedded secular and religious instruction. The achievement of literacy remained linked to both individual and social salvation. These were part of a moral paradigm that included literacy as a tool for moral development and academic achievement.

By 1840 it was popular to collect data on the relationship of literacy to crime and poverty. In his study of nineteenth-century Canada, Graff has commented on the "stark simplicity of the causal model" assumed by educational reformers: ignorance and illiteracy led to idleness, intemperance, and improvidence, which, in turn, resulted in poverty and criminality.[30] The high illiteracy rates of prison inmates were often cited as evidence of the causal relationships between illiteracy and profligacy. Of the high numbers of illiterates incarcerated in the Eastern State Penitentiary of Pennsylvania in 1838, the warden observed: "These numbers show the gross neglect which most of our personnel have experienced from parents and guardians of their moral and religious training—of their elementary instruction."[31]

Technical literacy, also, was an important matter in the late eighteenth and nineteenth centuries. Still in its infancy, it was one dimension of a broader movement to transform American culture both materially and ideologically into a modern nation. This movement cut across America's geographic and cultural topography, and its common elements can be found in the content, style, and context of printed materials designed to reshape attitudes toward technological progress.

Different audiences interpreted the message within their own experiences. Agricultural reformers and the "progressive" constituency within the farm population itself were familiar with and internalized the organization of technical knowledge. But the distinctions between the "frames" of knowledge of these innovators and of those who were the object of reform constituted one obstacle to the diffusion of technical knowledge. In some cases the message of reform itself was also set to the accompaniment of regional and socioeconomic differences. The path to technical literacy was precarious and obscured by the unfamiliarity between author and audience. Leaders of early agricultural societies (for example, the Philadelphia Society for the Promotion of Agriculture and the Massachusetts Society for Promoting Agriculture) struggled to find the style of expression and level of sophistication appropriate to the "common" farmer. They were reproached "for introducing articles which [were] above the capacity of common farmers."[32]

Like those who would save souls or promote economic progress through technical literacy, proponents of nationalism commonly looked to print as an efficient way to further their cause. Nineteenth-century educational reformers in the United States attempted to find the common ground for nation building and economic expansion and the sectarianism of evangelical Protestantism. It was the "civic-national" paradigm for literacy, however, that gradually came to dominate public schooling.[33] After the Civil War, that model seemed to have even greater urgency.

In 1883 the Reverend Joseph Cook was so impressed with the "Evils of Illiteracy" and their impact on free elections that he publicly spoke out for national aid to education as "the only adequate remedy for the national evil of illiteracy." Viewing the condition of illiteracy in the South following the Civil War, Cook cited an address by President Hayes that asserted that in "more than one-third of the Union the ignorant voters are almost one-third of the total number of voters." This boded ill for American democracy, according to Cook. The "war itself," he observed, "is not fought out until we enable the Southern States to conquer the perils of the illiteracy which came into existence there by the downfall of slavery, and by the enfranchisement of the blacks."[34]

Moral rhetoric denouncing illiteracy persisted even when the point of an argument had little relation to values or norms. Shortly before the turn of the century J. C. Zachos, curator of the Library of the Cooper Union, spoke of illiteracy as a "great evil through the whole country" and a "menace" to free institutions. Zachos's remarks were prompted by his concerns with recently emancipated southern blacks and a stream of "new" immigrants populating urban America as the nineteenth century came to a close. In his "Address to the Friends of Education, Especially Among the Illiterate Classes," he urged a national (rather than a state) policy to deal with illiteracy. If unchecked, he argued, it is a "fatal injury to the whole country, as a democratic republic."[35]

The remarks of Cook and Zachos were not unusual and echoed the continuing belief of earlier American educational reformers, from Jefferson to Mann to Stowe of Ohio, that illiteracy was a political and moral evil upon which war must be waged. Nor were Jefferson and Mann exceptional in their concern with the relationship between literacy and political well-being. As purveyors of the Enlightenment and liberal reform, they saw public education and individual enlightenment as partners in the cause of progress.

One of the basic features of campaigns against illiteracy after 1830 was their focus on the public school as an instrument of reform. Influence on educational matters was diffuse because of shared state and local power, but the common school became the critical institution in efforts to elevate and spread literacy in the United States. Years of schooling eventually became a surrogate for level of literacy in the twentieth century. Even by the fourth decade of the nineteenth century, however, common school reforms succeeded in bringing schooling to most children age ten and under so that becoming literate was closely associated with going to school. In the course of common school expansion the meaning of literacy became increasingly standardized and institutionalized, reflecting the values and purposes of those controlling the school. In short, becoming literate in the public school was an extension of the school's attempt to impose a particular form of socialization upon the young.

Nineteenth-century school reform, says Church, "was primarily an effort to reach down into the lower portions of the population and to teach children there to share the values, ideals, and controls held by the rest of society."[36] The promise of sharing the "proper" values and behaviors, including becoming literate, was a dream for success and upward mobility. In his study of school reform in Massachusetts, however, Katz found "educational reform and innovation represented the imposition by social leaders of schooling upon a reluctant, uncomprehending, skeptical, and sometimes, as in Beverly [Massachusetts], hostile citizenry."[37]

The moral fervor of early twentieth-century campaigns against illiteracy was muted compared to nineteenth-century evangelical rhetoric. The sense of urgency and crisis, however, continued. Hearings on various literacy legislation from World War I to the mid-1970s illustrate the crusading spirit of these campaigns, the expectations of their advocates, and the presumed causal and functional relationships among illiteracy, social ills, economic development, political stability, and personal well-being.

A great deal of the testimony on House Bill 6490 (1918), "To Require the Commissioner of Education to Devise Methods and Promote Plans for the Elimination of Adult Illiteracy in the United States" focused on matters of national security. For many, the wartime examination of army recruits had brought the scarlet letter of illiteracy to light. Even though a similar bill had been proposed four years earlier, suddenly it seemed that the efficiency and effectiveness of the United States Army were in jeopardy.[38] Thus the secretary of war issued the following directive:

There shall be established in each Development Battalion a school for the instruction in English of soldiers who have not sufficient knowledge of the English language to enable them properly to perform their duties. The instruction shall be sufficient to enable the student to receive, execute and transmit verbal orders or messages intelligently; also, as far as practicable, to read and understand ordinary written or printed matter as contained in the various drill regulations, soldier's hand books, etc.[39]

The school was to administer to both foreign-born and native-born illiterates.

In hearings on the bill, Commissioner of Education Philander P. Claxton told the committee that to deal with adult illiteracy a "great national campaign" was needed and that the "strength and safety of the Nation depends upon it. . . ." Illiteracy both contributed to inefficient soldiering and created problems of commitment, it was stated. "The people are asked to fight for democracy," said Claxton. "What may those who can not read be expected to learn about it?" Claxton also reiterated familiar arguments about the economic significance of illiteracy. Three-quarters of a billion dollars per year, he noted, were lost because of illiteracy. Perhaps of even greater moment was the situation in which illiterate persons held the balance of political power. Claxton cited the complaints of one exasperated citizen: "They've got us; this illiterate mass outvotes us; they have the balance of power, and we can do nothing."[40]

Those testifying before the committee spoke to the different purposes of literacy. Each had ample historical precedent and echoed the reasoning of common school reformers of the midnineteenth century. Illiteracy, poverty, and criminality were causally linked, as were social unrest and illiteracy. A more personal view of the problem was taken by some: John Abercrombie of Alabama asked the committee to consider "the millions of people in this country who are unable to read the laws that they are expected to obey and for the violation of which they are punished in our courts of justice."[41] And, in the metaphors of incarceration and liberation, Claxton urged: "We are asking that you will enable us to free the five-and-a-half-million illiterates from their prison walls" so that they might "hear any voice that is worth while at any time in the history of the world" and "become associate and companion of all the best and greatest in the world. . . ."[42]

Approximately one year later the House Committee on Education heard similar arguments in the hearings on the Smith-Bankhead Americanization Bill. Once again, the political and economic liabilities of illiteracy were emphasized, this time as they related to political and social unrest of the sort that anarchism spawned during the war. Of more immediate concern was the threat to safety posed by foreign illiterates who, according to the deposition, could not "understand rules and suggestions that are given as to their safety."[43] Industrial safety increasingly had become a concern for those studying the effects of illiteracy on national welfare. In the digest of the bill, Special Assistant to the Secretary of the Interior Herbert Kaufman asserted:

The extent to which our greatest industries are dependent upon [illiterate, foreign] labor is perilous to all standards of efficiency. Their ignorance not only retards production and confuses administration, but constantly piles up a junk heap of broken humans and damaged machines which cost the Nation incalculably.[44]

The cult of efficiency that swept through business and education in the early twentieth century was clearly evident in the testimony. The management of human resources dominated the thinking of the bill's advocates. This was linked to concerns with industrial efficiency, national security, and the national welfare.

Individual justice was also given some attention. The proposed law, said Kaufman, was really an attempt "to validate the estate of 8,000,000 Americans and potential Americans in all the facilities, in all the instruments of progress in the United States." Though he could not resist the conclusion that such validation would "lower the national overhead on every product which they learn to utilize," it was Kaufman's belief, also, that "most of the greatest benefits which our democracy has conferred upon its people are lost to these [illiterates]."[45] It was Commissioner Claxton, however, who spoke directly to the issue of the rights of illiterates. "These people have certain rights," he asserted, and for their defense of democracy at the risk of their lives "we owe these people something."[46] The rights of illiterates and the correlate issue of social justice, although of secondary importance compared to concerns for economic productivity, were not completely subservient to a management ethos guided by principles of utility.

Illiteracy after World War II

In the decades between the two world wars there was minimal activity in the attack on adult illiteracy in the United States. The 1940 Census did not ask a question on literacy, but, instead, focused on the number of school years completed. In 1947, however, a census study did estimate the illiteracy rate among those having completed fewer than five years of schooling in 1940. The study indicated that among male workers the illiteracy rate had dropped to 4 percent overall, and that much of this decline had occurred among farmers. Southern states continued to have "the majority of the poorly educated and illiterate," however. Among farm workers the illiteracy rate was still higher than for other occupational groups. American blacks continued to have a much higher illiteracy rate than white Americans.[47]

The army draft for World War II once again made it clear that illiteracy was a far greater problem than had been generally thought.[48] The excessive number of illiterates was the subject of one Colonel Holliday's memorandum to the Commanding School of the Third Army, San Antonio, Texas. Holliday reported that 815 of 2,410 selectees for the 367th Infantry were illiterate, by which he meant that the greater proportion could neither read nor write. He complained that such a large proportion of illiterates would "greatly hinder training and may make the rate of progress prescribed in the Mobilization Training Program impossible of attainment." Holliday's request was to "discharge these men for the convenience of the Government because of Illiteracy."[49] A similar complaint was reported a year-and-a-half later to the adjutant general of the U.S. Army by Captain Fleetwood of the Replacement Training Center at Camp Pickett, Virginia. Fleetwood's report noted that in a "shipment" of 230 "colored trainees" 120 were "completely illiterate."[50] The pressure of manpower shortage forced the army to abandon its literacy requirement in August 1942. From that date to May 1945, 260,000 illiterate men were inducted. These were given special literacy education before being enrolled in training in military specialties.[51]

Ginzberg and Bray's government manpower study of U. S. Army recruits in World War II sheds some light on the problem of functional literacy in twentieth-century America by assessing the relationship between literacy skills and job performance in the armed services. Like a number of other studies, they found illiteracy in the United States to be associated with race, region, population density, and lower socioeconomic status. Though they mustered little direct evidence, they contended that in 1940 the vast majority of the 4 million males in the work force who had less than five years of schooling "had somehow adjusted to life—they were able to secure employment [despite the decrease in low-skill jobs in the South], discharge familial responsibilities, and participate in community activities." Whatever the adjustment made in civilian life, however, wartime crisis accompanied by manpower shortages raised serious doubts about the efficacy of the undereducated in the armed forces. It seems to have come as a surprise that such a large percentage of draft-age males had such a limited education.[52]

The investigation of Ginzberg and Bray focused on the aims and results of the so-called Special Training Program of the army. This twelve- week course was designed to school illiterate and undereducated recruits to make them fit for army service. The aims of the program spanned both the instructional and socialization dimensions of military life. In the case of the former, the goals of the program were to bring the reading level of recruits up to fourth grade so that they might "be able to comprehend bulletins, written orders and directives, and basic Army publications. . . ." Recruits were also taught arithmetic to the fourth grade level so they "could understand their pay accounts and laundry bills, [and] conduct their business in the PX. . . ." Among the socialization objectives were included the acquisition of "sufficient language skills" for "getting along with officers and men," the facilitation of "adjustment of the men to military training and Army life," and the indoctrination of the recruits into the allied cause.[53]

Ginzberg and Bray's evaluation of the graduates of the program led them to judge the performance of the recruits as quite good. This finding, they note, ran contrary to the stereotype of these men by their superiors as bungling, inept, and of little use to the army. Of the graduates, 25 percent received the grade of corporal or higher, a surprising finding since 50 percent of them had been assigned to noncombat units where promotion was less likely than in combat units. Seventy-eight of the graduates were court martialed, but only five of these were "general" court martials for serious offenses. Thus, the authors concluded, they did not, as a group, constitute a serious disciplinary problem.[54]

When the performance of the graduates from Special Training Units was compared to a control group, 12 percent (compared to 7 percent of the control group) were found to be unacceptable or a loss to the army. Few (9 percent) of the graduates were judged to be "very good" soldiers, whereas 23 percent of the control group received this rating. A rating of "good" was assigned to 28 percent of the graduates compared to 34 percent of the control group.[55]

Upon discharge, a follow-up study of graduates from Special Training Units showed some carryover in the educational aspirations of these men. About one-half submitted claims for education upon reentering civilian life. Some of these (17 percent) turned out to have stayed in school less than three months. Twenty-five percent stayed only four to twelve months, but 30 percent and 25 percent stayed one to two years and two-plus years, respectively.

The value of these additional months or years in terms of occupational mobility was probably not very great for those who did not continue for at least two years. Thus, it came as no surprise that "there was no tremendous change in the general occupational and income circumstances of these men as a result of their military service, even with full allowance for their special training."[56] That an inordinate number of illiterates were concentrated in the South, particularly the Southeast, where there was a trend toward a decreasing number of low-skill jobs and hence fewer job opportunities for illiterates, probably contributed to the difficulty of upward occupational mobility for this group.

By 1959 a sample survey by the Bureau of Census showed an overall illiteracy rate of 2.2 percent in the United States: 1.6 percent among whites and 7.5 percent among blacks. In actual numbers, there were

2,619,000 noninstitutionalized persons unable to read and write and another 250,000 institutionalized ones. Age continued to be a major determinant of illiteracy rates, as did occupational status and wealth. Approximately 15 percent of male farm laborers and foremen were illiterate. Among other male laborers, excluding farmers and miners, the percentage illiterate was 8.2.[57]

United States Census surveys of illiteracy prior to 1960 were decidedly optimistic, even enthusiastic, about declining illiteracy rates. During the decades between 1960 and 1980, however, reassessments of the quality of literacy brought new problems to light. Recent measures of illiteracy have focused on "functional" literacy rather than the self-report system of the census. The results, at times, echo despair rather than enthusiasm. Of course, astonishment at the numbers of illiterate Americans was not new nor were statements about the presumed malevolent effects of this lack of proper education.

The 1960 Census reported information on grade completion but did not ask a specific literacy question. Thus, extrapolation of illiteracy rates from these figures is notoriously unreliable. The problem of "function" did not abate during the 1960s. Assessing functional literacy became increasingly difficult with the inception of federally funded adult education programs in the United States in the 1960s. Functional illiteracy was the nemesis of the Manpower Development and Training Act (1962) when it became evident that large numbers of enrollees could not complete the programs because they lacked the basic literacy skills. Though it cannot be said that the Economic Opportunity Act (EOA)(1964) solved the problem of functionality, it was the first federal program to subsidize literacy education directly. The longer-range effect of the EOA and the subsequent Adult Basic Education (ABE) Act (1966) was to raise the grade level equivalent for "functional" literacy. ABE programs, themselves, spawned a reevaluation of the school curriculum in order to address the problem of skills required to function in a "modern society."[58]

Bills to encourage state ABE programs were an integral part of the new attack on illiteracy. Exhibits of the hearings included current statements and written materials from the previous decade. They demonstrate the persistent appeal of certain standard arguments for the eradication of illiteracy. The types of appeals can be gathered easily from the statement of Albert Hayes, president of the International Association of Machinists: "Early lack of opportunity for at least a basic education has denied the adult illiterate of a fulfillment opportunity to qualify himself for a full personal life, a profitable economic existence, and the basic ability to understand and fulfill his role as a freeman in a democratic society."[59]

Other testimony reasserted the causal relationship of illiteracy to crime, poverty, poor health, and industrial accidents.Economic growth, national security, and the effective exercise of democratic principles were all associated with literacy. The liberal, constitutional ideal of free, educated persons deciding the form and content of a structure for self-governance was stated with little reformulation:

> The Founding Fathers envisaged an informed citizenry as the bulwark of the Republic. And a democracy, above all other forms of government, demands a literate population. How can one intelligently exercise one's suffrage rights and obligations unless one is literate? Or how can he participate in civic affairs understandingly?[60]

It was put forth again in a statement that was typical in its political appeal though atypical in its assumption about the link between quality of thinking and literacy:

> In order to function effectively in a democracy, citizens must possess facts about many things and people. If they are to exercise the kind of independent judgment which our representative form of government requires and are not to be unduly swayed by the rabble rousers, and the bombardment of mass media, they must think clearly and discriminatingly about those things and people. They cannot think clearly and independently unless they can participate effectively in the arts and skills of communication which is functional literacy.[61]

Of greater importance in the early 1960s than in the period immediately following World War I were appeals to social justice, personal adjustment, economic mobility, health, domestic relations, and "simple humanity." Said Richard Crohn of B. I. Mazel, Inc.: "Thinking of it in terms of simple humanity—the inability to communicate, to enjoy the pleasures of reading, to advance their education and economic status, because of a lack of these simple skills—places an obligation upon us to do something about it."[62] And from Willard Givens, vice president of Senior Citizens of America: "Our sense of justice, and equal opportunity should compel us to change this situation [of adult illiteracy]."[63]

Perhaps the most succinct and forceful statement of the relationship(s) between illiteracy and individual justice, however, was that of Glenn Jensen, executive director of the Adult Education Association of the United States:

> As important as all the implications indicated above [economic growth and mobility, citizenship, national security, etc.] are[,] the implications of literacy for the individual are much more important. The significance of our way of

life i[s] its emphasis on the individual, his worth, and his dignity, in contrast to material values. Helping to make an individual literate, therefore, is providing him with a means of achieving his right of life, liberty, and the pursuit of happiness.[64]

It became obvious by the end of the 1960s that functional literacy was more easily spoken of than defined. School grades completed continued to be the measure of function. If actual forms and documents (driver's license, bank loan, or income tax) and the presumed grade level needed to complete them are considered, functional illiteracy rates were high indeed. The average reading level of such materials is tenth-grade or higher. If it is assumed, as it was in the 1969 population survey, that everyone who had completed at least six years of school was literate, there is a large discrepancy between illiteracy calculated on the basis of these two different grade equivalents. If a ninth-grade education is taken as the equivalent of literacy, for example, there were in 1969 approximately 39 million people age fourteen or older who would be classified as functionally illiterate.[65]

By 1976 approximately $260 million of federal, state, and local monies had been spent on ABE.[66] The target population for ABE programs was some 54 to 64 million Americans, age sixteen and over, who were without high school diplomas and presumed to "suffer significant disadvantages because of their limited education."[67] It is notable that the diversity of enrollees rather than their homogeneity was more in evidence. Urban enrollees tended to be "young to middle age, . . . employed as unskilled or semi-skilled laborers or service workers" and of various ethnic and racial minorities. About two-thirds of them were women and 15 to 25 percent were on welfare. Many were teenage dropouts from school. The majority "had nine or more years of formal schooling. . . , and a few [were] high school graduates."[68] Their common bond was functional illiteracy.

Most of the enrollees in ABE programs were motivated by the desire for occupational and economic mobility. Other types, classified by motivation, included "concerned mothers" who wished to aid children with schoolwork, "self-improvers" who saw in literacy a way to greater self-respect, "troubled youth" who were socially deviant or emotionally disturbed, and "educated aliens" who wished to learn English. The hardcore unemployed did not tend to enroll in ABE and comprised only 14 percent of the total.[69]

The diversity of enrollees, including their differing aspirations, created a difficult task for the teacher who would be sensitive to their different motivations and expectations. Yet from the broader perspective of liberal social reform, the more disturbing fact was that of nonenrollment.

The United States Office of Education and the National Advisory Council on Adult Education estimated that only 2 to 4 percent of the total eligible population were ABE participants. It is clear that the poor participated at a far lower rate than those of moderate income. Thus, only 5.5 percent of those with an income under $4,000 participated compared to 15.5 percent of those with an income of $10,000 to $14,999 and 20.3 percent of those having an income of $25,000 or more.

The bulk of the hard-core poor did not participate in ABE. This disconcerting fact led Hunter and Harman to recommend "community-based initiatives" that would "require the adults themselves to contribute to designing programs based on concrete learning needs growing out of specific issues affecting their lives in their communities." An action-oriented, pluralistic approach was needed, said Hunter and Harman, an approach that would take greater account of ethnic, cultural, and socioeconomic differences, as well as different learning styles and motivations for learning.[70]

The thrust of Hunter and Harman's argument was that both the meaning and acquisition of literacy skills cannot be separated from the social fabric of those becoming literate. Political and economic disadvantages associated with race, class, and lack of access to power were interwoven with illiteracy. The value of literacy for the disadvantaged must be put (for them) in the context of such considerations as achieving "economic security, health care, greater power over decisions affecting their families, better schools for their children, community improvement, and the like." Simply learning to read and write would not solve their problems, though literacy would enhance their "formal credentials" in the "competition for jobs."[71]

Conclusion

A review of the problems of definition associated with the concept of literacy might easily lead one to despair of any successful solution to the problem. Yet three generalizations seem to be self-evident. First, it is clear that parameters can be established for the meanings of literacy. Second, the conceptual parameters for literacy are formulated by its potential meanings when considered in light of its purpose and function. Third, the operational parameters are set by the range of possible behaviors to which literacy is linked. Being literate, then, is a matter of both expectation and response. The crucial questions become for whom? and for what? Both meaning and behavior, of course, have individual and social dimensions. It is the relative melding of the two that determines the clarity and utility of any given definition of literacy.

The plurality of possible meanings for literacy has clear, though by no means hard and fast, implications for educational and social policy. On one level there are matters of utility and functional literacy, that is, matters of determining the economic and social priorities for which literacy is needed, at what level, and for how many. Functional literacy demands are often related directly to human resources development and the setting of national or regional agendas for economic productivity. At another level are those functional literacy demands that relate to political rather than economic citizenship. The basic questions in this regard are those of determining the level and type of literacy needed for the preservation of basic freedoms and the performance of citizenship obligations. Finally, there are those questions raised about the distribution of literacy and whether it conforms "to standards of social justice and human progress."[72] These latter questions are usually framed in terms of expectations, opportunities, and the just deserts of one's efforts.

Each level of implication mentioned relates in some way to empowerment, whether that is a matter of self-governance and the exercise of basic rights or of acquiring power through the meeting of obligations or the acquisition of material goods. The functional literacy demands placed upon individuals by corporate organizations or governments always occur within a context of purpose and function. For example, corporations interested in increasing productivity or eliminating waste caused by mistakes made by functionally illiterate people may establish criteria for functional literacy and implement programs to raise literacy levels. William McGowan has pictured this situation as follows: "Every day, SALES ORDERS are botched, bank transactions are bungled, messages are scrambled, and papers by the million are misfiled, all, to some extent, because of substandard reading skills. Mutual of New York estimates that 70 percent of its dictated correspondence has to be redone at least once because of error."[73]

McGowan points out that the "illiteracy problem is particularly acute in business and industry, especially in banking, telecommunications, and data processing where competent reading skills are most in demand." The problem, says McGowan, cuts across a large segment of industry and service corporations and affects everything from the reading of warning signs and the writing of memoranda to the interpretation of instructional manuals. Large-scale efforts to improve literacy levels have been few in major corporations, but employee reading and writing programs are increasing, as are remedial English courses. The anti-illiteracy program of Pratt and Whitney is probably the largest, and the corporation has hired a professional literacy coordinator.[74]

Literacy related to political citizenship has historically been a high priority in most nations. Often the critical issue is the tie to particular ideological commitments. For example, literacy may be seen as one of several guarantees of basic freedoms, or it may be seen, more conservatively, as serving the vested interests of those having power. Thus it is often a double-edged sword to be forged with caution and used only when the risks of misinterpretation are minimized by controlling the content of text. Literacy for liberation versus literacy for control is the issue here. The history of literacy programs in the United States shows that a fine line has been walked in this regard. Moreover, it is often a line that has disappeared altogether when the purposes of liberty and national security were at odds.

The relationship of literacy to justice occurs at two levels: procedural and distributive. These levels are related, but are separate problems. The first, of course, is primarily a matter of legal safeguards, but it also affects the rights of illiterates and those who, though they may be literate, are in an adversarial position (i.e., litigants) with respect to illiterates. Literacy is related to distributive justice across both political and economic domains. It is the latter that most frequently comes to mind when considering problems of distributive justice.

The relationship of literacy to justice is often thought of in terms of fairness—fair treatment and the fair distribution of society's rewards and resources. In countries where educational systems are directly linked to economic and political opportunities, issues of justice also become issues of educational policy. The distribution of literacy is thus linked, via education, to the distribution of resources and rewards. How a fair distribution is defined and how it is implemented are, in turn, related to the particular concepts of distributive justice that guide political and economic policies. The analysis of literacy and justice within the context of liberal and contractarian ideals is taken up in the next chapter.

2

Literacy and Justice

. . . .

This chapter defines selected political and philosophic parameters of the relationships between literacy and justice. These have received little attention from historians of education and literacy, though there seem to be some common operating assumptions about the role of literacy (and education) in helping to secure both procedural and social justice. Among these are the importance of shared knowledge (what John Rawls calls publicity) in making decisions about political governance, the importance of literacy skills in economic opportunity, and the importance of literacy in securing individual freedoms guaranteed by political systems.

The emphasis on social contract and contractarian theory in this chapter has the effect of emphasizing the rationalist interpretation of liberal theory while bypassing the empiricist/utilitarian interpretation. This, of course, is generally dictated by the thrust of the inquiry, but it also acknowledges the weaknesses of utilitarianism in matters of ethics and justice.

Raphael has pointed out that in Hume's thought the relationship between utility and justice is "curiously narrow" and is "more or less equated with rights in relation to property."[1] Hume was concerned with the rules of property in contradistinction and opposition to Locke's natural right to property. According to Raphael, Hume argued that the need for such rules arose "because there is a scarcity in the supply of many goods that are wanted and because men are predominantly selfish with limited generosity."[2] It would be difficult to argue with Hume's assertion about scarcity, but his presumptions about human behavior have been denounced by many liberals who are unwilling to give man over to acquisitiveness.

To be fair to Hume, we cannot discount his recognition that a moral sentiment of benevolence or generosity exists in some of our public actions. Though "man's first motive for joining in the conventions [of rules of property] is self interest," Hume acknowledged that some rules benefit society generally, and we give them moral approval even though they do not benefit us in some individual cases. Thus, self-interest in a particular instance is sacrificed to the general good because, in the long run, the system benefits most people. This, of course, is a generalized self-interest.[3]

When applied to the distribution of goods, utilitarianism has stressed the maximization of satisfaction, sometimes called happiness. For Bentham, human actions were motivated by the calculus of pleasure and pain. Political decisions were based on a calculation of whether or not they would maximize the pleasure of the community as a whole.[4] One could justify the unequal distribution of literacy on utilitarian grounds in ways similar to justifying the unequal distribution of goods, including education. From the standpoint of utility, there would be an optimum distribution of levels of literacy that would contribute to maximizing productivity and minimizing waste. In undemocratic governments, differentiated citizenship roles could set the limits to literacy. The point, of course, is that the criterion of utility could be used to justify inequalities in basic literacy and in levels of literacy as well as for any other commodity or attribute. Such differentiations would probably correspond to educational opportunities. The concept of justice as fairness is simply irrelevant to utility when the latter is purportedly a measure of aggregate satisfaction in a society.

The issue of functional literacy is usually formed on utilitarian grounds. For this reason it is subject to the same weaknesses as arguments for maximizing utility in general. When we speak of functional literacy, we must always return to questions for what? and for whom? That is, of course, unless the concept of utility itself is joined to morality and/or a concept of rights, in which case the answer to these questions need only presume a distribution of literacy that maximized the payoff for literacy in the aggregate.

A consideration of justice as it relates to illiterates may be directed to both the individual and group levels. Weinberger phrases it well when he says: "on the one side the concern is with just behaviour in the autonomous action of the individual with respect to fellow human beings, while on the other it is with the institutionalisation of just forms of life on the part of society."[5] At the individual level, for instance, a court might be concerned with whether justice is attained in a contractual relationship or whether an illiterate voter is treated fairly. When the concern is with illiterates as a class of persons, then attention is directed to the rules (general and special) governing the relationships of illiterates to the legal and political systems.

Any such analysis should keep in mind that the legal system is what Jenkins calls a "*supplemental* principle of order" to other institutions. Its functions, he reminds us, are to prescribe and prohibit certain modes of conduct, to "settle disputes and secure compliance," and "to reassert the threatened unity of the group."[6] The relationship of both literate and illiterate persons to law, then, must take these functions into account. Many of these relationships will be dealt with in detail later. The focus of this chapter, however, is the relationship of literacy to a broader system of justice, particularly that formed out of liberal and contractarian ideals.

It may be hypothesized that in an advanced contractarian society where documents play an important role in governing interpersonal and interinstitutional relations, illiterate persons experience greater injustice than literate ones. Confirmation of the hypothesis would rest upon an assessment of the degree to which a person's illiteracy is punished or compensated for by the legal system.

The problem of the illiterate voter or contractor is part of the larger problem of administering justice in a society that relies heavily on the printed word. Hart reminds us that a "central element in the idea of justice" is the maxim, "Treat like cases alike and different cases differently."[7] This simple guide to conduct is complicated by illiterate persons', in many ways, having the same qualities as the literate persons with whom they deal. Yet they are quite different in their inability to decipher the text of a document.

Historically, the problem of defining illiteracy and the class of illiterates is similar to that of defining sets and universals in philosophic discourse. The practical questions are what is to count as illiteracy? and who is to count as illiterate? The condition of illiteracy is peculiar because it seems alien to a system whose operation has depended so heavily upon documentation with its accompanying systems and conventions of language. Judges hearing cases involving an issue of illiteracy often have been in the position of trying to balance the "objective reality" of the text with the "subjective reality" of expectations arrived at independently of textual considerations.

Concepts of Justice

My analysis of the relationship between literacy and justice draws selectively from the immense body of theoretical literature dealing with the concept of justice. The emphasis throughout, however, is on the implications of contractarian/social contract theory for the illiterate person. In dealing with Rawls's theory of justice, for example, it is not my intent to defend or attack its antimeritocratic arguments, but rather to show how the conception of justice as fairness helps to clarify the role of literacy and the problem of illiteracy in theories of social contract. Moreover, I will try not to be taken too far into the epistemological and metaphysical mine fields of contractarian theory, but rather to treat those elements of social contract and justice that relate to the issue of illiteracy.

In his work *Social Order and the Limits of Law* Jenkins reminds us that theories of justice are based upon assumptions about the nature of the good society. "Opinions concerning both the good society and the role of law in securing it," he says, "are complicated by an additional factor: they depend not only upon abstract theories of the nature of man but also upon the actual circumstances out of which they arise." Societies respond according to the immediate problems to be solved.[8]

When we speak of *substantive justice,* we are referring to that justice which prevails in the ideal society, with the ideal distribution of resources and the ideal means for realizing all human potential and meeting all human needs. *Procedural (formal) justice,* on the other hand, is embodied in a system of law that is impartial and in which equality before the law guarantees fairness in treatment by the law. Whether we are speaking of substantive or procedural justice, the issue seldom arises outside the context of competing claims for limited resources. Thus, although justice is often the object of abstract philosophic study, the context for study is usually an immediate problem relating to the distribution of social, economic, and political benefits.

When justice is conceived of as fairness (that is, when fairness is seen as the essential element of justice), the problem of justice becomes one of avoiding distinctions and striking "a proper balance between competing claims."[9] The ancient Pythagorean formulation of justice was symbolized by the square number "in which like was united with like. . . ." In this ancient view justice meant equality "in the distribution or allotment of advantages or burdens." The link between equality and justice in contemporary theories is most evident in the theme of equality of treatment before the law.[10] Usually there are constraining factors in the application of this concept of justice. Thus, the principle of equality of treatment is applied to certain classes of people, but not to others. One of the functions for those administering a legal system is to decide the applicability of particular legal principles and precedents to particular groups. Justice, conceived of in this way, is the "correct application of a law, as opposed to arbitrariness."[11] What this means is that for all individuals subject to a general rule, that rule (not special rules) ought to apply. The problem in regard to illiteracy becomes one of deciding whether, and under what circumstances, the class of people called illiterate will be subject to general and special rules, respectively.

In his seminal work *Jurisprudence, Realism in Theory and Practice,* Karl Llewellyn observed that "justice must always . . . be sought under the dire influence of the principle of scarcity." "Rarely," he noted, "is there enough of good and warranted Justice to go around."[12] Yet he acknowledged that it made sense to talk of "net Justice" in a social scheme. His own concept of justice, he said, had four attributes, the first being that it was an "aspect of the Good." Second, he saw justice as a regulatory mechanism to handle conflict. The idea of fairness (evenhandedness) was also central to the concept of justice. Finally, justice "operates under the sad fact of scarcity" so that preference and compromise will always enter into its distribution.[13]

Llewellyn was far from being an egalitarian, yet with respect to justice as fairness he saw that fairness "includes a right portion of favor, of unearned aid or indulgence to those who need it. . . ." He added, "provided the favor be so handled as not to turn its beneficiaries into laggards, spongers, sluggards." The utility of justice was thus a concern for Llewellyn even though he observed that the "problem of net Justice looks . . . peculiarly to the development of the disadvantaged." This development, he explained, looks to both the "dignity of human beings" and wisdom because, as he put it, "refreshment out of the undeveloped is the way of hope for all."[14]

It is clear that Llewellyn saw, though he did not develop, the relationship between justice and knowledge. One of the major problems with legislative justice, he observed, was the slowly developing but "horribly effective growth of a barrier of ignorance between men and their rights—between men and their law."[15] (He was critical also of the delays in justice and the increasing paternalism of government.) The effect of ignorance on the "law of a democracy" was of dire consequence for Llewellyn. He shared some sympathy for Pollack's belief that "almost any rule of law could be translated into English which an ordinary man could understand."[16]

Llewellyn correctly identified the crucial link between knowledge of one's rights and one's expectations. The "inaccessibility of knowledge of the rules, and worse, of even the main lines that organize the rules, plays twice into the other barrier, that of uncertainty and expense." From the standpoint of administering the law, the results were added labor costs and uncertain advice. From the standpoint of what Llewellyn called the "law-consumer," it put a premium on specialized advocacy. To choose the wrong lawyer "is to lose."[17]

The concept of justice as fairness provides a useful link between two levels of justice: one social and the other individual. From a Rawlsian contractarian perspective the question of fairness "arises when free persons, who have no authority over one another, are engaging in a joint activity and amongst themselves settling or acknowledging the rules which define it [the activity] and which determine the respective shares in its benefits and burdens." "A practice will strike the parties as fair," says Rawls, "if none feels that, by participating in it, he, or any of the others, is taken advantage of, or forced to give in to claims which he does not regard as legitimate."[18] The heart of this relationship is clearly some sort of contractual or conventional arrangement in which mutual expectations are identified and understood. Out of these expectations comes the acknowledgment of all parties concerned that the arrangement is, indeed, fair.

The placing of these arrangements in an institutional context results in formal justice, itself "an aspect of the rule of law which supports and secures legitimate expectations." "One kind of injustice" occurs, says Rawls, when "judges and others in authority [fail] to adhere to the appropriate rules or interpretations thereof in deciding claims."[19] Rawls adds that even in a situation in which the laws and institutions themselves are unjust "it is often better that they should be consistently applied" so that those being treated unjustly will have a chance to protect themselves. At the very least, they will be able to erect defenses against consistently unjust procedures.[20] What is clearly called for in such a situation is reform. Formal justice, which is often a matter of procedural justice, cannot deal with the substantive justice of institutions. In the long run the force of the claims of formal justice lies in the acknowledgment that the basic institutions themselves are just.

Jenkins has argued that law (the legal system) is an "indispensable instrument of social justice" but that it cannot achieve goals that are identical with the goals of social justice. Instead, he says, the goals of social justice "undergo a distinct metamorphosis" when they become part of the "conceptual and procedural apparatus" of law.[21] This apparatus embodies both the power and the limitation of the law. Most importantly, notes Jenkins, "law is not an effective instrument for the formation of human character or the development of human potentialities."[22] "Law cannot create the spirit of cooperation and the sense of community that are envisaged by social justice."[23] Thus its power to achieve social justice is limited, though there is no question that it may serve a watchdog function with respect to those institutions more directly related to human development. This function of law described by Jenkins is basically conservative and "essentially protective rather than constructive."[24] For this reason it is possible that a legal system may protect a social system, such as apartheid or slavery, that is considered unjust by large numbers of people. A legal system may serve unjust purposes even though its procedures are fair, given the inequalities of the political and social system in general.

Whether institutional arrangements themselves are just in the long run determines whether particular groups and individuals are treated fairly. This leads us to consider the measures whereby institutions are judged. Shklar takes the position that we cannot realistically separate considerations of justice from the world of politics—that questions of justice must be considered within a political context and within the context of competing values.[25] Shklar's position runs counter to legalistic thinking in general and positive-law theory specifically. The latter, notes Bird, views positive law as the standard of reference to judge what is just, and the degree of justice as the degree of conformity to positive law.[26]

Positive law is not the only standard of reference to determine the justness of institutions. Its application to issues of justice and injustice is probably limited to conflict resolution within the existing system of law. A social-good theory of justice uses social utility as the measure of a just society, and "the origin and basis of justice lie in the good of society." Natural-law theory, on the other hand, uses natural law as its standard of reference. Justice under natural law is a wider concept than under positive law, and the resolution of questions of justice does not depend upon placing justice within the context of positive law.[27] This does not mean that positive law is ignored or rejected, but rather that it must conform to certain conceptions of the good society based upon natural law.

Natural-law theory is of considerable interest to this study because it is fundamental to our common-law heritage and our constitutionalism. Boorstin says, in his essay on "The Perils of Indwelling Law," that our common-law heritage and the Blackstonian view that "common law was a providential embodiment of Reason and Nature" have historically led American legal theory to "remain impressively inarticulate" and to content itself with restatements, but not to propose "sweeping revisions and codifications," nor to link explicitly legal theory and social purpose. This, of course, has gradually changed with the codification movement over the last fifty years. Of our propensity to constitutionalism, Boorstin has remarked: "We retain an incurable belief that constitutions are born but not made, and this despite the carelessness, prolixity, crudity, and proven ineptitude of many of our state constitutions."[28] Boorstin's criticism notwithstanding, however, much of legal thinking in the United States has been wedded to natural law theory. Like the concept of social contract, it provides an important reference point for considering the concept of justice.

The long tradition of natural law theory—from Aristotle to the scholastics, from theories of social contract to a defense of unrestricted freedom of contract—has regarded natural laws as immutable and eternal. Whatever the epistemological basis for natural law, it has been considered to be the fount of natural justice. Whether by inclination (as Aristotle would have it), revelation, or reason, a knowledge of natural justice was recognized as being important for governance. Its content, notes Jenkins, was "rooted in man's nature: its formulation is the work of reason; its enforcement is the task of government."[29] Social order was presumed to be patterned on natural law.[30]

Historically, theories of obligation and contract were often worked out on the basis of natural law. In the area of international law, Grotius had deduced from natural law the principle that "agreements were to be honored." The same principle was applied to relations of government and the governed. In the works of Hobbes, Locke, and Rousseau, principles of natural law and obligation were wedded to a contract theory of the state.

Natural-law theory has given high priority to the necessity of moral agreement by free and rational men. Such agreement, by extrapolation, was to lead both to greater social cohesion and to individual freedom. These seemingly dichotomous results were reconciled in the moral conception of natural law.

In the hands of social contract theorists, natural law provided an ideological defense for government by consensus, the sanctity of contract, and the protection of private property. Natural law was not the only theory that could be called upon to defend contract and property. Social utility, too, was a powerful argument for honoring contract and defending the rights of property. Yet the appeal to natural law was so explicit in eighteenth-century contract theory and in early-nineteenth-century arguments defining the freedom and honor of contract that it deserves special recognition as part of the ideological foundations of American law.

The concept of obligation was an important aspect of natural law theory and helped to give that theory its moral force. In its general meaning, the term *obligation* denoted a "moral oughtness," says Ladd.[31] This element of moral certainty and the obligation to honor it was easily applied, in turn, to theories of government by consensus. Natural law, after all, was part of the nature of things; it was for reasonable men to discover and to apply as best they could to ordering their lives. Reasonable men, it was argued, would recognize and acknowledge natural law as the origin of their fundamental agreements about how society and government should be ordered. It is in this sense that Shklar asserts that natural law, when applied to political theory, is "fundamentally an ideology of agreement," a conservative ideal that has the effect of overriding moral diversity.[32]

The idea of obligation is an important element in the idea of justice. We are obliged to do what is right, to be fair, to fulfill promises, and to honor the legitimate expectations of others. It is the latter that is problematic for the illiterate person when those expectations are conveyed by undecipherable print. To ignore the obligations of contract would be unjust and morally culpable in our dealings with others.

The obligatory nature of individual contracts or contracts between government and the governed was a logical extension of the "moral oughtness" of natural law. When obligation between individuals is spoken of, it arises from some situation "specifically related to the agent-obligor" and often is legitimized by a promise in the form of a contract.[33] The contract is reason enough, in a legal sense, for being obliged; it does not, however, explain why a contract or promise should be honored at all. For this, either an intuitive appeal, an appeal to prior principles, or an appeal to a higher moral authority must be made. In the latter case, the moral absoluteness of natural law was pressed into service, though an appeal to the greater good of society might also be made.

Problems of obligation would not normally arise if resources were inexhaustible. Given a situation in which scarcity did not exist, the problem of unfulfilled obligations might still be a moral problem, but it would have little practical significance because missing resources resulting from unfulfilled obligations might be replaced with ease.

Though they are poles apart philosophically, both Rawls's and Hart's remarks are helpful here. For Rawls, the larger problem of justice is occasioned by what he calls the "circumstances of justice" that "obtain whenever mutually disinterested persons put forward conflicting claims to the division of social advantages under conditions of moderate scarcity." "Unless these circumstances existed," says Rawls, "there would be no occasion for the virtue of justice."[34] It is likewise with natural law theory and obligations. One of the truisms that underlie natural-law theory in its simplest form, says Hart, is the fact of limited resources.[35] This fact, coupled with a division of labor in society, is an important context for explaining the presence of obligations in a society. The rules that govern the making of promises and foster cooperation help give substance to legitimate expectations. They function, moreover, as guarantors for the fulfillment of obligations. The successful operation of such rules, of course, assumes an appropriate level of understanding in the population to whom they are addressed, and, by inference, accessibility to and possession of those skills required for interpretation.

Rawls's treatment of the institutional context for obligations is particularly informative. "The context of obligations," he notes, "is always defined by an institution or practice the rules of which specify what it is that one is required to do."[36] Rawls has argued that there are "several characteristic features of obligations" that may be "covered by the principle of fairness." Among these he includes the following: that obligations "arise as a result of our voluntary acts"; that "these acts may be the giving of express or tacit undertakings, such as promises or agreements"; and that "obligations are normally owed to definite individuals, namely, those who are cooperating together to maintain the arrangement in question."[37]

Promising, as Rawls and others have recognized, is a key element in our understanding of the concept of obligation. Promises, says Rawls, must be defined in a way "so as to preserve the equal liberty of the parties and to make the practice a rational means whereby men can enter into and stabilize cooperative agreements for mutual advantages."[38] At the heart of promising is "mutual confidence," without which obligations would be meaningless.

In his recent study of *Legal Right and Social Democracy*, MacCormick has addressed the issue of promise as a moral obligation. Though he is not committed to the view of rule utilitarianism, he points out that it is "generally advantageous to members of a community to be able to regard promises as firm commitments from the moment they are made." This is so, he continues, "without regard to nice questions about the degree to which the promisee has perfected the promisor's commitment by acting in reliance on the promise." Legal systems transform the broad moral basis of promise into specific criteria by which obligations are enforceable. In large part the criteria involve a commitment in writing. To secure enforceability, private, noncommercial contracts generally require a written instrument.[39]

Sandel points out that unfair agreements occur for a variety of reasons, including coercion, misinformation, confusion over one's own needs, and unrecognized risks. He continues, "the fact that different persons are situated differently will assure that some differences of power and knowledge persist, allowing agreements, even 'voluntary' ones, to be influenced by factors arbitrary from a moral point of view."[40] To avoid the unacceptable solution of an infinite regress of agreements to keep agreements (or contracts) social, some contract theorists have appealed to an independent standard of reference called "natural law."[41] In acknowledging the reality of a pluralism of human goals and values, Rawls's deontological position cannot appeal to the metaphysics of natural law, nor the pure reason of Kant. His solution lies in "pure procedure," a device whereby he can acknowledge both a voluntarist and a cognitive account of agreement. For Rawls, the former emphasized the act of choice by a self that is prior to the choosing. For the latter, the principles of justice are discovered collectively rather than posited ontologically.[42]

The "common knowledge" of which Rawls speaks is that sense of justice that leads each person to assume that the other has an "effective desire to carry out his bona fide obligations."[43] Fundamentally, for Rawls, that sense of justice is fairness, without which we cannot expect people to be bound by a promise. Moreover, as Rawls argues elsewhere, obligation, as an ethical principle, must rest on just institutions themselves. "Obligatory ties," says Rawls, "presuppose just institutions, or ones reasonably just in view of the circumstances." This assertion is a logical outgrowth of Rawls's assumptions about the nature of the social contract and his distinction between obligation and natural duty. The principle of fairness, says Rawls, "holds that a person is required to do his part as defined by the rules of an institution when two conditions are met: first, the institution is just (or fair) . . . and second, one has voluntarily accepted the benefits of the arrangement or taken advantage of the opportunities it offers to further one's interests." "We are not," continues Rawls, "to gain from the cooperative labors of others without doing our fair share."[44]

In Rawls's contractarian theory of social justice the concept of obligation is tied to the assumption that one is dealing with an institutional arrangement that is genuinely if not completely fair. When justice is conceived of as fairness, we may follow Sandel's lead by inquiring into "the moral force of contracts and agreements generally."[45] The hypothetical, original contract that characterizes social contract theory, says Sandel, "would seem a kind of ordinary contract writ large."[46]

Some social contracts are more hypothetical than others, and contracts, legally speaking, are not hypothetical at all, but the justice of both may be assessed by asking two basic questions: (1) were the parties to the contract free or coerced, and (2) did each party receive a fair share? Thus, the morality of a contract, says Sandel, consists of "two related, yet distinguishable ideals." The first is that of autonomy or a voluntary act of will. The second is that of reciprocity or that of a fair exchange leading to mutual benefit.[47] Contractually, all other arrangements are spun around these two ideals and their variations.

The ideals of autonomy and reciprocity are coexistent though sometimes incompatible ideals. They are, in fact, different measures of the morality of contractual obligation both socially and legally speaking. In other words, they are different forms of justification. With the ideal of autonomy, notes Sandel, the contract *"imparts* the justification"; that is, the process justifies the outcome, "whatever it happens to be." The ideal of reciprocity, however, looks to the actual substance of the exchange and asks whether the result of the contract *"approximates* justice."[48] The ideal of reciprocity thus presupposes some "criterion of fairness independent of contract" that may be used to assess fairness. The tension between these two complementary though often competing ideals is the source of much debate about contractarian theory and underlies both the legal and political difficulties of illiterates.

The problem of reciprocity is dealt with nicely by Weinberger. As a concept of justice, reciprocity is a matter of the equality of inverse relations, performance and counterperformance, reciprocal rights and duties. Weinberger explains, however, that reciprocity does not have universal validity because not all interpersonal relations are affected by it. That it should be included among the principles of formal justice, then, is highly questionable. Reciprocity, he argues, is most appropriate for partnerships. Because it is a principle whose substantive aspect involves value, however, one must raise questions about the nature of equality involved. Are we speaking of equality of activity, worth of performance, readiness?[49] These are problems for any class of persons entering into agreements, but when the ingredient of illiteracy is introduced, the inequality of individual attributes looms even larger.

In an essay titled "Justice as Fairness," Rawls argues that the concept of fairness is "fundamental justice." It "relates to right dealing between persons who are cooperating with or competing against one another, as when one speaks of fair games, fair competition, and fair bargains." "A practice will strike the parties as fair," Rawls continues, "if none feels that, by participating in it, they or any of the others are taken advantage of, or forced to give in to claims which they do not regard as legitimate." "This implies," says Rawls, "that each has a conception of legitimate claims which he thinks it reasonable for others as well as himself to acknowledge." Thus, "a practice is just or fair . . . when it satisfies the principles which those who participate in it could propose to one another for mutual acceptance under the afore-mentioned circumstances."[50]

The concept of mutual acceptance is a formative idea in both theories of social contract and contractual agreements in a legal sense. Rawls, of course, was speaking of mutual acceptance in a collective sense, that is, what is called "publicity." Among the formal constraints of justice—generality, universality, publicity, ordering of conflicting claims, and finality—publicity is the most crucial in considering problems of illiteracy.

The constraint of publicity, says Rawls, "arises naturally from a contractarian standpoint" because parties to the agreement or social contract "assume that they are choosing principles for a public conception of justice." They assume that the principles of justice will be known by everyone and that these principles have "universal acceptance." The condition of publicity implies *explicitness;* that is, it differs from the condition of universality in that the latter asks that the principles of justice be assessed "on the basis of their being intelligently and regularly followed by everyone." Publicity asks that we follow these principles out of *explicit* recognition so that parties to the agreement "evaluate conceptions of justice as publicly acknowledged and fully effective moral constitutions of social life."[51] Publicity, then, helps to guarantee that common expectations will be recognized, that all will know what limitations are placed on their behaviors and what to expect from each other. It is this anticipation of legitimate expectations that creates the problem for the illiterate person in a documentary society since these expectations derive from information that is available, but inaccessible to the illiterate.

In his concepts of social justice and social contract, Rawls has proposed a moral conception of justice based not upon an appeal to a higher and external source of authority, but upon obligation resulting from a mutual acknowledgment of principles that might govern human exchange. It is central to Rawls's antiutilitarian argument that an appeal not be made to "a higher order executive decision" but that it rest on a consensus about rules that constitute fair human exchange.

It is fundamental to Rawls's conception of justice as fairness that parties mutually acknowledge a set of principles that will govern their dealings with each other. Rawls is speaking in the very broad terms of social contract here when he notes that "if participants in a practice accept its rules as fair, and so have no complaint to lodge against it, there arises a prima facie duty (and a corresponding prima facie right) of the parties to each other to act in accordance with the practice when it falls upon them to comply." Obligations resulting from such an agreement do not presuppose "a deliberate performative act in the sense of a promise, or contract, and the like."[52] Yet as we have seen earlier, conditions of fairness must also prevail if formal contracts are to be consistently honored.

Liberty, Opportunity, and Literacy

Both natural law and Rawlsian concepts of obligation and justice point to (not create) serious issues for a political and legal system administering justice for or to illiterate persons. The issues raised begin with the problem of consent—a dilemma common to constitutional democracies. Contract and covenant theories of government, whether inspired by natural-law theory or a more general ideal of fairness, assume that those subject to political and legal constraints have acted as free, rational persons and willingly accepted the demands and constraints placed on them. They have, then, the moral obligation to control their behaviors in accordance with the constraints.[53]

If the objection that one inherits a political order rather than voluntarily joining it is left aside (this problem clearly applies to the education of children), then if one "chooses" to accept the benefits of a particular order, the argument of consent is compelling because it makes of the relationship between individual and society a contractual or covenantal one. To abide by specific statutes and/or common-law principles that govern the benefits to be distributed in a society then becomes an obligation. Thus, for example, if it is assumed that political and economic institutions are justly organized or made in the image of natural justice, then it is just or fair to be bound by the laws that regulate such institutions.

For a contractarian theory of social justice there is a close connection between freedom and the legal principles of contract. A contractarian position postulates that free, rational persons will agree on rules for ordering their behaviors and that these rules will establish the greatest possible liberty under law.[54] In turn, it is assumed that laws will consistently apply rules and provide a procedure for adjudicating differences. It is imperative that the rules of law be public so that legitimate expectations may be based upon them. This is for the common good, but it is a matter of individual justice, also. Here, for example, the precept that "there is no offense without a law" "demands that laws be known and expressly promulgated [and] that their meaning be clearly defined. . . ."[55]

Both the literate and the illiterate person, of course, are bound by the implied agreement of the social contract (metaphorical or embodied in a political and legal system) and the explicit and specific agreements made under formal contracts. Persons are assumed to be rational, and the act of consent is presumed to be free for the literate and illiterate alike. Yet the act of consent is much more problematic for the illiterate. When written rules and contracts prevail, both obligations and expectations are secondhand for the illiterate person. Obligation and rational, free consent imply capacity, ability, and capability. It is the latter that is uncertain for the illiterate. There is little doubt that an illiterate person is capable of giving his consent, if by that term is meant the saying of "yes." But there is considerable doubt that the "yes" would correlate well with the substance or text of the agreement. The discharging of obligations, says Flathman, "is grounded in and limited by what is common to men as men or at least common to the members of a society qua members of the society."[56] When language, and print in particular, is that common bond, illiteracy is of both social and individual concern.

In constitutional democracies, in which a high value is placed upon free consent, a population with a high degree of illiteracy has difficulty consenting to and accessing information relating to both general and specific obligations. And perhaps more importantly for the individual, there is difficulty in exercising those rights that result from consent and participation. This last point is fundamental to securing justice in contractarian theory.

Rawls's theory of justice includes a lexical or priority ordering of two basic principles. His first principle is that "each person is to have an equal right to the most extensive total system of equal basic liberties compatible with a similar system of liberty for all."[57] These liberties include a "just procedure" and such basic liberties as liberty of conscience, freedom of thought, liberty of the person, and equal political rights.[58] Rawls's second principle addresses what Dworkin calls the "sovereign question of political theory" in the liberal state: "what inequalities in goods, opportunities and liberties are permitted in such a state, and why."[59] It postulates that "social and economic inequalities are to be arranged so that they are both: (a) to the greatest benefit of the least advantaged, consistent with the savings principle [intergenerational savings in the form of capital accumulation], and (b) attached to offices and positions open to all under conditions of fair equality of opportunity." The lexical ordering of these two principles is such that the first principle is prior to the second and "liberty can be restricted only for the sake of liberty." The second principle, in turn, is "prior to the principle of efficiency and to that of maximizing the sum of advantages; and fair opportunity is prior to the difference principle."[60]

The lexical ordering of these principles means that "liberty can be restricted only for the sake of liberty." Still, Rawls reminds us that there is an important distinction between liberty itself and the "worth" of liberty. This distinction is important when considering the problem of illiteracy. Poverty, ignorance, and illiteracy may be severe constraints on the ability to exercise one's rights just as they may be obstacles to fair, equal opportunity for social and economic advancement. Whereas liberty in general refers to the "complete system of the liberties of equal citizenship, . . . the worth of liberty to persons and groups is proportional to their capacity to advance their ends within the framework the system defines." Thus, although equal liberty may be present, the worth of that liberty may be unequal. From Rawls's perspective the unequal worth of liberty is compensated for by insisting that the basic structure of institutions is "arranged to maximize the worth to the least advantaged of the complete scheme of equal liberty shared by all." This, he says, is the goal of social justice.[61]

Before looking at the implications of Rawlsian theory for education, it is important to note certain basic tenets of a liberal theory of education. Gaus has contrasted the social contract theories of Mill and Rawls with the utilitarianism of Bentham. He has pointed out that they concur in "holding that one can achieve the classical liberal ideal of an independent agent pursuing one's own goals while simultaneously experiencing fairly intense identification with one's fellows."[62] In his essay "The Convergence of Rights and Utility: The Case of Rawls and Mill," Gaus argues that both theorists come to similar conclusions about the principle of individuality because they share what he calls a "developmental conception of human nature."[63] Other than general limitations that satisfy ethical demands, neither Rawls nor Mill gives us a blueprint for the outcomes of development. Their theories, then, are not utopian, but open-ended. Mill, for example, criticized a "cramped and contracted notion of human excellence, which cares for only certain forms of development."[64]

What Gaus calls a developmental model is an extension of the liberal view of rational man and suggests that any theory of education in a liberal society must likewise be open-ended with respect to self-fulfillment and goals. "No doctrine," Strike reminds us, "is as essential to liberal views as the idea that people are capable of rational self-directed action."[65] The premise is extended easily to education in general. The centrality of education (not necessarily publicly administered) in liberal-democratic thought is summarized by Strike: "A free democratic society relies on the competence of individuals to manage their private lives and to participate in public deliberation in rational ways."[66] The development of rationality thus becomes a major purpose of education in a liberal society. The means is a curriculum that emphasizes literacy, mathematics, and science, with literacy itself broadly interpreted as a "condition of assessing information in our society."[67]

In his work *Educational Policy and the Just Society*, Strike notes that rationality itself may be considered a "primary good." It is, he says, "quintessentially a universal instrumentality" and is assumed when we speak of developing a "rational set of private values or a life plan." It is also basic to the exercise of political rights and economic opportunity. In general, then, rationality is a "public good in the sense that primary goods are public" and is a "requirement implicit in having rights and liberties, opportunities and powers, and income and wealth."[68]

A number of prescriptions for the ideal education in a liberal society exist. It is not my purpose to weigh the strengths and weaknesses of these, however. Suffice it to say that most walk a fine line between education for virtue and education for freedom. In doing this, they recognize the tension between the plurality of interests to be served by schools and the demand for efficiency of instruction, between facilitating autonomy and satisfying social utility.

This tension is most evident in differing concepts of citizenship. The utilitarian accepts the necessity for a moral basis of education in order that citizens might serve the larger social good. Yet he is primarily interested in the "channeling" of citizenship, that is, in making educational institutions selecting and sorting devices for the social, political, and economic placement of future citizens.

In contrast to this are those educational plans that stress autonomy and rationality. Ackerman describes these in developmental terms and notes that the "distinctive character of liberal education has been established by the same dialogic methods used to discipline seemingly unrelated power struggles."[69] Citizenship, Ackerman argues, is a developmental process that requires that a child participate in the "dialogue that constitutes the liberal state" long before he/she reaches "political maturity."[70] The ultimate purpose of education for the liberal, he continues, is "to bring the child to citizenship in a way that, as nearly as possible, respects the questions of legitimacy he raises as he develops his own distinctive pattern of resistances to, and affirmations of, his earliest culture."[71] In short, education in the liberal state is a way of bringing future citizens to terms with the social compact both in its historical meaning and in its future plan. It is, to put it differently, a process of both renewal and rational change.

The implications of Rawls's theory for education rest upon what he sees as the serious shortcomings of the liberal and meritocratic ideals. In many respects, these weaknesses relate not only to a theoretical distribution of rewards but to the educational mechanism that makes such rewards possible. A system of natural liberty presupposes equal liberty, a free market economy and, says Rawls, a "formal equality of opportunity in that all have at least the same legal rights of access to all advantaged social positions." Yet such a system allows the "initial distribution of assets for any period of time" to be "strongly influenced by natural and social contingencies" so that the existing distribution of wealth, for example, "is the cumulative effect of prior distributions of natural assets— that is, natural talents and abilities. . . ." Rawls's major criticism of this meritocratic order is that it is arbitrary from a moral standpoint because "it permits distributive shares to be improperly influenced" by these former distributions.[72]

The liberal interpretation, according to Rawls, attempts to move beyond the meritocratic ideal by specifying that the condition of "fair equality of opportunity" must be present to be just. Says Rawls: "In all sectors of society there should be roughly equal prospects of culture and achievement for everyone similarly motivated and endowed. The expectations of those with the same abilities and aspirations should not be affected by their social class."[73] Thus, according to Rawls, the liberal position attempts to regulate economic and political behaviors in such a way that they will guarantee fair equality of opportunity. This can be done through equal educational opportunity so that "chances to acquire cultural knowledge and skills should not depend upon one's class position, and so the school system, whether public or private, should be designed to even out class barriers."[74]

For Rawls, both the meritocratic and liberal interpretations of social justice are morally defective because they do not alter the fact that the distribution of wealth and income is "determined by the natural distribution of abilities and talents." Says Rawls: "distributive shares are decided by the outcome of the natural lottery; and this outcome is arbitrary from a moral perspective."[75] The alternative to the meritocratic and liberal ideas for justice Rawls calls the "democratic interpretation." This, he says, is a combination of the "principle of fair equality of opportunity with the difference principle." Put simply, the difference principle holds that the expectations of those occupying a higher socioeconomic position are just only if "they work as part of a scheme which improves the expectations of the least advantaged members of society."[76]

The democratic conception of justice of which Rawls speaks is heavily dependent upon fair equality of educational opportunity and the basic skills that result from that. Two principles are relevant here: that of "redress" and the "difference principle." The principle of redress is a prima facie principle that is to be considered as one, but not the only, criterion of justice. "Redress" asks us to compensate for the natural but undeserved inequalities resulting from birth and natural endowment. It asks that society, in order to provide "genuine equality of opportunity," "give more attention to those with fewer native assets and to those born into the less favorable social positions." "The idea," says Rawls, "is to redress the bias of contingencies in the direction of equality." Thus, for example, greater educational expenditures might be in order for the "less rather than the more intelligent, at least over a certain time of life," such as the early years of schooling.[77]

The difference principle is not the same but is compatible with the principle of redress. Handicaps, per se, are not to be evened out to result in fair competition in the social and economic races. But, says Rawls, resources for education would be allocated "so as to improve the long-term expectation of the least favored." If it turned out that giving more to the more intelligent also resulted in the improvement of the least favored, then this would be an acceptable policy. The goals here are not only economic efficiency and the good of all, says Rawls. Rather, in the preceding example, the role of education is to enable "a person to enjoy the culture of his society and to take part in its affairs, and in this way to provide for each individual a secure sense of his own worth." The problem, as Rawls sees it, is to adopt a policy that allows for inequalities but does not further derogate the self-worth of the least favored. Resources for education, then, would not be allocated solely on the basis of the expected return on the investment. Rather, the object would be to allocate resources so that enrichment in the personal and social life of the least favored would result.[78]

The argument, hypothetically, need not be restricted to the allocation of resources for schooling, nor must it be restricted to those in the least favored social position at birth. It could apply equally well to basic education programs for adults who, having been excluded from early schooling for whatever reason, never became literate. It would apply likewise to those who attained such a low level of literacy that it was an obstacle to the exercise of the rights of citizenship, the opportunity for economic advancement, and the attainment of self-respect. Thus social/educational programs designed to remediate adult illiteracy would be justified, not simply from the viewpoint of utility, but from the standpoint of social justice. Given this line of argument, literacy becomes a "right" (not in a constitutional sense or in the sense associated with natural-law theory) much like that of which Oxenham speaks when he says we "regard literacy as a right contingent upon the circumstances of a given society."[79] The right to literacy becomes a second order or enabling right, not belonging to the human condition, but, rather, belonging to a set of societal obligations to the individual. It becomes a right because society is obligated to offer chances for the full operation of more basic human and constitutional rights.

The Rawlsian theory of justice asks that we deemphasize, though not abandon, the priorities of efficiency and social utility in our thinking about social justice. In such a scheme the technocratic imperative gives way to an ethical view while social utility and technological efficiency assume secondary importance. The reordering of priorities, in turn, has important implications for how the meaning and purpose of literacy are defined.

Conclusion

Considerations of justice as a concept and its relationship to literacy raise two basic questions: what is the worth of liberty for the illiterate person and how, given the existence of a class of illiterates, is social justice to be achieved in the liberal/contractarian society? In dealing with the first of these, some previous remarks about meaningful reading bear repeating. It will be remembered that Olson observed that in order to read something meaningfully several factors must be present, including decoding skills, appropriate background knowledge, and ability to imagine a situation of which the text would be a true description. The illiterate person, it can be assumed, lacks the first of these. The second two, although they may result from decoding skills, may or may not follow from them. Background knowledge presumably could be gained through experience unrelated to decoding skills. The third, imagination, might be primarily a matter of cognitive development rather than literacy skills.

When the question is one of the worth of liberty, the situation may be severe because the primary *sources of information* are legal and political documents. Even if a situation were imagined in which this were not so, the exercise of liberty would often depend upon reading and signing legal and political documents. The very concept of liberty, moreover, is not easy to understand and interpret. Its possible applications to legal and political behaviors sometimes require technical knowledge beyond what the "typical" citizen would have.

For the illiterate person, the worth of liberty is extremely problematic. Courts of law as well as administrative authorities have frequently been put in a position of devising compensatory measures for those who appear before them unable to read and write. In fact, as will become evident later, the attitudes of American courts varied considerably: from a sentiment to indulge the foibles of the illiterate to a stern censure of the illiterate's carelessness in entering into contractual agreements. It could hardly have been otherwise. Illiteracy is a burden on court proceedings, yet illiterate defendants and plaintiffs alike have a right to be heard.

At a more general level, court opinions frequently addressed the broader concern of the impact of illiteracy on political stability and social utility. In cases in which a disputed contract was at issue, for example, a judge might take the occasion to comment on the necessity for secure and stable contracts as mainstays of economic order. Where voting rights were in question, a case might serve as a forum for expressing the relationships between literacy and political well-being. It would be a mistake to label these discourses as explications of social and political theory, yet they did draw attention to the problem of illiteracy and social justice.

In a society ordered on contractarian principles, in a general political sense and in a specific economic sense, there is, first, the question of consensus. Closely related to this is the idea of publicity. Second are the problems of access to the social benefits deriving from a contractarian arrangement. Together, these problems of access constitute the problem of equal opportunity.

The voluntary consent by free, rational persons to rules for social order is the heart of the ideal of social contract. Though important for historical accuracy, the legend of the state of nature and the original social contract need not be assumed to recognize the ethical implications of social contract theory. Numerous political and legal obligations may be derived from the act of consent, and consent itself may be implied by a willingness to share in the benefits of a society even though that society may not be of one's own making. The crux of the matter for the illiterate person is the uncertainty of his consent. Conceivably, this could be a problem for the literate person also, but it is reasonable to assume that for illiterates, as a class, there are greater obstacles and hence less access to political and legal information than for literate persons. Illiterates are, as one title would have it, "information poor."[80]

Serious ethical questions arise given the condition of illiteracy and the resultant poverty of information. The ideal of social contract and the presumption of consent imply that the governing principles of justice will be understood and accepted by all. These principles, in other words, are public, and the agreement to abide by them has the force of an ethical commitment made willingly with full knowledge of its consequences. Moreover, the condition of publicity results in a common set of expectations that, if violated consistently, would presumably undermine all agreements predicated on mutual trust. In short, without the condition of publicity, the contractual basis for society would rapidly deteriorate and with it the possibility for principles of social justice emanating from free, rational choice.

It is apropos that the concluding remarks to this section deal with equal opportunity, for this ideal has been the foremost guiding principle of liberal reform in the United States during the last quarter-century. In their review of the conceptual difficulties that obfuscate the meaning of *equal opportunity* in education, Burbules, Lord, and Sherman point out that the term is one properly associated with social justice and that *equitable opportunity* is a better phrase to "denote opportunities that are both equal and fair, given relevant characteristics." It follows from this that criteria for access to opportunities "should be identical to these relevant characteristics, and that it is this identity that makes the opportunity equitable." Many of the authors' remarks are clearly inspired by Rawls's theory of social justice and the concept of justice as fairness. They urge that we reconsider the singleness with which the ideal of equal opportunity has functioned as a guide to policy. Instead they suggest that we place the ideal of equitable opportunity alongside other guiding principles, such as "broader conceptions of rights," so that the "consequences of policy decisions for the least advantaged groups in society are regarded, with serious concern, as inseparable from the provision of opportunities for all other groups. . . ."[81] Much of the equity and equal rights legislation that extended *Brown* (1954) to the handicapped, women, and bilingual population has, of course, been an attempt to extend equal opportunity to all children. Despite ABE programs, extending opportunities to adult illiterates has been far more difficult.

Rawls's lexical ordering of his two principles of justice states that "liberty can be restricted only for the sake of liberty," not social utility, for example, and that the principle of equal opportunity has priority over the difference principle. The latter principle states that the basic structure of society should "be arranged in such a way that any inequalities in prospects of *obtaining* [italics added] the primary goods of wealth, income, power, and authority must work to the greatest benefit of those persons who are the least advantaged with respect to primary goods."[82] Thus in the case of inequality of opportunity, it must also be shown that an inequality of opportunity "enhance[s] the opportunities of those with lesser opportunity."[83]

The lexical ordering of the difference principle and the principle of equality of opportunity poses a basic question for those studying illiteracy: how closely related are levels of literacy and the distribution of prospects for acquiring primary goods? This question is not unique to Rawlsian theory and states in a different way the ongoing concern with equal opportunity. Asking these questions in itself implies that we consider the problem of illiteracy within the context of social justice. To answer the questions requires an array of empirical evidence that could serve as a basis for defining levels and types of literacy needed for persons to share equitably in the benefits of society. Despite the use of batteries of standardized tests and the ongoing concern with functional literacy we know very little about these questions. For philosopher, educator, and policymaker alike, illiteracy thus becomes more than a technical problem or one of social utility exclusively. It becomes a concern with both individual and social justice. For those who would speak in terms of functional literacy, the standard of reference can no longer be only social welfare or technical efficiency. Instead, functionality itself must be defined in terms of the distribution of social benefits and access to justice.

3

The Political
Dimensions of Illiteracy

· · · · · · ·

This chapter examines the problem of illiteracy and the legal issues involving illiterate citizens within the context of Anglo-American political theories—theories that rest heavily on the ideal of social contract as
well as a general contractual ideal. The groundwork for this detailed
consideration is laid by treating the genesis of these ideals. Of particular
interest is the link between contract and natural-law theory. This relationship was basic to American constitutionalism with its defense of
both natural and contractual rights. The rights of Americans, particularly illiterate persons, then are considered in these contexts.

The liberal-democratic ideal of an enlightened public's freely participating in and contributing to the political decisions that affect them
has inspired a number of campaigns against illiteracy. Political participation has been seen as an exercise of autonomous decision making, as
part of the "worth" of liberty, and as a means to further social justice.
When restrictions on political participation have occurred, they have
often been interpreted as an infringement on liberty in general. Basic to
this spirit of democracy is the historic ideal of the *social contract* (compact), the situation of consent that allows for a constituency to promulgate self-imposed rules and laws for self-governance. In Anglo-American law and political theory, the ideal of social contract has in fact been
a mélange of medieval theories of natural law, an archetypal Biblical

paradigm of the once perfect state of nature, constitutionalism in its generic sense, enlightenment theories of human nature and psychological development, and common-law precedents involving property rights and obligations.

The interpolation of these diverse and oftentimes contradictory elements has been the subject of much commentary and controversy. The spirited dialogue over the relationships of the disparate elements in social contract theory, however, is not explored here in detail. What is important is that by the eighteenth century formal theories of social contract had been expostulated and principles of natural rights and property rights had been wedded to a theory of natural law and constitutionalism. The result was a theory of government by consent. The force of this theory was demonstrated, as were its eventual adaptation and implementation, in the new American republic.

The postulate of a social contract was basic to the evolution of the modern concept of constitutional democracy, and the contractual ideal was and is a mainstay of classic liberal thought. The latter, moreover, has seemed to cohere with a minimum of logical distress with other assumptions about natural law, human reason, and property rights. Along with its implications for popular sovereignty and its atomistic conception of political participation, the ideal of social contract has helped to explain (not cause) the sanctity with which the ideal of contract has been treated and the high priority placed upon property rights in American society.

At the same time, social contract, in the form of constitutional democracy, has promised equal liberty, a just system of legislation, and equality before the law. That there are tensions between the economic and political extrapolations of social contract is frequently recognized. What is important at this juncture, however, is that the ideal of social contract (compact) was recognized explicitly at a very early date by the United States Supreme Court. In *Calder et Wife v. Bull et Wife* (1798), Justice Chase noted: "the purpose for which men enter into society will determine the *nature* and *terms* of the *social* compact; and as *they* are the foundation of the *legislative* power, *they* will decide what are the *proper,* objects of it: The *nature,* and *ends* of *legislative* power will limit the *exercise* of it." Chase continued: "This *fundamental* principle flows from the very nature of our free *Republican* governments, that no man should be compelled to do what the laws do *not* require; *nor to refrain from acts which the laws permit.*" Thus, said Chase:

> There are certain *vital* principles in our *free Republican governments,* which will determine and over-rule an *apparent and flagrant* abuse of *legislative* power; as to authorize *manifest injustice by positive law;* or to take away that

security for *personal liberty,* or *private property,* for the protection whereof the government was established. An ACT of the Legislature . . . contrary to the *great first principles* of the *social compact,* cannot be considered a *rightful exercise* of *legislative* authority. The obligation of a law in governments established on *express compact, and on republican principles,* must be determined by the *nature* of the *power,* on which it is founded.[1]

There were immense problems to be solved, of course, with assumptions made about "social compact." The most notable of these, for the purpose of this study, were those about publicity and the nature of free, rational consent. These problems were both political and educational in nature. Their implications were recognized but not fully appreciated by early American political and legal theorists. Thus, for example, it was possible for Jefferson to plan for the perpetuation of agrarian democracy through public education, but apparently to overlook the tremendous demographic and economic problems associated with its support, including the maintenance of a literate population in an area of low population density.

Publicity (the sharing of legitimate expectations) has been assumed to be a fundamental condition for the survival of modern constitutional democracies. It is an assumption that, by implication, also leads to the necessity for mass literacy. Both publicity and literacy, moreover, had been interpreted as necessary though not sufficient conditions for consent as that principle is embodied in the ideal of social contract and self-government. Consent itself is a clear enough concept if it indicates nothing other than a behavior, such as the signing of a contract or a vocal affirmation. When it is associated with rational deliberation and a voluntary, willful act, however, the meaning of consent is not so easily construed. This was true time and again in nineteenth-century cases dealing with contract; it has proved, also, to be a source of difficulty in political theory that predicates sovereignty on a theory of consent.

Morality, Social Contract, and Natural Law

Within the evolution of natural-law principles and theories of social contract we see both the emergence and transformation of theories of liberty and "civic humanism." The development of these two dimensions of contractarian theory has historically established the ideological parameters for the economic and political purposes of literacy in Anglo-American culture. The analyses of Pocock and Skinner provide a useful context for considering the development of these critical ideas.

In his analysis of the political thought of Renaissance Florence, Pocock describes *civic humanism* as a "style of thought . . . in which it is contended that the development of the individual towards self-fulfill-ment is possible only when the individual acts as a citizen, that is as a conscious and autonomous participant in an autonomous decision-[m]aking political community, the polis or republic."[2] The republic per-sisted, he continues, only when equal, direct,and immediate participa-tion of autonomous citizens led to "the pursuit of the universal good."[3] The segmentation of that good through the abuse and unsurpation of political power was seen as a threat to political stability because it cor-rupted the good of the whole. This it did primarily because it "prevented the development of virtue among the groups excluded from power."[4] It was also a point upon which Machiavellian political theory was explicit:

> Only if we are prepared "to act in favour of the public," "to do good for the com-munity," to "help forward" and "act on behalf of" the common good, . . . to ob-serve and follow everything required to uphold it . . . can we in turn hope to avoid a state of tyranny and personal dependence.[5]

By the late-seventeenth and eighteenth centuries the ideal of civic humanism, says Pocock, was ensconced in the practice of inheritable freehold. The freeholder was the guarantor of the principle of autonom-ous decision making in politics—the independent citizen unentangled with the potential corruptions of government. The pressure of the mar-ket was slow to transform this agrarian civic ideal. An economy of ex-change relationships seemed to be the antithesis of the independent freehold. Market relationships trapped men in a web of dependent re-lationships from which they could not easily extricate themselves and over which they had little control.[6]

Late-seventeenth-century Americans—particularly those interested in political theory—were aware of Renaissance political ideals, espe-cially those that had been filtered and transformed by James Har-rington and John Locke. Harrington, says Morgan, "thought he had found in the England of his day the widespread distribution of property" that was a "necessary condition for republican government."[7] Morgan has noted that American clergymen were aware of Lockean political theory and "every generation learned of its duty to pull down bad rulers and to uphold good ones."[8]

American historians have frequently noted the widespread anxiety of colonial Americans over corruption. Wood has commented that "since the seventeenth century" Americans had "warned themselves re-peatedly against declension and social corruption."[9] It was a concern, however, born out of a knowledge of English government as well as fear of licentiousness and luxury. But republicanism, observes Wood, also was an "ideological response to great social changes," including "distinctions of prestige and status that were arising, the rate and the nature of mobility, and the distribution of power and wealth."[10] The fear of corruption eventually received its most widespread political expression in Jeffersonian doctrine. In turn, the agrarian freeholder ideal of Jefferson was assaulted by an emerging urban America in which large concentrations of capital helped to corrupt as well as limit the powers of the independent farmer.

The moral basis of the state posited by civic humanism and realigned in Anglo-American thought as the ideal of agrarian freehold assumed both a leveling tendency in landed wealth and a liberty (opportunity) to acquire new wealth. It assumed, moreover, a larger social good to be served—a community of values that functioned to assure political stability and liberty. Both the ideals of equality and liberty were thus a part of the ideal polis. The relationship between them, however, was not altogether sanquine.

In his celebrated essay "Two Concepts of Liberty," Isaiah Berlin pointed out that the classical English political philosophers spoke of liberty as noninterference by others.[11] The central question they sought to answer was how to establish the necessary conditions to make use of freedom. More recently Skinner has concluded that the idea of negative (unconstrained) liberty underlies the "entire development of modern contractarian political thought."[12] Following the lead of Taylor, he argues that negative liberty has operated as an "opportunity concept" divorced from the "pursuit of any determinate ends or purposes."[13]

One of the major theoretical tasks of contractarian theories from the late seventeenth century forward was the synthesis of liberty as an opportunity concept with the ideal of a larger social good on which the political stability of the state depended. The synthesis was consummated at the hypothetical level in the theory of social contract. This, in turn, was embodied in constitutional theories of political power. The logical tension of negative liberty and moral equality, however, persisted in debates over the public good versus private interests. This same debate was, and is, found in controversies over the role of public education in a democracy. It is, by extension, found in debates over the level and type of literacy best suited for democratic societies.

The Social Contract and Natural Law

It is important to note at the outset that whatever the theoretical incongruities of natural and positive law, historically the two did not operate independently. Kelsen has remarked that natural-law doctrine has tended "to view positive law not as a mere fact, but as a system of valid norms, as a legal order with normative validity, which exists side by side with a similarly understood natural law."[14] The writings of Blackstone are a good case in point. To Blackstone, the law of God, of Nature, and of England were tightly woven into a conservative fabric that glorified "the power of man's reason . . . the beauty of English institutions, and ultimately, . . . the Intelligence of God."[15] For Blackstone, the correlation between English law and natural law was both aesthetic and logical. In the harmony of man's reason with the principles of nature and English law was found the cause of the beauty and reasonableness of British institutions. As Boorstin has noted:

> When the *Commentaries* showed the close accord of English laws with the laws of nature, they were thus simultaneously proving to the eighteenth-century mind that English law had the aesthetic virtues of nature. And the converse of this also seemed true: if the English legal system could be shown to be at once "beautiful" and "sublime", this would reinforce the presumption that these institutions were part of Nature's scheme.[16]

In the departure of natural-law theory from the doctrine of scholasticism, the work of Grotius represented a transitional stage in the evolution of Western legal philosophy and the theory of property. Grotius, notes d'Entreves, was still "deeply imbued with the spirit of Christianity."[17] God is the author of nature in Grotius's now-classic definition of natural law as a "dictate of right reason by which, to every action . . . there attaches an ethical approbation or disapprobation . . . imposed or forbidden by God. . . ."[18] Although it is evident from Grotius's work that he views God as having an active part in the affairs of men, it is also apparent that his aim was to "construct a system of law which would carry conviction in an age in which theological controversy was gradually losing the power to do so."[19] Thus Grotius could assert that natural law "would subsist in some way or other even if we were to admit (an admission which cannot be made without risk of great impiety) that God did not exist or that he did not concern himself with human affairs."[20] Grotius points the way toward the separation of natural-law theory from theology.

That separation resulted in the division of social contract from the "contract of dominion." Grotius's starting point, says Bloch, was optimistic: "It was not the *drive for self-preservation* motivated by the *fear* of one's neighbor, but the social drive, *appetitus socialis,* that led to the social contract."[21] From the assumption of sociability came the view that injustice is all of that which "conflicts with an ordered community of individual rational beings." Justice, then, is all that which conforms to the community.[22]

Caponigri has observed that among those of the jusnaturalistic school, including Pufendorf, Grotius's doctrine of natural law gave him the reputation of a rationalist and a precursor of the Enlightenment. Thus, eventually, as in Locke, the essence of law is reason, not will. It is this very idea that, in the long run, allows natural-law theory to be divorced, etiologically, from theology; it is this idea that makes it possible for intellect rather than command to be the foundation of law.

The forcefulness of Grotius's statements, says Caponigri, threw into "greater relief his emphasis upon the basic character and immutable pirnciples of the natural law and the system of rights and obligations deriving from it." As a result, he continues, his concept of natural law led to "certain governing principles" in the areas of private and international law. The basic principle of property was thus taken to be "the power to dispose of things of a lesser nature which were conferred by God universally on the human race." Property was, then, a regulatory mechanism for commerce.[23]

According to Caponigri, Grotius believed that, in the area of international law, the basic principle was that "agreeements are to be honored," a principle that, it turns out, is easily applied to relations between a sovereign state and its constituency. Grotius, observes Caponigri, conceived of a contract as the "basic act and relation which binds members into a civil society and which relates government and governed." Grotius did not expand on this idea of contract; his work, nonetheless, contained a latent contract theory of state derived from his postulates of natural law.[24]

In the work of Locke, Hobbes, and Rousseau natural-law theory achieved prominence within the context of a contract theory of state. Locke and Hobbes are discussed here because it is their work that has the most direct bearing on the concepts of sovereignty, contract, and private property as these ideas developed in British and American law and political theory. Both Hobbes and Locke accepted the idea of man as a rational being capable of guiding his actions by intellect and discovering, through reason, those natural principles of justice that ought to rule when reason prevails. Yet it has been generally observed also that their inferences from this basic assumption were dramatically different—so different, in fact, that Hobbes became the forerunner of legal positivism and the rejection of natural law altogether.[25]

Hobbes's conception of natural law as the "moral basis and norm for statute law" enabled him to construct an argument independent of an "appeal to custom, precedent, or common law as the source of justice."[26] The "laws of nature," the "dictates of reason," and man's survival were inextricably woven together for Hobbes. The "faculty of right reasoning," he says in *De Cive*, was necessary to "observe the laws of nature"—laws that for Hobbes were "immutable and eternal."[27] Similarly, in *Leviathan* a law of nature "is a precept or general rule, found out by reason, by which a man is forbidden to do that which is destructive of his life or takes away the means of preserving the same." Thus, observes Kemp, Hobbes's concept of a law of nature "requires a certain kind of conduct—it does not merely permit it."[28] A natural right, or right of nature, explains Kemp, means that a "man may legitimately [morally] take the steps which he thinks necessary to the preservation of his own life; it does not mean that one man in a state of nature has any sort of duty or obligation to protect the natural right of another."[29] The formula was one in which self-interest held center stage and from which common interest was derivative only.

Hobbes's first law of nature, the "fundamental law of nature" as stated in the *Leviathan*, is *"that every man ought to endeavor peace, as far as he has hope of obtaining it; and when he cannot obtain it, that he may seek and use all helps and advantages of war."* From the first law, "by which men are commanded to endeavor peace, is derived this second law," says Hobbes: *"that a man be willing, when others are so too, as far forth as for peace and defense of himself he shall think it necessary, to lay down this right to all things, and be contented with so much liberty against other men as he would allow other men against himself."*[30] It is Warrender's thesis that "the validating conditions of law in the State of Nature or elsewhere, are the validating conditions of all law in Hobbes's system." "If any law is to be valid law . . . it must operate in a context in which the validating condition of 'sufficient security' may be said to be fulfilled," says Warrender. Hobbes's account of civil society, he argues, "is essentially an account of how these validating conditions may become satisfied."[31]

The second law of nature, for Hobbes, is the foundation of *contract*, "a mutual transferring of right," and *covenant*, a contract involving performance "at some determinate time after and in the meantime be trusted. . . ." Within the structure of the civil estate, the promise involved in a contract is obligatory, and "he which by the covenant is to perform first is obliged to do so."[32] It is important to point out that the promise to keep covenant does not originate with the state. The difference between obligations incurred by covenant in a state of nature and in a civil society, Warrender observes, "is a difference of circumstance and not of moral principle."[33] Thus, as Hobbes notes, in the common course of trade and commerce it is the prerogative and expectation of the commonwealth or sovereign "to appoint in what manner all kinds of contract between subjects—as buying, selling, exchanging, borrowing, lending, letting, and taking hire—are to be made, and by what words and signs they shall be understood for valid."[34] That knowledge of the law or knowledge of the conditions of contract constituted an important aspect of Hobbes's theory of obligation is evident.

In *Leviathan,* Hobbes says, "The law of nature excepted, it belongs to the essence of all other laws to be made known to every man that shall be obliged to obey them, either by word, or writing, or some other act known to proceed from the sovereign authority. . . . Nor is it enough the law be written and published, but also that here be manifest signs that it proceed from the will of the sovereign."[35] In a lengthy footnote to the second paragraph of *De Cive,* Hobbes reminds us that in the matter of belonging to a "constituted society among men" there are many "(perhaps most men) [who] either through defect of mind, or *want of education* [italics added], remain unfit during the whole course of their lives."[36]

In an oft-cited and frequently debated passage from *Leviathan* Hobbes explains that natural law and civil law "contain each other and are of equal extent." "Civil and natural law are not different kinds but different parts of law," he notes. Civil law may restrain "the right of nature—that is, the natural liberty of man," says Hobbes: "the end of making laws is no other but such restraint, without the which there cannot possibly be any peace."[37] In fact, it is the restraint of civil law that makes possible the administration of justice or equity. Even though the administration of equity might differ according to time and circumstances so that "what is done with equity at one time, is guilty of inequity at another," equity itself is still in accord with reason and, ultimately, natural law. This is true, says Hobbes, because reason does not change in terms of its purpose, "which is peace and defense"—concepts themselves that comprise the "first fundamental law of nature."[38]

In addition to a theory of sovereignty, Hobbes's treatment of covenant and contract is a transitional phase in the theoretical development of a will theory of contract. The concept of will, that is, of intent or purposeful choosing, and promise is fundamental to Hobbes's theory of contract. In his account of covenant in the English translation of *De Cive* (1651) (which he gives within the context of the "conveyance of right"), he points out that "covenants are made of such things only as fall under our deliberation, for it can be no covenant without the will of the contractor, but the will is the last act of him who deliberates; wherefore they only concern things possible and to come."[39] To covenant, he says in *Leviathan,* "is an act of the will—that is to say, an act, and the last act, of deliberation."[40]

When we turn to Locke we find again a theory that stipulates the general conditions under which consent and contract will be legitimate. In Locke's conviction that the world would be understood rationally, we find the roots of his concept of freedom. We are *"born Free,* as we are born Rational,"* he states, and "The Freedom of Man and Liberty of acting according to his own Will, is *grounded on* his having *Reason,* which is able to instruct him in that Law he is to govern himself by, and make him know how far he is left to the freedom of his own will."[41] For Locke, the limits of freedom are defined by the acts of "rational cooperation" and consent that allow men to found political authority. Membership in society is thus given by consent, but it is property, notes Laslett, that makes that membership tangible and functional.[42] Whether we are speaking of Locke or Hobbes or Rousseau the form of substance of the social contract, says d'Entreves, is unvaried:

> "Formally," the contract is a manifestation of individual will with the object of establishing a relationship of mutual obligation which would not otherwise exist by the law of nature. "Substantially", the content of the contract is the "natural right" of the individual, which is exchanged against a counterpart of equal or greater value—the benefits of society and the security of political organization.[43]

That the individual's natural rights are altered once having entered into the social contract is quite apparent from Hobbes's views of the absolute sovereignty of the state. Locke, on the other hand, devoted a good deal of time to explaining why these rights should go unaltered.

Through the act of consent and the establishment of political authority, according to Locke, men had created the civil order necessary to the preservation of private property. Atiyah has observed that Locke's emphasis upon consent and his rejection of promises or contracts "extracted by force of fear" helped to strengthen "the moral appeal of his position." "It was much easier," he says, "to support the idea that by 'Natural Law' consent was a valid source of political or legal obligations when it was at the same time insisted that the consent must be genuine and freely given."[44]

Seliger has observed that Locke did not elevate property above all other natural rights, but presented it as a "prototype of all natural rights."[45] Private property is a natural right not in contradiction to the scriptural lesson that God had given the earth to mankind in common, but rather, as a result of man's *"Property* in his own *Person,"* including the "Labor of his Body. . . ." In his *Second Treatise* Locke called upon the authority of God to explain the growth of private possession. Locke maintained that God gave the "World to Men in common" but had "also given them reason to make use of it to the best advantage of Life, and convenience," that He gave the world "to the use of the Industrious and Rational."[46]

Tully has pointed to the significance of the "workmanship model" in

Locke's analysis of property. This model, he says, comprises "two complex ideas: 'The *Idea* of a supreme Being, infinite in Power, Goodness, and Wisdom, whose Workmanship we are, and on whom we depend; and the *Idea* of our selves as understanding, rational Beings. . . .'" This model, which sees "God and man as makers," says Tully, aids in explaining "God's dominion over man and . . . why man is God's 'property'[;] it also explains man's dominion over and property in the products of his making: 'God makes him *in his own Image after his own Likeness,* makes him an intellectual Creature, and so capable of Dominion'. . . ."[47]

Locke went on to explain that a man's labor gave him title to his property. "The Condition of Humane Life, which requires Labour and Materials to work on, necessarily introduces *private Possessions,*" he observed. Moreover, the "different degrees of Industry were apt to give Men Possessions in different Proportions. . . ." This fact, added to the invention of money, said Locke, created an inequality of wealth, for it was money that gave man an opportunity to expand his wealth beyond his needs. The natural principles that helped account for private possessions also operated within the context of positive law. Political authority having been established, "Laws regulate the right of property, and the possession of land is determined by positive constitutions."[48]

In his wedding of natural and positive law, Locke was able to explain how it was that the sanctity of private property and the individual right to its possession were consistent with and not bridged by political authority. He had recognized the suitability of the idea of contract to provide the bridge between natural law (and natural rights) and the power of the State: "The idea of contract was the only possible means of setting the natural rights of the individual within the framework of the State."[49] Contract became the basis of the State, but, for Locke, the fact that the State itself was founded upon consent acted as a restraint upon the exercise of sovereignty. (Even the conqueror does not have absolute power in the "continuance of Government": *"without a Man's own consent* [property] *cannot be taken from him.)*"[50] Contractualism and the idea of consent made it possible for Locke to come to the conclusion that law made "men free in the political arena, just as reason makes men free in the universe as a whole." That law, notes Laslett, is "progressively codified by a legislative brought into being by consent[;] it is expressive of and in harmony with the law of nature, which continues of course in society."[51]

Law, freedom, and reason are mutually reinforcing elements in a social order in which law is the *"direction of a free and intelligent Agent* to his proper Interest, and prescribes no farther than is for the general Good of those under that Law." *"The end of Law,"* continues Locke, "is not to abolish or restrain, but to *preserve and enlarge Freedom. . . ."* But this freedom is qualified as it must be to satisfy the dictates of reason and the natural right to property. Thus, Locke says, freedom is not *"Liberty for every Man to do what he lists:* (For who would be free, when every other Man's Humour might domineer over Him?)" Rather, it is a *"Liberty* to dispose, and order, as he lists, his Person, Actions, Possessions, and his whole Property, within the allowance of those Laws under which he is; and therein not to be subject to the arbitrary Will of another, but freely follow his own."[52]

Natural Law and American Law

Locke's synthesis of the social good with liberty in the disposition of private property became a mainstay of American political thought. The natural-law tradition that emphasized the close link between the law of nature and the law of God also underlay the development of both British and American constitutional theory. American legal education included the study of Coke and Blackstone. In colleges where law was taught, the curriculum usually included a course on natural law.[53]

The importance of natural-law theory to the acceptance of English common-law principles should not go unrecognized. Eighteenth-century attitudes toward law linked the common law, the law of nature, and the law of reason. Common-law rules, like the law of nature, were *"founded in principles, that are permanent,* uniform *and* universal."[54] Yet, as Pound has commented in his *Formative Era of American Law,* the acceptance of English common law in "post-Revolutionary America was not a foregone conclusion."[55] Likewise, Hyman and Wiecek have pointed to the "republican ideological emphasis on the role of the legislature, Jeffersonian hostility to the decisions of the Marshall Court and democratic insistence on popular sovereignty" as obstacles to the continuance of common law tradition. All, they say, "combined to make the role of the judges suspect, especially when they thwarted popular or legislative will by holding a statute unconstitutional."[56]

It may be reasonably argued that without the tempering effects of natural-law theory with its appeal to universal principles of reason, English common law principles would have suffered a severe blow despite their usefulness in the day-to-day operation of the courts. In the absence of a *set* of clearly defined precedents that were unencumbered by English common law, natural-law theory provided a moral basis and hence a moral appeal for American jurists.

Nelson has observed that the America of the 1780s was not prepared to "abandon blithely the pre-Revolutionary ideal that human law must conform to fundamental principles of divine or natural law": "Post-Revolutionary Americans continued to maintain that they could rationally 'define the rights of nature' and learn 'how to search into, to distinguish, and to comprehend, the principles of physical, moral, religious and civil liberty.' "[57]

Yet the conflict between legislative will and immutable law was in evidence. In *Rutgers v. Weddington* (1784), notes Nelson, " 'the supremacy of the Legislature . . . *positively* to enact a law' was pitted against 'the rights of human nature' and the 'law of nature.' " Similarly, he observes, the case of *Trevett v. Weeden* (1787) challenged a Rhode Island statute that "penalized without jury trial anyone who refused to accept the state's paper currency" on the basis that it was " 'contrary to the laws of nature' and violative of the 'fundamental right' of 'trial by jury.' "[58]

Natural law, the social compact, and English experience were all brought to the defense of private property against legislative intrusion in *Vanhorne's Lessee v. Dorance* (1795). "The preservation of property . . . is a primary object of the social compact, and, by the late Constitution of *Pennsylvania,* was made a fundamental law," said the decision. "The right of acquiring and possessing property, and having it protected, is one of the natural, inherent, and unalienable rights of man." It was argued that every person has the obligation to contribute to the public welfare, but that, "no one can be called upon to surrender or sacrifice his whole property, real and personal, for the good of the community, without receiving a recompence in value." It was observed that even the English Parliament, with its "boasted omnipotence," "never committed such an outrage on private property. . . . Such an act would be a monster in legislation, and shock all mankind":

> It is consistent with the principles of reason, justice and moral rectitude; it is incompatible with the comfort, peace, and happiness of mankind; it is contrary to the principles of social alliance in every free government; and lastly, it is contrary both to the letter and spirit of the Constitution.[59]

Hyman and Wiecek have pointed out that "classical American constitutional jurisprudence absorbed Blackstone's higher-law principles." This was true in *Van Horne's Lessee v. Dorance* (1795), *Calder v. Bull* (1798), and *Fletcher v. Peck* (1810). After *Dartmouth College* (1819) the general appeal to higher law gradually disappeared from the opinions of the United States Supreme Court. The *Charles River Bridge v. Warren Bridge Co.* (1837) seems to have been its last gasp. Yet in state courts "higher law flourished." Here it came from demands that "statutes affecting property be general, not special" and "an insistence that such laws not be punitive or retroactive in application." Connecticut, Tennessee, Maryland, and Delaware used the language of *Calder v. Bull* when they wished to void state statutes that violated "eternal principles of justice," "obvious dictates of reason," "the nature and spirit of the social compact," and "the nature and spirit of our republican form of government."[60]

Pound has argued that natural-law theory was a stabilizing factor in the formative era of American law in the first half of the nineteenth century. It provided a link (however idealized) between the natural rights of man, as defined by continental jurists, and the "immemorial common-law rights of Englishmen as declared by Coke and Blackstone." The tie between natural law and morality, says Pound, provided "an absolute and universal system of legal duties and legal rights" that in the nineteenth century enabled American jurists to work out a "system of individual legal rights. . . ."

In other ways, also, natural-law theory provided stability and continuity to a legal system "shaped by judicial decision." Ideal positive law and natural law were, if not identical, closely identified with each other. Legal anachronisms, many of which were associated with English common-law elements rooted in feudal landholding patterns, were seen as incompatible with natural law. It was argued that positive law should be made without these "unreasonable" restraints. Commercial law, too, was interpreted within the framework of natural-law theory. Finally, argues Pound, "a conception of an ideal of comparative law as declaratory of natural law gave direction to judicial development of the law."[61]

Pound, however, was sceptical of the applicability of natural-law theory to twentieth-century circumstances. Said Pound in an essay that helped lay the groundwork for a sociological jurisprudence:

> Perhaps nothing has contributed so much to create and foster hostility to courts and law and constitutions as this [natural law] conception of the courts as guardians of individual natural rights against the state and against society, of the law as a final and absolute body of doctrine declaring these individual natural rights, and of constitutions as declaratory of common-law principles, which are also natural-law principles, anterior to the state and of superior validity to enactments by the authority of the state, having for their purpose to guarantee and maintain the natural rights of individuals against the government and all its agencies.[62]

It was Kant, Pound observed, who gave the "death blow" to natural-law theory as it was thus conceived and who premised a theory of rights on the concept of freedom of will. It was Kant who thus reconceptualized the problem of law in terms of "conflicting free wills" and determined the "course of nineteenth-century juristic theory." The "transition was complete," argued Pound, "from the idea of justice as a maintaining of the social *status quo* to an idea of justice as the securing of a maximum of individual self-assertion."[63] It was this Kantian view of freedom of will that profoundly affected contractual theory in both its political and economic dimensions.

The Constitutional Ideal

The contractarian ideal in the form of a social compact theory and the continued presence of natural-law theory had, by the late eighteenth century, set the stage for the development of American constitutionalism. Together, they formed the moral foundation for a theory of consent in public life while retaining the concept of liberty necessary to the exercise of private interest.

The heart of American constitutionalism was the act of consent, rationally and freely given, that led to the social contract. Contract itself was a matter of mutual obligation resulting from a bargain freely and rationally made, but its origin in willful actions presumed a freedom of action. The material bases for constitutionalism were the freeholder ideal and the inviolable right to private property. The nature of sovereignty itself was found in the willful act and the consent. Natural law, the legal theories of covenant and contract, and the historic ideal of civic humanism helped to define the limitations of freedom and obligation and to reconcile (structurally at least) the tension of liberty and equality.

Virtue and liberty were the pillars supporting public responsibility and private initiative. Together with the principle of consent rationally and freely given, they provided the political rationale for a commitment to mass literacy leading to an enlightened, self-governing public. The virtuous freeholder (and even the virtuous craftsman and trader) was he who understood the moral foundations of ownership and citizenship—of the relations among men that must prevail if free exchange and political participation were to survive. Both the law of nature and the utility of political and economic participation demanded such an understanding. Thus, it was argued, both economic survival and political reality demanded a literate, well-informed public.

American constitutionalism did not logically reconcile the competing claims of liberty and equality. Rather, its solution was to contain conflict through process and structure. Given the hypothetical nature of Locke's and Hobbes's solution to the problem of consent, this should not surprise us. Neither Hobbes nor Locke argued that men were actually equal in virtue, yet for both equality was a premise necessary to civil order. As McWilliams observes: "for Locke as for Hobbes, man's natural freedom and equality of force made it necessary to regard human beings as equals, despite their inequality of worth, in order to make civil government possible."[64] Pure consent was a fiction, yet majority rule, says McWilliams, "corrected that defect by relying on the only equality that counted in politics, the equality of force and freedom."[65]

McWilliams's conclusion is that for Locke and Hobbes "equality was a concession to political necessity, a recognition of the rights inherent in the individual and the basis for orderliness, not a reflection of equal worth."[66] The arguments of Locke and Hobbes on equality were fundamentally ways of structuring inequality. For American constitutionalism the mechanism to preserve inequality was representative rather than participatory government. In his essay "The Compromised Republic: Public Purposelessness in America," Barber has summarized the effects of eclecticism on American republicanism and what he calls "surrogates for pristine republican institutions":

> private property became the surrogate for public norms, self-interest binding men to their public obligations no less surely than shared values once did; that procedural consensus became the surrogate for substantive consensus; that representation replaced participation, as accountability replaced self-government, and autonomy was traded for rights.[67]

The structuring of inequality is only one side of the constitutional fabric. The premise of a common good—a civic humanism—was acknowledged in law and political theory alike. Moreover, it became the incentive for many arguments to support public elementary schooling. Vague as it might be, consent to a common set of values was presumed by educators and political leaders. Whether the moral basis of consent was founded on God's law or the law of reason remained a matter for debate, the latter surfacing repeatedly in attempts to formulate an ideology of public education. Civic humanism, altered to take account of American constitutionalism, provided the rationale for much of primary education and the goal of a literate population. Functional literacy, including that related to technical reading and economic well-being, did not emerge as a serious competitor for inclusion in the curriculum until the fourth decade of the nineteenth century. Even then, however, it could not take the measure of moral instruction and civic education. Proponents of the economic value of literacy and education would have to wait until the second half of the nineteenth century for their arguments to receive wide recognition and approval in public education.

The Civic Life of the Illiterate Person

The Colonial Period

We have seen that as a matter of principle literacy and education had a great deal to do with conceptions of civic life in general in eighteenth-century America. They had little relationship to legal requirements for civic participation, however. Illiteracy rates measured by the inability to sign one's name varied widely at the opening of the nineteenth century in the United States. It has been estimated from army enlistment records that illiteracy rates fluctuated between 25 and 63 percent during the period 1799-1829 depending upon region, ethnicity, and occupation. Prior to the last half of the nineteenth century, literacy was not, however, a common device for enfranchisement. Though rare, it did, however, have some application. Thus, in seventeenth-century colonial New Jersey in the town of Newark, one "Richard . . . [was] admitted a freeholder, upon Condition of his setting his Name to our Agreements, and Hath the Priviledge of Commonage for Fifty Pound Estate, without Deduction; and He Hath Promised to set About Learning to read—which was an Encouragement unto Them herein." Probably Richard eventually would have been admitted as a freeholder even without literacy, but clearly this was, at the time, a stipulation accompanying his political participation.[68]

The concern with freeholder literacy, however, was certainly less important than the concern for property qualification, the latter being a notable feature of voter eligibility in colonial America. It is quite probable that concern with literacy and political stability in the early nineteenth century was not translated into voter qualifications simply because the problem did not seem to be formidable and its solution was perceived in educational, not political terms. The tremendous faith in education as the guarantor of political stability was reflected among educators and politicians alike. Historically, arguments regarding the need for education, the problem of illiteracy, and the close conceptual relationship between public enlightenment and democratic governance have been waged in terms of nation building, economic well-being, and moral and social stability. Though the concern with all three was the making of the good citizen, exclusion from this status was not perceived in terms of equal protection until the latter part of the nineteenth century and did not become an issue of minority rights until well into the twentieth century.

In colonial America, the illiterate person was involved in a wide range of important political, economic, and legal behaviors. This is quite clear from an examination of colonial court records, though such records do not permit an accurate assessment of difficulties that arose because of the inability to read or write. Participation of a more direct political nature, for example, involved the founding of a new town. Thus, in 1626 Rhode Island petitioners committed themselves to the rules and regulations of a corporate way of life. Five of the thirteen men signing the following petition signed with a mark:

We whose names are hereunder, desirous to inhabit in the town of Providence, do promise to subject ourselves in active and passive obedience to all such orders or agreements as shall be made for public good of the body in an orderly way, by the major consent of the present inhabitants, masters of families-incorporated together in Towne fellowship, and others whom they shall admit unto them only in civil things.[69]

Other types of political agreements also included illiterate persons. A New York resolution "adopted by the commonality of the Manhattans" in 1643 included nineteen markers out of the forty-four signers. These men had been "invited to a fort to express their opinions on a proposition and procedure for electing representatives to review and render judgment upon regulations passed and representatives chosen by the director and council of the Fort."[70] Similarly, a Maryland resolution of 1638 giving the power of representation to one Henry Bishop was signed by six men, five of whom were markers. Their basic act of political commitment is shown by the following:

(We) chose for the Burgess of the hundred of Mattapanient Henry Bishop and have Given unto him full and free Power for (us) and for every of them to be present in their names at the next Assembly as their Burgess or deputy and in witness thereof have herento sett (our) hands.

> The mark of Richard X Garnett
> The mark of Richard X Lusthead
> The mark of Joseph X Eldo
> Robert Wiseman
> The mark of Anum X Benum
> The mark of Lewis X Freeman[71]

Still of general civic importance but of considerably greater significance for legal proceedings were jury duty, witnessing, testimony, and depositions. Illiterate persons often performed these functions, and we must assume that no great stigma was attached to their participation. Jurors were frequently illiterate. Of twenty-five New Plymouth Colony juries in 1652, 11 percent of the jurors were illiterate. A jury hearing a case of land disposition in Kent County, Delaware, in 1705 was 58 percent (seven of twelve) illiterate, and a jury of inquiry in Talbot County, Maryland, in 1676 was 67 percent illiterate.[72]

Illiterate persons were often asked to confirm or testify to the accuracy of transactions or to serve as witnesses to possible criminal activities. In some cases, their expertise was called upon to appraise the value of land or chattels. In a case of nonsuit before the County Court of Kent,

Delaware, in 1681, for example, four illiterate men and a literate sheriff appraised the land in question and found "the said Land and appertences Belonging unto Itt to Bee worth one hundred and twenty pounds starling mony of England. . . ."[73] A year later, a similar instance may be found in which four markers appraised, as part of probate, a parcel of land, finding it to be the equivalent or "true vallue of the six mares mentioned in the Execution."[74]

In the matter of witnessing, being literate was not necessarily crucial to understanding the issue at hand. A correct reading of the document or deposition, however, was critical, and it may be surmised that seemingly insignificant changes in wording could result in substantial changes in meaning. In the following description, which might be confusing to one not accustomed to markings on livestock, there was probably minimum room for error by William Ward, an unlettered man who agreed to testify that "Francis Martyns steere had these particular markes viz. a white starre that went crosse the forehead the towe hynder feete whyte about halfe and a small white tippe on the tayle cropped on the right eare, and a Flower de luce on the lefte eare. . . ."[75]

On the other hand, the testimony of Susanna Gleison against Phillip Reade, a physician residing in Concord, for swearing and cursing was of a nature that could be easily misworded. The wording was even more important, for there had been conflicting testimony in the case and blasphemy was a crime punishable by death in Massachusetts Bay. Gleison testified as follows and signed with a mark:

> Susanna Gleison aged ab^t 55 yeares, being Sworne do say, that Sometime ab^t may last, Shee being present at ye house of Philip Read at Concord, whose wife was y^n weak & neer death (as her friends thought) her mother mentioneing ye name of ch^t Hee ye Said Read replyed, ye Devill take you & yor ch^t and a motion being made of praying to God for her He said ye Divel take you & yor prayers. And ye wife of David fisk Soone after comeing in, this depon^t took occasion to manifest her trouble at ye s^d Read, for his evill speaking Whereupon his mother in law Goody Rice replyed he blasphemed he blasphemed. And after this ye^e Said Read comeing to ye house of this Depon^t shee told him of his curseing & evill speaking, to wch ye replyed, excusing his rage y^t he was then:—Saying y^t The woman (his mother in law) had made him mad, and Said the Devill take her for shee had brought him to
>
> Her
> Susanna   X   Gleison[76]
> Mark

In addressing the question of participation by illiterates in the economic and political system in the colonial period, one repeatedly encounters situations in which the illiterate person was involved in the mainstream of political and economic life. Frequently, however, he or she was probably dependent on the lexical skills of others. Thus, although the illiterate was not marginal in the sense of being on the fringe or actually isolated from these important behaviors, his position was one of dependency and, in this sense, precarious. Because he lacked the skills associated with literacy, he probably was rather the victim of circumstance, the conditions of his participation more likely the result of others' generosity and benevolence than of his own abilities. He was, to put it differently, less the maker of his destiny than the literate person.

This is not to say that there is a correlation between literacy and the successful performance of specified political and economic tasks. It is difficult to tell, in general, whether this was true or not in the colonial period. What can be said is that the illiterate person should not be presumed to be alienated and marginal; rather, he should be presumed to be more dependent than the literate person.

Literacy and the Franchise, 1800-1965

The major dilemma for the late-eighteenth-century founding fathers, insofar as education and political theory were concerned, was to create a system that would avoid the anarchistic tendencies of pure democracies while guarding against "the creation of a formal American aristocracy." Their solution, as Kaestle has observed, was a republican form of government "in which the general will would be refined and articulated by the best men." Freedom and order were reconciled by an education that would prepare men to vote intelligently and prepare women to train "their sons properly." In the concept of Republicanism, virtue, balanced government, and liberty all found a place. A virtuous and educated yeoman citizenry was to be one guarantor of political and social stability.[77] Jefferson's remarks on education, for example, were usually placed in at least one of the three following contexts: the need for enlightened leadership, the threat of arbitrary power exercised by a government over its people, and the moral progress of the populace. Public enlightenment and the free exchange of information were thus safeguards against the propensity of governments to tyranny as well as protection against moral decay. Though Jefferson's own plan of a three-tiered system of education did not meet with success in Virginia (and Benjamin Rush's plan went down to defeat in Pennsylvania), they did establish a base from which the common school movement of the midnineteenth century could proceed.[78]

The conviction that the establishment of expanded common school education was a unique feature of American society with important political implications was widespread. The enthusiasm of David Buel at the New York State Constitutional Convention in 1821 was evident:

> The provision already made for the establishment of common schools will, in a very few years, extend the benefit of education to all our citizens. The universal diffusion of information will forever distinguish our population from that of Europe.[79]

Later, the appeals of Horace Mann, Henry Barnard, and Calvin Stowe helped to secure the relationship between education and political well-being enunciated by Jefferson years earlier. Said Mann in his Tenth Annual Report: "the minimum of this [public] education, can never be less than such as is sufficient to qualify each citizen for the civil and social duties he will be called to discharge." He continued:

> such an education . . . as is indispensable for the civil functions of a witness or a juror; as is necessary for the voter in municipal affairs; and finally, for the faithful and conscientious discharge of all those duties which devolve upon the inheritor of a portion of the sovereignty of this great republic.[80]

In the minds of political and educational reformers, free public education increasingly became the great panacea for social and political ills. As property qualifications for voting were gradually eliminated, first in favor of taxpayer qualifications and then in favor of age, sex, and race qualifications, education assumed a greater burden for political socialization and the cultivation of civic virtue. The experience of property ownership was also presumed to be a socializing experience leading to both independence of judgment and a sharing of fundamental social norms, but it was no longer preeminent in importance for proper political participation. Education, not real property, seemed to be capable of fulfilling Blackstone's dictum that "the true reason of requiring any qualification with regard to property in voters is to exclude such persons as are in so mean a situation as to be esteemed to have no will of their own."[81]

To stress the role of education in political socialization should not be construed to mean that property became irrelevant as a determinant in voter qualifications. It surely did not. Rather, it was a matter of degree, region, and state. During the first half of the nineteenth century, midwestern states moved toward the norm of resident white males, over twenty-one, having the right to vote. Some states, such as Virginia and Massachusetts, vacillated frequently among various degrees of property ownership and taxableness.[82]

The Use of The Literacy Test

Establishing qualifications for voting was one way of defining the nature of a "community" of interests. These interests were, and are, frequently assumed to be an extension of certain accepted social, political, and economic norms that represent some consensus of fundamental values. Whether we are speaking of race, sex, wealth, or literacy, it is evident that the use of any or all as determinants of eligibility for voting is simply a means of defining the nonmembers of a community of values and interests. The use of literacy as a tool of voter exclusion is strong testimony to the belief that certain values were understood by literate persons and that these values were expected to be evidenced in voting behavior. In short, it was testimony not only to racial bigotry and discrimination but to the power of what has elsewhere been called an "ideology" of literacy.[83]

The development of mass literacy in the United States during the first half of the nineteenth century was accompanied by a certain irony in the use of literacy tests as tools for excluding some segments of the population from voting. The reason for this, however, is not difficult to discern. Despite the fact that basic literacy became more widespread, its acquisition still differed with respect to wealth, nativity, and race. The very poor, especially those below the thirtieth percentile of the wealth distribution, the foreign-born, and American blacks, shared in the achievement of literacy far less than did the rest of the population.[84]

On a North-South gradient, illiteracy rates increased as one moved from New England to the South in the early nineteenth century. Thus among army enlistees in North Carolina between 1799 and 1829 the illiteracy rate was 0.58, while in Connecticut and Massachusetts the rates were 0.26 and 0.21, respectively. The North-South vector of illiteracy held true throughout the nineteenth century, but the surge in public schooling, the widespread availability of inexpensive newspapers, and the increased availability of cheaply printed books eventually resulted in a decline to 0.07 in the nationwide illiteracy rate by 1895. As with the beginning of the nineteenth century, however, the overall rate masked substantial differences according to ethnicity, race, region, occupation, and wealth.[85]

Suspect groups were easily identified by a test of literacy for voter eligibility. The depressed literacy rates among poor and minority groups, in turn, made them easy targets for discrimination and reinforced, as well, the beliefs that they were basically unfit for suffrage by virtue of their inferior lexical skills. The formula proceeded in a straightforward, syllogistic manner. From the assumptions that political participation ought to be preceded by acceptance of prevailing social/political norms and that literacy and schooling were the sources of these norms, it followed that literacy was necessary for proper voting behavior. The fact that certain specifiable groups in the population were far less literate than the population in general made them, in turn, unfit for suffrage. Administrative abuse of literacy tests leading to their selective application were viewed by the perpetrators of discrimination simply as a way to guarantee that the formula would work.

In addition to the ideological context for literacy requirements, the passage of the Thirteenth, Fourteenth, and Fifteenth Amendments to the Constitution also provides an important context for understanding the development and implementation of literacy tests. With the adoption of the Thirteenth Amendment slated for implementation on 18 December 1865, Congress faced the politically volatile question of a new apportioning of representatives. This would, in turn, alter the historical pattern of using only three-fifths of the slaves in determining representation.

Section Two of the Fourteenth Amendment was the battleground for reapportionment. The proposals of Schenck of Ohio and Stevens and Broomall of Pennsylvania to apportion on the basis of suffrage (legal voters) were strongly opposed by New England, where restrictions on aliens and educational requirements for voter eligibility excluded sizable numbers from voting. In addition, New England "had a disproportionately large number of women (who were universally excluded from voting at the time) due to the extensive emigration of her males to the West. . . ."[86] James Blaine of Maine attacked apportionment by suffrage, noting that the elimination of literacy requirements would "cheapen" suffrage everywhere. The lines that were drawn for the debate on the Fifteenth Amendment were apparent beforehand on Section Two of the Fourteenth Amendment. Shellabarger of Ohio thus attacked a restrictive franchise by arguing that it was contrary to the "constitutional requirement guaranteeing states a republican form of government."[87]

The debate over Section Two was not exhausted with the passage of the Fourteenth Amendment. It reappeared more than once in the context of census taking. The ninth census (1870) was the first testing ground for the operation of Section Two. The Census Committee of the House compiled a list of categories and distribution of states that excluded people from voting. The most prevalent category of exclusion was local residence requirements (thirty-seven states), followed by state residency (thirty-six); pauperism, idiocy, and insanity (twenty-four); race or color (sixteen); property or nonpayment of taxes (eight); and oaths (five). Other reasons included armed forces service (two), character or behavior (two), literacy (two), U.S. residency (two), residency on lands ceded to the United States by a state (two), and other causes of exclusion (two). The list provides a good look at the restriction of suffrage in the United States, but it is significant that illiteracy was only a reason for exclusion in two states in 1870. Though the secretary of the interior directed marshals to list in tables the number of male citizens of the United States twenty-one and above as well as those whose right to vote was denied for reasons other than rebellion or crimes, the accuracy of these numbers was highly suspect—the number of adult male citizens reportedly disfranchised was a mere 0.5 percent.[88]

The next serious attempt to deal with Section Two of the Fourteenth Amendment followed the twelfth census with the Apportionment Act of 1901. By this time, Democrats had regained political control of the South. Through grandfather clauses, white primaries, poll taxes, and literacy tests, black voters almost disappeared in the South. The debate over apportionment saw Republicans attempt to reestablish themselves as a viable party.[89] By this time the issue of literacy and literacy tests for voter qualification had degenerated to the point that it could not be divorced from the issue of racism.

The problem of the uneducated voter was re-formed in the new context of pure, fair, and orderly elections in the early twentieth century. The issue of discriminatory behavior and denial of suffrage remained but became clearly distinguished from that of protecting the integrity of the ballot. The latter concern emerged forcefully with the use of the Australian ballot. The difference in the two issues was put well by Representative Edgar Crumpacher of Indiana in the debate over apportionment:

> Restrictions upon the exercise of the elective franchise, reasonably necessary for the integrity of elections, are not denials or abridgments of the right itself within the meaning of the law. The people, in adopting the fourteenth amendment, intended it to have a practical operation, and it must be construed in conformity with the custom and necessity for holding elections under reasonable safeguard. . . .[90]

Debates over the Fifteenth Amendment in the Fortieth Congress raised important questions about whether Congress had contemplated the use of literacy tests. Avins has argued on the basis of these debates that "the history of the fifteenth amendment in the House and Senate leaves no doubt that the framers contemplated continued use of literacy tests which might in fact have discriminatory effects."[91] Whether or not this inference can be made on the basis of statements of original intent is questionable; it is clear, however, that issues about education, wealth, and the franchise in a republican form of government were debated. It is well known, also, that these debates were provoked in part by Republican attempts to "encourage the enfranchisement of Negroes in the expectation that they would swell the ranks of the Republican party."[92]

Ohio Republicans Shellabarger and Bingham helped to lead the fight against loose language that would allow the status quo to continue. Bingham, a radical Republican, warned against the dangers of an aristocracy of property and intellect that would result from educational and property qualifications for voting. John Broomall, a radical Republican from Pennsylvania, also "argued against suffrage based on distinctions of wealth, intelligence, race, family, or sex." The House version, however, turned out to be a compromise settlement.[93]

It was a similar story in the Senate, where Republicans led the fight to protect the franchise of the lower classes. Republican Warner of Alabama explained to his Senate colleagues that they would "fail to protect the only classes of your citizens who need protection." Those with knowledge and wealth, the "learned and the rich, scarcely need the ballot for their protection." It was the "poor, unlearned man, who has nothing but the ballot, to whom it is a priceless heritage, a protection, and a shield," continued Warner.[94]

Others had similar concerns though the emphases varied on a continuum of concern for the plight of the poor to discrimination against blacks. Some arguments, however, went beyond the concern with the rights of specific groups to a more general concern with the preservation of political principles through minimal educational requirements. In a curious blend of naïveté about the level of educational attainment in the nineteenth-century United States and a grasp of the relationship of the political obligations incurred through citizenship, James Patterson of New Hampshire argued that the restriction of a literacy test "is no wrong done to the voter, for it simply protects the purity and integrity of the Government under which all rights are secured. . . ." Though Patterson was willing to concede that an "educational test may not be necessary" it would do no harm. "If the people have the intelligence prerequisite to self-government an educational test will not limit very much the extent of suffrage. . . . It is simply a safeguard against a possible evil."[95]

The constitutional right of states to regulate suffrage within their boundaries was never in serious doubt before the War between the States. Chief Justice Taney's opinion in *Martin Luther v. Luther M. Borden et al.* (1849) with respect to voter qualification, though only a small part of the issue posed by the Dorr insurrection, expressed the prevailing view well:

> certainly it is no part of the judicial functions of any court of the United States to prescribe the qualification of voters in a State, giving the right to those to whom it is denied by the written and established constitution and laws of the State, or taking it away from those to whom it is given; nor has it the right to determine what political privileges the citizens of a State are entitled to, unless there is an established constitution or law to govern its decision.[96]

The right of suffrage was clearly not perceived to be a right of citizenship, nor was it construed as a natural and inalienable right. Looking back upon the period before the Fifteenth Amendment, the court in *United States v. Miller* summarized the condition with respect to state control of voter qualifications:

> Before the adoption of the fifteenth amendment, it was within the power of the state to exclude citizens of the United States from voting on account of race, age, property, education, or on any other ground however arbitrary or whimsical. The constitution of the United States, before the adoption of the fifteenth amendment, in no wise interfered with this absolute power of the state to control the right of suffrage in accordance with its own views of expendiency or propriety.[97]

The Fourteenth and Fifteenth Amendments to the United States Constitution did not extend suffrage to all adult citizens. If qualifications were applied without discrimination, the criteria might include literacy, age, sex, or other "relevant" criteria. In 1874 the Supreme Court of the United States attempted again to put to rest the issue of state prerogatives to regulate suffrage. *Minor v. Happersett* had arisen because one Virginia Minor of Missouri had been denied registration to vote. Happersett, the registrar, had refused to register Minor because she was a woman and was disqualified by the provision of the Missouri state constitution that "Every *Male* citizen of the United States shall be entitled to vote."[98] In its opinion, the court reviewed the purpose for which political communities are organized. It noted that the founding fathers of the nation had not intended "to make all citizens of the United States voters. . . . So important a change in the condition of citizenship as it actually existed, if intended, would have been expressly declared."[99]

There was no question, said the court, that the right to suffrage was protected and that a citizen might be deprived of it only by due process of law. Such protection, however, could only be claimed if the right had been given. This was clearly not the case and the court was adamant:

> Certainly, if the courts can consider any question settled, this is one. For nearly ninety years the people have acted upon the idea that the Constitution, when it conferred citizenship, did not necessarily confer the right of suffrage. . . . Our province is to decide what the law is, not to declare what it should be.[100]

Attempts to use the literacy test as a tool for the exclusion of ethnic and racial minorities in the United States have a well-documented legislative and constitutional history. Among the earlier attempts at exclusion, the most noteworthy were in Connecticut and Massachusetts.

Here, the efforts to restrict the "foreign" vote through literacy tests were quite successful. The constitutional amendment passed in 1855 in Connecticut prescribed that the ability to read the constitution or statutes should be a requirement for exercising the right of suffrage. This, says Porter, "was aimed directly at the foreigners, although natives must have come under it also." In Massachusetts, the requirement to be able to read the constitution and write one's own name was combined with the qualification that a literacy test was not to apply to anyone over sixty years of age. This attempt to reduce the foreign vote was further reinforced by another constitutional amendment "requiring foreigners to remain in the state for two years after naturalization before they could vote."[101]

In general, the effect of such voting restrictions was to prevent sizable portions of the male population from voting. Three percent of the male population over twenty-three years old was prevented in New York by residence and registration laws. In Massachusetts, one-sixteenth of the population was eliminated by educational qualifications. Said one author of the "Legal Aspect of the Southern Question" in 1889: "an educational test like that in Massachusetts would reduce the voters about one-half [in South Carolina and Alabama]." It was no doubt accurate when the same author observed that reading and writing requirements for voting in southern states "would disfranchise a large proportion of negroes and many whites."[102]

Literacy for Americanization and its negative correlate, the exclusion of undesirable, illiterate immigrants, were major themes in the literacy campaigns of the early twentieth century. The former, as expressed by Winthrop Talbot, saw literacy as a requisite for a democratic society. Said Talbot, "Unless means are provided for reaching the illiterate and near illiterate, every social problem must remain needlessly complex and slow in solution, because social and representative government rests upon an implied basis of universal ability to read and write."[103]

The baser tones of ethnic bigotry linked the peril of illiteracy to the barbarism of the "new" immigrants. In the tortured rhetoric of missionary zeal, A. D. Mayo spoke of what he called "the upper section of the grand army of illiteracy"; the "millions . . . who know just enough about everything to miss the valuable knowledge of anything that most deeply concerns the private life or the public welfare of the nation." Part of Mayo's anger was directed at those of privilege and great wealth who exploited illiterate persons of the lower classes. The most threatening illiteracy, he maintained, was not ignorance of letters but of the "inevitable laws of human society and the conditions of Republican government." Mayo's real target was the peril of unrestricted immigration. Quick action was needed to stop "the inflow from everywhere that, in one generation, would make this Republic the mental and moral sewer of all nations." Literacy tests for voting and immigration restriction were moral and political imperatives needed "to prevent that massing of the forces of Illiteracy which, now, in every city and in the most cultivated states of the north, no less than in the Black Belt and the mountain wilderness of the South, has already become the peril of the Republic."[104]

Other states, too, debated the issue of the literacy test as a tool for exclusion. New York, for example, addressed the problem in 1846 and again in 1855, yet was unable to frame a constitutional amendment that would exclude the "undesirable" foreigner while sparing favorite native groups.

Using data from the United States Census of 1900, the New York State Education Department prepared a report in 1906 that showed the extent of illiteracy among the voting population.[105] New York, like other states with large immigrant populations, was concerned with the political participation of these newly arrived and often illiterate persons. Published tables showing county illiteracy rates tell us that the proportion of illiterate persons ranged between 0.016 and 0.179. Overall, the state had an illiteracy rate of 10.7 percent in 1900. The proportion of the voting population who were illiterate ranged between 0.021 and 0.24, depending upon the county.

Having found that the highest illiteracy rates among the voting population were in rural areas, the commissioner of education concluded that the "better and more convenient school accommodations in the cities are breaking down illiteracy more satisfactorily than is being done in the country districts."[106] This did not alter the fact that illiteracy rates were high among recently arrived immigrants. Foreign-born illiterates were 81 percent of all the illiterates, noted the report. But, the report continued, there was a greater "appreciation of school privileges, or some other fortunate factor, among foreign born than native born parents."[107] This conclusion was reached by noting that "the percentage of illiterates born in this country of foreign born parents (5.7 percent) is much lower than the percentage (9.2 percent) of illiterate children of native born parents."[108] Most of the illiterate children of native born parents were located in rural districts. Eventually New York was able to pass a constitutional amendment in 1921 requiring that all voters be able to read and write English. The amendment passed thus read:

> After January 1, 1922, no person shall become entitled to vote by attaining majority, by naturalization or otherwise, unless such person is also able, except for physical disability, to read and write English; and suitable laws shall be passed by the Legislature to enforce this provision.[109]

The decision in *People ex re. Chadbourne v. Voorhis et al.* (1923) heard in the Court of Appeals of New York effectively put an end to possible discrimination occurring as a result of the arbitrary administration of literacy tests by boards of registration and inspectors of election in that state. It was the intent of the New York state legislature, said the Court, "to do away with the test of literacy by the inspectors and to substitute therefor the proof by certificate": "No sanction remains for literacy tests of new voters to be conducted by the inspectors of election."[110] The burden of administering literacy tests in New York state was thus shifted solely to The Board of Regents of the State of New York. Tests were administered through the public schools. The use of the literacy test undoubtedly had the effect of excluding large numbers of the foreign-born from voting, particularly in the city of New York, but the test itself was not of an arbitrary or discriminatory nature.

The literacy test in New York State was straightforward and left little room for arbitrary interpretation. The following is one of the sample tests from the early twentieth century.

New York State Board of Regents Literacy Test

Read this and then write the answers. Read it as many times as you need to:

In New York State a general election will be held on November 6, 1923. On election day every voter should go to the polls and vote. The polling place is a room where several election officers meet for the purpose of receiving and counting the ballot of each voter of an election district. When a voter enters the polling place he gives his name to the election officer. A citizen votes either by ballot or by a voting machine. A ballot is a slip of paper. Both the ballot and the voting machine contain the names of the great political parties and the names of candidates of each party.

1. On what day will the general election in New York State be held in 1923?
2. Who should go to the polls and vote on election day?
3. What is the place called where voters go to vote?
4. What is it that election officers receive and count?
5. What does the voter give to the election officer when he enters the polling place?
6. How does a citizen vote?
7. What is the ballot?
8. What else besides the names of the candidates of each political party do both the ballot and the voting machine contain?

The various tests were about one hundred words in length and were drawn from the first four thousand words of the Thorndike list of the ten thousand words most frequently used in the English language. A scoring key was used to rate the examinations. Complete sentences were not required in the answers, but illegible answers were disqualified. Unless grammatical and spelling errors indicated "actual misreading," they were "overlooked."[111]

After the passage of the Fifteenth Amendment and the end of southern reconstruction, a number of southern states succeeded in keeping most black voters from the polls. One of the most notorious attempts at disfranchisement occurred in Oklahoma in an amended constitution (1910): "No person shall be registered as an elector of this state or be allowed to vote in any election herein unless he be able to read and write any section of the Constitution of the State of Oklahoma." It then proceeded systematically to exclude black voters by a grandfather clause.[112] One of the most remarkable aspects of the litigation over this amendment was the language of the Oklahoma Supreme Court. With biblical phrasing, geneticism, and Darwinian logic hand in hand, the court observed:

> and the presumption follows as to his [a person previously entitled to vote] offspring; that is, that the virtue and intelligence of the ancestors will be imputed to his descendants just as the iniquity of the fathers may be visited upon the children unto the third and fourth generation.[113]

In the South, South Carolina was a leader in the move to disfranchise southern blacks. At the Constitutional Convention of 1895, Benjamin Tillman, a political leader at the state convention, explained the aim of the new literacy test: "The only thing we can do as patriots and as statesmen is to take from ["the ignorant blacks"] every ballot that we can under the laws of our national government."[114]

In Louisiana the application of a literacy test in the period 1896–1900 reduced the number of registered black voters from 127,263 to 5,354. Slightly more than 1,000 of the latter had registered under the property and grandfather clauses; thus, "all but 4,327 . . . had been excluded by registration officials because of their illiteracy."[115] Flagrant discrimination had, by 1962, virtually eliminated the black vote in some southern counties. Two counties in Alabama had no blacks registered to vote despite the fact that blacks represented 80.7 and 77.9 percent of the county populations. Similar instances could be found in Georgia, Louisiana, and Mississippi. Six counties in Georgia, thirteen in Mississippi, and four parishes in Louisiana were without registered black voters even though they numbered well over half the county populations.[116]

Numerous judicial decisions regarding voting rights accompanied the increased disfranchisement of minority groups between 1870 and 1966. Many of these involved the use of literacy tests to eliminate large groups of unwanted voters arbitrarily. It was the pattern in such cases to find that literacy tests, per se, were not unconstitutional and that states had the right to demand literacy of their voters. The Supreme Court of Massachusetts in 1893, for instance, found that the state had the right "to deny or abridge the right to vote of the male inhabitants who are 21 years of age. . . ." In a number of states, said the court, an "impartial and uniform rule" had been used to deny the vote to those who were "thought not to possess the qualifications necessary for an independent and intelligent exercise of the right."[117]

The move to a standard test of literacy administered through the public schools in New York state had gone a long way toward eliminating the discriminatory administration of literacy tests. Other states, however, did not necessarily move in this direction and continued to keep in force vaguely worded statutes and/or administrative practices that did little to prevent discrimination. In *Davis, et al. v. Schnell, et al.* (1949), it was found that vaguely worded phrases such as "understand and explain" did not constitute a reasonable standard for interpreting articles of the federal Constitution. Such open-ended wording, said the court, leaves the way clear for arbitrary application of literacy tests:

> A simple test may be given one applicant; a long, tedious, complex one to another; one applicant may be examined on one article of the Constitution; another may be called upon to "understand and explain" every article and provision of the entire instrument.[118]

Under such circumstances, applicants for registration might be rejected solely on the basis of whether the board "likes or dislikes the understanding and explanation offered." It continued, citing *Yick Wo v. Hopkins,* that this type of power was not discretionary but "a naked and arbitrary power to give or withhold consent."[119]

Given the right of the states to regulate suffrage, the issues for courts in regard to literacy tests generally became ones of statutory and constitutional discrimination, unreasonable standards for interpreting literacy, and unfair administration of the tests. In dealing with the "grandfather" clause of the suffrage amendment to the constitution of Oklahoma, the court in *Frank Guinn and J. J. Beal v. United States* (1915) accepted the argument that the clause was of such a nature as to exclude most blacks from voting.[120] That argument itself, however, did not question the constitutionality of all literacy tests. *Guinn* expressly recognized the right of a state to control voting privileges. Moreover, it was of the opinion that the suffrage qualification of literacy could (perhaps ought to) "bear a reasonable relation to the good of the whole, because it would confine the elective franchise to those most competent to exercise it, while each man so disfranchised would remain equal to, and equal in freedom with every other man who could not read and write."[121]

The ideal of the educated voter's intelligently expressing his will through suffrage was a common way of buttressing arguments in favor of literacy tests. Both *Darby v. Daniel* (1958) and *Lassiter v. Northhampton County Board of Elections* (1959) are cases in point. Each found in favor of the particular literacy tests being challenged. At a time when the cold war, red-scare climate of the 1950s had not yet dissipated, the opinion of the court in *Darby v. Daniel* clearly reflected a concern with the survival of constitutional government. "When alien ideologies are making a steady and insidious assault upon constitutional government everywhere," said the court, "it is nothing but reasonable that the States should be tightening their belts and seeking to assure that those carrying the responsibility of suffrage understand and appreciate the form and genius of the government of this country and of the States."[122]

The language in *Lassiter* was less pointed, more deliberative, and free from the censorious remarks that characterized *Darby*. It is a case, however, that bears a more detailed scrutiny and some explanation of the context in which it was heard. The civil rights movement of the 1950s and the decision in *Brown* had placed minority rights first on the agenda for social reform and made discriminatory behavior the paragon of political vice. Presumably the court could have reasoned that statutes or practices that have the effect of or tendency to discriminate or result in treatment that denotes inferiority are unconstitutional. Yet it did not. To understand this better, *Lassiter* must be put within the contexts of realistic jurisprudence, minority rights, and legal precedent.

In its initial stand on the Fourteenth Amendment to the United States Constitution, the Supreme Court interpreted the purpose of the first clause to be the establishment of "the citizenship of the negro." The Court went on to say in the *Slaughter-House Cases* (1873) that the "equal protection" clause was designed to redress the "evil" of discriminatory laws against "newly emancipated negros."[123] By 1883, however, the United States Supreme Court had become more cautious with its invalidation of the Civil Rights Act of 1875. It then took only seven more years to reaffirm the separate-but-equal doctrine in *Louisville, New Orleans and Texas Railway Company v. Mississsippi* (1890) and six more to reach *Plessy v. Ferguson* (1896).[124]

In his *Supreme Court and Social Science* Rosen has argued that the decision in *Plessy v. Ferguson* "was based on several social science postulates that were interwoven" with the "definition of the fact situation of this landmark case." The majority of the court (excluding Justice Harlan) had clearly accepted the position of social Darwinism that artificial interference with the natural order of things was a threat to social progress and "was to be regarded as oppressive and arbitrary." Characteristics belonging to race were seen as racial instincts, not as environmentally determined behaviors. Brown's opinion for the majority in this case, says Rosen, was an "affirmation of the factual existence of racial instincts." From the standpoint of legal precedent the court had also confirmed the separate-but-equal doctrine laid down almost fifty years earlier in the Massachusetts case of *Roberts v. City of Boston* (1849) in which "separate facilities from railway cars to schools, indeed, the entire system of racial segregation, was condoned and put on a legal footing by the court."[125]

Cumming v. Board of Education (1899), *Berea College v. Kentucky* (1908), and *Gong Gong Lum v. Rice* (1927) applied the separate-but-equal doctrine to schools. By the 1930s, however, the activities of the National Association for the Advancement of Colored People (NAACP) and the vigorous "fact-finding" of the court in *Norris v. Alabama* (1935) and *Missouri ex rel. Gaines v. Canada* (1938) had opened the way to a closer look at social segregation. The blatant racism evident in the Japanese-American cases during World War II was a temporary setback, but by 1950 *McLaurin v. Oklahoma State Regents* had shown the Supreme Court willing to expand its reasoning to the psychological considerations involved with racial segregation. This was to be important groundwork for the hearing of *Brown v. Board of Education of Topeka* (1954).[126]

In *Brown* the court was faced with an extremely difficult fact-finding situation regarding the psychological effects of racial segregation. The argument of biological inferiority was still present in 1954 as it had been in 1896, yet, as Rosen has argued, the "dominant cultural standard of rationality" had replaced mythology. Both the nature and method of science had become refined as the experimental method held sway. To ignore the empirical findings of social science was to risk an inconsistency with social reality.[127] The court, which was giving a consolidated opinion involving four cases, explained that its decision could not rest on a mere comparison of facilities and programs of "separate-but-equal" schools, but rather that it "must look instead to the effect of segregation itself on public education."[128]

The court, of course, concluded that children were indeed deprived of equal educational opportunity by virtue of their segregation. Segregation by race, said the court, "generates a feeling of inferiority as to their status in the community that may affect their hearts and minds in a way unlikely ever to be undone." Even the Kansas court from which appeal was made (but which had ruled against the negro plaintiffs) had acknowledged that "segregation of white and colored children in public schools has a detrimental effect upon the colored children" and denotes "the inferiority of the negro group," thus affecting the "motivation of a child to learn." The U.S. Supreme Court explicitly rejected *Plessy v. Ferguson* and concluded that the "doctrine of separate-but-equal has no place."[129]

Given the climate of opinion, *Lassiter* seems at first a decision outside the judicial mainstream. Though the decision in *Lassiter* was conceptualized in terms of the rights of citizens, it was not conceptualized in terms of minority rights. Both the attorney general of North Carolina and the Supreme Court of the United States spoke directly to the political implications of illiteracy but did so in terms of the larger collective good. The attorney general, acting as amicus curiae, took the opportunity to quote from Robert M. Hutchins in defending the use of literacy tests:

> The faith [in a democratic form of government] rests on the proposition that man is a political animal, that participation in political decisions is necessary to his fulfillment and happiness, *that all men can and must be sufficiently educated and informed to take part in making these decisions,* that protection against arbitrary power, though indispensable, is insufficient to make either free individuals or a free society, that such a society must make positive provisions for its development into a community learning together; for this is what political participation, government by consent and the civilization of the dialogue all add up to. (Emphasis ours)[130]

The court explained that discrimination was not the charge in *Lassiter;* nor was the legislative context of North Carolina the same as in *Davis et al. v. Schnell et al.* (1949) in which the "great discretion . . . vested in the registrar made clear that a literacy requirement was merely a device to make discrimination easy."[131] Given these factors, the court followed precedent in interpreting Section Two of the Fourteenth Amendment within the context of state provisions regulating the right to vote. But it also appealed strongly to the democratic ideal of an enlightened citizenry intelligently using the ballot. "The ability to read and write . . . has some relation to standards designed to promote intelligent use of the ballot," said the court. "Literacy and illiteracy," said the court, "are neutral on race, creed, color, and sex. . . ." Like most courts before it, the Supreme Court was not willing to equate literacy with intelligence, but it was willing to acknowledge the importance of printed material in influencing and providing a basis for democratic decision making. Said the court: "in our society where newspapers, periodicals, books, and other printed matter canvass and debate campaign issues, a State might conclude that only those who are literate should exercise the franchise."[132] The court, of course, was not advocating such a policy, but it did allow the reasonableness of such a decision.

The passage of the Voting Rights Act of 1965 was the culmination of concern with a long history of abuses. Both the 1957 and 1960 voting rights acts had sought unsuccessfully to put an end to discrimination in voting practices. The 1957 act had empowered the attorney general of the United States "to institute a civil action or other proper proceeding for preventive relief, including an application for a permanent or temporary injunction, restraining order, or other order, to end discrimination in voting practices." The 1960 act had made it possible, in suits on voter discrimination brought by the federal government, for the attorney general to "ask the court to determine whether the individuals concerned were deprived of their rights pursuant to a *pattern or practice* [italics added] of discrimination." If such a pattern were determined to exist, "any person of the same race in the affected area [was] entitled to apply to the court for an order that he is qualified to vote at any election." Qualified applicants were then issued certificates entitling them to vote. Neither the 1957 nor the 1960 voting rights act was sufficient to end "wholesale discrimination in many areas." Unfair literacy tests and moral character were still employed to eliminate otherwise qualified voters.[133]

On the eve of the debate over literacy tests in the United States Congress in 1962, the United States Commission on Civil Rights reported that it had 382 sworn complaints from "persons alleging that they had been denied the right to vote or to have their vote counted by reason of race, color, religion, or national origin. . . . " All of these, excepting three from New York, were from southern states. The three in New York involved persons literate in Spanish but unable to pass the state literacy test in English. The situation had drastically altered since 1932, when twelve southern states had effectively disfranchised black voters.

In the early 1930s, "considerably fewer than a hundred thousand [blacks] were able to vote in general elections and virtually none was permitted to vote in the primary elections." The elimination of white primaries through private lawsuits and the voluntary abolition of the poll tax were the major factors in increasing black voter registration by about 1.25 million in the early 1960s. The commission presented a very politic account of present injustices and progress over the preceding thirty years. The majority of "Negro American citizens do not now suffer discriminatory denial of their right to vote," said the Commission, even though in eight southern states over two-thirds of blacks were not registered to vote.[134]

Aside from the issue of states' rights (an issue that dominated the arguments of literacy test proponents in the 1962 Senate debates), one of the most controversial aspects of the 1961 Civil Rights Commission's deliberations concerned the level of education that might reasonably be used as a mininum standard for voting.[135] This, of course, was not a constitutional issue itself, but it did supply a standard of reference that became part of the Voting Rights Act of 1965. Level of literacy forced a reconsideration of the basic relationship between education and republican government.

One of the recommendations (Number Two) of the committee was that Congress should enact legislation that stipulated that if a literacy test were in use by a state, "it shall be sufficient for qualification that the elector have completed at least six grades of formal education."[136] Such a recommendation would have the effect of substituting a congressional standard of literacy for the various state-imposed levels as measured by literacy tests. In this form it did not mean that literacy tests could not be used by states; rather, persons who had not completed six grades could be required to take a literacy test, or "a state could, if it chose, apply in every case a standard of literacy below that evidenced by a sixth grade education."[137]

It is quite clear that Congress did not expect a lower grade level of literacy to be used. Senate Bill 480 (1962) included a statement about the sixth-grade level as a measure of literacy and implied that this was functional for purposes of political judgment:

> The Congress further finds that illiteracy is rapidly disappearing in the United States; that the quality of elementary education furnished by the Nation's schools is of high caliber; that persons completing six grades of education in a State-accredited school can reasonably be expected to be literate; that a literate electorate can be assured by affording the right to vote to any otherwise qualified person who has completed six grades of education; and that any test of literacy that denies the right to vote to any person who has completed six grades of education is arbitrary and unreasonable.[138]

The eventual determination on this question, though not without prompting from the Civil Rights Commission *Report* of 1963, appeared in Public Law 89-110, the Voting Rights Act of 1965. Among its provisions was one that made the "sixth primary grade" the standard educational level for voting. A caveat to this standard was included in Sec. 4, e (2), which read, "except that in States in which State law provides that a different level of education is presumptive of literacy, he shall demonstrate that he has successfully completed an equivalent level of education. . . ."[139]

In 1966 the Supreme Court of the United States heard the case of *State of South Carolina, Plaintiff v. Nicholas DeB. Katzenbach, Attorney General of the United States. South Carolina v. Katzenbach* was the constitutional test for certain portions of the newly legislated Voting Rights Act of 1965. In bringing a bill of complaint, South Carolina had sought a determination on the validity of selected portions of the act and sought, also, an injunction against enforcement by the attorney general.[140] As is well known, the Warren court rejected the states' rights arguments (arguments expressed, as well, by Senator Sam Ervin in his opening statements before the Senate Sub-committee on Literacy Tests and Voter Requirements). It found that Congress had correctly assumed its power to prescribe remedies for racial discrimination in voting. This it had done under Section Two of the Fifteenth Amendment to the United States Constitution.

Congress heard extensive testimony in drafting the Voting Rights Act of 1965. A great deal of this offered evidence of the abuse of voter registration requirements and procedures, not the least of which concerned the unconstitutional use of literacy tests. The unworkability of previous statutes designed to correct abuses was obvious and was duly noted in Justice Warren's opinion a year later:

> White applicants for registration have often been excused altogether from the literacy and understanding tests or have been given easy versions, have received extensive help from voting officials, and have been registered despite serious errors in their answers. Negroes, on the other hand, have typically been required to pass difficult versions of all the tests, without any outside assistance and without the slightest error.[141]

"Tests or devices" measuring literacy, educational achievement, or knowledge of a particular subject that were employed in a discriminatory way as prerequisites for voting or voter registration had been banned by the Voting Rights Act. The unconstitutionality of the discriminatory application of these "tests or devices" had been declared by the Court.

The 1965 Voting Rights Act was designed to eliminate both obvious and subtle forms of discrimination. Among the latter, of course, were literacy tests. The United States Code forbids the use of tests or devices that contravene the guarantees of suffrage as set forth in the code. It defines "test or device" as follows:

> any requirement that a person as a prerequisite for voting or registration for voting (1) demonstrate the ability to read, write, understand, or interpret any matter, (2) demonstrate any educational achievement or his knowledge of any particular subject, (3) possess good moral character, or (4) prove his qualifications by the voucher of registered voters or members of any other class.[142]

States or counties that had been targeted as offenders and that came under the court's jurisdiction were subject to action by the office of the attorney general of the United States. This allowed the attorney general to "appoint federal officials to enter the polling places and observe the voting process."[143] The targeting of potentially culpable states and political subdivisions and particularly the use of a percentage cutoff formula for judging a district's probable violation of voting rights were also the provisions that received the greatest constitutional challenge. The Supreme Court, however, upheld the method:

> Congress began work with reliable evidence of actual voting discrimination in a great majority of the States and political subdivisions affected by the new remedies of the Act. The formula eventually evolved to describe these areas was relevant to the problem of voting discrimination, and Congress was therefore entitled to infer a significant danger of the evil in the few remaining States and political subdivisions covered by . . . the Act. No more was required to justify the application to these areas of Congress' express powers under the Fifteenth Amendment.[144]

The 1965 legislation also provided what was called a "bailout" standard whereby states could exempt themselves by satisfying a standard prescribed by legislation. Bailout standards were extended in the 1970 and 1975 amendments to the act. The extension of the bailout dates made it unrealistic for jurisdictions that had a history of discrimination to bail out prior to the fixed dates. The 1982 amendments found the previous bailout provision to be "unnecessarily stringent in that it offered no bailout opportunity for jurisdictions that eliminated discriminatory voting tests and practices that were used at the time of initial coverage." The 1982 amendments to the Voting Rights Act altered the process for seeking bailout by placing the initiative on counties rather than states to satisfy standards of nondiscrimination.[145]

Between the time of the 1982 amendments and March 1985 bailout litigation was initiated by three towns in Connecticut; the state of Alaska; El Paso County, Colorado; and Honolulu County, Hawaii. The United States did not accept the argument of the state of Alaska. In the cases of Connecticut, El Paso County, and Honolulu County, sufficient evidence was provided that literacy tests had not been used to discriminate against voters of large minority groups. The case of El Paso County was particularly significant from the standpoint of educational policy. Here we see the bilingual initiatives of the 1970s being implemented on a sufficiently large scale to "demonstrate that a substantial majority of its citizens of Spanish origin were fluent in English and that an effective bilingual election program had been implemented to meet the voting needs of the citizens who had difficulty with the English language."[146]

Hancock and Tredway have argued that the new bailout provisions are far more discriminating because single districts may satisfy new standards irrespective of other districts in a state. The new standards are not easy to satisfy and generally require "positive steps." These include expanding "opportunities for minority participation (or demonstrating that such action is unnecessary)," eliminating "voting procedures that inhibit or dilute equal access to the electoral process," and preventing "intimidation and harassment of minority voters." Proportional formulas are no longer part of the bailout standard. The criterion, instead, is that minorities have equal opportunity to participate with nonminority citizens. The new bailout standard was a compromise reluctantly agreed to by leaders of minority groups. Yet, as Hancock and Tredway point out, it provides an incentive for public officials and minority communities to lay the groundwork for fair election practices.[147]

Conclusion

The theory of social contract (compact) and the ideal of constitutional democracy envisioned an enlightened, sovereign people making rational decisions in the best interests of a larger social good while preserving a wide latitude for individual initiative. Theory was implemented in state statutes defining voting qualifications. Courts had repeatedly upheld state prerogatives in this matter.

Citizenship often turned out to be a halfway covenant. Constitutional decisions had consistently defended state prerogatives to control voter eligibility. Historically, voting privileges were qualified by property-holding requirements as well as sex and sometimes race. Thus, it was not unusual for illiterates to be marginal persons in terms of their participation in self-government. They were not, that is, part of the community of interest that underlay the social contract. Citizenship did not necessarily include the right to vote; equality before the law (procedural equality) did not guarantee the equal worth of liberty through suffrage.

Liberty, more often than not, was equated with the intelligent exercise of freedom, and literacy tests were seen as a method for guaranteeing the truth of this equation. Of course the same tests were sometimes avowedly, sometime covertly, used as a method of exclusion for and an assault upon aliens and racial minorities by nativists and racial bigots. The misuse of literacy tests, however, did not alter the fact that the right to vote was not interpreted as an inviolable natural right allied with the conferring of citizenship. Positive law, not natural law, was the rule.

After the Civil War, new patterns emerged for the restriction of suffrage. The first was a direct outgrowth of Amendments 13, 14, and 15 to the United States Constitution and resulted in the discriminatory exclusion of minorities from voting. The second emerged in the late-nineteenth and early-twentieth centuries and linked the movement for efficiency in government with the issue of protecting the ballot from fraud and corruption.

Discriminatory restriction of voting through literacy tests was only one of several devices through which minority groups could be excluded from the franchise. Though present in a number of states where blacks or "new" immigrants constituted a potential threat to the political status quo, literacy tests became associated primarily with the attempt to restrict the franchise of black voters in the South. Discriminatory application of literacy tests by voting registrars and constitutional provisions that arbitrarily or unreasonably restricted the franchise were two common means for disfranchisement. Outright violence and intimidation were the most dramatic instances of racism and exclusion. Many of the reasons for exclusion were openly political and stemmed from the fear of upsetting status quo power structures. It was difficult to tell, at times, whether political or racial fear was the more powerful instigator of injustice.

In large part the body politic had entrusted the franchise to schools where basic literacy skills and lessons of civic virture came together in one of the major purposes of public schooling—political socialization. In the latter nineteenth century, schooling itself became a measure of literacy both in function and quality. Schools increasingly legitimized their curriculum in terms of economic opportunity though civic virtue also remained a central purpose of instruction. By the twentieth century, grade level became a measure of level of literacy so that reformers of education, both lay and professional, judged the quality of educational output by the average grade completed.

Both education and political leaders defined literacy in terms of utility. They defined illiteracy in terms of deviance. The adult illiterate was unquestionably a deviant from the expected norm. The link between literacy and suffrage, however, was problematic. On the one hand it was assumed that an intelligent exercise of the franchise was best carried out by a literate population. Yet intelligence (native capacity) was obviously not the same as literacy. Literacy as a personal attribute was enabling, not definitive. The critical question thus became, at what level did the attribute of literacy need to exist to enable the application of native intelligence to decisions of self- governance? The problem was essentially one of establishing a criterion level that would satisfy the demands of public virtue yet preserve the suffrage dimension of citizenship.

The problem of functional literacy as it relates to suffrage was not solved. Yet the problem of criterion level was. Criterion levels are usually established on the basis of function. In the case of voting, however, a truly functional level was difficult to establish. Thus a sixth- or eighth-grade level came to be used as a minimum criterion level not because it was functionally related to intelligent voting but because a great deal of periodical information related to public matters was published at that level of reading difficulty. Whether this readability level was an acknowledgment of the level of literacy in the population or whether the level was considered sufficient to access information of public value is unknown.

There is no question that the level of literacy demanded by most literacy tests was a product of particular situations. Literacy is an attribute that has been used to classify people as competent or incompetent. This use logically followed from its perceived relationship to self-governance. Yet the relationship between self-governance and literacy often turned out to be a matter of who should govern rather than at what level they should be competent. Thus literacy tests became a means of exclusion and discrimination unrelated to any reasonable level of functional literacy. Ethnocentrism, racism, and political ideology, rather than competency in self-governance, were the contexts for exclusion. Ironically, the abuse of the literacy test was made easier by the absence of any well-founded measure of function and competence.

That this was the case should not be surprising. The ideal of a literate, self-governing population often operated at the level of ideology, not the level of function. As an extension of the political system, public schooling could do little to link its curriculum to the functional rather than the ideological demands of public virtue. The problem has been both institutional and conceptual. Though ideology played an important part in political socialization, there was, and has been, very little articulation between school and community in these matters. (Competency testing as it presently exists cannot solve this problem.) At the conceptual level efforts have been misguided by a singular normative approach to the problem. The problem is no more likely to be solved by a cutoff score on a literacy test than a cutoff score on an intelligence test. Function is a matter of performance, not cutoff scores. Only in a closed system such as schooling can tests predict performance. Given the current technology of testing and the multiple dimensions of citizenship, including voting, it is virtually impossible to predict performance from test scores. Yet perhaps this is to misread the situation and to demand a technical solution to a conceptual problem.

The problem of functional literacy is not fundamentally a technical one. It is, rather, a matter of reconsidering what the relationships are between citizenship rights on the one hand and literacy and education on the other. To what extent are these relationships dependent and independent, singular or plural? Can the ideological and the functional be separated? Should they be? Proposals to answer these questions are obviously beyond the scope of this study, but they are critical to broader social as well as educational policy.

Illiterate Voters and Jurors

Assistance to Illiterate Voters

Many who advocated literacy tests as a means of safeguarding democratic principles and constitutional government probably interpreted the difficulties of illiterates at the polls as empirical evidence substantiating their arguments. Certainly this tended to be true in those cases dealing with the Australian (secret) ballot. Illiterate voters did, indeed, experience difficulties when casting their votes, and these problems were periodically dealt with by state courts or officials responsible for interpreting state statutes governing conduct at polling places. It is interesting, for example, that Pennsylvania very early allowed for assistance to illiterates at the polls. A 1705 statute in that state provided that an illiterate voter submitting his choice of names would have his ballots opened by the sheriff or appointed judges of said elections, who could then "read the persons' names contained therein, and ask such selector whether these are [the] persons for whom he votes." If the voter answered in the affirmative, the ballot was then deposited with the other electors' papers in a box.[148]

We do not know whether assistance to illiterate voters was ever a political issue in colonial Pennsylvania. One hundred and eighty-eight years later, however, it was. The situation was one in which the chairmen of the Republican and Democratic committees in Beaver County had petitioned for an interpretation of the so-called Baker Ballot Law. Section 27 of this act provided that "if any voter declares to the judge of election that, by reason of disability, he desires assistance in the preparation of his ballot, he shall be permitted by the judge of the election to select a qualified voter of the election district to aid him." The issue arose over whether or not the voter was required to specify his disability and whether or not the election board should approve his selection of an assistant in voting.[149]

The judge to whom the petition was made observed that no proof of disability was required and that a simple and general declaration of disability was all that was necessary. The voter was the sole judge of the disability, the basis for which might be "ignorance of the law, inability to read or write, defective vision, palsy, excessive nervousness producing abnormal self-distrust, or other causes." The choice of an assistant was the "absolute right" of the voter, said Judge Wickham, and the "choice must be respected by the election board."[150]

The issue in Beaver County, Pennsylvania, did not result in litigation and so was less complicated than many of the cases heard in other states. The first of these discussed here, *Freeman et al. v. Lazarus et al.* (1895), was heard by the Supreme Court of Arkansas and involved, in addition to election fraud and a jurisdictional dispute, the status of votes cast by illiterates in a local option election. The act regulating elections in the state of Arkansas allowed two election judges in the presence of an elector to aid in the preparation of a ballot of an illiterate voter. The intent of this stipulation, said the court, was to protect the "will" of the voter. No solicitation or influence was permitted by the election judges in this procedure.[151]

Evidence presented before the circuit court, from which appeal was made, showed that many of the voters in Bragg Township (the pivotal township in the election) were "unable to read." The election judges, however, "did not wait to be requested by the voter to prepare the ballot, but at times solicited the voters to allow them to prepare their ballots." Over half the ballots cast in the township were, in fact, prepared by the judges, the electors involved apparently having directed the judges to vote their ballots "For license." Yet many of these ballots in fact were written "Against license." Given the violation of the will of so many voters and the lack of compliance with the statute requiring the assistance of *two* judges, the circuit court thus decided that the voting returns from Bragg County were invalid. Upon appeal this judgment was upheld.[152]

Many cases involving illiterate voters arose because of contested elections in which the vote(s) of an illiterate elector(s) affected the outcome of the election. Some of these were concerned only with technicalities, such as that of *Shaw v. Burnham* (1939), in which an election was contested because the person endorsing the ballots of four illiterate voters had placed the endorsement on the wrong side of the ballot.[153] Whether the issue was technical or substantive, however, it was nonetheless significant from the standpoint of the candidates.

Montgomery v. Oldham (1895), adjudged by the Supreme Court of Indiana, was heard because an illiterate voter had not declared his illiteracy. The voter, Clinton Parker, had stated to the election judges that he could read, yet he said, also, that "he had no confidence in his own ability to properly stamp his ticket. . . ." Parker, as it turned out, was "unable to read and write the English language intelligently, or to read his . . . ballot." In giving its decision, the court allowed Parker's vote to be counted, noting that it is the "inability to read the English language, that entitles the voter to the services of the poll clerks to prepare his ballot according to his direction, and not his declaration of the fact." Substance had outweighed procedure in this instance.[154]

It was likewise with the case of *Huston v. Anderson* (1904) heard by the Supreme Court of California. As with *Montgomery v. Oldham,* the situation was one in which illiterate voters were reluctant to admit their illiteracy. A contested election had revealed a problem with twenty assisted voters who had sworn by affidavit that they could either read the Constitution in English, write their names, or mark their ballots. It became evident, however, that some were unable to mark their ballots, that others were unable to write, and that one was unable to read the Constitution in the English language. The court's conclusion was generally favorable for illiterate voters in the sense that it acknowledged their right to assistance. In the absence of fraud and gross irregularities in the voting procedure, there was no reason to discount their votes.[155]

In situations such as that in *Marilla v. Ratterman* (1925) in which fraud was a distinct possibility the position of the court was different. *Marilla v. Ratterman* was a case referred to the Court of Appeals of Kentucky in which evidence was offered of massive election fraud in more than sixty precincts. The similarity in the conduct of election officers also suggested a conspiracy:

> This conclusion is borne out by the fact, that in nearly all of these precincts, one of the Republican officers of election or the challenger would immediately inquire if the voter understood or knew how to vote the city ballot, and whether requested or not would proceed to show him, either by pointing a finger to the place where the ballot should be stenciled to vote for the contestees, or by making a cross mark, dot, or dash upon the ballot, or else by going into the booth with the voter, or else stencil the ballot for him. . . .
>
> Frequently, when a Democratic challenger or officer insisted upon the voter showing by his oath, that he was entitled to assistance, as being of one of the classes to which assistance may be rendered, the oath administered was not that he could not read, but was that he did not know or understand the ballot sufficiently to vote it intelligently, or some other form of words, which would make a pretense, that the voter had been sworn.[156]

In their efforts to control the outcome of the election, Republican precinct captains had illegally aided illiterate voters in marking their ballots. Illiterate voters had not been asked to swear to their illiteracy and had been shown how to mark the Republican candidates on the ballot. Behavior in the twelfth precinct of the ninth ward is illustrative:

> the Republican "captain" of the precinct came in and directed the clerk, a negro woman, that she should show all the voters how to vote the city ballot,

and, when a protest was made, he represented that the election commissioners directed that to be done. After that when a voter came in he was asked if he
could read and write and understood the city ballot. If he answered that he
could read, the clerk then showed him on the ballot the Republican groups
and where to stencil to vote for them. If he answered that he could not read,
the clerk would make a cross mark with a pen in the squares to the left of the
Republican groups and tell the voter to stencil there. No voter was sworn that
he was illiterate.[157]

In giving its opinion the court recognized the existence of fraud and included, as well, a brief rehearsal of the several "certain principles relating to elections and voting . . . which are too well established for controversy." Among these, it noted that "where an election officer or other
person goes into the booth with a voter and assists him in stenciling the
ballot, the vote should be rejected, whether or not the voter is an illiterate." It added: "to mark the ballot of a voter with a pen or pencil, or to
point out on the ballot, where to stencil it, without the voter having been
sworn to the effect, that he cannot read, or is blind or physically dis-
abled" should result in the rejection of the ballot regardless of whether
the voter then proceeds to a booth and stencils it. Each of these principles
was a corollary to the more general precept that valid elections were to
be "free and equal" and the ballot to be secret.[158]

To safeguard the intent of the voter, to prevent fraud, and to secure orderly procedure in voting were all concerns of the courts. Increasingly,
courts took a "hard" position with respect to illiteracy. The introduction
of the Australian ballot in the late nineteenth century brought to courts
a number of cases involving illiterate voters. Like the foregoing, these
were concerned with free and equal elections conducted in secrecy without fraud. Yet the Australian ballot had the effect of exacerbating already existing problems encountered by illiterate voters. Five such cases
will be discussed here, including three from the late nineteenth and
early twentieth centuries and two Ohio cases heard in 1950.

The contested election and demand for a recount in *VanWinkle v. Crabtree* (1899) stemmed from a situation in which the Xs designating the
voters' choices were misplaced in such a way that their intent could not
be determined. In giving the decision, the court stressed that the intent
of the Australian ballot law was "to protect the elector from intimidation, to accomplish which the secrecy of his ballot must be preserved." In
addition, however, the court spoke to the educational implications of the
law. The Australian ballot, it said, was "well calculated to promote the
cause of general education by compelling the masses to learn to read and
write as a condition precedent to the exercise of the right of suffrage. . . ." The same ballot, it continued, would "punish the illiterate[s]

by compelling them to admit their ignorance in public, by asking aid in the preparation of their ballots.[159]

As in *VanWinkle v. Crabtree*, the court in *Hunt v. Campbell* (1918) generally took an unsympathetic view of the illiterate voter. Said the court: "If the voter is not held to a substantial compliance with the directions of the statute in the expression of his choice of candidates, the spirit of the Australian ballot system is ignored."[160] In Arizona, the court reminded its listeners: "educational qualifications are a prerequisite to the exercise of suffrage. One too illiterate to mark his ballot substantially as the statute directs cannot for that reason be assisted."[161]

Concern with ballot reform in the late nineteenth and early twentieth centuries occurred within the context of political progressivism. The spirit and rhetoric of antibossism, good government, and municipal reform were as evident in legal prose as they were in journalism and political campaigning. The case for the ballot reform, as for progressive reform in general, often rested on the principle of social efficiency. The principle was explicit in arguments for municipal reform, for example, with pronouncements on the failure of local city government to operate efficiently and without corruption. Said one author in 1892: "The result has been that municipal matters have been left to the petty schemer or the corrupt politician and offices have too long been treated as the legitimate reward for political services. . . ."[162]

State legislative interference, decentralized decision making, and the lack of restrictive suffrage were all seen as causes of the evil. The "common feeling" among those who perpetuate bossism, said another spokesman for good government, is one "which regards the agencies of the public as mere private spoils."[163] Similarly, in an oration on the secret ballot (1891), George Hill argued that the only sure way to diminish corruption was to "take away the opportunity and the profit." The "element of secrecy" was the "corner-stone of the system" that would help guarantee a "truthful expression of the people's choice." It was, said the author, also necessary to prevent fraud in the ballot itself so that "no deception should be practiced upon the voter, by means of ballots which are not what they purport to be."[164]

Concern with social efficiency and good social order was a powerful motivating factor in ballot reform, but the voice of constitutional law was equally as forceful. Courts were mindful of Hamilton's caution in "Federalist No. 59" that "every government ought to contain in itself the means of its own preservation."[165] It was a caution that was legitimatized in Article I of the United States Constitution and reiterated strongly in the late-nineteenth-century case of *Ex parte Yarbrough and others* (1884).

This case, also known as the "Klu-Klux Cases," was a test of the power of the federal government to protect elections from violence, fraud, and corruption. It elicited a spirited defense and explanation by the court of its right to protect a republican form of government. A government "whose essential character is republican," said the court, "must have the power to protect the elections on which its existence depends, from violence and corruption." Continued the court: "If it has not this power, it is left helpless before the two great natural and historical enemies of all republics, open violence and insidious corruption."[166] The court concluded: "It is essential to the successful working of this government that the great organisms of its executive and legislative branches should be the free choice of the people, as that the original form of it should be so."[167]

Interestingly, the court also commented on the nature of "instruments of writing," noting that "what is implied is as much a part of this instrument as what is expressed." The context of the deliberations in *Yarbrough* was the Constitution of the United States and the doctrine of implied powers, but the following words of the court were a keen observation on both the limitations and vulnerability of written expression: "This principle [of implied powers], in its application to the constitution of the United States, more than to almost any other writing, is a necessity, by reason of the inherent inability to put into words all derivative powers. . . ."[168]

The adoption of the Australian ballot in Ohio in 1891 led to several cases in which courts were required to face the issue of educational and literacy qualifications for voting. *State ex rel. Weinberger, a Taxpayer v. Daniel T. Miller et al.* (1912) provided the basic argument for the constitutionality of Ohio statutes governing the secret ballot. In delivering its opinion the court also cited the precedent in *State ex re. Bateman v. Bode* that identical ballots give equal protection to all and that inequalities inhere not in the law but in voters themselves. "It is always much more difficult for some electors to cast their ballots than for others," that court continued. "Before the law, all stand equal, . . . and if their condition becomes such as not to enable them to enjoy the protection or reap the benefit, it is their fault or misfortune, and not the fault of the law."[169]

Equal opportunity was the theme of the court's analysis in *Weinberger.* The general nature of law, said the court, affords "everybody equal opportunities under the law." But, the court added, "it is not possible for constitutions or legislation to make all men equal in understanding, intelligence and education. . . ." State legislation, it was noted, tended in the direction of equality of education even to the point of "compelling the youth of our country to take advantage of these opportunities."[170] The court acknowledged that "in every phase of our social and civic life the uneducated man is at a disadvantage." The opportunities are the same for the educated and uneducated, the court observed, but the uneducated person "is not in a position to take advantage of these. . . ." In commenting on the use of a printed ballot, the court concluded that the state is "powerless" to give the uneducated voter "further aid": *just so long as we are to have elections by written or printed ballot, just so long must the uneducated man find it a difficult matter to vote for the candidate of his choice.*" [171]

When the issue of aid to illiterate voters arose again in 1950, both *Bateman* and *Weinberger* were cited by the court. The situation in both *State ex re. Melvin v. Sweeney* (1950) and *Simmonds v. Eyrich, et al.* (1950) was unusual. The secretary of state of Ohio, having conferred with the attorney general of the same state, issued a directive to boards of election authorizing them to assist illiterate voters. The attorney general's opinion was such that it did not advocate assistance to illiterate voters under the statute in question, but did acknowledge that if said statute were "*construed* to prohibit assistance to illiterate voters, to that extent it is unconstitutional. . . ." Moreover, the section of the Ohio General Code under question, he noted, "prescribes a reasonable procedure for assisting voters unable to mark their ballots for the candidates of their choice. . . ."[172] The procedure to which the attorney general referred was the same as that for assisting those whose physical disability prevented them from casting their ballots, namely:

> Any elector who declares to the presiding judge of elections that he is unable to mark his ballot by reason of physical infirmity . . . may upon request be aided by a near relative who shall be admitted to the booth with such elector, or may receive the assistance in the marking thereof of the two judges of elections belonging to different political parties, and they shall thereafter give no information in regard to this matter. . . . Such assistance shall not be rendered for any other cause.[173]

The issue of aid to an illiterate voter became acute at this point simply because the format of Ohio's ballot was being changed for the upcoming election. Candidates on the ballot were to be voted for separately and their names "rotated" so that it might "be difficult for a voter with little education, as well as for a voter who cannot read or write, to properly express his choice." In its opinion in *Simonds v. Eyrich* the court followed the reasoning of *Weinberger,* finding no reason why legislation "should be shaped to meet [the] convenience [of the illiterate voter]."[174]

In its conclusion to *Simmonds v. Eyrich* the court explained that the election law in question contained no "positive provisions requiring active compliance therewith on the part of an illiterate voter." Instead, it said, the law was "negative" in the sense that it did not provide a method for assistance in cases in which a voter was illiterate or educated at a level insufficient to enable him to express his will. There was nothing in the Ohio law, the court continued, that imposed a duty upon the legislature to assist a class of voters who by education or intelligence were incapable of casting their votes. The illiterate voter surely could attempt to "prepare" for voting, said the court, by consulting others more knowledgeable prior to the election: "His [the illiterate's] disability to mark the ballot may by sufficient effort on his part be cured. His disability does not necessarily continue with him into the voting booth."[175] As with *State v. Sweeney,* the court in *Simmonds v. Eyrich* essentially took the position of its 1912 decision that it was powerless to remedy the difficulties of the uneducated in social and civic life.

Conclusion

Exercise of the voting franchise was unquestionably the most significant dimension of civic life affected by illiteracy. The concept and practice of self-governance went to the very heart of the democratic ideal. Functional literacy as it pertained to voting rights raised difficult questions about the nature of freedom, consent, community, and self-government, as well as problems of due process and fraud. As an essential element in self-governance, consent was conceived in both individual and collective terms. For the individual voter and voters taken collectively, casting the ballot was an expression of purpose, intent, or will. The democratic process of voting was taken to be the embodiment of the purpose(s) of free persons. Unobstructed voting, the guarantee of due process, and the avoidance of fraud were imperative to safeguard the intent of voters. Not to do so would be to undermine the entire purpose of consent in the social contract. Moreover, the worth of liberty and citizenship themselves depended heavily upon proper administrative surveillance and constitutional guarantees of the right to vote.

In most cases of discriminatory exclusion from the franchise, the absence of due process and equal protection formed the legal bases for court action. This was true, also, in cases of fraud and corruption, but the "purity of the ballot" issue went beyond discrimination per se. By their very nature, cases involving the secret ballot and exclusion based on illiteracy dealt with the level of education needed to make intelligent use of the ballot. The Australian ballot presented an issue quite different from fraud, though the perceived need for this type of balloting arose within the context of bossism and election fraud. Many of the illiterate and uneducated were effectively disfranchised by the secret ballot. Yet the exclusion did not lay in discrimination as that term denotes an unreasonable judgment made upon a class of persons. The issue was conceived in terms of individual rather than group inadequacy. Moreover, solution(s) to the problem were conceived in educational terms, not political ones. In an age with expanding educational opportunity (uneven as it was) the problem was only of short-term duration, it was thought. Disfranchisement, then, was seen as only temporary, and the larger collective good of the unspoiled ballot could be served with a minimum of dislocation.

The Illiterate Person and the Jury

The effect of illiteracy on jury selection has both similarities and differences to that involved with the exercise of the franchise. With both we are dealing with constitutional guarantees. With the franchise, the difficulties that arise from illiteracy directly affect the illiterate person and, by extension, the electoral process and outcome. From the standpoint of social and political theory, consent is the issue. From the standpoint of procedural justice, the exercise of citizenship rights is the difficulty. In the case of jury duty, it is primarily the rights of others that are affected. Illiteracy is still a social issue as with the exercise of franchise, yet the effects on the illiterate juror are minimal. Insofar as the outcomes of criminal or civil proceedings affect the legitimate expectations of defendants and community, jury duty is both a political and socially significant process. Considered in this light, illiteracy affects the capability of the political and judicial systems to administer justice.

Questions of juror qualifications, like those of franchise, generally arose in two contexts. The first was that of cultural pluralism and minority representation; the second was that of individual rights. Two of the five possible exclusions from jury service presently listed by the United States Code are related to language. Inability to read, write, and understand the English language "with a degree of proficiency sufficient to fill out satisfactorily the juror qualification form" may be cause for disqualification. Likewise, inability "to speak the English language" may disqualify.[176]

Opinions in recent court action have not deviated substantially from those over the past 100 years, though there seems to be an increase in the sophistication with which jurors are examined. Utility and underrepresentation have been the central questions. Legally this was often a matter of applying state codes on jury selection to the particulars of litigation. Jury questionnaires used to determine proficiency in English were upheld recently in *United States v. Santos* (1979).[177] Once jury selection has been made, courts of appeal have not been willing to disquality or alter judgments on the basis of challenges to English proficiency.[178] Moreover, courts have exercised great discretion in assessing English proficiency. Competency in all aspects of language use is not required.

Thus, for example, proficiency in understanding English when accompanied by difficulty in speaking does not necessarily disqualify a juror.[179]

Challenges to Illiterate Jurors

In the second half of the nineteenth century a number of cases challenged the competency of illiterate jurors. In reviewing these, what one observes generally is that court judgments about competency are differentiated by context, that is, by the functional situation to which the illiterate juror must apply himself. Jury duty was a civic obligation and was normally linked to the responsibility of good citizenship. To serve on a petit or grand jury required one to be an eligible voter.

Different states varied in their statutory requirements for jurors, but a large number had some provision for literacy. Many states, as Proffatt observed in *A Treatise on Trial by Jury* (1880), required "a person to be well-informed and intelligent; and in some, it is further required that a person must be able to read and write the English language." In New York City, he noted, a person may not serve "'unless he shall be an intelligent man, of sound mind, and good character, free from legal exception, and able to read and write the English language understandingly.'"[180] In Iowa, "all qualified electors of the state, of good moral character, sound judgment and in full possession of the senses of hearing and seeing, and who can speak, write and read the English language, [were] competent jurors in their respective counties."[181] In Mississippi, jurors were to be qualified electors and "able to read any section of the constitution of this state. . . ," and in Alabama the statute as of 1914 expressly provided that "if a person cannot read English, yet, if he has all the other qualifications prescribed and is a freeholder or householder, his name may be placed on the jury roll and in the jury box."[182]

In dealing with illiteracy and juror competency it is important to remember that justices of the court were concerned with the function of the juror as it was affected by language skills in general. Thus the ability to understand the language of the court was of first consideration. *Oral literacy,* if we may use the term, was of equal importance with visual literacy in interpreting evidence.

From the court's viewpoint, functionality was the primary concern, and the adequacy of communcations skills was interpreted according to the context of the case being heard. Many times this involved *literacy* in the traditional use of the term, but the problem of literacy was not exclusively a problem of print. In *The Lafayette Plankroad Co. v. The New Albany and Salem Railroad Co.* (1859) heard before the Indiana supreme court, the justices agreed with the counsel for the appellants that a "competent juror must be a man of sound mind, of ordinary intelligence, and having a sufficient acquaintance with the English language to understand the evidence of the witnesses, and the instruction of the Court."[183] This included the ability to understand spoken English even though the juror may have been literate in another language. What was important was that the juror be functional within the context of legal proceedings; not to be so was to be effectively illiterate. Again, in *State of Louisiana v. Albert Push* (1871) it was held that "a person who only understands German, and does not understand English, is no more capable of sitting as a juror in the First District Court of New Orleans, where the proceedings are conducted entirely in English, than if he were deaf and dumb."[184] The position of the state of Louisiana was reaffirmed in *State of Louisiana v. Jean Gay Fils, et al.* (1873): "Jurors, to be competent, must be able to understand all the pleadings and proceedings, as they must be considered by them."[185]

Several cases in a twelve-year period between 1867 and 1879 are helpful in illustrating the position of the courts with respect to level of education, literacy, and juror competency. The first of these was *The Commonwealth v. George W. Winnermore* (1867), a Pennsylvania case appealed to the supreme court of the same state. A lower court had overruled the "challenge for cause of a juror" and this was upheld at the supreme court level. The juror was not classified as illiterate, but his low level of education raised essentially the same problems for the court.

In giving its decisions the court noted that the ground for challenge of the juror "was want of education, rather than natural capacity or intelligence." The juror, observed the court, "could read but little; only read newspapers; never read a book; and did not know his age." Although this demonstrated a low level of education, said the court, "it did not show want of capacity to reason and judge of what was orally communicated." No statutory provision demanding a specified degree of learning as a prerequisite to be a juror existed in Pennsylvania, and "it does not follow that, because a man may not have read books, or may have confined his reading solely to the literature of the newspapers, he is not intelligent enough for a juryman."[186] Illiteracy, per se, was not a measure of juror competency in this case, although the court's dim view of reading only the newspapers reflects its own expectations of the "educated" man.

Several years later in the Mississippi case of *Henry White v. The State* (1876) illiteracy was the point of contention. This case, which involved the murder of an infant child, was appealed, in part, on the grounds of juror incompetency. The court held that the inability to read and write was not a statutory disqualification of a juror for incompetency. "The law," said the court, "does not define an intellectual or educational standard."[187] In the same year in *State of Louisiana v. Andrew Louis* it was decided that "the law does not declare ignorance a disqualification in a juror which will authorize a party to challenge him for cause."[188] And again in 1878 in *The American Life Insurance Company v. Zenora F. Mahone and Husband* the Mississippi court held that juror qualifications as defined by statute did "not erect a standard of education or learning."[189]

The gravity of misunderstanding directions of the court and testimony presented was probably most crucial in capital offenses. Though the situation of one or two illiterate jurors was common, a most uncommon case was *George B. Lyles v. The State* (1874) heard on appeal in the state of Texas. The case was one of murder and had initially involved five men indicted for the murder of José Gamboa. Three of the five were jointly tried before a jury, nine of whom "did not speak nor understand the English language," and who were objected to as jurors by the defendants. The court's charge was written in English and translated orally. The court refused to translate the charge in writing despite the plea of counsel for the defendants.[190]

Lyles v. The State was appealed on several grounds, but a good share of the court's opinion dealt with the illiterate jurors. Thus we are offered a more detailed picture than usual of the court's position on this matter. With minor exceptions the language of Texas courts was English and, said the court, "it would seem . . . a necessity that the jurors should have a reasonable knowledge of the language in which the proceedings were conducted, to enable them to perform their duties." The "inviolate right" of trial by jury could not be protected "when the jurors can neither speak nor understand the language" of the proceedings. The court suggested that without the jurors' "capacity" to understand the charge and the proceedings the trial would only be a "legal fiction." The Texas code did not exclude jurors because of illiteracy. The opinion of the court, however, was that neither the framers nor the legislature contemplated impaneling jurors who were ignorant of the language used in court.

The fact that the charge had been incorrectly translated confounded the situation even further. An incompetent translator had orally translated the word *murder* as *assassination*. The jury had no written translation of the charge to take with them to their deliberations. Thus the three literate jurors could not help the illiterate ones. Moreover, it was obvious that the literate jurors could have given a misconstruction to the others. In any case, a fair trial by jury was not possible.[191]

A similar case to *Lyles v. The State* followed in 1880 with *J. Campbell v. The State,* also heard on appeal in the state of Texas. All peremptory challenges to jurors had been exhausted, and eight jurors were impaneled over the defendant's challenges that they could not speak or understand the English language. When arguments were heard, the privilege of addressing the jury in Spanish (the language of the eight challenged jurors) was denied. Citing the decision in *Lyles v. The State* the court concluded that the jury had been forced on the plaintiff "in violation of his constitutional privileges" and that the error was magnified by the refusal to permit defendant's counsel "to address them in a language they could comprehend, or to consume at least a part of the time allotted him for argument in that language." The court noted that counsel had been forced "to resort to pantomime."[192]

Other decisions that involved the question of juror competency as it relates to the ability to read and write English followed in the next two decades. Four of these were from Texas and Colorado; others were from Iowa, Mississippi, and Alabama. Two Texas cases demonstrate the critical importance of determining the competency of a juror on the basis of his literacy skills. In each, the presence of an illiterate juror was material in determining the outcome of the case. In *James Wright v. The State* (1882), adjudged in the Court of Appeals of the State of Texas, it was determined that the requirement for jurors to read and write employed in a Texas statute meant the ability to read and write English. The case, which was an appeal from a conviction for horse stealing, involved a challenge to a juror who possessed "a very fair knowledge of English," but who could only read and write German. In this court's opinion, the "defendant was deprived of a fair and impartial trial when there was forced upon him one juror who could not read and write the English language, and could not read the charge of the court for himself. . . ."[193] Thus the ability simply to understand English was not a sufficient qualification.

In the far West, the decision in *The Town of Trinidad v. Simpson* (1879) used a similar line of reasoning in regard to a juryman selected for a trial in Las Animas, Colorado. The statutes of Colorado did not include the inability to read and write among the grounds for challenging a juror. The question the court had to answer was whether or not an interpreter could be used when the court was confronted with the difficulty of an illiterate juror. In responding to the challenge, the court noted that the case stood at common law and cited Coke's heading of *propter defectum* (on account of some defect) as the most appropriate category under which to decide the case.

In delivering its opinion, the court observed that "knowledge of a language other than a person's vernacular is but an accomplishment [and] want of it argues nothing respecting mental culture." High intellectual attainment and aptitude for jury duty were not precluded by lack of such knowledge. Yet, said the court, a juror cannot competently discharge his duties if ignorant of the language of the court: "Ignorance of the language, as a matter of fact, is as conspicuously a disqualifying circumstance as though he were deaf, unless the court may aid him in the discharge of his duties through the instrumentality of an interpreter."[194]

In commenting on the legality of using an interpreter, the court first took a historical view of the subject, noting various English statutes relevant to the language of the court in English-speaking countries. Although English was clearly the language of the court in this instance, it did not follow that *only* English would be used in judicial proceedings:

> Contracts in a foreign tongue are to be dealt with, and must be translated. Non-English speaking witnesses are put upon the stand and must "bear witness" through an interpreter. Non-English speaking prisoners are put upon their trial, and the indictment and other proceedings of the trial are made known and manifest to them by the same instrumentality. The proposition, therefore, that all judicial proceedings must be in the English language must be taken *sub modo*.[195]

The spirit of Colorado law was to "secure a record in English," and the use of an interpreter did not defeat this purpose, said the court. A full panel of English-speaking jurors would be preferable, and "a wise discretion would excuse from jury duty persons ignorant of the language." Still, use of an interpreter was proper, and persons ignorant of the language of the court were not necessarily disqualified by that ignorance.[196]

Ten years later *In re Allison* (1889) reaffirmed this position. The court was disturbed that the use of an interpreter "renders court proceedings more tedious and expensive." Nonetheless, court procedure was bent to the practicalities of administering justice. A Spanish-speaking juryman with the use of an interpreter, it said, "may perform the duties of [a] juror far better than many English-speaking citizens." Thus, bowing to expediency and the force of history, the court said:

> In certain counties of the state where the great bulk of the population originally were, and a very large proportion thereof still are, Mexicans, it would, for many years, have been practically impossible to have administered justice, under our system of jurisprudence, without their aid in this capacity. Since [*The Town of Trinidad v. Simpson*] . . . the legislature has expressly declared that neither the county commissioners, the courts, nor the judges shall "discriminate against, reject, or challenge any person, otherwise qualified, on account of such person speaking the Spanish or Mexican language, and not being able to understand the English language."[197]

In *Albert Johnson v. The State* (1886), a case appealing a conviction for rape, the court concluded that one of the jurors was incompetent because his degree of literacy did not extend beyond his ability to write his name. Unlike in most previous judicial decisions, the court in this case attempted to distinguish among levels of a literacy and urged that a functional definition of literacy ought to be employed. The statute governing juror qualifications, said the court, "must have intended something practical":

> That a person can write his name certainly does not fill the measure of the statutory requirement that the juror should be able to *write*. We think that he should be able to express his ideas in words upon paper with pen and pencil.[198]

The import of the Florida case of *The County of Jefferson v. B. C. Lewis and Sons* (1884) was similar to that of *Johnson v. The State*. This former case centered around a suit brought by the defendants B. C. Lewis and Sons to recover damages upon bonds issued by Jefferson County. Among the various grounds of error upon which the appeal was made was that concerned with juror competency. In hearing the case in lower court, plaintiff's counsel was permitted to examine the jurors " 'as to their ability to calculate interest, and to work interest in case of partial payments such as might arise upon the pleadings and proofs in this case.' " No error was committed in this procedure, observed the state supreme court, for the object "is to procure a jury sufficiently intelligent to understand the testimony and to render a proper verdict upon it." The statute cited was one of 1877 that provided "that when the nature of any case requires that a knowledge of reading, writing or arithmetic is necessary to enable a juror to understand the evidence to be offered on the trial, [then] it shall be a cause of challenge if he does not possess such qualification. . . ."[199]

The problem of juror selection was frequently complicated by discriminatory exclusion and was similar to the problem of voter participation in some states. Two constitutional questions have been at issue in the law of jury exclusion. The first is related to the right to serve on a jury, the second with the right to be tried by an impartial jury. Even when a prima facie case of racial exclusion has been made, however, certain explanations have been legitimate in "explaining away," for example, the exclusion of blacks from juries. Thus when "minority" jurors have been excluded over long periods of time, or their proportion has been far less than would be expected from their proportion in the population, there are "acceptable" explanations of this, including lower rates of literacy, fluency in English, schooling, high incidence of criminal convictions, or high rates of unemployment.[200]

Despite the passage of the Civil Rights Act of 1875, the record of impaneling racially balanced juries has been dubious. In 1880 the United States Supreme Court struck down a West Virginia statute that barred blacks from juries. They also invalidated a Virginia law that allowed state selection officials to "exclude blacks from jury lists." Yet in

Virginia v. Rives (1880) the court ignored the fact of all-white juries when speaking to the issues of impartial juries.[201]

It was common knowledge as late as 1960 that blacks and other minorities were systematically excluded from juries.[202] This was true not only in the South, but, for example, in Colorado, where people with Spanish surnames in Logan County seldom appeared on jury lists and even less often on juries themselves. The result in the particular case of *Montoya v. People* (1959) was a reversal of a conviction of a Spanish-American defendant on grounds that Spanish-Americans constituted a "substantial segment" of the county, that there were members of this class of people qualified to serve as jurors, and that there had been only token representation of them over an "extended period of time."[203]

The ability to "read, write, speak, and understand the English language" as a federal jury qualification remained part of the 1957 Civil Rights Act.[204] In 1962, a United States Court of Appeals in *United States v. Henderson* upheld a district court judgment that allowed jury selection on the basis of literacy. The words of the court, however, bear closer scrutiny, for they did allow an eighth-grade level of education to be used as an indicator and confirmation of "the required ability to read, write, speak and understand the English language and [to] indicate the existence of an intelligence level which certainly is not unreasonable as a requirement for the selection of efficient jurors."[205] The mixing of level of *literacy* with level of *intelligence* was a strange choice of words for the court, but it is significant that one concurring statement of Circuit Judge Schnachenberg pointed out the possible confusion and misconceptualization that would occur when level of education and intelligence are linked in a functional way, if not necessarily in a causal way:

> While I concur in Judge Castle's opinion in this case, I make an exception to that sentence which holds that defendant has no constitutional or statutory right that "ignorance" be represented in the jury box. I do not find that defendant has made any contention for "ignorance" in the jury box. He has directed his attack to the requirements of a *literacy* test, i.e., a formal eighth grade education. In this case we are concerned with an intelligence test which is measured, in part, by *literacy*. A lack of literacy denotes *illiteracy* not ignorance. An illiterate person may be a wise person. 28 U.S.C.R. § 1861 does not disqualify as jurors persons because they are ignorant; it disqualifies them because they are *illiterate,* i.e., unable to read, write, and understand the English language.[206]

In cases involving challenges to prospective jurors on grounds of illiteracy, judges have been allowed wide discretion within state codes to determine whether a challenge to proficiency is warranted. In the 1904 case of *State v. Greenland,* for example, the Supreme Court of Iowa noted that there was no special interrogation of one of the jurors' competency in English even though the juror's qualifications were challenged. In fact the only evidence of inability to read and write was that the grand juror used a mark as a signature. In the absence of other evidence, the court did not accept this challenge because the juror in question explained that he had a physical difficulty in signing.[207]

More recently, the opinion in *State of Louisiana v. Jasper Brazile* (1956), heard in the Supreme Court of Louisiana, acknowledged the wisdom of a holistic approach to English proficiency. *"A prospective juror's competence or incompetence,"* said the court, *"cannot be limited to isolated answers given during the course of his examination. It must be judged from his entire examination."* In addition the court held that it was proper for the defense counsel to ask that a juror read a document "to test his ability to read," even though the document was unidentified. This latter point proved to be exceedingly important. The court could not really judge the competence of the juror on the basis of the ability or inability to read the document. Yet the fact that a peremptory challenge (which exhausted the number of peremptory challenges allowed) had to be used resulted in the defendant's having to accept a juror who was "obnoxious to him." Thus, said the court, "he is . . . entitled to have the conviction set aside and to be given a new trial."[208]

A discussion of two recent cases concludes this section. The first is *A. D. Scifres v. State of Arkansas* (1958), and the second *The People of the State of California v. Ronald Dale Jones* (1972). Both cases deal extensively with challenges to illiterate jurors.[209] The opinions of the courts speak both to the technicalities of juror examination and to the larger educational and social context for a fair trial by jury.

Scifres v. State was a case of robbery appealed to the Supreme Court of Arkansas. Russ, "a negro who had reached the seventh grade in school," was challenged by the appellant on grounds that "he lacked sufficient education to understand or comprehend the court's instructions." In this case, challenge was made by asking the prospective juror to define certain legal terms and terms related to legal issues. The questions and answers are as follows:

> **Q.** Can you define . . . the words bias and prejudice?
> **A.** You have something within you against.
> **Q.** Can you define . . . the word duress?
> **A.** No, sir.
> **Q.** Can you define . . . the word intimidation?
> **A.** I am sorry.

Q. You have no idea?

A. No, sir, why I wouldn't express.

Q. Can you define . . . presumption of innocence?

A. That he is not guilty.

Q. Can you define . . . present ability.

A. I am sorry.[210]

The court found this line of questioning unobjectionable. It cited the general opinion, offered in *American Jurisprudence,* that it was unnecessary for a juror to be a "scholar and understand the definition of every word used in the course of a trial by witnesses, counsel, and the court." The court's opinion also included the broader context for constituting jury membership. It reached back to the 1873 United States Supreme Court case of *Sioux City and Pacific Railway Co. v. Stout,* reiterating the opinion on the "ideal" jury under our jury trial system. It was a picture of democratic membership acting in a democratic way to resolve litigation with a unanimous conclusion:

> Twelve men of the average of the community, comprising men of education and men of little education, men of learning and men whose learning consists only in what they have themselves seen and heard, the merchant, the mechanic, the farmer, the laborer; these sit together, consult, apply their separate experiences of the affairs of life to the facts proven, and draw a unanimous conclusion.[211]

This ideal has no doubt persisted. It is the average man, golden mean theory of justice and trial by jury, according to which wisdom emanates from the proper balance or proportion of human ingredients. As *Sioux City v. Stout* expressed it:

> This average judgment thus given it is the great effort of the law to obtain. It is assumed that twelve men know more of the common affairs of life than does one man; that they can draw wiser and safer conclusions from admitted facts thus occurring, than can a single judge.[212]

What *Sioux City v. Stout* called "average judgment" in some ways runs counter to the criterion of utility and what might be called the expert theory of judgment. The average judgment theory assumes inequality of condition (wealth, education, and learning) and is, in some ways, less of a theory than a faith in the law of averages. Somehow, it is assumed, the meshing of inequalities will produce the best average result. Different types and different degrees of knowledge are averaged to some acceptable outcome.

As a theory of justice, the average judgment theory is of dubious logic. As a theory of representative knowledge, it makes sense. It assumes, moreover, a minimum level of language facility and intelligence for each juror and a representation of groups presumed to have special knowledge and perspectives, such as women and minority groups. The final case considered in this section, *People v. Jones* (1972), illustrates just how difficult it has become and to what lengths challenges can go to address the problems of representation and competency.

People v. Jones was an appeal from a manslaughter conviction in the Superior Court, Los Angeles County. The points of contention were two aspects of jury selection: representation and language facility. The legal issue was whether or not the lower court had erred in disallowing presentation of evidence to support a motion "to quash the complete jury venire."

The motion of the defendant's counsel was to "quash the complete jury venire for the Southern Judicial District of Los Angeles County." The motion charged that the "inexorable operation of the system" had excluded "large and disproportionate numbers of [the] economically oppressed, the educationally disadvantaged, and [the] culturally different, black people and Mexican-Americans in particular." Statistical analysis of the system was offered to show that a disproportionate percentage of white middle-class persons were accepted for potential jury duty. Specifically, "the percentage of the eligible population taken from the middle-class white section was thirteen times as great as the percentage from the black area."[213]

Among the four causes of this was the use of a written "competence" test that included both reading comprehension and vocabulary. This was attacked because it allegedly was "irrelevant to the criterion of intelligence" and discriminated against prospective jurors from "lower socioeconomic strata." Sufficient knowledge of the English language did not mean ability to read, it was argued. The court disagreed, saying that jurors must be "fully able to understand spoken and written English."[214]

The reading comprehension part of the test was not included in the court record. The vocabulary test follows:

	1	2	3	4
1. *fraud*	deceit	remark	wife	flood
2. *involve*	implicate	wrong	ruin	turn around
3. *credible*	unbelievable	estable	estimated	believable
4. *aquit*	refuse	mediate	discharge	go away
5. *plaintiff*	arraignment	one who brings suit	overseer	evidence

	1	2	3	4
6. *allege*	assert	to own	reduce	reflect
7. *intent*	application	purpose	service	extent
8. *larceny*	large opening	theft	Swedish	market
9. *trustee*	leader	orphan	traitor	a safe keeper
10. *ratify*	select	import	approve	rate
11. *valid*	highly valued	having legal force	perfect	uncertain
12. *proper*	appropriate	ordinary	respectful	expert
13. *impute*	prefer	impure	to ascribe or credit	prove
14. *legacy*	to delegate	operation	bequest	loan
15. *assign*	sign	bring into	lessen	make over to
16. *accede*	donate	rise up	agree	excel
17. *expend*	terminate	payout	detest	grow longer
18. *justify*	warrant	expect	to reprove	fortify
19. *immoderate*	trustworthy	temporal	ashamed	to excess
20. *provoke*	put together	catch	remove	to cause
21. *malice*	sadness	force	unpleasant	ill will
22. *marital*	judged	military	referring to marriage	reduced to rank
23. *apprehend*	apprise	seize	rob	precede
24. *waive*	give up	move violently	make note of	march
25. *duress*	overcome	length	existence	complusion

It is obvious that the test contains a disproportionate number of legal terms. The test was devised in the 1930s by a professor at University of Southern California. (Defense had proposed to call the professor as a witness.) Test items had been correlated with intelligence quotient (IQ), the purpose being "to construct a test of average verbal ability, which did not exclude anyone of ordinary intelligence." The large proportion of legal words was "to make the test appear relevant and 'motivating' to the prospective jurors." The passing grade corresponded to an IQ of 90, and it had been the practice of the jury commissioner to fail prospective jurors scoring lower than 17 of 25 correct answers.[215]

The court's discussion of the test does not include a statistical analysis. It focuses on substantive, but nontechnical questions. The court pointed, first, to the disproportionate number of legal terms, saying that they were "stressed almost to the point of excluding all others. . ." It noted that the test seemed "designed to eliminate persons whose interests and day-to-day contacts have nothing to do with the law." Among the legal terms, said the court, there were some that would naturally be more familiar to "persons in the higher economic brackets." Words like *trustee, ratify, legacy,* and *assign* were found more frequently "in stock brokers' offices than on construction sites or in factories and unemployment lines." The court also pointed out that some of the synonyms were culturally biased. English spoken in black neighborhoods probably had a synonym for the word *impute,* but it was probably not *assign* or *credit.* These were words more likely found in legal opinions or among university faculty members "given to somewhat precious usage." Finally the court pointed to the absence of answers (synonyms) that would have counterbalanced the cultural bias toward upper socioeconomic groups. "Why," said the court, "is the examinee asked to define 'fraud' rather than 'con,' 'larceny' rather than 'ripoff'? Why is the correct answer to 'acquit' not 'cut loose' but 'discharge'?"[216]

In reviewing the plaintiff's response, the court had little patience and less sympathy. The People claimed that the test was used to "obtain qualified jurors" and that there was no evidence to support "intentional or systematic discrimination." "Large segments of the population," however, were discriminated against, regardless of intent, said the court. The test, it continued, was not designed to make good jurors. Furthermore, it was the discriminatory effect, not the intent, that counted. Looking at the matter in its entirety, the court concluded that the defendant was entitled to a hearing and reversed the judgment.[217]

Conclusion

Literacy as it relates to juror competency has historically meant the ability to understand the language of the court, to read court directives, and to read documents germane to making a judgment about guilt or innocence. The inability to read and write often could mean exclusion or marginality for the illiterate person. The question of marginality was fundamentally a question of who "belongs": that is, it was a question of who was allowed to participate in this aspect of civic life. The condition of marginality was determined by the expectations of "significant others." To be marginal in a functional sense was often a product of the discretionary power of a judge.

In general, the normative nature of the law required that it be interpreted within a specified cultural context. The link between juror competency and illiteracy was no exception. In many cases the illiterate person was specifically the target of statutory law, although the application of that law was left to justices of the courts. In dealing with the literacy requirements for juror competency, the legal significance of literacy transcended the fortunes of the illiterates themselves; rather, it is clear that the lives and fortunes of others were at stake. Its utility was immediately evident. Literacy acquired a greater significance than if only the illiterate party were affected. More than voting, jury duty was an expression of service to the community and a symbol of the larger community interest.

In facing the problem of illiterate jurors, courts were dealing with two constitutional principles: the right to serve on a jury and the right to be tried by a fair and impartial jury. Thus, both issues of equality and equity were involved. Questions arising in either case were often framed within the context of discriminatory exclusion; questions involving the latter principle often involved juror competency. Competency, insofar as the illiterate person was concerned, was a matter of whether or not reading and writing or a specified level of education were needed to understand the proceedings of the court or the intricacies of a particular case. Courts exercised great discretion in determining these matters and frequently made decisions that excluded those who were below a requisite level of education. The "facts" of the case were the functional standard of reference for these decisions.

The issue of discriminatory exclusion was invariably colored by local and state politics and prejudices. It could involve a deeply felt position that members of a so-called inferior race ought not to sit in judgment on a "superior race," or, conversely, that members of one race were "made" to sit in judgment on another. Expressed in this manner, the position represents a cultural divide that was not likely to be overcome by legal or educational means. It was a matter of "knowing one's place" and accepting the basic racist position of an inferior/superior dichotomy. Racism expressed as discriminatory exclusion was operationalized, in part, through literacy requirements. Such requirements, moreover, were often tied to suffrage requirements in a given county and state and, in this way, could be extensions of exclusion from the franchise itself. A state or local political hierarchy, whether avowedly racist or simply following tradition, could thus become the basis for jury exclusion. The network of discrimination woven in this way reached to the very heart of civic life.

Recent cases on juror qualifications have been sensitive to the link between tests of competency and discriminatory exclusion. There is no question of counsel's right to question the competency of a prospective juror, nor is there a question of whether or not jurors must understand the language of the court. Yet the level of competency and its potential effect on excluding large minority and underprivileged segments of the population are critical. What are underscored in these recent cases are both the complexity of the issue and subjectivity of judgment. Functional criteria are difficult enough to establish because of their contextual relativity. When the criteria themselves are used to make judgments about representation and intent, their inadequacy is brought to light. The difficulty with juror qualification remains because the relationship of competency and utility, on the one hand, to fairness and representativeness on the other is unclear. Clarity, moreover, requires a philosophic, not a technical, solution. Competency is not a matter of criteria levels. It is a matter of context, both historical and social.

4

The Economic Dimensions
of Illiteracy

. . . .

This chapter provides an overview of the economic participation of illiterates and the financial and legal difficulties they faced as a result of their illiteracy. Chapter 5 will, in turn, focus specifically on illiteracy and contract. The diversity of judicial decisions in which illiteracy was an issue reflects the broad range of economic activities in which illiterates participated. The extent of illiterates' participation in different financial transactions precluded their appellation as marginal people. Illiterates' involvement in property transactions was often greater than would be expected from their numbers in the general population. Illiterates, then, were not peremptorily excluded from these activities. Yet, the marks of illiterates and their competency did not go unchallenged in courts of law. Challenges to the mark and the competency of the illiterate person were common. Cases concerning these problems may be found throughout the nineteenth and twentieth centuries. The many cases dealing with the legitimacy of the mark that involve disputed deeds, wills, and contracts illustrate the dependency of illiterate persons on the lexical skills of others. Judges frequently warned of the difficulties associated with using the mark, yet, just as often, courts affirmed that the mark had the authority of the law behind it.

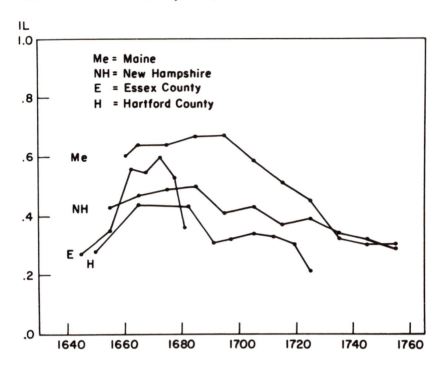

Figure 1. Illiteracy rates (IL) in Essex County, Massachusetts (1640–81), Hartford County, Connecticut (1635–1729), and New Hampshire and Maine (1641-1750). (Source: *The Probate Records of Essex County, Masschusetts,* vols. 1–3 [Salem, 1916]; *A Digest of the Early Connecticut Probate Records,* comp. Charles Manwaring [Hartford, 1904]; *Probate Records of the Province of New Hampshire,* vol. 1 [1635–1717], ed. Albert Stillman Batchellor [Concord, 1970]; *Probate Records of the Province of New Hampshire,* vol. 2 [1718–40], ed. Henry Harrison Metcalf [Bristol, 1914]; *Probate Records of the Province of New Hampshire,* vol. 3 [1741–49], ed. Henry Harrison Metcalf [Concord, 1915];*Probate Records of the Province of New Hampshire,* vol. 4 [1750–53], ed. Otis G. Hammond [State of New Hampshire, 1933]; *Probate Records of the State of New Hampshire,* vol. 5 [1754–56], ed. Otis G. Hammond [State of New Hampshire, 1936]; *Probate Records of the Province of New Hampshire,* vol. 6 [1757–60], ed. Otis G. Hammond [State of New Hampshire, 1938]; John T. Hull, *York Deeds,* vols. 1–13 [Portland, Me., 1887]. Maine and New Hampshire points are averages of three decadal periods.) Previously printed in Lee Soltow and Edward Stevens, *The Rise of Literacy and the Common School in the United States: A Socioeconomic Analysis to 1870* (Chicago: University of Chicago Press, 1981), p. 35.

Illiteracy among Testators

It will be remembered that in the case of illiterates' participation in civic activities it was difficult to construct a firm statistical base for considering their difficulties in coping with this dimension of citizenship. Fortunately, it is far easier to do this for the economic activities of illiterate persons. The data presented in this first section are intended to be illustrative, not comprehensive nor exhaustive. Nonetheless, they give a fair representation of illiterates' involvement in basic, though selective, economic activities. It is well known that during the colonial period numerous testators signed their wills with a mark. Lockridge and Soltow and Stevens have used these marks as a basis for estimating the level of illiteracy during that era.[1] There are several difficulties with making such estimates, but for the purpose of this study it is sufficient to note that Lockridge's estimates for New England over the 145-year period from 1650 to 1795 show that 10 to 45 percent of male testators and 55 to 70 percent of female testators were illiterate.[2] For both female and male testators in New England during the period 1640–1760, Soltow and Stevens found an illiteracy rate ranging between 25 and 65 percent.[3] Geographically, the picture is that presented in Figure 1.

The complexity and quality of writing found in colonial wills varied dramatically as it does today. The following will by an illiterate is distressingly brief, and the testator's poverty is evident in the meager belongings that he had to convey to his godchild:

> I give unto my god Childe Grace Shed a sowe shott [shoat] and bleue blanket And this is my last will and testament. I have here unto set my hand this leaventh day of September 1638.

The marke of Thomas   X   Lee[4]

It was likewise with the following, in which both the testator and the witnesses were illiterate:

> If it please God I doe dye my debt beinge discharged with debt [?] do remayne I give to Goodman Fisher and he to see me Layd in the ground like a man.

The marke of John   X   Wilkinson
The marke of James   X   Granne
The mark of William   X   Briar[5]

These wills may be contrasted with that of Elizabeth Bridgham, who, though illiterate, made her bequest in several portions. The accompanying inventory indicates that the value of the estate was £213, 12 s:

In the name of God Amen

    I Elisabeth Bridgham of Boston Widow, being sick of body, but perfect in memory, blessed bee God, Doe make this my Last Will & Testament as followeth—Inp^{r}mis I commit My Soul into the Mercifull hands of God my Creator & Redeemer, & my body to earth from whence it came, hoping that at the last day it shall arise a glorious body, Like unto the body of my Lord & Saviour Jesus Christ; & my Estate, which my Late Husband Henry Bridgham by his last Will Left mee to dispose of, (that is to say) one hundred pounds & all the household goods, the which I doe give & bequeath as followeth First I give & bequeath unto my eldest Son John out of the one hundred pounds aforemencioned to buy bookes with the Summe of Fifty pounds, & the other fifty pounds I give & bequeath as followeth (that is to say) forty pounds unto my Son Joseph, & the other ten pounds unto my other four Sons to bee equally devided between them; Further I give unto my Son John a new paire of blew Curtainses & vallants, that haue not bee vsed. Itm. I give & bequeath unto my Son Jonathan the best paire of green Curtains & vallants, my best greene Rugg, the best Feather bed & boulster, with the best bedsteede, & the rest of my household goods, I give & bequeath unto all my six Sons to bee equally devided between them.

    Itm. it is my further minde according as in my saide Husband's Will is provided, That in case of any of my saide Sons shall take any indirect course, it shalbee in the power of my overseers hereafter names to cut short & lessen what I haue given unto them & bestow the same on such of them as shall better deserve the same.

    Itm. I give unto my Sister Hannah Buttall my best cloth gowne my best black Cloake & my best wearing Linnen, & the rest of my Wearing apparrell, I give unto such poor persons as the discretion of my Over Seers shall thincke fit; And I doe appoint my Son Jonathan Executor^r of this my last Will & Testam^t & m^r Anthony Stoddard, Deacon Robart Sanderson & Deacon Henry Allen Deacons of the first Church of Boston Over Seers of this my saide Last Will & Testament, & all other former Wills, gifts & bequests I revoake & make voide for ever by these pu^{r}sents. In Witness whereof I the saide Elisabeth Bridgham haue hereunto Set my hand & Seale, this second day of August in ye yeare of or Lord, one thousand six hundred Seventh two.

Elisabeth Bridgham

Attested Copy   her X marke & a Seale[6]

    Illiterate persons were also found in a number of testamentary-related procedures. Illiterate witnesses to wills were common, and numerous instances may be found of claims against estates and debts due to estates by illiterate persons.

    For a later period there is ample evidence of illiterates' participation in testamentary activity. A data set from 1780 to 1900 taken from Kent County, Delaware, and Washington County, Ohio, provides two groups of signatures or marks useful in measuring the participation of illiterate persons in the important legal and economic activity of making a will.[7] Illiteracy rates among both testators and witnesses to wills are shown in Figure 2.[8]

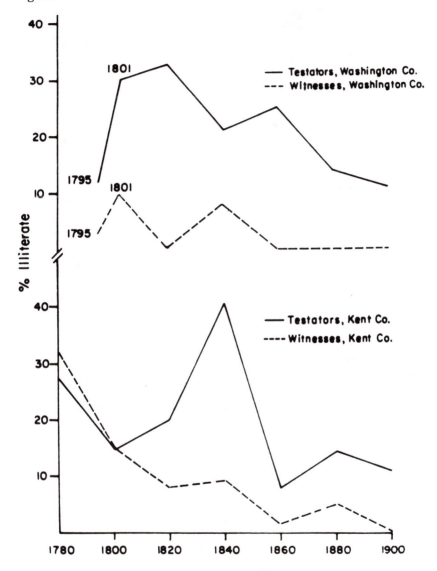

Figure 2. Illiteracy rates among testators and witnesses, Kent and Washington Counties, 1780–1900. Previously printed in Edward Stevens, "Literacy and the Worth of Liberty," *Historical Social Research,* 34 (April, 1985), p. 68.

The most obvious fact when comparing levels of illiteracy among testators and witnesses is the lower percentage of markers among witnesses. Only between 1780 and 1800 in Kent County did the percentage of markers among witnesses exceed that of testators. By 1820 the number of illiterates among witnesses had dropped below 10 percent. From 1860 to 1900 in Washington County there were no illiterate witnesses in the sample of wills. This was also the case in Kent County by the year 1900.

The highest percentage (40 percent) of illiterate testators was found in 1840 in Kent County. In Washington County the highest figure was 33 percent, found in 1820. In both Kent and Washington counties the patterns were curvilinear. In both counties, also, the level of illiteracy among testators had dropped to 11 percent by 1900. Thus between the years 1800 to 1900 a slow downward trend in illiteracy is observable. This is what would be expected, given the decrease in illiteracy on a national scale.[9]

Illiteracy among Grantors and Mortgagors

Agreements or covenants, debts, contracts, and conveyances of land were as common among the unlettered as they were among the literate. As with wills there was a wide range of complexity and level of comprehension needed to understand the documents. In the seventeenth century, the promise of Henry Elliott of Suffolk in 1679 was simply to deliver a squaw:

> I underwritten do hereby promiss and oblige my Selfe to deliver to George Danson or his Order an Indian Squaw named Sarah. belonging to the s^d Geo: Danson and now in my possession at demand. Witness my hand.
>
> Henry X Eliott[10]
his mark
>
> Witness.
> Nath: Colson
> Daniel Mascroft

The agreement of William Still of North Carolina was a little more complex but still relatively simple and bound him

> to pay or Case to be payd unto Thomas Durant or to his order the full and Just sum of one pound ten shillings in oyle and in Good tite Cask full and Good to the Liking of the said Tho. Durant and to be delivered att sum Conveent

Landen nere your one house one tenth day of febery next Ensueing the date here of as witness my hand this 27 day of July 1696.

The mark of William   X   Still[11]

Teste

John Durant

The mark of Rebecka Peterson

Other agreements were considerably more elaborate. One of these from the state of New York involved a lease of a bowery by a baker to two brothers. The terms of payment were to continue over six years and included the exchange of livestock, farm implements, and produce, including specified amounts of butter and grain.[12] A second example comes from the county of Kent in Delaware. This provided for a partnership of five years' duration between the unlettered persons of Thomas Wilsham and Thomas Shaw. The agreement stated that they be

> copartners togather In the trade of occapation of planting or any other thing whatsoeuer that Is to say in planting Buying selling uttering vending or Relating of all kinde sorts of Corn tobbacco Chattells Goods Land moueables Eather Bought purchased procured or by Labor Increased By [one] or Both of us as allsoe prouidgions [sic] or any other thing or things Raised planted or Improued By the Care or Industry of Eaither of us aboue mentioned. . . .[13]

The agreement went on to provide for mutual indebtedness and recovery of debts as well as improvement of land and purchase of livestock. Both examples make it quite apparent that unlettered persons could be parties to elaborate agreements. It is evident, also, that they would require the help of court authorities and probably literate friends and neighbors to enter into these arrangements.

When we turn to the nineteenth century, once again the samples from Ohio and Delaware give us a portrait of illiterates' participation in important economic activities.[14] The sample of 1,463 grantors and 865 mortgagors from Kent County, Delaware, and 3,225 grantors and 1,238 mortgagors from Washington County, Ohio, makes possible a detailed analysis of illiterate persons' participation in two very fundamental economic activities—deeding and mortgaging.

Illiterate individuals (markers) were not evenly distributed over the years from 1780 to 1900. In both counties there was a curvilinear pattern during these 120 years. In Washington County in 1790, for example, there were no illiterate grantors, whereas in 1860 15 percent were illiterate. In 1900 the county had 6 percent illiteracy. The same curvilinear pattern of illiteracy is also evident in Kent County.[15]

There was an increase in the illiteracy of grantors in the year 1840 that needs some explanation in view of the fact that illiteracy rates were decreasing overall in the country. The number of deed transactions during this period rose rapidly. It could be that broader participation by people at the lower end of the wealth distribution in the purchase of land accounts for an increase in the proportion illiterate.

Literacy and wealth have been shown to be related in the nineteenth century. Soltow and Stevens have noted that the top 10 percent of wealth holders in 1860 and 1870 included enough illiterate persons to account for only 3 percent of the male illiterates; the top 20 percent of wealth holders in 1860 had only 8 percent of the illiterates. If illiterates were evenly distributed along the wealth scale, then approximately 10 percent of the illiterates would be in the top decile range for wealth and 20 percent of the illiterates would be in the top two decile ranges.[16] The hypothesis that a greater proportion of the poor and hence of illiterate persons began participating in 1840 is substantiated in Kent and Washington counties. In both, the average values of deeds decreased substantially in the samples for this year, although they rose again by 1860.

Another explanation for the illiteracy rates in 1840 and 1860 may have been the increasing proportion of female grantors.[17] The male/female ratio of participation altered dramatically during the 1790-1900 period. In Washington County, Ohio, in 1790 only 6 percent of the grantors were female; this percentage rose steadily to 1900, when 47 percent of the individuals were female. This pattern was not apparent, however, in Kent County, where female participation varied only 5 percent over the years 1800-1900. (In 1780 female participation was only 38 percent, however.)

It is known that illiteracy was greater among females in 1840 at the national level. A breakdown of the data by sex and illiteracy shows male illiteracy to have risen somewhat to 1860 in Washington County and to 1840 in Kent County. In both counties the proportion of illiterate females, however, was much larger than that of males. This was true in both counties, particularly during the period 1820–60. In Washington-County female illiteracy persisted at a high level until 1880. Female illiterates throughout these years outnumbered male illiterates by a margin ranging from two to one to eighteen to one. The increasing proportion of illiterate female grantors in Washington County probably tended to increase illiteracy overall in that county.

Because data for mortgagors are for only 1840–1900 in Washington County and 1860–1900 for Kent County, it is not possible to make complete comparisons with illiteracy figures for grantors. From 1840 on, however, the pattern of illiteracy (marking) among mortgagors is very similar to that of grantors. There is a steady decline in the proportion of illiterate mortgagors during the latter part of the nineteenth century.[18] In Washington County this drops from 0.17 in 1840 to 0.05 in 1900; in Kent County the decline is from 0.12 in 1860 to 0.07 in 1900.

The link between illiteracy and sex among mortgagors is significant as it was with grantors. Men outnumbered women as mortgagors between 1840 and 1880, but by 1900 the proportions were approximately equal. Before 1900, also, illiteracy rates for females (proportion of markers) were far larger than for men. In 1860, for example, illiteracy among females was 0.19 and 0.23 in Kent County and Washington County, while for males the rates were only 0.06 and 0.09 for the two counties, respectively.

The largest difference in literacy rates between males and females was found in 1840 in Washington County, where 40 percent of the females were markers compared to 6 percent of males. Female literacy gradually rose to the level of male literacy over the sixty years for which mortgage data are available. Thus by 1900, female markers were only 8 percent of female mortgagors in Kent County, whereas the rate for males was 7 percent. In Washington County, the proportion of markers was 5 percent for both males and females in 1900.

Wealth and Literacy

It has already been observed that rising illiteracy rates in the sample from 1840 may have been caused, in part, by the involvement of a greater proportion of grantors and mortgagors from the lower end of the wealth distribution, in the conveying of land and borrowing of money for this purpose.[19] The average value of land conveyances and degree of indebtedness among markers was far below that among those signing their names. This does not mean that investments by illiterate persons were less significant from a personal standpoint. We do not know the income of the literate and illiterate persons represented in the sample, but it may be that illiterate persons had to make a greater sacrifice than literates.

The upper end of the range of values for deed transactions was much lower for illiterate persons (markers) than for literate persons. There was tremendous wealth inequality among both literate and illiterate transactors. In Kent County the range of deed values was $13 to $75,000 for literates and only $12 to $8,400 for illiterates. The value of Washington County deeds averaged less, in general, but the difference in the range of values between literates and illiterates was still sizable.[20]

When values of deed transactions are cross-classified by literacy, the degree to which the average value of transactions among literates exceeds that among illiterates is expressed by the following ratio: Average value, literates/Average value, illiterates. In all years sampled this shows the higher transaction levels to be among literates, with the ratios ranging from 1.1 to 3.4 and averaging 2.3. Thus, as a general guideline, we would expect the value of deed transactions among literates to be about two and one-third times greater than among illiterates.

The findings for literate and illiterate grantors are also applicable to mortgagors. In all years sampled, the degree of indebtedness among literate persons exceeded that among illiterates. In terms of the ratio (Average value, literates/Average value, illiterates) the range of differences was between 1.3 and 3.0 with the average ratio of values being 1.9 in Kent County and 1.7 in Washington County. The degree of indebtedness among literate persons was generally about twice as great as among illiterate ones.[21]

Illiteracy and Dependency

The data from Kent and Washington counties show that approximately 10.7 percent of the grantors, and 10.7 percent of the mortgagors were markers, who may be presumed to be illiterate. There were proportionately more female markers than males. In Washington County, at least, this contributed to the surge upward in illiteracy rates for the years 1840 and 1860. A similar link between sex and illiteracy may be found among mortgagors.

Both male and female markers probably encountered difficulties in interpretation of written instruments, though the problems may be assumed to be more severe among females. In midnineteenth-century America the problems may have been exacerbated by the increasing proportion of female participants in deed and mortgage tranasactions. This would have been true particularly in Washington County. In Kent County, where female participants were persistently a higher proportion of grantors and mortgagors, the problem of interpreting and negotiating sophisticated written instruments may have been more continuous if not more severe.

Many illiterate persons were probably dependent upon literates to interpret written documents and give advice about their accuracy and intent. Such advice was probably available if the illiterate transactor were a coconveyer or comortgagor with a literate person. If the illiterate person were the sole participant or one of several illiterate persons who were parties to a transaction, then outside help would have been required or such advice would have been absent. The question may be asked, then with what frequency did illiterate persons find themselves in situations in which they had to seek advice from a literate person not involved with their transactions? Conversely, it may be asked, to what extent were the problems of illiteracy minimized because the illiterate person was a coparticipant in a transaction with a literate person? Table 1 displays the data used to answer these two questions.

Many illiterate transactors had literate partners to a deed or mortgage agreement. These cases ranged from 8 to 10 percent of the total separate transactions and usually involved husbands and wives. Most often the husband was literate, the wife illiterate. This, however, was more often true in the first half of the nineteenth century than in the second half. It is presumed that questions of intent and accuracy could be clarified to some extent by the literate party. This would have been more convenient than consulting outsiders even though it was no guarantee of protection against duplicity. The success with which problematic wording or terms in an agreement were understood would, of course, depend on the level of literacy and the familiarity of the literate party with the proper forms of deeds and mortgages.

Single markers, female or male, were in the most precarious position in terms of available advice. In Kent County, single, illiterate markers were 4 percent of the grantors in separate deed transactions and 1 percent of those in separate mortgage transactions. The majority of these were male, although the rate of illiteracy was greater among females in general.

Table 1
The Dependency of Illiterate Grantors and Mortgagors in Kent and Washington Counties, 1780–1900

County (Years)	Percentage of Deed Transactions with		
	Single Illiterates	Two or More Illiterates but no Literates	Literates and Illiterates
Kent (1780–1900)	4	3	8
Washington (1790–1900)	2	2	8
	Percentage of Mortgage Transactions with		
	Single Illiterates	Two or More Illiterates but no Literates	Literates and Illiterates
Kent (1860–1900)	1	3	8
Washington (1840–1900)	2	4	10

Source: The sample of deeds and mortgages from Washington and Kent counties.

In Washington County, single transactors constituted 2 percent of both separate deed and mortgage transactions. Separate transactions including no literate parties but having two or more markers comprised 3 percent of the separate deed and mortgage transactions in Kent County. In Washington County the proportions were 2 percent and 4 percent, respectively, for separate deed and mortgage transactions involving two or more illiterates with no literate parties.

In both Kent and Washington counties, the preponderance of these were husbands and wives. Overall, then, in Kent County, 7 percent of deed and 4 percent of mortgage transactions were conducted by illiterate persons without the aid of a coconveyor or mortgagor who was literate. In Washington County the figures were 4 percent and 6 percent for grantors and mortgagors who had no immediate help in the form of literate partners to a deed or mortgage agreement. For those illiterate persons who had no literate partners to a transaction, the problem was surely more acute than for those with literate partners. The only source of help for the former would be an outside literate party—a neighbor or relative, perhaps, or a lawyer. It is probable that it was more difficult for an illiterate person than for a literate one to hire a lawyer. The majority of illiterate persons were found at the lower end of the wealth distribution.

Court Appearances by Illiterate Persons

In addition to determining the extent to which illiterates participated in the economic activities of a community—activities that might result in litigation— it is important, also, to know, where possible, the extent of court appearances by illiterates. This latter problem is not easily solved. For Washington County, however, a method was devised for estimating court appearances between 1790 and 1840 by locating names of illiterate grantors and mortgagors in the records of the Court of Common Pleas of Washington County. Court records are indexed alphabetically by plaintiff and defendant. Thus, it is possible to locate the names of illiterates in these indexes. The search for each name was made for a forty-year period—twenty years before and twenty years after the date when the name was recorded in the deed or mortgage records. For example, a name recorded in 1820 in the deed records was searched in the court indexes for the period 1800 to 1840; for 1840, indexes were searched from 1820 to 1860. In order that illiterates' appearances before the court could be compared to appearances by literates, a random sample corresponding in number to the illiterate sample size was taken from the literate names recorded in the sample of grantors and mortgagors. The results of the analysis are shown in Table 2.

Table 2
The Number of Literates and Illiterates Appearing in Cases before the Common
Pleas Court of Washington County, Ohio, 1793–1860.

Year	LI	ILL	Percentage of Literates Appearing as			Percentage of Illiterates Appearing as		
			Plaintiffs	Defendants	All	Plaintiffs	Defendants	All
1790-1800	9	9	22(N=2)	22(N=2)	22(N=2)	22(N=2)	11(N=1)	22(N=2)
1820	16	16	56(N=9)	75(N=12)	75(N=12)	19(N=3)		19(N=3)
1840	109	109	23(N=25)	33(N=36)	43(N=47)	12(N=13)	7(N=8)	12(N=13)
1790-1840					45.5(N=61)			13.4(N=18)

Source: A subsample of 218 from the sample of 3,225 grantors and 1,238 mortagors from *The Records of the Court of Common Pleas*, Washington County, Ohio 1793–1860.

Most of the actions brought before the court were for debt or trespass. A few were for criminal offenses, including attempted rape and assault. It was not unusual for the same person to appear in several different cases. When this occurred, the person was counted only once in the calculations. If a person appeared as both a plaintiff and a defendant in two cases that were related, then he was used both times in the calculations. Dudley Woodbridge, for example, was involved in more than fifty cases. For the most part, Woodbridge was a plaintiff. Unlike Woodbridge, who was literate, Thomas Hutchinson, freeholder, was an illiterate tavern keeper who found himself in debt a good deal. Hutchinson appeared in court a number of times to free his creditors or to recover monies owed to him. He was six times a plaintiff, twenty-two times a defendant. As defendant he was ordered to pay his debts twenty-one times, and in an action of trespass he was acquitted. As plaintiff, he recovered his money in all six cases.

Overall, 13.4 percent of the illiterate mortgagors and grantors appeared in the local court of common pleas. This figure may be contrasted with that of 45.5 percent of the literate mortgagors and grantors in the subsample who made court appearances. Literate mortgagors and grantors, then, appeared before the court a little over three times as often as illiterates, a fact that may well reflect the greater wealth of the literates and hence the ability to pay lawyers' fees and court costs, if necessary. It may also reflect greater knowledge, gained through reading, concerning court procedures and available remedies at law. The simple lack of knowledge and the insecurity that comes from that ignorance may have been major obstacles to illiterates seeking remedies in court.

The Symbolic Mark

The ancient history of the use of the mark by illiterate persons has been described by Sisson. The symbolic cross, often referred to in nineteenth-century cases, was used to represent the consent of the marker as early as the seventh century. In England, the cross is known to have been specifically used as a substitute for a signature because of the marker's illiteracy. Subscribing to a deed on behalf of an illiterate party, says Sisson, goes back to the first century.[22] Marks as personal marks of identification sometimes denoting the marker's occupation were also in evidence by the late Middle Ages. An interesting late sixteenth-century example illustrates both the testamentary purpose and the status value of the mark:

> Anthony Farrard, of Lynstead, Kent, husbandman, aged 59, deposes in 1598 "That he is vnlearned and never could nor can wryte or reade but when he hath bene sometymes called to set his hande to wrytings he hath made his mark, wch he allwaies made as neere as he could the lykenes of a hooke such as carters vse in the lodinge of their carts, called an ovle hooke."[23]

In the American colonies, personal marks were also common (see fig. 3). From a legal standpoint colonial courts were not particularly interested in the formalities that later accompanied the making of a will. The presence of witnesses and sometimes even the signature of the testator were not required. The important matter was to carry out the wishes of the deceased testator and to avoid the "mechanical distribution" authorized by the intestacy laws.

If a court were convinced that the will were basically accurate, then it ordered a distribution of property "as neere as may bee according to the minde of the deceased." Although the relative informality of the probate procedure may at first be surprising, it should be remembered that it was not until the English Statute of Frauds (1677) that signatures were required on wills involving land. Even in this case, the English Statute did not apply to the colonies unless they accepted it.[24]

The signed and witnessed will was not required in early colonial America, but was still common and became the model for later practice. In the post-Revolutionary period, greater standardization of wills was necessitated by the increasing volume of land transfers. "The will, like the deed, was a fundamental instrument of transfer," and "probate was to the will what recording was to the deed."[25] Wills of land were authorized by the Ordinance of 1787 and required proof. Their signing and witnessing were important elements in the probate procedure. In the case of transferring real property, they were important in establishing titles.

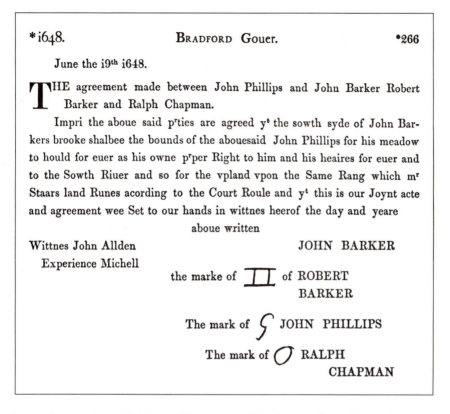

On the image:

*i648. BRADFORD Gouer. *266

June the i9ᵗʰ i648.

THE agreement made between John Phillips and John Barker Robert Barker and Ralph Chapman.

Impri the aboue said pʳties are agreed yᵗ the sowth syde of John Barkers brooke shalbee the bounds of the abouesaid John Phillips for his meadow to hould for euer as his owne pʳper Right to him and his heaires for euer and to the Sowth Riuer and so for the vpland vpon the Same Rang which mʳ Staars land Runes acording to the Court Roule and yᵗ this is our Joynt acte and agreement wee Set to our hands in wittnes heerof the day and yeare aboue written

Wittnes John Allden
Experience Michell

JOHN BARKER

the marke of ⊔ of ROBERT BARKER

The mark of ʃ JOHN PHILLIPS

The mark of ⊘ RALPH CHAPMAN

Figure 3. From David Pulsifer (ed.), *Records of the Colony of New Plymouth in New England, Deeds, and Books of Indian Records for Their Lands* (1620–1651), vol. 1 (Boston: William White, 1861), p. 163.

The passage of the British Wills Act of 1837, requiring a written, witnessed will for both real and personal property, established a model for a number of American states and "imposed the same formal requirements on wills of land and on testaments of personal property." This did not necessarily mean, however, that courts became inflexible and rigid.[26]*

---

*On occasion there was inflexibility. *In the Matter of the Succession of Mary Carroll* (1876) in Louisiana (a state with the legal heritage of French civil codification) illustrates not only the unbending position of a court but its narrow view of illiteracy as well. The testatrix in this case was illiterate and made her mark to the will. Prefixed to her mark were the words "that the said testatrix, being illiterate, has made her mark." In interpreting these words, it was noted that in the precedent case of *Margaret Brand v. N. A. Baumgarden* the testatrix had declared her inability to write with the words "The testatrix, having declared that

The will could be an intensely personal document, and the dispositon of one's lifelong accumulations of property could be a soul-searching experience. The testator's wishes were thus the main issue in the courts. Still, the frequent willing of land required "certainty, routinization, and predictability." What was achieved was a compromise that procedurally solved the problem, though it did not dissipate the tension between standardization of form and flexibility of interpretation.[27] Thus rules for construing of wills were less rigid than those for other written documents. The decision in the case of *Florence E. Miller v. William I. Cline, et al.* (1916) illustrates the point well. Variations on the writing of wills were so numerous, said the court in this case, that "to lay down any positive and definite rules of universal application in the interpretation of wills is impossible. . . ." "Every will must stand or fall upon the language used therein and the test that is applied to it, and therefore courts are not inclined to follow rules of construction blindly, but interpret reasonably in each particular case."[28]

The Problems of Witnessing

Witnessing a will was a common activity of unimposing but immense importance in the titling of land and the distributing of wealth to future generations. Cases involving the witnessing of wills were not usually dramatic, though they might determine the vicissitudes of fortune for plaintiffs and defendants. By the nineteenth century, states usually had in place statutes similar to that of the English Statute of Frauds under which the symbolic mark was a valid subscription to a will. This remained true under the English Statute of Wills that also served as a model for many revised state statutes. The mark remained a valid form of signing in the twentieth century; in some cases, this was true even when it was not witnessed.[29] In *Meazels v. Martin* (1892), for instance, a Kentucky court upheld the signing of a mortgage with a mark because the plaintiff Sarah Meazels had acknowledged before a county clerk that

---

she could not write, has made her usual mark," said words being equivalent, according to the court, "to the declaration that she did not know how to sign." The court continued, however, that the words "being illiterate, has made her mark" did not mean she could not write. In making this judgment the court observed that the word *illiterate* "means unacquainted with letters" and it follows "that very often illiterate persons can sign their names." Said the court: "We meet every day with persons who are illiterate and who can sign their names." Thus, "from the fact that a person is illiterate it can not be concluded that he knows not how to write or sign his name." The will in question was found to be defective (28 La. Ann. 388).

she was unable to write her name. The acknowledgment, certified by the county clerk, was sufficient evidence (even in the absence of an attesting witness) that the mark was that of the appellant.[30]

Challenges to the mark were common, and it remains to examine briefly under what conditions the validity of the mark was challenged. The requirement of the Statute of Frauds that wills be signed, which included the disposition of real property, was a common ground for challenge. The English cases of *Harrison v. Harrison*(1803) and *Addy v. Grix* (1803) both involved illiterate witnesses to a will. It was the judgment in each case that the Statute of Frauds did not prohibit witnessing to wills by persons able to sign only with a mark. The court in *Harrison v. Harrison* cited *Gurney v. Corbet* (1710), a case heard in common pleas. It was noted that "there might have been a great deal of argument upon it originally," but that the mark of a witness was sufficient.[31] These cases, in turn, were cited as authoritative in the New York case of *Jackson, ex dem. and others v. VanDusen* (1809) and later in the New Jersey Supreme Court case of *John Den and others v. Samuel Mitton* (1830).

The case of *Jackson v. VanDusen* was an "action of ejectment, brought to recover the third part of a farm." It involved a question of evidence and arose because of the difficulty in identifying and hence authenticating the mark of an illiterate witness (Wheeler) to a will. The appeal of this case (1809) included testimony from one of the witnesses to a will drawn for Johannes VanDusen. The defendant argued that a "comparison of hands" was not authoritative for a marker, that the "general character" of handwriting could not be judged for a person making a mark. The decision in the case, however, hinged on the fact that Henry VanDyck had actually observed Wheeler's making his mark at a time previous to the will. The so-called comparison of hands was not really a comparison, said the court. Rather, it was a direct observation of the illiterate's making his mark. The mark, therefore, was held to be legitimate.[32]

Den v. Mitton originated in the Sussex Circuit Court in 1827. The decision of the chief justice noted that the choice of an illiterate marker as a witness may have been unwise, yet nonetheless permissible. The legitimacy of the mark was upheld in the appeal. In its opinion the court outlined the difficulties of illiteracy in cases of alleged fraud:

> He who is unable to write his name, and makes his mark is, notwithstanding, a competent and legal witness to the execution of a will. It may be more difficult for him than for one who writes, after a lapse of time, to identify the instrument and to make the necessary proof; and in the case of his absence or decease, it may be more difficult to obtain the requisite secondary proof, but the multiplication of difficulties, however imprudent the use of such a witness may be thereby rendered, or however commendable to select, where feasible, another person, does not amount to a legal disability or exclusion.[33]

Near the end of the nineteenth century the link presumed to exist between competency and illiteracy as indicated by the use of a mark is made explicit in the Georgia case of *Gillis, et al. v. Gillis, et al.* (1895): "A witness who signs by his mark, if so capable of testifying, is just as competent a witness under the statute of frauds, our act of 1852 and section 2414 of the code, as one likewise capable of testifying who writes his own name."[34]

No inference about the incompetency of a witness to a document should be made simply from the condition of being illiterate. Likewise, no inference about competency may be made either. The fact was simply that in the eyes of the law competency and witnessing a document by a mark were not related. The illiterate person was not presumed to be any less intelligent than the literate one. Fundamentally, it was a matter of priorities: the act of making one's last will and testament was too important to be undermined by "eyesight, the continued sanity, the integrity, the memory, or the accessibility of witnesses." The court in *Gillis v. Gillis* recognized that certain "evils" may stem from having illiterate or infirm persons, otherwise competent, attest to wills by their marks, but it did not deviate from the position that, other measures of competence aside, "all witnesses, learned and unlearned, vigorous or infirm," are placed "upon the same footing"; that "illiteracy or infirmity will not count against them. . . ."[35]

The British case of *Henry Spencer Cooper v. David Smith Bockett, Thomas Cooper and Jermyn Pratt* (1844) offers an interesting contrast to the case of *Den v. Mitton* and illustrates well the influence of social class on the testimony of an illiterate witness to a will. The document in question was written by Captain Robert Henry Spencer Cooper and witnessed by two of his servants, both of whom were illiterate. Two issues were at hand: whether Cooper had signed the document previous to the witnessing and whether changes had later been inserted into the will. The two illiterate witnesses, George and Mary Crittenden, had witnessed the will by tracing their signatures in pen over the penciled signatures made by Spencer for them.

In dealing with the issue of the timing (order) of signatures, both Crittendens offered testimony. For our purposes the importance of the case lies in the arguments given to dispute the illiterates' testimony and the court's response to those arguments. In arguing for the respondent Bockett, the attorneys attacked the legitimacy of the Crittendens' testimony by questioning their competency on the grounds of social class and illiteracy:

> Too much importance must not be given to the evidence of the attesting witnesses, who are illiterate persons; it would be dangerous to the interests of

society, if witnesses of the class here subscribing were enabled to cut down a Will when called upon to depose to the exact order of circumstances attending the execution.[36]

The court's response approved the line of argument offered here. It stated that the evidence of George Crittenden pertaining to the timing (order) of the signatures "ought to be received with caution and great reserve. . . ." The court pointed to the contrast between the captain's social station and education and that of the servants. It was highly improbable, the court said, that a well-educated, well-informed man of the world would make a mistake in ordering of the signatures to a will. The evidence of the witnesses, on the other hand, was considered suspect because of their station in society, their probable degree of education, and their lack of knowledge with respect to business dealings. In short, the court concluded that the memory of the witnesses was not to be trusted and that, in the absence of fraud, the probable intent of the educated person was to be trusted more than the testimony of lower-class illiterates.[37]

One other aspect of the difficulty in using illiterate witnesses should be mentioned. In the second half of the nineteenth century the issue of the substitute and "helping hand" signature—a literate person's signing for or guiding the illiterate's hand—was adjudged in several cases. One of these, *Wiley B. Horton and another v. Alexander Johnson and wife* (1855), decided in the Supreme Court of the State of Georgia, held that the illiterate witness to a will should have made his mark and that another literate witness signing for him was insufficient attestation under the Statute of Frauds. This was reaffirmed in *Gillis v. Gillis* (1895). The illiterate witness, said the court in *Horton v. Johnson,* should have made his mark.[38]

The solution to the problem of the "helping hand" signature was not a settled one and differed from case to case and state to state. In *Montgomery v. Perkins* (1859), heard before the Court of Appeals of Kentucky, two witnesses unable to write had their names subscribed to a will by letting the draftsman of the will guide their hands in the configuration of their signatures. When such a procedure was challenged in court, it was held that the Kentucky statute governing the witnessing of wills should not be interpreted too literally: "that a substantial conformity with the spirit of the statute [requiring a witness to a will to subscribe his name in the presence of the testator] is all that reason or sound policy requires."[39]

The case of *Lord v. Lord* (1876), a New Hampshire probate appeal, was similar to the Georgia cases of *Horton v. Johnson* and *Gillis v. Gillis* but differed from the case of *Montgomery v. Perkins* in that a substitute signature was made for the illiterate witness. The court held in *Lord v. Lord* that the purpose of witnessing was satisfied by an agent's subscribing the name of a person unable to write: "the validity of the attestation depends upon the signing of the name of the witness by his authority and in his presence, and not upon the fact of his making a mark, or doing any other manual act in connection with the signature."[40]

The authority of the mark was firmly established by American courts throughout the nineteenth century in matters pertaining to the witnessing of documents. The competency of witnesses was not necessarily suspect for their having been illiterate. It remains to look briefly at decisions involving illiterate witnessing under different circumstances.

The few nineteenth-century cases involving illiterate witnesses in circumstances other than the signing of a will do not demonstrate a consistent pattern with respect to witness competency. Justices in these cases took note that some testimony of illiterate persons ought to be viewed with suspicion, but they were careful to avoid ruling out such testimony. In the Louisiana case of *Louis Pillié v. Henry B. Kenner* (1842) the court took the position that when an unimpeached witness is illiterate and "his statement extraordinary," it is admissible to substantiate it by demonstrating that the same statement was made at the time of the transaction.[41] In other words, the credibility of the illiterate witness was under some suspicion. The English case of *Johnson v. Todd* (1843) in the following year is instructive by way of comparison. The case, insofar as it pertained to illiteracy, involved the veracity of an affidavit signed by an illiterate person. The court, after referring to the general "infirmity of affadavit evidence," went on to comment specifically on illiterate witnesses:

> When the witness is illiterate and ignorant, the language presented to the Court is not his: it is, and must be, the language of the person who prepares the affidavit; and it may be, and too often is, the expression of that person's erroneous inference as to the meaning of the language used by the witness himself; and however carefully the affidavit may be read over to the witness, he may not understand what is said in language so different from that which he is accustomed to use. Having expressed his meaning in his own language, and finding it translated by a person on whom he relies into language not his own, and which he does not perfectly understand, he is too apt to acquiesce; and testimony not intended by him is brought before the Court as his.[42]

Although the case was not tried before an American court, it clearly sets forth the dangers of witnessing by an illiterate person.

In the matter of witness competency, it is worth considering, also, the late-nineteenth-century case of *In the Matter of Adam A. Cross* (1895).

The case involved the appeal of Captain Cross, a New York City police officer who had been convicted of bribery in part by the testimony of an illiterate witness. The bribe had been offered by the manager of a house of prostitution in New York City. The presiding justice observed that persons involved in business "who cannot read and write, have their faculty of memory more acutely educated, for the reason that they are compelled to depend upon their memory and cannot rely upon written memoranda."[43] The moral destitution of the manager of the "house" served finally to persuade the court that her testimony was not to be trusted. Yet the analysis of her illiteracy and its bearing upon her memory is significant:

> The fact that this woman could not read and write, according to common experience, tends to create in her a more accurate and retentive memory, because it would be upon that faculty that she must rely in the conduct of her affairs. Instead, therefore, of her incapacity to read and write accounting for her loss of memory, it seems to make it more remarkable.[44]

A theory of faculty psychology stressing the exercising of mental faculties provided the foundation for explaining why illiterates commonly were able to demonstrate superior recall skills. Strangely, the court used this assumption regarding the link between illiteracy and memory to discredit the witness's testimony. It concluded that "upon a consideration of the whole of her testimony that she was willfully forgetful and had not the slightest regard for the truthfulness of her testimony."[45] Although the profligacy of the witness persuaded the court to discount the testimony, it also made clear that illiteracy, far from being a detriment to the offering of proper testimony, could actually enhance its value.

Courts adjudicating cases involving challenges to the mark of an illiterate person were faced with the issue of literalness versus intent. The rise of formalism in American law and the consequent standardization of written documents had put new pressures on illiterate persons. The numerous land transfers that accompanied will making had made standardization desirable, yet the dispositive nature of the will made the intent of the deceased the focal point of probate. Witnesses to this intent were important to the satisfaction of the testator's wishes. Illiterate witnesses signing with a mark were suspect, but their inability to write did not make them legally incompetent. They were not marginal persons in the sense of being excluded generally from the legal system. They were, however, considered more vulnerable than literates to perpetrators of fraud and misrepresentation. Their vulnerability was very apparent when dealing with the substitute or helping hand signature.

Administering an Estate

The final situation studied in testamentary activity is that of administering the estate. In *Nusz, et al. v. Grove* (1867) the right of a formerly
separated widow to administer her late intestate husband's estate was
upheld. The court confirmed the argument presented for the the widow
that the Maryland Code did not disqualify the administrator of an estate
because of illiteracy. The principle, it was argued, was the same as that
governing the making of a valid deed or contract, namely, that "all valid
testamentary papers should be executed by a person of sound and disposing mind, and capable of making a valid deed or contract and signed by
the party executing the same. . . ." According to precedent, signature by
mark was a "sufficient signing." Under both the Statute of Frauds and
the Maryland Code, the attorney argued, "capacity to execute a valid
deed or contract is a necessary ingredient to the validity of every
will . . . and the mark of an illiterate person has been held a sufficient
signing, and confers validity upon the instrument. . . ." The inference
was "irresistible" that the "incapacity of the person applying for letters
of administration to write or read writing is no evidence of incapacity to
execute a valid deed or contract, and no impediment to the granting of
letters of administration."[46]

Two cases following *Nusz, et al. v. Grove*—both from Pennsylvania—
reached similar conclusions. In each, the court observed that the ad-
ministratrix was possessed of good business sense. In *Bowersox's Appeal*
(1882) the widow was "rather illiterate," could not "read printing unless
it be in German," and did not have a "business education." She was, in
this latter respect, said the court, "like a large majority of the widows in
the Commonwealth." However, the court continued, "the preferred right
[of the widow] to administer" the estate "of her deceased husband" was
not legally disqualified by an "imperfect or defective education." What
was required were "a good mind and sound judgment, a knowledge of the
values of property, and of the practical business transactions of life. . . ,"
all of which the appellee had. This, concluded the court, would "enable
her to select competent assistants and able advisors" and would "secure
an efficient and faithful discharge of the trust."[47]

Wilkey's Appeal (1885), an appeal to the Supreme Court of Pennsylvania, involved a similar situation. Here the right of a widow to be
granted letters of administration was challenged on the grounds that
she was "aged, illiterate [and] unduly influenced [by her youngest son]
and generally incompetent to administer the estate." In negating the
challenge and issuing letters of administration, the court found that testimony showed Mrs. Wilkey to be competent and to have as "good business capacity as the ordinary run of farmers' wives."[48] Like *Nusz, et al. v.*

Grove and *Bowersox's Appeal* before it, the court in *Wilkey's Appeal* was not willing to view illiteracy as a legal disqualification, nor as implying lack of good business sense. The suggestion was that in the absence of other evidence showing incompetency the illiterate person was not to be excluded from this important family and civil function.

Similar reasoning was applied in *Bell v. Fulgham,* heard before the Supreme Court of Alabama in 1918. The court basically applied an educational norm as a test in its decision to allow an illiterate as administrator of an estate. Illiteracy, per se, was not a disqualification for administration of an estate. Even though he could not read and write, said the court, the appellant "is a man of good intelligence, accustomed to transact his own affairs, and, we infer from the evidence shown in the bill of exceptions, has a memory for the details of past transactions superior to that of the man of average book learning."[49]

The Problem of Fraud and Misrepresentation

The problems of fraud and misrepresentation in the making of a will are similar to those in other dimensions of economic and legal behavior. The focus of this section is on the reading of wills and deeds in which the general problems of intent and imposition are encountered in the more specific legal issues of fraud and misrepresentation. The rules governing the signing of deeds are closely related, both historically and legally, to those governing the signing of contracts in general. Discussion of these latter, however, will be left to Chapter 5.

Intent and Undue Influence

The dependency of the illiterate testator is obvious in cases in which his inability to read the will requires that it be read to him. When a will was executed by a marker, precaution and prudence, said the court in *Chaffee and Chapman v. The Baptist Missionary Convention of the State of New York* (1843), require that the "whole will should be deliberately read over to him in the presence and hearing of the witnesses, and the fact of such reading in his presence should be stated in the attestation clause." At least, continued the court, "the witnesses ought, by inquiries of the illiterate testator himself, to ascertain the fact that he was fully apprised of the contents of the instrument which he executed and published as his will, as well as that he was of competent understanding to make a testamentary disposition of his property."[50]

In the latter half of the nineteenth century a number of cases dealt with the issue of reading a will to an illiterate, incompetent, or otherwise handicapped testator. Often, the problems of age, infirmity, incompetency, imposition, and fraud were entwined in the more general issue of testamentary capacity. *Lyons v. Van Riper and others* (1875), heard in Chancery in New Jersey, is virtually a stereotype of misfortune in which one Miss Van Winkle, "seventy years of age, entirely blind, profoundly ignorant, unable to read or write [and] utterly unacquainted with business matters and the ways of the world," was misled by a trusted friend into conveying her land by deed, when, she thought, she had only granted authority to sell it. It was clear, also, that Van Winkle "fully understood" the contents of her will, which included the land conveyed to the complainant in this case. It was equally clear that the deed in question was misrepresented as authority to sell the property. The court, for this reason and others, nullified the deed.[51]

Not all cases were so stereotypical. Some decisions emphasized the competency or incompetency of the testator in general business affairs. Others stressed the sanctity of the will and demonstrated their concern with the right of the testator to dispose of his/her property as desired. In the execution of a will the critical point was whether or not the testator or testatrix knew the contents of the will and approved them. As a general rule, it was held that when a testator was "in health, and of ability" it was unnecessary to show that the will was read to him or that he knew its contents. In *Guthrie, et al. v. Price, et al.* (1861) the Supreme Court of the State of Arkansas noted in its decision: "The legal presumption in such cases is always in favor of the will; and he who seeks to impeach it, must show, conclusively, that the testator was imposed on, or that there was some mistake, whereby he was deceived."[52]

In cases in which the testator was unable to read the will, witnesses to a will might provide testimony to the fact that a will was read to an illiterate testator; however, other evidence might also be used to confirm that a testator had a knowledge of its contents. When the will of an illiterate testator was challenged, the important point was that the burden of proof was shifted so that "it became the duty of the person offering the will, to show that the contents of the paper were fully made known to the testator": "So if the testator is incapable of reading the will, whether the incapacity arise from blindness, or any other cause, the rule is the same, and the burthen of proof is thrown on the person offering the will."[53]

The position of the courts in the foregoing cases was designed to preserve the right of the testator to dispose of property according to his wishes, and to guard against the possibility of fraud. This twofold concern also was carried forward to twentieth-century cases. Consistently (*In re Beck's Estate* [1914], *Barlion v. Conner* [1917], *In re Gluckman's Will*

[1917], *In re Cummins' Estate* [1935], *Mann et al. v. Cornish* [1950], *Pepe et al. v. Caputo* [1951], *Morrow v. Person et al.*[1953]), courts held that a testator's inability to read a will did not constitute, prima facie, that the testator did not know the contents of the will.[54] "We are aware of no rule of law," said an Ohio appeals court, "that fixes any age beyond which a man loses a testamentary capacity or which prevents an illiterate from executing a will."[55] The burden of proof rests upon those who "allege fraud and undue influence," said a federal appeals court in *Mann et al. v. Cornish* (1950), and a testator's inability to read does not create the presumption that he is ignorant of the contents of his will.[56]

Most courts assumed that the use of the mark indicated the inability to read and write. They did not assume, however, that a testator or testatrix did not know the contents of his or her will.[57] Nonetheless, courts were cautious when confronted with testators who had no or little facility with English. The shades of understanding and the plurality of situations were so numerous that courts often found themselves in a morass of subjectivity. Both illiteracy and lack of education were enough to cause doubts about intent and undue influence. The principal contention in *In re Beck's Estate* (1914), heard in the Supreme Court of Washington, was that the will "was not the will of the testatrix" because she did not understand the English language and did not understand what was being said when the will was being read to her. The court took the inability to understand English as prima facie evidence that it was not her will. The court also ruled on the "suspicious" circumstances surrounding the making of the will, namely, the drawing of the will by one of its beneficiaries. This situation did not raise the "presumption" of undue influence, but it did raise a "suspicion which ought to appeal to the vigilance of the court." The lower court erred in not allowing for this. Thus the original judgment was reversed and remanded for further proceeding.[58]

As in the case heard in Washington, the suspicion of undue influence was also involved in *In re Gluckman's Will* (1917), heard by the Court of Errors and Appeals of New Jersey. The testator in this case could "talk and understand" English, but could not read or write in English, except for his signature. Because of potentially contradictory provisions in the will and the testator's limited facility with English, the will was challenged. As was often the case the court took a holistic view of the situation. The testator's illiteracy did not defeat the will since the court assumed that he understood what was read to him. Much of the reasoning of the court was based on the fact that Gluckman was an astute businessman, that he knew Hebrew lore, and that he had been a close friend of Judge Roberson for twenty-five years. This, added to the fact that he had responded to the reading of the will by saying, "All right.

That's good," was sufficient to convince the court that the will should be admitted to probate.[59]

Fraud in Deeds and Mortgages

We have seen that the illiterate persons were often the objects of fraudulent practices. These commonly occurred in the making of a will but were also common in disposing of land through deed and securing a loan by mortgage. The problems were similar to those with wills and deeds. *Olson, et al. v. Goetz, et al* (1930) and *Ida Cromwell v. Sharon Building and Loan Association* (1959) illustrate the latter. The first of these involved improper behavior of a public servant. In *Olson v. Goetz* a district court in Pennsylvania ordered an affidavit of defense to be filed on the basis of its finding that a notary public "took the acknowledgment of two ignorant, illiterate persons to a deed when they thought and she knew and had informed them that they were acknowledging a mortgage": "She appended her official seal and certification that they had acknowledged a deed; . . . she . . . had substituted the deed which she certified had been acknowledged in place of the mortgage which they thought they were acknowledging."[60]

In the case of *Cromwell v. Sharon Building and Loan,* Ida Cromwell, an elderly and illiterate woman, had undertaken to modernize her home by placing new shingles on the roof and repairing the porch. Financing was accomplished by a mortgage, but within a year payments were in arrears and foreclosure proceedings were begun. These were discontinued when payment was made, but were reinstituted and concluded the following year.

Cromwell began suit independently of the foreclosure proceedings, asking that the mortgage be annulled on the grounds "that its execution was induced by misrepresentation, fraud, undue influence and mistake." The appellant did not claim lack of mental capacity due to lunacy or insanity. She did, however, claim she did not understand the terms of the mortgage because of ignorance. During the hearing, Cromwell did not explicitly testify to fraud, undue influence, misrepresentation, or deceit. She did claim ignorance and offered testimony that she did not finish first grade in school. In giving its decision, the court observed that "literacy is not a prerequisite for the owner of land to have full dispositive power thereover" and that the law "does not attempt to designate the amount of education required to execute a valid deed or contract." The law, continued the court, "presumes that one who executes a deed is possessed of sufficient mental capacity to make a valid and binding contract." A competent person cannot impeach his own deed unless fraud, undue duress, or mistake is evident; this was decidedly not the case, concluded the court.[61] The court might well have given the advice heard in an earlier case, *Modern Security Co. v. Lockett, et al.,* thirty-one years earlier. The court spoke of those entering into installment contracts in the following words: "An installment plan is always attractive to one who desires a thing, and is based principally on hope. Now that the day of settlement has arrived, the petitioners, I think, regret the action which they have taken; but it is . . . too late."[62]

Fraud in the making of a deed was a common occurrence for the illiterate person. The case of *Sun Oil Co. v. Rhodes, et ux.*(1934) was one in which an illiterate husband and wife conveyed mineral rights to seventy acres of land in Polk County, Texas. The verbal agreement, said the appellees, was different from the written one, which had been fraudulently worded so as to convey a greater interest in the minerals than they intended. The deed, said Rhodes and his wife, was not read or explained to them: the "agent knew that neither of them could read or write, and knowing this did not read the deed to them or have the notary . . . do so. . . ." The civil appeals court concluded that the circumstances under which the deed was signed and "the failure of the notary to take the acknowledgment of Mrs. Rhodes to the deed in the manner required by law, rendered the deed void. . . ." The judgment against the Sun Oil Company was thus upheld.[63]

Like the previous case, both *Bieranowski, et al. v. Bieranowski, et ux.* (1942) and *John Lloyd Mills and Rosella Mills v. W. H. Lynch* (1963) involved accusations of fraud in the making of a deed. The first of these concerned a misrepresentation of a document signed by Mrs. Bieranowski, an illiterate woman of Polish nationality who could not write her name and who understood only a few words of English.

The situation in the case was simply this. Mrs. Bieranowski, having been seriously ill, asked her son to attend to the making of her will. A real estate agent, her lawyer, and her son Michael were all present when the preparation of the will was discussed. The mutual understanding of the discussion depended upon Michael as an interpreter of his mother's wishes. In language reminiscent of nineteenth-century contract theory, the court said, "the meeting of their minds obviously depended upon the integrity of his [Michael's] interpretations." A deed conveying the property to Michael without consideration had been "marked" by Mrs. Bieranowski "in the belief that it was the will she had requested." Later, after family differences had arisen between Michael's wife and Mrs. Bieranowski, Michael announced that he was owner of the house. The issue in the case thus hinged upon the "veracity . . . between mother and son." In making its decision, the court noted that Mrs. Bieranowski was entirely dependent upon Michael's honesty. Michael's substituting a deed for a will made clear that her confidence in her son was "grossly abused."[64] The deed was therefore cancelled.

Mills v. Lynch (1963) was a complicated case involving the transfer of land and the misrepresentation of a deed as a deed of trust. The details need not be described here. What is important is the court's explication and application of rules governing fraud and misrepresentation in the execution of deeds. In deciding cases of contract, courts frequently enunciated the principle that it is the duty of a party to a contract or a deed to read or to have it read before signing. In the absence of fraud, misrepresentation, or mistake, there can be no relief in law or equity for failure to read. In *Mills v. Lynch,* however, it was clear, said the court, that "plaintiffs were prevented from reading the paper or having it read to them by the positive assertion that this was unnecessary because they knew what it was, a deed of trust."[65]

Plaintiffs alleged fraud in the factum; that is, they contended that there was a "disparity between the instrument executed and the one intended to be executed." It was evident to the court that the illiterate plaintiffs had been misled by misrepresentation of the written instrument, that they had acted with "reasonable prudence," and that they were not "obligated to the one who had deceived [them]."[66] Thus in this case, which was brought in a motion to nonsuit, the original decision against the illiterate plaintiffs was reversed.

New Dimensions of Fraud

The twentieth century brought an increasing variety of circumstances that might involve the illiterate person in litigation of some sort. In a number of cases it is evident that the increasing complexities of financial and economic activities in the late nineteenth and early twentieth centuries brought new difficulties and continued legal problems for the illiterate person. The new demands of economic citizenship were apparent in cases involving checking and banking and workmen's compensation. *Burrill v. The Dollar Savings Bank* (1879) dealt with a problem common enough among literates and illiterates alike: a temporarily lost savings passbook. Burrill, an illiterate black who later learned to read and was employed as a waiter in Philadelphia, had brought suit to recover $195 that had been fraudulently withdrawn from his account by a person unknown to him. He had been unaware of the impersonation until he had attempted to withdraw money himself and found that none remained.[67]

The case of Samuel Burrill was brought in assumpsit against the Dollar Savings Bank to recover the amount of the deposit. In arguing for the plaintiff it was observed that Burrill could not read "and his attention was not called to the provisions of the rule" that a depositor keep his deposit book safely. The attorney for Burrill stated that the plaintiff "knew nothing about these by-laws, and never assented to them, nor agreed, either expressly or impliedly, to be bound by them." In delivering his argument for the bank, the attorney cited the Massachusetts cases of *Goldrick v. Bristol Co. Savings Bank* and *Levy v. Franklin Savings Bank*. These had ruled that a depositor is obligated to assent to the by-laws. The agreement between depositor and bank thus becomes a "contract between the parties, though the depositor could neither read nor write. . . . " The court's ruling noted "the depositor must be presumed to know what the printed rules and regulations of his book require. . . . If he cannot read he should inquire what they are. Common sense tells him they are there for some purpose; and common prudence would dictate that he should inquire of some one what they are, and how they may affect him." The court's per curiam opinion noted that "savings banks like the defendant in error are really charities for the benefit of the poor." "The fact that the plaintiff was illiterate, and could not read the rules in the bank book delivered to him, made no difference," continued the court. "He ought to have requested it to be read to him."[68]

Other cases in the twentieth century illustrate the variety of situations in which illiteracy might be a problem associated with banking and checking. *Navar v. First National Bank of Breckenridge* (1923) was a case heard by the Court of Civil Appeals of Texas. This involved an illiterate Mexican laborer, "unable to either speak, read, or write the English language and unable to sign his name."[69] The facts of the case made it apparent that Romulo Navar had taken out his passbook under an X, but subsequent transactions had been under a written signature. The case hinged upon the question of identity and the impersonation of the original depositor Romulo Navar by another who signed his name. The bank was unwilling to pay the money lost to the impersonator. In hearing the case on appeal, the court found the bank negligent because it knew Navar was illiterate but had accepted a signature in place of his mark.[70]

Another banking and checking case was that of *Louis Weiner v. Chase National Bank of City of New York* (1913). The plaintiff in this case was illiterate "with the exception that he could read numbers." He operated a lunch wagon and employed a man named Steinberg as a manager and cook. He also entrusted him with paying bills and writing checks. When paying bills, the plaintiff, Weiner, would compare the amount of the figures on the check with the figures on the check stub and the bill. If they matched, he would sign the check that Steinberg had made for him. Steinberg's ruse was quite simple: "[he] wrote in the amount on the check to which he intended to change the figures and when the check was signed made the necessary changes in the figures to make them the same amount as the writing."[71] Thus, for example, $9.00 was easily changed to $19.00 or $17.00 to $47.00. Fifty-one such checks were altered, according to Weiner, although only twenty-four totaling $1,053.60 were offered for evidence. The remainder were destroyed by Steinberg. Steinberg, as it turned out, was convicted of third-degree forgery, but Weiner still sought to recover $434.00. In the opinion of the court, the bank was not negligent for having overlooked the forgery, said forgery having been so inconspicuous as not to have aroused suspicion. Moreover, the court concluded that the plaintiff drew his checks in "a negligent and unbusinesslike manner" and that "the crudeness of his signature" was not "a warning to the bank of his illiteracy." The plaintiff's complaint against the bank was thus dismissed, although he was allowed an exception and sixty days to make a case.[72]

The banking and checking transactions discussed in the foregoing were common activities for a large number of Americans in the early twentieth century. They were not overly demanding in technical knowledge, nor did they presume a special aptitude for business. Above-average intellectual capacity probably was not a prerequisite for carrying out these activities successfully. It is clear, however, that illiteracy could be an obstacle to their orderly pursuit. Fraud was easily practiced on the unsuspecting whether illiterate or literate, yet illiteracy made fraudulent practices considerably easier. Thus, aside from procedural niceties, fraud was the focus of a court's inquiry.

Insurance

Cases involving misrepresentation by insurance companies increased in importance as the sale of life insurance became more common. Courts generally acknowledged the difficulty of reading and interpreting the technical language of policies. As a corollary to this they placed a great deal of emphasis on the veracity of the insurance representative. They acknowledged that many people do not actually read their policies, but, having come to an agreement with a representative, rely upon his word that the policy is the one agreed on. The case of *Summers v. Alexander* (1911) gives a good overview of the problem.[73]

The case itself was a peculiar one because the insurance agent admitted to fraud, yet nonetheless maintained that the policy should be in force because the insured "was negligent in not discovering that plaintiff had perpetrated a fraud upon him." This was an "inversion" of the doctrine of estoppel (a bar to speaking against one's own act or deed), said the court, because it was being applied to the victim of fraud rather than the party "practicing the deception."[74]

The illiteracy of the victim was certainly a factor in not recognizing that the policy issued was not the one agreed to. The court was sympathetic to the insuree's reliance on the representations of the salesman: "Having relied on these representations, it cannot be said that he was charged with the duty of having read and explained to him the terms and conditions of the policy received."[75] It cited approvingly the opinion of *Cooley's Briefs on the Law of Insurance:*

> The principle that the insured is not bound to know the contents of the application, and may rely on the agent's assurances that his answers have been correctly written, will, of course, apply with special force where the insured is illiterate and unable to read, or is ignorant of the language.[76]

In delivering its opinion the court provided an unusual number of synopses of previous cases involving illiterate insurees. Among these were *State Insurance Co v. Gray* (1890), *Lewis v. Mutual Reserve Fund Loan Association* (1900), and *Caldwell v. Life Insurance Company of Virginia* (1905).[77] Though the circumstances were different each of the cases acknowledged the difficulty and relevancy of illiteracy to the judgment. Each resulted in a finding for the illiterate person. *Lewis v. Mutual Reserve* made the point most forcefully: "How can it be inexcusable negligence not to read, when one cannot read? How can one be bound by an obligation he never signed, and whose contents he never knew?"[78]

Compensation for Bodily Injury

The first four cases discussed in this section involve the signing of releases by illiterate persons. These are discussed initially because they bring into perspective the issue of illiteracy and contractual or quasi-contractual responsibility. Three other cases involving illiterates are then reviewed primarily for the light which they throw on the courts' attitudes toward illiteracy in general. All are reminders, however, that the growth of an industrial economy brought new difficulties for illiterates—that the social organization of work was increasingly complex, as was the web of statutory law governing it. Contractual relations themselves, though more standardized, were more sophisticated and required greater discrimination by contracting parties. The printed word was ever more conspicuous as a guide to the jungle of rules and regulations governing the formal relationships within business and industry. Within the milieu of print and documentation, illiterates and courts alike struggled to confront problems of liability and breach of contract resulting from misunderstanding and ignorance stemming from the inability to read.

In attempting to recover damages for bodily injury, Henry Spitze brought suit against the Baltimore and Ohio Railroad. Spitze, a blacksmith, was injured in a trip hammer accident, the result of which was a "seriously crushed right hand." As a member of the Baltimore and Ohio Employees Relief Association, to which he had contributed a percentage of his monthly salary, Spitze was entitled to and received benefits for his injury and signed a release discharging the railroad company from further liability for the injury. In *Spitze v. Baltimore and Ohio Railroad Company* (1892) suit was brought against the railroad company on the grounds that the plaintiff "was induced to enter the relief association on the faith of agreements made by the railroad company with the association." Said agreements, however, were not carried out because the company did not make its proper contributions.[79] No injury from the company's insufficient contributions was claimed and this part of the suit failed. Spitze then attempted to show that the release he signed was not read to him and that he could not read English. He "believed he was signing a receipt to the Baltimore and Ohio Employees Relief Association. . . ." It was therefore incumbent upon Spitze to show fraud.

The court, in delivering its opinion, said:

> there is not the faintest suggestion that the agents of the railroad company or the officers of the relief association knew, or had reason to believe, that the appellant could not read English, or that they made any statement or held any inducement which influenced him to sign the releases without inquiring as to their contents.[80]

In further explaining its position the court noted that the plaintiff had it within his power to inform himself of the contents of the release and that it was not a matter of fraud by the railroad but, rather, the "carelessness" of the plaintiff. A scolding tone was evident in the court's opinion when it pointed out that the plaintiff "cannot invoke his own heedlessness to impeach his solemn release, and then call that heedlessness someone else's fraud. If he did not know what he was signing, it was his plain duty to inquire."[81] If carelessness were allowed to impeach a solemn agreement, it was clear that all such agreements would be threatened and rendered meaningless.

Two other late-nineteenth-century cases reached essentially the same conclusion as *Spitze v. Baltimore and Ohio Railroad Company*. These were *Albrecht v. Milwaukee and Superior Railway Co.* (1894) and *Granson*

Mosby v. The Cleveland Street Railway Co. (1898).[82] In the first of these, Albrecht, a brakeman for the Milwaukee and Superior Railway Company, was injured in a switching accident for which, it was argued, the engineer was to blame. Ten days after the accident, the plaintiff signed a settlement under seal for $225, thereby releasing the company from further liability. Conflicting testimony was presented in regard to whether or not Albrecht knew the contents of the release and whether it had been read to him. The jury hearing the case in county circuit court had awarded Albrecht a total of $3,000, $2,775 plus the $225 under the settlement with the company. The Milwaukee and Superior Railway Company appealed the case, winning a reversal of the circuit court judgment. In its opinion, the Supreme Court of Wisconsin found that there was no fraud, misrepresentation, nor pretense in the manner in which the company's agents had secured the release. That the plaintiff was unable "to read English or understand the contents of the paper is no excuse." He should have, said the court, "sought the assistance of someone capable of properly informing him." The court concluded: "It cannot be tolerated that a man shall execute a written instrument, and, when called to abide by its terms, say, merely, that he did not read it or know what it contained."[83]

Granson Mosby v. The Cleveland Street Railway Company was also a situation in which an illiterate laborer had authorized a settlement for bodily injury. Mosby's business was hauling with a horse and wagon. It was his misfortune to be hit by a streetcar, the result being property loss and serious personal injury. The case was first heard in Cuyahoga County Common Pleas Court, Cleveland, Ohio, and a settlement of $500 was awarded to Mosby. The release was signed, but Mosby later was dissatisfied with the settlement. The case for Mosby, "a colored man who could neither read nor write," was simply that he was "very ignorant of the methods or proceedings of this kind, and it was undue advantage to settle with him in the absence of his attorneys and without their knowledge." The court did not find that fraud had been practiced on Mosby and concluded that it would be "bad precedent to establish, that an ignorant man, merely because he has not an attorney when he makes a contract, and because he can neither read nor write, and no advantage taken of him in any way or manner, may avoid his contract. . . ." This, said the court in deference to tradition, "would lead to quite an upheaval of contract relations" and was "too radical a ground to take."[84]

Eleftherion v. Great Falls Manufacturing Co. (1929), a case heard in the Supreme Court of New Hampshire, is an interesting contrast to the foregoing and illustrates the increasingly wide domain of statutory law in the area of contractual relations, particularly in situations concerning the rights of plaintiffs seeking monetary awards for injury. Like the previous cases involving releases, *Eleftherion* involved misunderstanding the nature of a signed instrument.

The plaintiff had signed an agreement with the insurance company carrying the defendant's liability insurance. The plaintiff believed this agreement to be "a notice to the defendant of the accident," but it was, in fact, a release in return for compensation. The negotiations for the agreement had been conducted by what turned out to be an inept interpreter furnished by the defendant. The court noted that the plaintiff and interpreter "generally misunderstood each other" and concluded that "the plaintiff was not, while the defendant was, negligent in the use of the interpreter."[85]

In its decision, the court made several telling points on the nature of contractual relations, particularly as they involved illiterate persons. It noted, first, that the agreement in question was valid as a contract only if "there was consideration moving from both parties." The agreement, the court said, imposed no obligation on the insurer as consideration for the plaintiff's decision to accept compensation, because the "insurer incurred no liability by the agreement which the law did not already impose on it. . . . It agreed to pay no more than the law required as compensation, and its agreement [t]o assume the defendant's liability was already an imposed duty by virtue of the policy it had issued."[86]

The court's second major point in *Eleftherion* went to the heart of the contractual relationship, including both the "will" theory of contract and the principle of mutual consent so prevalent in the nineteenth century, but clearly not set aside in the twentieth. "On the ground that the agreement was not in fact a concurrence or meeting of minds of the parties," said the court, "the invalidity of the agreement as a contract is further shown." "From his own standpoint the plaintiff had acted in ignorance of his rights but without knowing what he was apparently doing," observed the court. Despite the fact that he had signed the agreement, "it cannot be said that he meant to enter into any contractual relation." Moreover, the defendant "did not do what reasonable care required to see that the plaintiff was informed about and understood the nature of the transaction. . . ."[87] In fact, said the court: "In a mental way the defendant, not purposely, but negligently, set a trap with the result that the plaintiff acted with consequences unintended by him. The law does not permit the defendant to take advantage of them."[88] Thus, the unanimous conclusion of the court was that the "plaintiff did not intentionally, and hence in the statutory sense, give notice to accept, or accept, compensation."[89]

Unlike the previous four cases, the following do not deal with the contractual nature of the release agreement. Instead, they illustrate other dimensions of the problem of illiteracy in the area of compensation for bodily injury. More important than the determination of fault in these are the attitudes of the courts toward illiterates and illiteracy. It is quite clear that each court in these twentieth-century cases was willing to indulge the foibles of the illiterate working man more than in cases of contractual relations. Each displayed a remarkably sympathetic, though paternalistic and sometimes condescending, attitude toward the illiterate person. This latter attitude was more true of the court in *Mayon v. Jahncke Service Inc.* (1937) than in the other cases.

The plaintiff in *Mayon* was a "swamper" whose severely fractured leg had resulted in disability and the consequent lawsuit. The issue in this case centered around the choice of a physician to treat the injury and also the plaintiff's alleged failure to follow through with the prescribed treatment. The court, however, noted that Mayon was an "illiterate, partly deaf, and rather simple laborer, unable to speak or fully understand the English language" and that he was "dependent on others for advice as to what to do in getting relief from his injury." Moreover, it noted, he had submitted to treatment for several months.[90]

The insurance company discontinued the services of the plaintiff's first physician, and the plaintiff went to see a physician in New Orleans. He soon ran out of money and returned home, where he continued treatments under his former physician. Of the decision to be treated by his family physician, the court observed: "frequently illiterate country people have more confidence in their country family physician than in physicians and surgeons enjoying national reputations, and we are of the opinion that the plaintiff was justified in relying upon the advice of his own family physician; at least he should not be penalized for relying on his opinion and advice."[91] The court decided that compensation should be awarded for a period not exceeding four hundred weeks.

There is little hint of condescension, though a good deal of paternalism, in *Firestone Tire and Rubber Co. v. Industrial Accident Commission, et al.* (1954), a case heard in a California district court of appeal. In this case an award to an injured employee of the Firestone company was challenged. In reversing a referee's recommendation, the court observed that the conduct of the company nurse was improper in telling the employee he would lose his job if this were an industrial accident: "For an illiterate working man that sort of threat is about as bad as a threat of death."[92] The court continued: "We do not hold an illiterate, frightened employee to the same meticulous standards of conduct that we would expect from a trained medical or legal mind."[93]

The same paternalism had been present in the case of *Zobes v. International Paper Co.,* decided by the Supreme Judicial Court of Maine in 1917. The plaintiff was a young adult Russian immigrant who worked for a paper mill loading and unloading pulpwood. He was unable to read

English and had little oral command of the language. The plaintiff had entered an elevator shaft to urinate and was crushed severely by the descending elevator. The result was disability "for hard labor for the balance of his life."[94]

It was determined that there had been no barrier to the shaft at the ground level and the only sign was one on the side of the elevator reading, "Elevator, employees not allowed to use." The court observed that the plaintiff, "this foreigner . . . [who was] fitted by his life and training to be a mere hewer of wood and drawer of water" was not guilty of contributory negligence. Rather, the defendant was at fault:

> For its roughest work it employed many illiterate laborers, of no high order of intelligence or refinement, of all nations and all tongues, needing for this work brawn and muscle and not brains. Their habits, customs, and training should be taken into account, and their safety provided for. The shaft opening, though containing a serious hidden peril, was unguarded and unlighted. . . .[95]

Judgment was made for the plaintiff in the amount of one thousand dollars.

Judgment by Default and Nonappearance in Court

The prevalance of litigious activity in American society also surfaced in ways indirectly related to the making of contracts. The many decrees, summons, and directives issued by courts could be a source of difficulty for both the illiterate person and the courts. These usually involved a default of the case because of the ignorance of the illiterate that a suit was being brought against him.

In all of the cases cited in this section (*City of Gainesville v. Johnson, et al.* [1910], *Paltro v. Gavenas* [1917], *Daly v. Okamura* [1923], the companion cases of *McNac v. Chapman* [1924] and *McNac v. Kinch* [1925], and *Languein v. Olson* [1929]), the courts applied the general rule that a judgment rendered by default for a failure to answer ought to be vacated when it was clear that a defendant did not understand that he was to appear in court to defend himself. In three of the six cases the illiterate person was of foreign birth and claimed to have little facility with written English; in one case (*City of Gainesville v. Johnson, et al.*) the illiterates were "ignorant and illiterate colored people"; in two others (*McNac v. Chapman* and *McNac v. Kinch*) they were husband and wife who were "illiterate, mixed-blood Indians and negroes, unable to read and write, and had no notice of the case being set for trial."[96]

In all of these cases the element of subjectivity was very strong. The courts were in the unenviable position of assessing both the degree of illiteracy of the defendants and whether or not the lack of facility with the English language was of such magnitude as to be an obstacle to the defendant's appearance in court. In both *Paltro v. Gavenas* and *Daly v. Okamura* the court looked sympathetically on the illiterate's ignorance of the English language. It was clear, said the court in the former case, that "the petitioner has a defense against the unrecorded mortgage. . . . He did not understand the English language, and was led to believe by counsel for respondent that his rights were not being affected, and, for that reason, he did not appear to contest the foreclosure of the unrecorded mortgage."[97]

A similar finding was delivered in *Daly v. Okamura,* a suit upon three promissory notes each of the value of six hundred dollars. The appeal of the plaintiff to the Supreme Court of Arizona was from the order vacating the judgment. The high court affirmed the lower court's decision to vacate. In doing so, it acknowledged the validity of the lower court's reasoning: "the failure to answer within the time allowed by law, seems to have been the inability of the defendants and their attorney to understand each other, the defendants being Japanese with little knowledge of the English language or of the laws of the country."[98]

In both *City of Gainesville v. Johnson, et al.* and *Languein v. Olson,* the courts did not find the defendant's alleged illiteracy to have interfered with the judgment by default. The first of these cases was an appeal from the decision of the chancellor to set aside a final decree upon a petition made twenty days after the decree. The situation was apparently one in which Primius Johnson and other "ignorant and illiterate colored people" had part of their real estate condemned by the city in order that the land might be used for sidewalks. Johnson, acting as agent for the rest, spoke with the city attorney about remuneration for the real estate. He was told, in turn, to talk with a certain Mr. Hampton of the board of public works. It seems Johnson was told that Hampton would bring the matter before the board of public works and let Johnson know the outcome. He had heard nothing further, said Johnson, "until his attention was called to the advertisement of the property under the decree."[99]

In giving its opinion on the decision to vacate the final decree, the Supreme Court of Florida noted that this action was most unusual and ought only to have been performed under "extraordinary circumstances." These circumstances were not present, the court said, and the "allegations fail to show deceit, surprise, or irregularity, in legal acceptance. . . ." There was no sufficient excuse for the delay by the defendants. Most revealing of the court's attitude, however, was its comment on the illiteracy and the race of the defendants as well as the paternalism of some judges: "The facts set forth may appeal to the sympathies of a judge reared in the atmosphere of that tender consideration so generally shown to the illiterate negroes by the descendants of the slave-owner class, but they do not come up to the rule so frequently enunciated."[100]

The limits of the court's indulgence were also measured in *Languein v. Olson,* a case tried before the Supreme Court of South Dakota. The defendant Olson came to the United States at age five years from his native Sweden. This fact, it was claimed, accounted for his meager education in English and his inability to understand court papers. "Business reverses," moreover, made it impossible for him to hire counsel. Thus, he did not appear before the court as summoned in an action on four promissory notes held by the plaintiff.[101]

In reviewing the case, the supreme court found evidence conflicting with Olson's contention that he was unaware of the import of the summons. In addition to this contrary evidence, the court reasoned that the inability of the defendant to understand the summons was "reason enough to lead any intelligent mind to inquire and ascertain the import of those papers." The defendant, observed the court, did not claim to lack intelligence. His claim was that he had a "meagre education in the English language so that he is unable to read court papers understandingly." Yet, in the opinion of the court, it was clear that his statement regarding the severity of his pecuniary position and his inability therefore to hire counsel was itself evidence that he was aware that something was amiss. Furthermore, said the court, it was improbable that anyone brought up in the United States from age five forward would be ignorant in the extreme as pleaded by the defendant. "In fact," the Court continued, "the perception and intelligence with which appellant seeks to maintain his allegation of ignorance furnishes logical refutation of his averment." The conclusion of the court was that "a line must somewhere be drawn": "Some measure of stability must be recognized in judgments by default regularly entered after personal service of process." Although the court allowed that it was as liberal as any in allowing relief from default judgments, it was not willing to grant relief simply because the defaulting defendant "did not know the import of the summons and complaint. . . ."[102]

Conclusion

In this chapter the legal and economic significance of illiteracy was studied by examining both the degree of participation of illiterate persons in the economic mainstream and a number of court proceedings that involved illiterate persons as they encountered a broad variety of difficulties in dealing with financial matters.

Raw literacy rates provide a useful context for studying the significance of the problem of illiteracy as it relates to participation in fundamental economic activities. Single grantors and mortgagors were in the most precarious situation. These illiterate persons could seek outside help and probably many did. This was a double burden, however, and placed them in a much less secure position than if they had literate partners. When the illiterate person was also poor, or at least in a position in which legal assistance was not affordable, then he or she was extremely vulnerable to exploitation by scheming and unscrupulous persons. Poverty and illiteracy may help explain why appearances in court by illiterate persons were less frequent than appearances by literates. It is also clear that judgment by default could be directly related to the illiterate person's inability to read a summons. It may have been that relatively low wealth and illiteracy combined to discourage legal redress among illiterate persons. Those appearing before courts were frequently described by the presiding justices as poor and ignorant and having a low occupational status. They were often from racial and ethnic minorities.

Judicial proceedings involving illiterate participation in a variety of economic and financial activities suggest several important themes in the relationships of illiterate persons to the legal system. These, in turn, tell us a good deal about the difficulties faced by illiterates when entering into a broad range of business and contractual relationships. The opinion of a court, it is true, must be interpreted within the particular context of the suit before it. Yet, at the same time, it is characteristic of courts to search for general guidelines in making their decisions. This interplay of context and principle, of the particular and the general, makes it possible for us to define the problems of illiterates with greater precision.

The making of a will is an intensely personal undertaking, and courts have historically responded with an attitude bordering on reverence for the testator's wishes. But the will, also, is a major instrument for the distribution of wealth, including land transfer, to future generations. The standardization of testamentary forms and conveyancing practices gradually made testamentary activity more certain. Yet intent and consent remained subjective. The will remains a highly flexible document, more so, for example, than the deed, mortgage, executory contract, or commercial paper. Its flexibility also allows a greater variation in format and expression.

In many ways the will is a document for the particular not the general. It remains an expression of the subjective, undisturbed by the objectivity of the market even though subject to statutory rules for filing, witnessing, and administering. Its personal nature, however, requires that it be drawn and administered in an objective way. In the case of the latter, particularly, courts have used a standard of reference similar to good business practices.

Challenges to the "mark," it will be recalled, were not infrequent. These were sometimes based upon possible misidentification of the person affixing the mark. More common, however, were questions of testamentary capacity, intent of the testator, and ability of a witness to know the intent of the signer. In cases dealing with the administration of an estate by an illiterate person, the good business sense of the executor became a relevant factor.

In fact, the court frequently invoked this standard in other types of cases. The standard of reference was often the average, intelligent businessman or citizen—a person who has status within the community and whose opinion would be honored. Because courts emphasized the right of a testator to dispose of property as he saw fit, the problem of intent usually became the most important issue for the court to resolve. Generally, the burden of proof was upon the party attempting to impeach a will. An illiterate witness to the signing of a will was frequently put in the awkward position of testifying to the legitimacy of the will without knowing the testator's intent. Thus evidence from an illiterate witness could be suspect especially if it supported the impeachment of a will.

Of the many issues addressed by courts when dealing with the validity of documents, the problems of fraud and misrepresentation were perhaps the most severe. The disposition of property was often the context for fraudulent activities, but the making of contracts, in general, proved a situation bounded only by the imaginations of those who could perpetrate the fraud. Courts generally distinguished between fraud resulting in a disparity between the document signed and the one intended to be signed (fraud in the factum) and fraud resulting from some misrepresentation, pretense, or misapprehension regarding the document. In this latter case, the party has signed the document he intended to sign, but has been deceived as to its contents. Whichever type of fraud we are speaking of, the disadvantages of illiteracy are evident though the remedy for justice may differ.

Courts did not view illiteracy and lack of education as legal restrictions for the making of contracts and the disposition of property. There was, in the absence of contrary evidence, the assumption that parties to a contract had a sufficient capacity to understand the agreement. Moreover, courts consistently refused to assume a link between illiteracy and a lack of intelligence.

The emergence of a general theory of contract in the nineteenth century (a topic treated in more detail in the following chapter) was accompanied by treatises and statutes attempting to unify and objectify the rules for dealing with market activity. This process, however, was uneven in its development. The area of commercial law developed rapidly in the wake of the industrial revolution, and "various specialities," including negotiable instruments, sales, and insurance, arose before the general theory of contract appeared. Theory then responded in the latter nineteenth century. Standardization and codification were pursued rapidly in some areas and lagged in others.[103] There was disagreement among jurists about the desirability of codification. In his "Report on the Codification of the Common Law" in Massachusetts in 1837, Justice Joseph Story expressed great reservation about the codification of all the common law. It would, he said, be "either positively mischievous, or inefficacious, or futile." Yet he also specified areas of commercial contracts that could benefit from codification.[104]

General theories of tort liability and contract liability emerged at approximately the same time in the midnineteenth century. Though a general theory of tort liability developed more slowly, it eventually emerged in the twentieth century as a more powerful legal tool than contract liability. The slower development was probably a result of the "proliferation of the common-law forms of action" in tort. A general theory of contract probably developed sooner because of the need in commercial dealings to standardize and stabilize market transactions.[105]

In his work *The Death of Contract* Gilmore has spoken of the sharp breaks with the past of the Holmesian formulation of consideration and contract. This break was a masterpiece of adjustment to the problems of stability in market relations. The restricted meaning of consideration also moved the theory of contract away from the subjective basis of motive toward the objective basis of inducement to make a promise binding.[106] Consent and the meeting of the minds were objectified in the bargain sealed by consideration. The movement of contract law, then, was toward the "formal and external": "Unless the formalities were accomplished, there could be no contract and, consequently, no liability. The austerity of doctrine would not be tempered for the shorn lambs who might shiver in its blast."[107]

Free-market principles, the doctrine of freedom of contract, and the value of individual initiative did not disappear in the twentieth century. Yet their application became far more restricted by the operation of the market itself. It is ironic that the vigor of market activity itself should have resulted in its own restriction. Corporations, spawned out of the necessity to control human and natural resources and to reduce individual liability, were formed in the legal image of the individual. Their operation, however, effectively circumscribed individual autonomy. Nineteenth-century individualism expressed through the entrepreneurial will had been met and conquered by the reality of interdependent relationships in the twentieth century. The result, observes Hurst, was that contract law became "less important to the market than it was in times when transactions were more likely to be single dealings not woven into continuing patterns between contracting parties."[108]

In the late nineteenth and early twentieth centuries both the codification of the common law in uniform codes and statutory regulation of commerce, insurance, banking, and liability helped to soften the hard lines of freedom of contract. By the twentieth century a strict bargain theory of consideration had won general acceptance (New York excepted), but many judges chose to "estop" agreements in which a plaintiff, to his detriment, had "relied on a defendant's assurances without the protection of a formal contract." Within the restrictions of a formal contract, the idea of consideration diminished in importance. This was accompanied by the decline of the idea that "tort liability is, or should be, based on negligence or other fault."[109] The result, of course, was to acknowledge the lack of autonomy in human behavior and the increasingly complex (usually bureaucratic) environment in which most people worked.

At the heart of contract theory there was the principle that an agreement represented a "meeting of the minds." This principle assumed that each party understood the legal import of making a contract as well as the substantive part of the contract. Deliberate misinformation given by one party to another was grounds for fraud, as were threats inducing a person to sign. Yet a party whose illiteracy was an obstacle to understanding the contract still had the positive duty of having the agreement explained or read to him; to avoid this obligation was to be negligent. In the absence of deliberate misinformation, equal access to information contained in the contract was assumed, a difficult situation at best for those unable to read. Thus, courts were often in the position of having to determine the *context* for ignorance if the illiterate party were indeed ignorant of the obligations to which he had agreed.

Though increasingly regulated, the stability of contractual relations was still seen as necessary to the success of commercial and business enterprise. To protect against fraud, yet to preserve the sanctity of the contract was the balance that courts sought to achieve. The benevolence and paternalism of the courts, sometimes expressed when dealing with the poor, the ignorant, and the illiterate, did not alter the commitment of courts to preserving the rights and obligations of contracting parties. The increasing sophistication of financial and economic arrangements in the late nineteenth and early twentieth centuries probably placed additional burdens of understanding upon illiterate persons. Courts struggled with the question of how far into the levels of ignorance their sympathy should reach—how far, that is, the principles of equity and law could be merged.

5

Contract and Illiteracy

. . . .

In the previous chapter it was seen that illiterate persons entered into a wide variety of financial relationships. Many of these relied upon implicit or explicit agreements of a contractual nature, though not necessarily belonging to the law of contract, as such. To convey one's meaning and intent to another party was seen as critical in making a transaction successful. In this chapter illiteracy and contract law are treated in greater detail.

It is thought that the increasing complexity of a documentary society in which contractual agreements played a major role also made it more difficult for the illiterate person to successfully enter into financial agreements. This did not necessarily mean that they were alienated from the legal and economic system however. In fact it will be evident that the legal system did not lose sight of fairness and equity despite the sometimes harsh doctrine of freedom of contract.

Having achieved suitable recognition in law and in political theory in the seventeenth century, the ideal of contract became pervasive in the eighteenth century in governing formal agreements of a personal and commercial nature. By the second decade of the nineteenth century it was difficult to think of formal agreements in any other terms. As a principle of social ordering, contract had become deeply embedded in American society. It probably operated (and continues to operate) at more than one level, however. As Fuller has pointed out, we can talk of contract as an ordering principle in a strictly formal sense in which the "influence of contract in human affairs derives entirely from the state-made law of which he is the official custodian and expositor." But a judge might also approach contract in a different spirit, recognizing that the principle of contract can "serve as a source of social ordering" even when contracts are not enforceable at law. Even with formal contracts, this distinction sometimes blurs, for the "interactions" of parties to a contract and a customary standard of reference may give meaning to a contract not readily apparent in the written instrument. The actual behaviors of the parties prior to the signing of a contract give rise to many possible differences of opinion over the meaning of a contract. Such differences may also allow courts to give a so-called practical construction to a contract.[1]

As a principle of social ordering and as a statement of an explicit negotiation followed by performance, the contractual relationship asks for a "common conception of the nature of the game" being played. The give-and-take and the trade-off of the contractual agreement mean that each party "must accept the other's right to work for a solution that will best serve his own interests." It demands "an uneasy blend of collaboration and resistance" between contracting parties.[2] If expressed in the market language of Bentham, a view of considerable legitimacy in nineteenth-century America, the virtue of contract lay in its "capacity to increase human satisfactions through an exchange." The advantages of the exchange "for each of the contracting parties is the difference between the value which they put upon what they give up, and the value of what they acquire."[3]

The principles of free will and a free market for negotiating one's own best interests helped create a hostile environment to those unable to read documents, which, both symbolically and in fact, were expressions of individual will, intent, and purpose. Yet principles of equity and fairness were never purged from legal principles despite periods of vigorous formalism in law. The idea of equity remained as a buffer to the mindless application of conventions and a literalism that could easily be taken to extremes. That the idea of equity remained was fortunate for the illiterate, whose inability to read made him excessively dependent on others in a documentary society. In this chapter the interfacing of the idea of equity with formalism in American law provides the context for considering the problems of illiterate persons and the extent to which they were either victims or beneficiaries of American justice.

Antecedents to a Law of Contract

By the seventeenth century in England transactions supported by written evidence were common, so that the written transaction came to supersede the informal, oral one. The impressive court system—the Bench, Exchequer, eyres, and common pleas—organized between 1100 and 1300 itself had fostered the growth of written records. In turn, increased documentation prepared more people to come to terms with the practical uses of literacy. Sealing, a common practice after the Norman conquest, "helped to bridge the gap between the literate and non-literate."[4] Royal initiative in the use of documents and the pragmatic concerns with conveyances and charters fostered by this initiative gradually led to a "widening literacy."[5]

In the evidentiary sense (though not necessarily belonging to the law of evidence as such) the written word came to dominate because of its permanence compared to oral language and its "physical aptitude for proof."[6] The written word expressed in the form of a document became evidence of intent. This, of course, was most obvious in transactions that included such phrases as "I agree," "I promise," "I devise," "I bequeath," or similar statements that are dispositive.[7] In other cases where the intent, or perhaps a factual issue, was ambiguous, veneration of the written word often excluded oral evidence pertaining to intent or fact. The belief in the superiority of written expression was put well in the late seventeenth-century case of *Jones v. Morley*. Coke, reporting on Chief Justice Popham's decision, says:

> it would be inconvenient that matters in writing made by advice and on consideration, and which finally import the certain truth of the agreement of the parties, should be controlled by averment of the parties, to be proved by the uncertain testimony of slippery memory. And it would be dangerous to purchasers and farmers and all others in such cases if such nude averments against matters in writing should be admitted.[8]

For all its merits written expression was and is imperfect and subject to ambiguity and misinterpretation. Nowhere is this more evident than in attempting to construe the meaning of a document or to interpret the intent of two or more parties to a contract. In the late-eighteenth-century case of *Gibson v. Minet* (1791), the rule of construction of words in a document was simply put: *"that the words may bear the sense,* [italics mine] which by construction, is put upon them. If we step beyond this line, we no longer construe men's deeds, but make deeds for them."[9]

Ambiguities were to be resolved, fraud was not to be tolerated, and misrepresentation was to be avoided. Yet as Gulson reminds us, "the end and object of a contract or other similar transaction is, not to furnish a statement of the intentions of the parties, but to perform a substantive act, to the validity of which their actually existing intentions, if incompatible with that act, are practically immaterial."[10] By the nineteenth century the literalness of the document was trusted above all else. Fraud and mistake were to be avoided, but the latitude for these had become increasingly narrow.[11]

It is common for legal historians to issue a number of qualifying remarks when discussing the history of the concept of contract. Generally, these may be reduced to the fact that in ancient and medieval England the concept of contract, in any modern sense, was unknown and that the abstract and generalized notion of contract did not appear until the rise of the action of assumpsit and the doctrine of valuable consideration.[12]

The difficulty in discussing the concept of contract before the seventeenth century is compounded by the fact that common law courts were slow to develop remedies for breach of contract.[13] Rather, it was ecclesiastical courts prior to the emergence of chancery that generally dealt with contractual issues that could be said to involve a breaking of faith between parties. It was the morality of the obligations (or the immorality of the breach of faith) that was the issue.[14]

A theory of property, not agreement, continued to dominate land transactions. Under the common law, a "conveyance of any interest in land necessitated, where possible, the transfer of physical possession. Where that was impossible, a deed-symbol had to be manually transferred in the place of the land." There was apparently no exception to this rule. Later, under the Statute of Frauds (1667) and the Real Property Act of 1845, the deed-symbol and the supremacy of the written instrument itself became evident.[15]

Even by the fourteenth century the common law generally dealt only with formal agreements.[16] When the question of debt and the proof of debt involved a written and sealed instrument such as a deed, questions of proof were excluded as in covenant. The seal settled the controversy. The controversy could, however, be handled in terms of fraud with the defendant's denying the deed. This plea, says Milsom, "was eventually extended from a simple allegation of forgery to cover certain kinds of duress, and also to the case of the illiterate to whom the deed had been read wrongly."[17]

Illiteracy seems to have been an important factor in the application of the Writ of Debt. Debt could be classified as Debt either upon an Obligation or upon a Contract. The dichotomy can be better understood if one recalls the importance of the seal in an illiterate age. In over half of the cases of Debt "in the reigns of the first three Edwards the plaintiff relied upon a sealed instrument." These instruments were in the form of either writing (deed) or a tally. When a deed or tally with seals attached could be produced, the Debt "lay on an obligation." All other cases were said to "be on a contract," the "essential feature" of which "was the receipt by the defendant of a material benefit." In this use of the concept of contract, however, liability was not a result of a promise, but, rather, of the receipt of some material benefit.[18]

Unlike an action in convenant in which the complainant had a deed under seal and sought justice in the common law courts, informal agreements without writing were brought before chancery. Barbour has shown that in the fifteenth century, agreements in dispute brought before the chancellor were often informal and simply stated that there was "an agreement or bargain, or that the defendant 'sold' the land to the complainant." These were often brought against vendors who failed to deliver land as promised. Because of the informality of the agreement, these types of agreements probably "represent a large number of ordinary transactions of daily life,"[19] and, it should be added, many of whom were probably performed by persons unable to read and write.

Trespass, Assumpsit, and Consideration

The concept of *assumpsit* (generally an undertaking, in the sense of an assurance) became a key element in the development of the modern concept of contract. In the fifteenth century, however, it was one of a number of ways of "pleading a trespass action." The action of assumpsit was severely restricted at this time.[20]

The *critical* development of the action of assumpsit did not occur until the beginning of the seventeenth century with the hearing of Slade's case (1602). This celebrated case involved a seller of wheat, Slade, and a buyer, Morley, who promised to pay. When no payment was forthcoming from Morley, Slade sued in *indebitatus assumpsit*. The jury found that Morley had indeed bought the wheat and rye from the plaintiff, Slade, and that "there was no other promise or assumption between the plaintiff and the defendant except the said bargain. . . ." The crucial question was whether a case could be brought on the action of *indebitatus assumpsit* when, after the sale, no subsequent promise had been made. It was decided that the bargain with an agreed-upon price and without a subsequent promise was a "sufficient basis for an action of assumpsit." (The problem of "the unpaid seller who had delivered goods to another without an express agreement on the price" was not solved by Slade's case.)[21] Although Slade's case did not seem a major breakthrough at the time, the opinion delivered "became the foundation of modern contract law" and, in practice, allowed assumpsit to displace the action of debt.[22]

The doctrine of consideration, like the action of assumpsit, was one of the cornerstones to the development of modern contract theory. It, too, was slow to be put in place. In medieval law the nearest relative to the modern concept of consideration for informal contracts (as differentiated from a deed, for example) was the doctrine of quid pro quo. This doctrine applied only when "it could be shown that the debtor had actually received a material benefit from the creditor; this benefit was the *quid* in return for which (pro quo) the defendant was saddled with the liability in debt." Without quid pro quo the contract was not binding on the defendant.[23]

The doctrine of consideration also suffered from some ambiguity, though not to the extent of quid pro quo. Simpson observes that it is commonly thought that cases that accepted the principle "that a promise could count as a good consideration for the promise sued upon" represent "a dramatic step forward in the history of the law of contract." The step forward he interprets to mean "the recognition that an agreement involving mutual promises became *binding* when the promises were made." Sixteenth-century cases were not concerned with the question of when is a promise binding, but, rather, with the question, when is a breach of promise actionable? The doctrine of offer and acceptance that answers the "when" question was unknown in the sixteenth and seventeenth centuries. What was required at this time was that the plaintiff "show that a *promise* [not a contract] had been made for good consideration and broken."[24]

However undeveloped the doctrine of consideration might appear at this point historically, the important point is that by the seventeenth century English law recognized "that a valuable consideration is a benefit given or promised to the undertaker, or, some loss or liability incurred by the promisee, in return for the promise given by the undertaker."[25] Thus the benefit principle derived from the action of debt and the liability principles derived from the action of assumpsit and trespass had come together to form "the twin bases of our modern doctrine of consideration."[26]

The emergence of the theory of "simple contract" resting upon "valuable consideration" and necessitating no particular form for the agreement was not an unmixed blessing, even though transacting business on a contractual basis became far easier. Havighurst has noted that between 1602 (Slade's case) and 1677 (Statute of Frauds) "contract plaintiffs, good and evil, had a rather easy time of it" bringing actions on assumpsit.[27] The doctrine of consideration, says Havighurst, "was almost the only means of control which a judge had over a jury unable or unwilling to detect perjury and still permitted to decide upon its own knowledge of the facts."[28]

Fraudulent practices generally resulting in perjury and subordination of perjury escalated in number in the first half of the seventeenth century. To deal with this alarming situation, the House of Lords in 1673 gave a first reading to "An Act for preventing many fraudulent practices which are commonly endeavoured to be upheld by perjury or subordination of perjury." This was to become in 1677 the famous Statute of Frauds, which in the matter of contracts stated:

> noe action shall be brought . . . whereby to charge the defendant upon any speciall promise to answere for the debt default or miscarriages of another person . . . unlesse the agreement upon which such action shall be brought or some memorandum or note thereof shall be in writing and signed by the par- tie to be charged therewith or some other person thereunto by him lawfully authorized.[29]

By the seventeenth century the written word was authoritative far beyond what might have been imagined in medieval England. Its pre- sence, moreover, was proof of a contract willfully made. Atiyah has argued that the statute demonstrated "a belief in the unreliability of evidence of the spoken word, and a dread of perjury and fraud about the spoken word." Wholly executory contracts required some "solid proof" in writ- ing for their existence. Contracts for the sale of goods required writing only "if the goods [had] not been delivered and accepted, or if no part of the price has been paid." It might well be, as Atiyah has suggested, that the statute was "an attempt to hold back the advance of the consensual contract and to require parol contracts to be part-executed before they were enforced." The statute is, from this point of view, a compromise sta- tute between twelfth-century requirements for valid contracts of sale and seventeenth-century concerns with (evidentiary) requirements for proving a contract of sale.[30]

British Common Law in the American Colonies

American law was heavily dependent on British legal principles and, in many instances, case precedents themselves. The degree of dependence, however, has been a matter for debate among legal historians. In his essay "Reception of English Common Law in the American Colonies," Stoebuck has noted that explanations of the influence of the common law in the American colonies fall into certain standard theories. The first of these was generally accepted throughout the nineteenth century and was supported by Judges Story, Kent, and Shaw. It was succinctly stated in 1829 by Justice Story in *Van Ness v. Pacard:* "The common law of England is not to be taken in all respects to be that of America. Our an- cestors brought with them its general principles, and claimed it as their birthright; but they brought with them and adopted only that portion which was applicable to their situation."[31]

This view assumes that, allowing for modifications for their new circumstances in America, the American colonists adhered to English common-law principles. The view may be contrasted with a second theory, which emerged in the early years of the twentieth century. This theory, among whose advocates were Paul Reinsch, Charles Hilkey, and Max Radin, deemphasized the importance of English common-law to the American colonists. Instead, it relegated the common-law heritage to a secondary position of importance. Reinsch stressed the idea that the colonial administration of justice was rude and popular. Hilkey stressed the importance of two other sources of law: the Mosaic code and local innovations. Radin emphasized the importance of natural law to the colonists. A third theory was advanced by Goebel in his study of Plymouth Colony. It stressed the importance of legal procedures in English borough and manor courts as a backdrop to the colonists' administration of their courts.[32] The fact that the Pilgrims came from parts of England where the effects of the enclosure movement were profoundly felt made them wary of copyholds. Thus, says Goebel, landholding in early Plymouth Colony "was conceived in the image of the English freehold."[33]

In Connecticut the English common-law system with its reliance upon precedent was rejected. The rule of law was in the form of statute law— The Fundamental Orders—and, by an act of 1672, every family in the colony was required to purchase a printed copy of the state's statutes. Court opinions were not published in any colonies. This made it more difficult to introduce "English common law into the colonies," but it also "prevented the development of a common law of their own."[34] In 1784 Connecticut formally took the step toward establishing its own common-law system.[35]

In both land law and the law of succession, Stoebuck found that British principles were basic in Massachusetts, but that important modifications were made. These included the nonrecognition of feudal tenures and the provision for transferring land and personalty by will.[36] In other respects such as the law of dower, English law prevailed. "It may not be without significance," notes Haskins, "that it was in 1647 that the Massachusetts General Court voted to purchase several English law books, including a copy of Coke on Littleton." Forms of action characteristic of English common law such as debt, replevin, trespass, and trespass on the case were employed.[37]

Skilled conveyancers were generally not present in seventeenth-century colonial America. Thus, simplified forms for the transfer of land were a necessity. Friedman writes that "in some colonies, land passed from person to person in a free and easy way" and "conveyancing habits developed that were unheard of in old England."[38] Conveyances of land were sometimes made by signing the back of the original patent like endorsing a check "until some purchaser, to be on the safe side, would decide to record his ownership by enrollment in court." Such recording practices eventually helped to convert land transactions "from status to contract, from a matter of family and birth, to the subject of a free and open market." The supremacy of the written record was plain as the record itself came to guarantee title to lands. An unrecorded deed did not have the validity of a recorded one when tested in a court of law. The recording system that "began as a tool of state policy" to simplify the "governance of settlements" became, in time, a "tool of the market."[39]

The opening of the eighteenth century brought an upsurge in the use of English common-law forms. Reports from the colonies to a Privy Council request in 1700 asking for information on court procedures show differences in the administration of justice in Barbados, Massachusetts, New York, Rhode Island, Maryland, and Virginia. Yet it is equally as clear that the court systems of these colonies were products of the English common-law and equity courts. In Virginia, said the report to the Privy Council, "[T]he proceedings are in English and Judgmts: grounded & passed according (or as near) to ye Common & statute Laws of England & ye Circumstances of ye Country will admitt & to such peculiar Laws as are made amiable to ye present state of ye Country."[40]

South Carolina, North Carolina, and Pennsylvania all adopted some provision for the use of English common law. Court decisions from North Carolina and Maryland show the use of English precedents.[41] By the time of the American War for Independence, English common law, including the intricacies of pleading, was very much in evidence in the colonies.[42]

In an instructive sidelight to common-law practice in Massachusetts, Nelson has noted that even in 1760 the recognition of social status played an important part in pleading. The precise identification of the parties to litigation included information on name, residence, and "addition," that is, "the occupation or social rank of both plaintiff and defendent." Says Nelson: "More suits were abated or dismissed from improper additions [such as *gentleman* rather than *yeoman*, or *esquire* rather than *gentleman*] than on any other ground." In the twenty-five year period from 1760 to 1785, however, this situation altered radically, and by the latter year "misnomers and errors in additions were freely amendable."[43] The reform of "additions," however, did not completely solve the problem of expense. As of the 1790s, pleading still remained an obstacle to access to court remedies.[44]

In post-Revolutionary America there were numerous instances of antipathy to English common-law principles. Ignorance and distrust both were motivating factors in the popular demand for rejecting English precedent. Yet, as Aumann remarks, the commercial "needs of the day" were instrumental in overcoming popular protest.[45] As might be expected, different states experienced different levels of protest and acceptance of common-law principles. In South Carolina during the post-Revolutionary period, says Ely, critics of English law saw "the persistent deference to English law as an undemocratic and potentially dangerous survival of the conservative legal system of Britain. . . ." Despite the criticism, however, he says, "the place of English law in America was never seriously threatened."[46]

In newly settled areas after the War for Independence, English common-law principles, allowing for modification by new circumstances, were in operation. Brantley has noted the heritage of English legal practices in Alabama, and Brown has observed that, with variations, twenty-six of the twenty-eight jurisdictions organized between 1776 and 1836 provided for the use of English statutes. Blume's analysis of the Wayne County, Michigan, Court of Common Pleas records indicates that the English common-law forms and fictions constituted the procedural basis for a good share of litigation.[47]

The simple fact was that "English Law was the only law that post-Revolutionary American lawyers knew anything about." Their sources were limited, says Gilmore, and included the "crabbed and incomprehensible pages of Coke on Littleton to the elegant superficialities of Blackstone." Treatises on American law did not exist, nor were there "published collections of American case reports."[48] American law only gradually was weaned away from English common law.

Principles of Equity

The English Precedent

Courts of equity in England were especially important as feudalism and the land tenure system declined. In their place emerged the impersonal world of land as a commodity. The impress of increased foreign activity in English trade and the deficiencies of common-law actions as applied to trade and commerce became increasingly evident.[49]

The highly technical forms of common law rooted in both land tenure and the system of pleading were not amenable to fluid commercial activity. It was not only merchants who were affected, however.[50] Peasant property holding had become a true property right in the face of the increasing "unreality" of the lord's jurisdiction.[51] These "people of humble life" often were the victims of the technical constraints of the common-law forms. Agreements to sell land or to make a marriage settlement, in which no clerk nor learned man was present, were not unusual. Under these conditions, the agreement remained formless because literate people were unavailable to incorporate such agreements in deeds. When challenged, these events were difficult to bring within the forms of common-law pleading. Settlement of a dispute by the principles of reason and conscience, however, was possible at chancery.[52]

From the viewpoint of legal effectiveness, the increasing number of cases heard in chancery was probably indicative of the inadequacies of common law to deal with land tenure problems in times of rapid social change. The problem was compounded by a general level of educational attainment insufficient to deal with legal and financial documents.

Because the informal method of striking a bargain was not enforceable at common law, it was necessary, or at least reasonable, to give some protection to participants in these transactions, when a written document was not at odds with an oral agreement. This became a matter for equity to be settled by the chancellor.[53]

Equity as administered by the English High Court of Chancery was an extension of the king's justice. In a particular case in which failure of substantial justice was apparent, there was no remedy in the common-law courts. Precedent (*stare decisis*) was always in danger of running counter to principles of natural equity. Thus, fraud, accident, mistake, and forgery, for example, could not be dealt with at common law. Chancery, by the application of the principle that the "essence of equity is the correction of positive law where that fails because too generally formulated," administered "relief according to the true intentions of the parties." Equity, notes Katz, "was thus an attempt to make law supple enough to do substantial justice throughout the broad range of human experience accessible to the power of the state."[54]

In seventeenth- and eighteenth-century colonial America there is evidence that feelings of hostility toward the procedures of chancery courts were coupled with a desire to retain the principles of equity. New Jersey, New York, Maryland, and South Carolina operated chancery courts over a long period of time. In New York proceedings in chancery became "as formalistically rigid as their English counterpart."[55] In other colonies the prerogative nature of courts of chancery was probably a source of opposition.[56]

The potential flexibility of the common law when separated from the social fabric of England was apparent. By the late eighteenth century, equitable defenses against perjury, mistake, and fraud were permitted. By the Constitution of 1776 in Pennsylvania the "common pleas courts were given the power of a court of equity so far as [it] related to perpetuation of testimony, obtaining of evidence from places outside the state, and protection of the property of the insane." Ironically, the illiterate person was at a temporary advantage at least at common law. "Mistake was a defense at common law only when [the] defendant was unable to read." The advantage was small, however, for common law generally held that a contract or conveyance in writing superseded an oral one. Thus, the "writing was conclusive as to the terms of the contract or conveyance." If the writing did not actually express the intent of the parties (as might frequently be the case with an illiterate person) injustice might easily occur. In Pennsylvania, the implicit power of equity was lodged in courts of law by the courts' willingness to accept proof of the "actual intention of the parties and enforcing the bargain which the parties intended."[57]

The result of this mass of equity legislation in the long run was to extend equity jurisdiction to the courts. As it became apparent that various species of private acts could be classified, general acts giving jurisdiction to the courts, in turn, superseded them. Analysis of these private acts prior to 1836, according to Cowan, shows that "most of these general acts were preceded by private acts granting relief to individuals petitioning for some equitable remedy." The special (private) acts functioned as a catalyst to grant the courts themselves power "to give equitable relief in cases similar to those represented by the private acts." Eventually, by the Constitution of 1874, the legislature was forbidden to "exercise powers already granted to the Courts."[58] In this very fundamental sense, the juridical dimension of popular sovereignty intersected with common-law tradition and the principles of equitable relief.

A review of the impact of English common law and equity principles in the period immediately following the War for Independence indicates no slavish acceptance of these principles. Overall, it may be said that American attitudes toward the English common law ranged from outright hostility to acceptance with provisos for extenuating local circumstances. A general attitude of ambivalence characterized much of the American reception of English common law with most criticism being reserved for the niceties or sophistries of pleading. Resentment was sometimes linked, in turn, to high court costs and lawyers fees, which were seen as obstacles to justice for the poor or common man. Nonetheless, English common-law principles kept the courts in order both substantively and procedurally. By the opening of the nineteenth century English precedents both in common law and in equity helped to lay the groundwork for an American law of contract.

Contract in the Nineteenth Century

It has been noted already that American constitutionalism is heavily imbued with the ideal of social contract and the contractual ideal in general. Economic due process and freedom of contract have been hallowed principles guarded by the American constitution. Historically, due process of law as applied to contract has meant that a person's right to property cannot be abridged, nor the property itself be taken for the benefit of another without compensation. State laws that had the effect of violating the right to acquire property were met with the countervailing principle that laws that prohibited entering into contracts or prevented the acquisition of property were invalid.[59] Yet the interplay of rights, the tension produced by differing estimates and ordering of priorities, a conspicuous feature of liberal thought, was also apparent in the limitations on freedom of contract and property rights. Justice Shaw's decision in *Commonwealth v. Alger* (1851) illustrates the point well:

> Rights of property, like all other social and conventional rights, are subject to such reasonable limitations in their enjoyment, as shall prevent them from being injurious, and to such reasonable restraints and regulations established by law as the legislature, under the governing and controlling power vested in them by the Constitution, may think necessary and expedient.[60]

It was likewise with freedom of contract, as the decision of *Holden v. Hardy* (1898) illustrates:

> The right of contract . . . is itself subject to certain limitation which the State may lawfully impose in the exercise of its police powers. While this power is inherent in all governments, it has doubtless been greatly expanded in its application during the past century, owing to an enormous increase in the number of occupations which are dangerous, or so far detrimental to the health of employees as to demand special precautions for their well-being and protection or the safety of adjacent property.[61]

The inviolability of contract was expressly recognized by the United States Constitution. The sanctity of contract and its importance to social stability were expressed often in the decisions of Chief Justice John Marshall, whose opinions were often concerned with the protection of contractual relations from legislative power. Thus, in *Fletcher v. Peck* (1810), *New Jersey v. Wilson* (1812), and *Dartmouth College v. Woodward* (1819) the Marshall court found that the impairment of contracts by the states was in violation of the United States Constitution. In each of these cases the nature and foundation of a particular contract were thoroughly explored.

The later case of *Ogden v. Saunders* (1827), however, gives us a broader perspective on the way in which Marshall incorporated natural rights and natural law theory into his reasoning about contract. It is this case that is of most concern in this context. It is not the intent here, however, to explore the decisions of Marshall as they relate to his attempts to "resolve the great political issue of his time"—whether "popular will or fixed principle should be the source of law—by . . . the appeal to consensus."[62] Suffice it to say that this political context of Marshall's decisions is also important to understanding Marshall's interpretation of contractual rights and obligations as outgrowths of accepted and fixed legal principles.

Ogden v. Saunders, like *Sturgis v. Crowninshield* (1819) and *M'Millan v. M'Neill* (1819), was a case involving the constitutionality of a bankruptcy law. The case of *Sturgis v. Crowninshield* involved "the validity of a discharge in bankruptcy under a State statute passed subsequent to the date of the making of the contract." Marshall's opinion "declared the statute . . . invalid inasmuch as it was a bankruptcy statute which granted discharges and so annulled contracts, and so was a law impairing the obligation of the original contract." The statute was declared unconstitutional. *Ogden v. Saunders,* on the other hand, involved "the validity of a discharge in bankruptcy under a State statute enacted before the claim on which suit was brought had come into existence." Marshall's opinion was a dissenting one, along with those of Story and Duvall. The majority of the court "limited the doctrine of *Sturgis v. Crowninshield* to cases where the bankruptcy law was passed subsequent to the creation of the contract."[63] Marshall, Story, and Duvall argued that, whether prospective or retrospective, such laws ran counter to the Constitution's express language that "no State shall pass any law" "impairing the obligation of contracts."[64]

Ogden v. Saunders offers Marshall's most explicit argument for the rational and natural law basis of contractual relations. In his dissenting opinion, Marshall noted that the original power and right of individuals to contract was not derived from government, but brought with them into society. The right was "intrinsic," not derived from positive law, Marshall argued. It resulted from "the right which every man retains to acquire property, to dispose of that property according to his own judgment, and to pledge himself for a future act." Although these rights are controlled by legislation, they are not given by it: "beyond these actual restraints the original power remains unimpaired." The "wise and learned men whose treatises on the laws of nature and nations have guided public opinion on the subjects of obligation and contract," said Marshall, concurred "that contracts possess an original, intrinsic obligation, derived from the acts of free agents, and not given by government."[65] Thus the sanctity of contract was reaffirmed though in a dissenting opinion.

Marshall's reasoning in *Ogden v. Saunders* was an extension of Hobbes's distinction between obligation to fulfill one's promise as expressed in a contract and obligation to perform according to a contract because the law compels obligation by the threat of punishment: "a man is obliged by his contracts, that is, . . . he ought to perform for his promise sake; but . . . the law ties him being obliged, that is to say, it compels him to make good his promise, for fear of the punishment appointed by law."[66]

Marshall concluded that the constitutional provision prohibiting a state from passing any law impairing the obligation of contracts was meant to apply both prospectively and retrospectively: "a prohibition to pass any law impairing [a contract] does not imply a prohibition to vary the remedy; nor does a power to vary the remedy imply a power to impair the obligation derived from the act of the parties." The sanctity of obligation of contract thus lay in its being derived from natural law *and* in being a natural right. Legislative provisions governing the remedies for nonperformance, although affecting the process whereby obligations might be met, were not construed as affecting the obligation itself. The latter derived from "the act of the parties, not from the grant of government. . . ."[67]

Joseph Story, like Marshall, was committed to the contractual ideal, the sanctity of private property, and the protection of individual contractual rights and obligations. Story's defense of contract, however, was clearly grounded in natural law theories of moral obligation rather than theories of consent. In *Joseph Story and the American Constitution, A Study in Political and Legal Thought,* McClellan has commented extensively on Story's "Natural Law," noting the uncommon close relationship between "nature's rules of human conduct" and divine law. In the vein of Coke, Blackstone, and Burke rather than Locke and Hobbes, Story maintained that both constitutional and common law should be understood as "the substratum of the legal system" expressing a "philosophy of morals" that is the "foundation of all other laws." "Conservative religious orthodoxy" thus lay "at the heart of [Story's] natural law philosophy." It was not an orthodoxy rooted in the doctrine of any sect but rather in a heritage of natural law theory extending from the thirteenth century forward.[68]

Story, McClellan points out, saw common law "as being in part declaratory of natural law moral precepts." Moreover, the "enjoyment of liberty and the security of property" in no small way might be "'traced to the principles of the common law as it [had] been moulded and fashioned from age to age, by wise and learned judges.'"[69] From natural law and common law Story derived his firm belief in the sanctity of contract: "The obligation of contracts . . . may . . . be deduced from the plainest elements of natural law,—that is, if such contracts are just and moral, and founded upon mutuality of consideration. . . . [They are] conformable to the will of God, which requires all men to deal with good faith, and truth, and sincerity in their intercourse with others," said Story.[70] For Story property rights were the foundation of civil rights and freedom. In his inaugural address as Dane Professor of Law he proclaimed that "the sacred rights of property are to be guarded at every point . . . because if they [are] unprotected, all other rights become worthless or visionary." It was this faith that underlay Story's dissent in the *Charles River Bridge* case,"his magnum opus" in the defense of property and contract.[71]

Newmyer has argued that the struggle for power that Story asserted was the fundamental question in the *Charles River Bridge* case was a struggle between law and politics, of "who should make and maintain the rules of republican society." In challenging an 1828 statute incorporating the proprietors of the Warren Bridge it was alleged by the proprietors that the construction of the new bridge threatened to destroy their profits. They argued that their charter included an implied guaranty that "the legislators would not authorize another bridge, especially a free one, in the same line of travel." In dissenting from Taney's opinion, which, in effect, justified the new charter on the grounds of the "rights of the community," Story based his argument on the law of contract. Story rejected Taney's argument that the Charles River Bridge charter rested on the common law of royal grants. From Story's viewpoint, says Newmyer, the issue was a contractual one, a litigation involving what "contracting parties of equal authority" meant by their agreement.[72] For Story, the issue of contractual obligations itself was a moral one—one which bound a legislature entering the economic arena quite as much as an individual. "Our legislatures neither have, nor affect to have, any royal prerogatives," said Story.[73] In the world of Justice Story's moral consensus, legislature, corporation, and individual were bound by the same obligations.

Story's view of property rights and contractual obligations did not prevail, although his dissent helped promulgate a conservative tradition in American law. The *Charles River Bridge* case turned out to be symptomatic of a fundamental alteration in the conception of property rights that Horwitz has described as a change "from a static agrarian conception entitling an owner to undisturbed enjoyment, to a dynamic, instrumental, and more abstract view of property that emphasized the newly paramount virtues of productive use and development." In short, the common-law conception of property rooted in a feudal view of property had been significantly altered to reflect a society undergoing phenomenal population growth and rapid economic expansion.[74]

A Will Theory of Contract

Lockean contractarianism had made use of the ideas of implied contracts and implied assent, and it was but a small step from a theory of political assent to one of economic assent. This is not to say that there was a causal link between the two. Rather, the relationship is better described as consanguine. The eighteenth-century "notion of contract, and the role of contract in society" says Atiyah, "were a great deal broader than they are today":

> Men thought their relationships with each other, and their relationship with the State, to be of a similar character. And over and above that, there is a sense in which they perceived the role of choice or consent in the one relationship to be the precondition for the proper role of choice or consent in the other.[75]

The Natural Lawyers saw willful action as the cornerstone of agreements. Promises themselves were expressions of willful acts. For some, such as Francis Hutcheson, natural law both was aesthetically appealing and served a utilitarian purpose. "The obligation to perform a promise," says Atiyah, was to the eighteenth-century mind "a basic principle of Natural Law." Justifications for the principle varied. For Hume it was a matter of "mutual self-interest"; for Paley, "a fear of punishment in the afterlife"; for Bentham, a "principle of utility"; for Adam Smith, a matter of "self-interest."[76]

The individualism of the classical economist and utilitarians fit well with the emphasis on free choice and assent in contractual theory. As consumer, buyer, earner, worker, and investor, the individual was at the center of the free market, his choices confirming both economic theory and his own potential. Through education men were taught to choose intelligently and to recognize their own best interests. In fact, the law itself served an educative function. Nineteenth-century law often displayed the moral didacticism that characterized the religious and educational rhetoric of the same period.

By the time of the emergence of a relatively free market economy in the eighteenth century, the traditional emphasis in law on property rights and transactions relating to property had been refocused on contractual relations in the transferring of property. Concern with property rights had shifted "from their use value to their exchange value." Concurrently, focus on the law of part-executed contracts was shifting to that of truly executory contracts. The seminal decision of *Chesterfield v. Janssen* (1750) "had decided that an unfair bargain would become binding if freely and voluntarily confirmed by the losing party." This, says Atiyah, was a revolutionary change from the principles of equity practiced in the past by the Court of Chancery, where unfair contracts were set aside "because they were unfair, not because they had not been properly assented to." This shift from a principle of unfairness to a principle of will, however, should not blind us to the strength of paternalism in eighteenth-century equity, and the "extent of the protection afforded by the law to poor and ignorant persons who were led into unfair, oppressive, or extortionate bargains."[77]

Formalism in legal action accompanied the emergence of a will theory of contract. The formalistic approach to legal decision making viewed the court's role as "purely passive and interpretive." It was a noninterfering posture, which, quite unlike equity, aimed to preserve the *literal* meaning of contracts. From an economic standpoint, it fit nicely with free market principles and the emphasis upon self-reliance and freedom to negotiate one's own risks and opportunities. The model of contract theory that thus emerged was that of the free market economy.[78]

The free market model for contract was a model in which free will and consent were overriding concerns. Any hiatus between the will of the parties and the fairness of the bargain usually turned out to be explained by the free market principle of caveat emptor.[79] The free market model that lay behind the will theory of contract was extended beyond the assumptions of Hume, Smith, and Bentham. They had all agreed, says Atiyah, that "bare expectations were less important than expectations allied to present rights, especially rights of property."[80]

Contract, Free Will, and the Free Market

As the United States entered a period of rapid westward expansion and, soon following, manufacturing and commercial growth, natural law theory, British precedent, and constitutional law all served to buttress the idea that contractual relations were, at the least, necessary to good moral order and, at the most, necessary to social stability. The idea of contract thus served the interests of both individual and society. "Solemn contracts" were not to be set aside lightly, for fear that grave social consequences would follow.[81] Hurst has described the opinions of state court judges between 1830 and 1860 as ringing with the "tones of natural law" and the principle of social compact designed to serve the "practical purpose of trying to preserve a broad arena for maneuver by private contract and property dealings within the market."[82]

Hurst has characterized the middle-class response to an expanding economy as placing "a high premium on the active will, on striving and improvising to adopt circumstances to a restless demand to increase the range of human satisfactions, particularly by acting on the economic dimension of life."[83] This "cluster of middle class attitudes and values" he describes as follows:

(1) regard for rational, peaceful order under the constitutional ideal, (2) favor for a diversity of outlets for active will, (3) belief in people's capacity to erect ideal values on an increasing material base as the foundation of justice, and (4) assertion of the quality of the individual life as the ultimate criterion of the good society.[84]

The high regard for the inviolability of contractual relations was part of the deference paid to property in general.[85] A series of cases decided by federal courts beginning with *Dartmouth College v. Woodard* (1819) had helped "to secure property interests, and to protect ownership and management rights from shifting, temporary winds of public opinion." Reformed recording practices and the appearance of simple, standardized deed (warranty and quit-claim) forms also helped to assure that rights in property were secure.[86]

The law of contract as it was understood in early-nineteenth-century America was generally in accord with the free market—a model that assumed that the individual was the basic economic unit and had complete mobility and freedom in decision making. Thus, in a market where all goods were presumed fungible and land was a commodity for exchange, individuals were expected to negotiate in their own best interests. Contract involved a meeting of individual wills or intent to be validated by valuable consideration.[87] The bargain was considered to be a give-and-take situation—not a situation in which "one could prevail only at the complete subordination or defeat of the other."[88] Nineteenth-century market-driven principles of contract assumed a general balance of power among those making a contract.[89] The market itself was presumed to be a major means for allocating market resources, and was seen as serving the best interests of society in general.[90]

The increasing use of the executory contract and the emergence of a will theory of contract were accompanied by the demise of principles of equity as applied to contractual relations.[91] Yet evidence of the fairness doctrine was still found in early-nineteenth-century American courts. The fairness doctrine accompanied by a benevolent paternalism found in *Butler v. Haskell* (1816) is clear evidence that not all courts were willing to abandon principles of equity:

> wherever the Court perceives that a sale of property has been made at a grossly inadequate price, such as would shock a correct mind, this inadequacy furnishes a strong, and in general a conclusive presumption, though there be no direct proof of fraud, that an undue advantage has been taken of the ignorance, the weakness, or the distress and necessity of the vendor: and this imposes on the purchaser a necessity to remove this violent presumption by the clearest evidence of the fairness of his conduct; and the relief is given by the

Court, either by refusing to enforce the contract, or by setting it aside altogether, according to the circumstances of the case.[92]

In courts of law (rather than equity) the equivalent of the fairness doctrine was found in the awarding of damages by juries. The substantive doctrine of consideration allowed juries to determine whether or not there was adequate consideration before awarding damages. Inadequacy of price was a ground for setting aside contracts in Pennsylvania (*Armstrong v. McGhee* [1795]). Said Chief Justice McKearn: courts had the obligation to turn to juries for "an equitable and conscientious interpretation of the agreement of the parties." In Massachusetts, too, the amount awarded in damages might be reduced by demonstrating inadequacy of consideration. As late as 1822, Chancellor Kent was writing that in contract disputes in which a jury determined damages, "relief can be afforded in damages, with a moderation agreeable to equity and good conscience, and . . . the claims and pretensions of each party can be duly attended to, and be admitted to govern the assessment."[93] Even when a more formal and literal approach to contractual obligations was becoming dominant, then, a fairness doctrine still could be applied to offset a so-called weaker party.

The market model highlighted the unencumbered will of the contracting individual, his ability to negotiate for his own benefit, and his responsibility to abide by the words (expressing his intent) of the contract. These features, in conjunction with the propensity of courts to formalism and literalness in judging intent—the words speak for themselves—helped to give contractual relations the impersonal quality of the free market itself. Offer, acceptance, and consideration were the manifestations of intent. Consideration was evidence of a price freely fixed, of a willing seller and a willing buyer.[94] The sound price doctrine of the eighteenth century, the inference that some objective value could be attached to the object of the transaction, gave way to the doctrine of caveat emptor.[95]

In interpreting the meaning of contracts, courts searched for a meeting of the minds, of assent, which itself was presumed to be an objective reality capable of identification. (The value of the transaction, of course, was subjective and determined by the will of the contracting parties.) Given the limits of probing the intent of parties to a contract, however, reality usually turned out to be the document itself and the "plain meaning of the words." As courts moved from a subjective, moral basis for liability and contract toward an objective (scientific, unitary) foundation what was thought or intended became secondary to what was said or written. They moved increasingly from questions of fact to questions of law. The particular was removed in favor of the general.[96]

As was the case with land law and the law of negotiable instruments, contract law thus came to put its faith in the written word above all else.[97] The operational subjectivity of a will theory of contract (subjective because of the difficulty in discovering intent itself) in actuality was made subordinate to the objectivity of the written word. A written contract ought to conform to the intent of the parties, of course, but when it did not, the rules of law and language prevailed in its construction. The substance of the contract, accessible through grammatical and syntactical analysis, could be made objective through the rules of language.

The reification of contract law and tort law also meant that determinations of liability should be objective; that is, it was the action that should speak, not the motivation. The law of contract became a doctrine, and the entire process of entering into a contract grew more formalized. Consideration became a matter of form signifying the existence of a bargain, a "reciprocal conventional inducement."[98] Agreement was not the point, nor was good faith. Formal signification was what counted. It is easy to see how limited liability was under such a doctrine and how broad the range for initiative.

The objective theory of contract effectively reduced the number of situations under which mistake could be used as a plea for not fulfilling a contract. There were justifiable or excusable mistakes, but they were measured against "generally accepted standards of the community." Not just any failure of the meeting of the minds would do. Thus the theory of contract moved toward absolute contractual liability. This was the theory, but, as Gilmore reminds us, absolute liability was only rarely found in practice. It was likewise with good faith, as courts often acknowledged a "pre-contractual duty to bargain in good faith."[99]

The impersonal free market model for contractual relations and the accumulation of American case law precedents for adjudicating contractual disputes helped American jurists to formulate a set of general principles to aid in their decisions during the first half of the nineteenth century. This foundation, in turn, made it possible for the treatise writers of the latter half of the nineteenth century to present contract law in a "scientific" manner. The work of Kent, Story, and Blackstone before them provided an impetus for a "scientific" study of the law, which, by the latter nineteenth century, had been incorporated in Langdell's scientific case study method for training young advocates.[100]

Prior to the Civil War, the free market model for contract law allowed courts to facilitate economic growth and market processes and permitted creative lawmaking.[101] At the same time, the attempt to reduce the vagaries of experience to a systematic set of rules tended to formalize contract law and to produce a doctrine of contract that protected the winners in the competitive market situation. If one were to express this in terms of economic class distinctions as Horwitz does, one would say that contract came "to serve the interests of the wealthy and the powerful." The law "had come simply to ratify those forms of inequality that the market system produced."[102]

The golden age of contract and a free market model had made the just or fair price doctrine a seeming anachronism. Yet the banishment of an objective theory of value from the realms of theory did not necessarily mean that courts were unsympathetic to fair dealings in individual cases. Friedman has remarked of the late nineteenth and early twentieth centuries that in matters of fraud, mistake, and misrepresentation courts followed tendencies not rules. It is not unlikely (and is well illustrated for illiterates) that throughout the nineteenth century courts allowed an eighteenth-century paternalistic mode of adjudication to protect the weak, ignorant, and illiterate when their cases reached adjudication.

By 1850 most economic actions were in some way subject to the law of contract. At the same time, however, the increasing number of statutes governing economic activity and the increasing complexities of business disputes themselves lessened the business of the courts in the matter of contract. Marginal and unusual cases occupied the courts' attention more and more between 1850 and 1900. Contract doctrine, having facilitated an expansive economy in the early nineteenth century, now became less important in supporting an expanding economy. Decisions involving contractual disputes tended to be particularized not generalized, the object in appealed cases being to interpret the unique circumstances or facts of a particular case.[103]

In several areas the laissez-faire, contract-oriented, market mentality was challenged by protective measures. Thus state legislators began to respond to issues of industrial accidents, factory safety, and consumer protection. Common law recognized the duty of an employer to pay for on-the-job injuries, but this depended on the "moral quality of will involved." The employer was liable if he were negligent in not providing safe working conditions. But an employee might also have assumed a risk and in that case could not recover damages. If an employee were negligent (contributory negligence) or were injured by the negligence of a fellow employee, then he might not recover damages. Statute law and common law were at odds in these domains. Thus the concept of a bargain struck between "equal" parties was used to challenge statutes designed to "even out" the bargaining position between buyer and seller and employer and employee. Between 1880 and the mid-1930s proposed regulatory statutes were struck down repeatedly by state courts. Thereafter the United States Supreme Court judicial review moved toward a "presumption of constitutionality" in "economic regulatory legislation."

Administrative commissions multiplied, also, especially in public utilities, insurance, banking, public health, and industrial safety.[104]

In the latter nineteenth century, courts became increasingly passive in the sense that they functioned more in a reviewing capacity and less as institutions that self-consciously devised doctrines to promote economic and social policies.[105] This did not mean that formalism had been abandoned. (It certainly was not if judged by treatise writers.) Rather, it meant that the creative work of the first half of the nineteenth century had been bureaucratized, that administrative machinery and statute law had subordinated the policy-making roles of judges, leaving them to focus upon the merits of particular cases.

Contracts and Illiterate Persons

In a social order in which contractual agreements prevail in economic life, it was likely that already existing inequalities were perpetuated when contracts were made between unequal parties. In some instances, the inequality was simply a matter of knowledge or ignorance of the law. In others, such as the case of the illiterate, inequality was based on a broader ignorance of the written word. Settlements at equity in some cases would be expected to compensate for illiteracy, but setting aside contracts, whether in law or equity, was a serious matter. It obviously affected the personal ambitions and economic welfare of the parties involved, but it also forced courts to consider the effects of such decisions on the assumed relationships between contract and social order.

The setting aside of contracts to which illiterate persons were party was particularly troublesome. Illiterate persons were not, by virtue of their illiteracy, incompetent in the legal sense as were lunatics, idiots, and drunkards. Nonetheless, mutual consent and an intelligent understanding of contractual terms were required if a valid contract were to exist.[106] To determine whether such consent and understanding were present was not an easy task, especially if the fairness of the contract were in question.

Competency and intelligence were not linked to literacy in any special way, and courts assumed that an illiterate person was, unless demonstrated otherwise, both competent and intelligent enough to enter into contractual obligations. This was true throughout the range of cases studied here. The court in *Nathaniel Atwood v. James Cobb* (1834) noted that many illiterate persons enter into contracts. These agreements create problems, the court admitted. Nonetheless, "in construing all instruments, and especially those which are formal, illiterate, hastily and unskillfully drawn," said the court, "the intent of the parties, if possible, is to be ascertained, without regard to technical rules; . . . the intent of the parties when thus ascertained, is to be the governing rule for carrying the contract into effect."[107] In the late-nineteenth-century case of *Willard v. Pinard* (1892), adjudged in the Supreme Court of Vermont, the court observed that "the defendant and his wife were unable to read or write, much more than to write their names." Yet, it was "not found that they were not possessed of ordinary faculties of mind, and ordinary memory and judgment in regard to property and its value." The court, moreover, did not seem surprised at the contractual arrangement by illiterates and noted that the "parties sustained to each other the ordinary relation existing between an educated, honest, businessman and an ordinarily bright and capable man, possessed of memory and judgment, but uneducated in knowledge of books, and the art of reading and writing, except to a limited extent."[108]

The Obligation to Read

The obligation to read or to have read a contract to which one is a party was explained by Blackstone and compiled in the *Commentaries*. Most American judges of the early nineteenth century probably began with Blackstone's formulation as their reference when faced with the problem of illiteracy and the understanding of contracts. For the literate person, the issue was quite straightforward. If the party to a contract had it within his power to understand the terms, but "reposed a blind confidence in representations not calculated to deceive a man of ordinary prudence and circumspection" then the "law affords no relief."[109]

The issue of "understanding" a contract was considerably more complicated for the illiterate than for the literate party. Verification of claims of ignorance without negligence are extremely subjective, and courts often operated in a gray area of evidence. Several nineteenth-century cases (*Francis Seldon v. Lawrence Myers, Philip Pike, Walter Lenox, and James C. McGuire* [1857], *Suffern and Galloway v. Butler and Butler* [1867], *Pennsylvania Railroad Co. v. Shay* [1876], *Charles Green v. John Maloney* [1884], *Chicago, St. P., M. and O. Ry. Co. v. Belliwith* [1897], and *Bates v. Harte* [1899]) illustrate this point well though all need not be discussed here.[110] The same difficulty was evident in cases of a third party for surety on a note. In *Craig v. Hobbs* (1873), for example, a note bearing the signature of the illiterate Hobbs but actually signed for him by one Grissom was held to be valid under the circumstances. The court concluded that Hobbs had placed his confidence, "blind confidence" though it might have been, in Grissom and that "the act of Grissom in signing it was the act of Hobbs, so far as the act of affixing the signature is concerned."[111]

Seldon v. Myers was heard by the U.S. Supreme Court with Chief Justice Taney presiding. In filing a bill to obtain an injunction staying the sale of his property (the court thus had equity jurisdiction), Seldon claimed that when he had executed the note and deed, he could neither read nor write and that he "did not know that the whole of said property was included, and was under the impression that it conveyed only a portion of it." In delivering the opinion, Taney noted that Myers and Company were under the obligation "to show, past doubt, that he [Seldon] fully understood the object and import of the writings upon which they are proceeding to charge him; and if they had failed to do so, the above-mentioned testimony offered by the appellant, as to the state of the accounts between them at the time, would have furnished strong grounds for inferring that he had been deceived, and had not understood the meaning of the written instruments he signed."[112] Clearly it was incumbent upon the literate party to make certain that the illiterate person understood the terms of the agreement. Testimony offered by a witness present at the negotiations supported Myers and Company and could not be refuted by other witnesses called in Seldon's behalf. The court had little faith in the "recollections" of other witnesses or in Seldon's memory. Interestingly, and in contrast to the assumption of the illiterate person's well-developed memory *In the Matter of Cross* (1895), the court noted that Seldon's inability to read and keep accounts would most likely result in a "confused recollection of these conversations and might, without any evil intention, confound what had been said in relation to dealings subsequent to the note with conversations which passed at the time it was executed."[113]

In dealing with illiterate parties to a contract, what courts generally required was a fair reading of the written instrument. This would normally be a complete reading, but, at the least, it would include all the critical parts of the agreement. Reading the written instrument correctly was as material to its validity as was signing the agreement.[114] If an illiterate party did not demand a reading of a written instrument, he was guilty of negligence. Neither law nor equity protected the negligent person.[115] The obligation to locate a reliable person to read and explain a contract was one that lay with the illiterate party. By the late nineteenth century this principle is noticeably more forceful in decisions of the courts. Parol evidence was not admissible to invalidate a written contract, and, regardless of what an oral agreement might have been, the written contract was sacred unless fraud was perpetrated on one of the parties. A similar attempt to protect the written contract is evident in the principle of negligence.

What courts wished to avoid was the use of negligent ignorance as an excuse to invalidate a contract. It was unnecessary to prove that an illiterate party actually understood the contract before signing or marking. Understanding was presumed. The reasoning was clearly put forth in *Green v. Maloney* (1884):

> It is of course not necessary, in such case of reading or explanation, to show that the illiterate did understand its contents and their nature; if, after a paper has been read or explained to him, he sign it, making no objection to it, nor request any explanation of it, he must, in all reason, be taken to have known what he was signing. And, in the absence of proof to the contrary, a paper read to a party and which he signed, is to be presumed to have been understood by him, and he will not be allowed to aver against it, unless he can show to the satisfaction of a court and jury that the paper was falsely and fraudulently read or explained, with intent to deceive and obtain the advantage of him.[116]

Both the parol evidence rule and the principle of negligent ignorance showed no diminution in early-twentieth-century cases. If anything, courts tended to state them with greater confidence and with greater explicit recognition that their observance was crucial to sound commercial dealings.[117]

Relief in Equity

It has been observed previously that the will theory of contract had generally superseded the theory of equitable limitations on contractual obligations that was characteristic of eighteenth-century contract law. Despite this shift in thinking about contract, the idea of a "fair exchange" still had its proponents. Not all courts were willing to accede to the rigors and punctilious demands of formalism, nor the austere will theory of contract. Relief from the rigors of common law was frequently found in equity. The early-nineteenth-century case of *Thomas Butler, William Butler, James Butler and the Hiers of Charles Butler v. E. Haskell* (1816) heard in South Carolina, a state noted for the persistence of equitable doctrines, has already been cited, but a more thorough consideration will be given here because it illustrates so well the application of equity solutions to contractual disputes.

In *Butler v. Haskell* the stage was set for a classic encounter between poverty and wealth. The complainants (appellants) were the alleged "ignorant and necessitous men, in an humble condition of life" facing the defendant, "an intelligent man, of great skill in the management of business, and of high standing and influence in society." Illiteracy, ignor-

ance, and financial ineptitude characterized the complainants though
no claim nor pretense to idiocy was made. Wealth, learning, and business acumen characterized the defendant, who had been employed by
the complainants to help resolve claims made upon the estate of one
Miss Margaret Butler.[118]

The suit in *Butler v. Haskell* was brought on the charge that the defendant had used his "superior judgment and skill" to obtain property from
the complainants at a "very inadequate price"; that the defendant, having been in the confidence of the complainants and obtained important
information, then took advantage of their "ignorance and distress":

> the defendant being the agent of the Butlers, possessed of all their informa-
> tion and papers, had opportunities of making discoveries relative to their
> prospects of establishing the rights of the complainants; and that availing
> himself of this knowledge, and of their entire confidence in him, and profiting
> by their necessities, he made purchases from them of their rights at most in-
> adequate prices.[119]

Witnesses were present for the signing of deeds, and there was no
claim of irregularity in their execution. No witnesses, however, were present for the "discussions and representations" that led to the signing of
the papers, and this was a decisive point in the court's verdict. "The rule
is quite clear," said the court, "that in all cases of this kind, where a great
advantage is gained in a contract by an agent from his principal, the
proof lies on him to show that the transactions were perfectly fair and
pure." To the objection by defendant that the signatures of some of the
brothers to the deeds were evidence of fairness, the court answered that
had the men "been intelligent or judicious men, this evidence would
have had great weight; but they were generally illiterate, and they were
all discouraged and hopeless; and their judgment upon the subject before them does not seem to be entitled to the high consideration attempted to be given to it."[120]

Inadequacy of price, as the court noted, was not, independently,
grounds for vitiating contracts. Yet inadequacy might be "so gross" as to
imply presumptive fraud, and under these conditions a sale might be
nullified. In recounting precedents for the case at hand, the court cited
Chesterfield v. Janssen for its position that fraud might be presumed
from the "circumstances and condition of the parties" and the "intrinsic
unconscionableness of the bargain." Though it avoided the language of
consent so evident in many nineteenth-century cases, what the court
was saying, in effect, was that consent is absent in cases of gross inadequacy of price. When advantage is taken of weakness, necessity, and ignorance, the rights of the contracting party are violated. The great principle

of equity that disallows bargains of "an enormous and unconscientious disproportion" is "the safeguard of society," said the court. "It is proper," the court continued, "that there should be perfect accordance between the principles of the contracts of the citizen, and the great principles of constitutional liberty which they enjoy. The former should be as pure as the latter are liberal and extensive." With the moral rhetoric typical of the period, the court observed that "the only solid foundation for the liberty of the country is the virtue of the citizen."[121]

The issue in *Butler v. Haskell* was adequacy of price. Two later cases also show that equity proceedings could deal with specific performance and reformation of contract. *Swint v. Carr* (1885) was heard before the Supreme Court of Georgia, where the complainant asked for specific performance on indebtedness secured by a deed. The defendant was an illiterate man who "took what he believed to be notes for the correct amount of the indebtedness to him."[122] In 1882 the complainant claimed that the notes were no longer valid because of the statute of limitations. He then threatened to prosecute the son of the defendant for illegally removing and storing brandy unless the defendant agreed to a new note. The defendant agreed to take the new note at less interest. It was claimed that the new note was freely accepted.

The court considered only the issue of specific performance on an "illegal, fraudulent and unconscionable agreement" that reduced the larger debt due to the defendant. It ruled that the new note was "extorted from the defendant's fears," that "being an ignorant and illiterate man, he was otherwise overreached and duped." Quoting Judge Story, the court said that in a court of equity no specific performance is required on a "fraudulent, illegal or 'hard and unconscionable' bargain."[123]

In *Kinney, et al. v. Ensmenger* (1889) the issue formed over a bill to reform a deed. The case was heard on appeal from the chancellor to the Supreme Court of Alabama. In hearing the case, the court concluded that there was no issue of culpable negligence involved. Thus it was willing to consider relief though it warned that great caution must be exercised so as not to "unduly encourage the want of ordinary prudence on the part of persons signing important papers."[124] It was careful to acknowledge the duty to read. It found, however, that both the complainant's "illiteracy and inability to understand the English language" and his misplaced trust in an agent who negotiated for him were sufficient to acquit him of culpable negligence and thus to seek remedy in a court of equity.[125]

The Question of Fraud

The principle of negligent ignorance was easily applied when no question of fraud existed. When, however, fraud or misrepresentation was thought to be a possibility, the issue was not so clear. The presumption of fraud was not easily made, and its presence was usually to be clearly established by proof. In his treatise *Contracts Not Under Seal* (1844), however, Story, observed that even though "fraud must be clearly established by proof" it is not "necessary, that positive and express proof [of fraud] . . . should be given; for whenever it is manifestly indicated by the circumstances and condition of the parties contracting, it will be presumed to exist. But it will not be implied from doubtful circumstances, which only awaken suspicion."[126]

Although fraud in a written instrument might be more observable than in an oral agreement, the difficulty was often the same because oral interpretations were so crucial to the illiterate person. The case of *Walker v. Ebert* (1871) delineated the issue of fraud in terms of a will theory of contract. When a contract is falsely read to an illiterate person, "the mind of the signer [does] not accompany the signature," said the court.[127]

The defendant in *Walker v. Ebert* was a German by birth, unable to read or write the English language. Ebert had entered into an agreement to be the sole agent for a "certain patented machine" and was to receive a percentage of all the profits on his sales. He had signed what he thought to be a contract, orally agreed upon. The instrument bearing his signature was, in fact, a promissory note. The action before the court was on a promissory note by the holder, who claimed to have purchased it for full value, before maturity. A lower court had ruled that the testimony by the defendant was not admissible, and the defendant had challenged this decision. In ruling upon the admissibility of evidence, the court applied a basic rule of intent governing the validity of an illiterate's mark to a contract:

> It seems plain on principle and on authority, that if a blind man, or a man who cannot read, or for some reason (not implying negligence), forebears to read, has a written contract falsely read over to him, the reader misreading to such a degree that the written contract is of a nature altogether different from contract pretended to be read from the paper, which the blind or illiterate man afterwards signs, then, at least, if there be no negligence, the signature so obtained is of no force; and it is invalid, not merely on the ground of fraud, where fraud exists, but on the ground that the mind of the signer did not accompany the signature; in other words, that he never intended to sign, and therefore, in contemplation of law, never did sign the contract to which his name is appended.[128]

The signature, noted the court, was no better than a "total forgery," and the defendant clearly had not intended "to endorse a bill of exchange."[129] This was fraud in the factum, a trick or artifice having been perpetrated on the illiterate victim. Obviously no meeting of the minds had taken place in a general sense, although the immediate issue was one of a deliberate misrepresentation. Ebert, the court concluded, was deceived as to both the "legal effect" of the instrument and its "actual contents."[130]

It was a common situation for the illiterate party to a contract to claim that, in fact, two contracts existed—one oral, one written. The written contract, as we have seen, was not defeated by parol evidence. This rule, however, said the court in *Sigfroid Trambly v. Hubert Ricard, and another* (1880), did "not exclude evidence which tends to show that the written contract was by some fraud or imposition never in fact freely and intelligently signed by the party sought to be charged."[131]

The case of *Trambly v. Ricard* involved what was probably a common occurrence in settling a home: the purchase of furniture. The plaintiff in this instance had purchased furniture on credit and contended that, by oral agreement, he had agreed upon a price, part of which was paid down, the rest to be paid by installments. The agreement was then committed to writing. The plaintiff testified that the written agreement was not that agreed upon orally and that the written agreement had been obtained by fraud. Nothing, said the plaintiff, had been said of borrowing or renting the furniture. Later, when the defendants came to remove the furniture from the premises, suit was brought for trespass to real estate. In delivering the opinion of the court (which had only to decide whether or not a jury might find fraud in this case) it was noted that the illiteracy of the plaintiff was of "controlling importance." Citing *Walker v. Ebert,* it noted that the literate party was "bound to show that he [the illiterate party] fully understood the object and import of the writings sought to be enforced against him": "A party who is ignorant of the contents of a written instrument, from inability to read, who signs it without intending to, and who is chargeable with no negligence in not ascertaining the character of it, is no more bound than if it were a forgery."[132]

The issues of consent, negligence, and fraud were closely related, and the resolution of each was always determined within a particular context. The point was well made in *National Exchange Bank v. Veneman* (1887), a case heard in the Supreme Court of the State of New York. The situation was one in which an illiterate German farmer signed what he believed to be a contract but which turned out to be a promissory note. Negligence was one of the issues to be resolved by the court. Because Veneman could not read the instrument and feared it might be a promissory note, he had asked the agent negotiating the supposed contract for assurances that it was nothing but a contract. Veneman had also asked his wife to read the instrument, but "she informed him that she was unable to read it, and did not understand its meaning." There was, however, a boy tending the horse nearby. As it turned out, the boy was literate but had not been asked to read the instrument. Thus, although it was clear that the agent had perpetrated a fraud, the issue of negligence still arose.[133]

In delivering its opinion, the court focused on the context of the negotiation. "It cannot be said," the court observed, "that it was negligence *per se* not to seek his neighbors and learn from them the contents of the writing." Noting that the content of the instrument was not particularly complicated and could be easily expressed by a literate person, the court reminded the parties that "the nature and character of the paper intended to be executed must always be considered in determining the question of the defendant's negligence, so far as it is based on the omission to inquire of others for the purpose of ascertaining from them the contents of the writing."[134] The argument was buttressed by the following example:

> If a farmer who could not read, should sell and deliver to a mill a load of grain and receive pay therefor, and should then be requested to sign a voucher in the miller's counting room, and should sign a paper prepared for that purpose and it turned out to be a negotiable instrument, could it be said that the farmer was guilty of negligence, as a matter of law, because he did not seek some third person for the purpose of ascertaining the import of the writing?

The question was rhetorical, and the court acknowledged that although there were some differences between the example and the case before it, it nonetheless illustrated that "the question of negligence is not always one of law and often becomes a question of fact for the consideration of a jury."[135]

Conclusion

The utility of the written instrument to assure contractual stability was an assumption deeply embedded in nineteenth-century contract law and carried forward to the twentieth century. The written contract itself helped to achieve stability in contractual agreements, and it was a matter of the highest priority to protect the integrity of written instruments. A written contract, said Justice Sanborn in *Chicago St. P., M. and O. Ry. Co. v. Belliwith* (1897), "is the highest evidence of the terms of an agreement between the parties to it . . ." and the contracting party "owes it to the public, which, as a matter of public policy, treats the written contract as a conclusive answer to the question, what was the agreement?"[136] To allow avoidance of contractual obligations by the plea that the contract had not been read nor understood, or to deny that a written contract expresses an agreement made, would be to destroy the foundation for achieving stability in business and commercial dealings. To plead ignorance of the stipulations of a contract in the absence of fraud "would absolutely destroy the value of all contracts," said the court in *Burns v. Spiker, et al.* (1921). Five years later in *Austin v. Brooklyn Cooperage Co.* (1926) the court, citing *Crim v. Crim,* reminded the plaintiff that "the written contract is conclusively presumed to merge all prior negotiations and to express the final agreement of the parties." To ignore this rule would undermine the "stability" of written agreements and "would absolutely destroy the value of all contracts and negotiable instruments."[137]

The written word was associated with reliability and durability. The idea of permanence went hand in hand with the written document. Insofar as a document itself was employed to convey a right or interest in property, it helped to protect these rights and interests. Certainly a gap between a person's intent and the meaning expressed in a written instrument could be expected to persist, and, in this sense, some ambiguity was characteristic of the written word as it was of the oral. Still, the sense of a document was based upon the construction of the words in a document. The standardization of common written instruments such as deeds, wills, mortgages, and two-party contracts helped to reduce ambiguity in the written message. One of the purposes of contracts was to minimize the risks of economic gain, and the standardized, written contract reduced those risks even further. As expanded commercial activity invited risk taking, new forms of agreements emerged to protect the venturesome entrepreneur.

The idea of contract as it developed from the sixteenth through the nineteenth centuries had both moral and legal dimensions. Contractual obligations were moral obligations in the sense that agreements to which free consent had been given were to be honored. In the settling of contractual disputes in equity, conscience and a sense of justice were to prevail. Even with the shift away from equity in the nineteenth century, a fairness doctrine was still in force when dealing with contractual disputes involving weaker parties.

The impact of natural law theory on the principles of contract was evident after the eighteenth century. Performance of promises was a principle of natural law, and consent based upon an intelligent evaluation of an agreement was not to be dishonored by a refusal to carry out the provisions of the agreement. The constitutional theory of Chief Justice Marshall, resting as it did, in part, upon the principles of natural law, recognized that the obligation of contract derived from the free choice of the parties, not from government. Remedies for breach of contract might be founded on government decree, but the making of a contract resulted from free consent. Though not derived from natural law theory, the prin-

ciples of offer and acceptance and consideration were amenable to a natural law interpretation. All, in effect, became ways of validating "intent," of determining whether a "meeting of the minds" had occurred.

Many of the problems of "intent" in contract were evidentiary in nature. Thus, the commission of fraud or misrepresentation was a matter
of ascertaining what evidence ought to prevail in a particular context or
with a particular document. It was assumed that the contract itself was
a stable form in which the "meeting of minds" was embodied. Yet, contracts were just as clearly agreements representing self-interest and the
desire to get the best of a bargain. The application of the principle of
literalism was often the only way to determine the intent of the parties.
Both the commonsense meaning of a disputed instrument and its structure were thus guides to the intent of the parties. It was but a short step
to saying that written expression was not simply symbolic of intent, but,
in fact, was the intent (as will) of the parties to a contract. It is difficult to
know whether this metaphysic of law was ever more than the abstraction of treatise writers. In practice, literalism was modified by the doctrine of fairness.

As offer, acceptance, and consideration came to be the validating
criteria for contract, the tension between literalism and fairness also became greater. Some of this may be attributed to technical difficulties in
assessing a person's intent in a contractual arrangement, but a more
basic difficulty resulted from differing estimates of the degree to which
persons were free and rational in their behaviors. The free, rational, self-
reliant person was the cornerstone of utilitarian atomism in which the
individual negotiated and assented to contractual arrangements in his
own best interest. The written accord was then taken to be the final expression of the individual's will, purpose, or intent. From this, there
could be no appeal, barring fraud or misrepresentation. On the other
hand, there was the question of fairness, of equity. Literalness in contract could be powerfully instrumental in confirming an unfair bargain,
and, in the case of the illiterate person, the questions of accuracy in interpretation and expectations had to be raised. How free and self-reliant
could the illiterate person be? Time and again, judgments had to be
made upon subjective consideration of this question.

The extenuating circumstance of illiteracy in a contractual agreement did not alter the general postulate that obligations had to be met
and contracts fulfilled. Natural law theory, with its roots in Christian
axiology, had long taught the moral obligation to perform a promise. Obligation to perform, too, had a utilitarian justification in the good order
and welfare of society. Arguments for both moral order and social order
were often brought to the defense of contract. Just as readily, however,
contract could be defended in terms of flexibility. This had been true in

Great Britain, where the theory of simple contract had developed, in contradistinction to a theory of property, as a response to the demand for ease and flexibility in commercial transactions. In the United States in the nineteenth century, economic growth and opportunities for profit easily justified business arrangements that would maximize mobility, freedom of decision, and economic self-improvement. Negotiation of a contract was often perceived as a process of attempting to win the race for pecuniary gain, the obstruction of which seemed contrary to the Protestant ethic itself.

The modification of common-law practice in its transmigration to colonial America probably aided the semiliterate person. Simplified conveyancing procedures and the general rejection of common-law forms (not substance) in the name of democracy helped to simplify property transactions as well as court proceedings. The gradual merging of common law and equity proceedings, also, probably made it easier for the illiterate person to gain recompense when the claim of mistake was made. Yet the respite from form and literalism was short-lived. By mid-nineteenth century, formalism and literalism had been reasserted, and questions of intent, assent, and expectations for the illiterate person were raised anew. What was the relative accuracy of the expectations of the illiterate compared to the literate person? How free and how fair was the negotiating process for the illiterate? These questions received no absolute answers; rather, their determination was usually a product of special circumstances surrounding a case.

Though it certainly implied a lack of education, illiteracy did not, in the eyes of the courts, usually imply a lack of intelligence or competence. Thus it was the presumption of courts that, in the absence of evidence to the contrary, illiterate persons ought to have the same responsibilities and freedoms in the matter of contract as literate persons. The right to contract had been buttressed by constitutional decisions. Assumptions about the free will of the individual and the natural law tradition, though they proceeded from different premises, both asserted the obligation to honor contracts. None of these assumptions, however, could resolve the problem of fairness. Mutual understanding was an essential element in the contractual ideal around which the forms of contract could be built. In practice, form might overrule suppositions about mutual understanding, but it would not eliminate that understanding as an essential part of the contractual ideal. Nor could proper form eliminate considerations of fairness.

As a general rule it was presumed that a free, intelligent person would act in his/her own best interest. When grossly unfair bargains were made, therefore, it seemed appropriate to search for a cause. In the case of the illiterate person, that cause was readily apparent. With the knowledge that fraud, deception, and misrepresentation were more easily practiced on the illiterate person, a doctrine of fairness made good sense in gauging the adequacy or inadequacy of price. The signing of a contract still implied understanding and assent, and negligence was not an excuse for invalidating a contract. Yet, in the name of equitable dealing for illiterates, courts were compelled to strike a balance between form and literalism on the one hand and fairness on the other. The balance was not always precise as economic expansion and concerns with individual justice competed for the attention of the courts and the loyalty of judges.

Contracts in the Twentieth Century

In his *Law and the Conditions of Freedom in the Nineteenth-Century United States* Hurst observes that nineteenth-century United States was characterized by a "release-of-energy principle" expressed "chiefly through contract." Contract, however, was "inherently too limited an institution" to serve the need of competing interests and the balance of power within a community, says Hurst. The very strength of contract— its focus on the initiative of bargaining parties—was its limitation as an organizing principle for social action. Yet these observations are more accurate for "freedom of contract" than for the contractual ideal in general. Freedom of contract unquestionably served private interests. It was this particular interpretation of contract that no doubt led courts to reserve the power to "refuse enforcement to contracts which they found to offend public policy" and to use a community standard when judging whether or not certain suspicious contracts should be enforced.[138]

The larger concentrations of money and power that began to characterize the twentieth century undermined the assumptions of a free market. Increasingly, bureaucratic structures and specialized technical knowledge restricted the flow and the intelligibility of information. Tighter controls were the trademark of institutions that relied more and more on specialization of labor and knowledge. Interdependence, planning, and cooperative enterprise gradually replaced unobstructed individual initiative as an institutional priority. Gradually contract law became less important than in former decades, when the pattern for contracting was single dealing:

> As markets enlarged their reach and became more and more interlocked, more and more people became subject to the impact of inflation and deflation, unemployment, and disturbance of credit. In proportion to their elaboration,

market processes made greater numbers of individuals vulnerable to basic unsettlment of their life expectations and hence made society more vulnerable to widespread unrest and loss of morale. Particularly from the mid-1930's on, the legal order showed a broadening range of responses to such market-borne vulnerability—by providing unemployment insurance, by fiscal and monetary policy designed (however imperfectly) to moderate swings of the business cycle, by insurance of bank deposits, and by enlarged welfare services.[139]

It was quite clear that no absolute freedom of contract existed. Justice Hughes in *Chicago, Burlington and Quincy Railroad Company v. Charles L. McGuire* (1911) had observed within the context of legislative action:

> freedom of contract is a qualified, and not an absolute, right. There is no absolute freedom to do as one wills or to contract as one chooses. The guaranty of liberty does not withdraw from legislative supervision that wide department of activity which consists of the making of contracts or deny to government the power to provide restrictive safeguards. Liberty implies the absence of arbitrary restraint, not immunity from reasonable regulations and prohibitions imposed in the interests of the community.[140]

Still freedom of contract and free market principles were not easily swept aside.

In 1923 the Supreme Court announced in *Adkins v. Children's Hospital:* "Freedom of contract is the rule and restraint the exception." Market autonomy was still recognized, but reined in. The change, observes Hurst, meant that "market autonomy was not henceforth a preferred value; statutes regulating dealings in the market would be upheld as long as the Court could find that reasonable legislators could believe that a given regulation would serve public interest by means reasonably adapted to the end."[141]

Freedom of contract by the early twentieth century had become an ideology, a weapon that could be used to protect group interests from governmental interference. It had, says Friedman, become an "arsenal of afterthoughts" available to litigants but "usable primarily as judicial techniques rather than as expressions of norms of behavior. . . ." By the midtwentieth century, particular suits were settled more and more by invoking justice, common sense, and public policy to complement precedent and established doctrine. By the midtwentieth century particularly, many disputes in contract (a major exception being family transactions) were dealt with through arbitration or settlements that simply had the effect of cutting one's losses to preserve stability and reputation.[142] Contract law, however, retained its identification with free enterprise and market-oriented decisions. This was so despite the fact that its domain had shrunk as legal specialities arose parallel to the division of society's labor.[143] The fair or equitable result under the specific circumstances of the case became, increasingly, the concern of the court. The formalism and literalness of an earlier period receded; in their place, not as a substitute but as a highlight, came practicality and a higher regard "for what parties did, and how they acted, rather than what their documents or agreements said."[144]

It would be too strong a statement to say that this tendency signaled a reappearance of natural law doctrine as such. It was not a matter of dredging up doctrinal support. Rather, it was a reemergence of a protective, paternalistic attitude toward those who, through ignorance, fared poorly in a contractual agreement. As the decision in *Wood v. Lucy, Lady Duff Gordon* (1917) would have it: "The law has outgrown its primitive stage of formalism when the precise word was the sovereign talisman, and every slip was fatal."[145] The tradition of paternalism in equity and the free market model for contract were competing for dominance in theory but complementing one another in individual cases. The result was a heightening of concern, expressed in terms of fairness, with the moral foundations of contract.

The development of mass markets, standardized contracts, and specialities in law no doubt diminished the importance of *general* contract *theory* and altered the structure of liability. Freedom of contract in the nineteenth-century sense no longer was viable as a concept to explain or represent commercial dealings. We should not interpret this to mean, however, that the principle of contract was brushed aside as a means of ordering agreements and the exchange of property.

Courts continued to be concerned with the relationship between the duty to read, negligence, and fraud. The written contract was still a fundamental expression of agreement, and release from liability was not the inevitable consquence of ignorance or failure to read.[146] Occasionally a court also found it necessary to probe more deeply into the conceptual difficulties of fraud, negligence, and contract. In *Bancredit, Inc. v. Lynn Bethea and Tony Bethea* (1961), for example, the appellate division of the Superior Court of New Jersey dealt with alleged fraud involving a promissory note. This case did not involve an illiterate person. The issue before the court, however, was that often found with illiterate persons. The opinion included lengthy discussion of fraud in the factum. The opinion first noted that the heart of the issue was the "absence of that degree of mutual assent prerequisite to formation of a binding contract"; the absence of the "proverbial 'meeting of the minds.' " The court observed that these ingredients were part of "basic contract doctrine."[147]

As part of its developing argument, the court reasserted the warning that a person entering into contract must be "reasonably prudent" "to determine the character of the paper upon which he has purposefully placed his signature." This was required to preserve the "general confidence in commercial paper" and to protect innocent persons from wrongful acts of a third party.[148] The court then pointed out that to judge upon a defense of fraud in the factum an inquiry was necessary into the "precise manner and mode in which the maker was deceived." This, in turn, required an "illumination of his actual knowledge at the time of signing."[149] The latter, of course, was also basic to determining whether negligence were present. But the "elements of knowledge and negligence cannot feasibly be isolated in determining the viability of the defense of *non est factum* under a given set of circumstances," said the court. [150] Illiteracy, among other disabilities, might have been cause for believing that fraud had occurred. In this case, however, the defendent was literate and it appeared that freedom from negligence was not established. Thus liability on the note remained.

Illiterate Persons and Contract

Historically, courts had refused to equate incompetency and a lack of intelligence with illiteracy. Nor did they necessarily identify education with competency and literacy. Thus, the allegation (or defense) that one was uneducated did not imply that one was illiterate or incapable of understanding a written instrument. In *Baker v. Patton* (1915), for example, the court noted that there was "a wide difference between an allegation that one is illiterate and an allegation to the effect that he is "'an uneducated man.'" The court continued:

> As all of us know, a very large percentage of successful businessmen who every day enter into important contracts are uneducated men; and a mere allegation that petitioner was an uneducated man, in a petition like that which we have under consideration, falls far short of an allegation that he is illiterate, and it is unnecessary to quote definitions given by the lexicographers to show this.[151]

In making many of the assumptions and distinctions about the relationships among illiteracy, competency, intelligence, and education, courts were helping to buttress a defense against what they perceived to be a threat to the stability of the written contract. The contractual foundations of social stability and economic success had been clearly explicated by political theorists of the eighteenth century, and these became part of the working knowledge of the courts by the opening of the nineteenth century. Parties in *Furst and Thomas v. A. D. Merritt, et al.*

(1925) were reminded that "successful enterprise and the advancement of individual and national wealth and prosperity" depended upon the "integrity of men" conducting "transactions of business, trade and commerce. . . ."[152]

Courts were not of one mind on the limits of duty to read. Historically some had insisted that in cases in which ability to read was impaired, it was the duty of the party to have a document read to him (her). This was ordinarily considered prudent. It should be remembered also that appeal cases involving fraud, misrepresentation, and possible negligence were often heard in equity, where greater flexibility was present.

The early-twentieth-century case of *Grimsley v. Singletary* (1909) shows a very flexible attitude toward the illiterate person. This case involved an illiterate black woman named Caroline who had unknowingly signed a deed to convey her land. Caroline's husband was also illiterate. She apparently made no attempt to have what she thought was a note read to her. In giving its opinion, the court acknowledged the duty to read but did not find that the failure to have someone else read it implied negligence. In fact the document had been read by the other party to the conveyance. In cases involving illiteracy, it was reasonable to "rely upon the representation of the other party as to what the instrument is or as to what it contains."[153]

Misrepresentation of an instrument and the actual, physical substitution of one instrument for another continued to be common occurrences for illiterate persons. *First National Bank of Watonga, et al. v. Wade, et al.* (1910) is a good case in point. This case, heard on appeal to the Supreme Court of Oklahoma, involved an "aged, infirm negress, of poor eyesight and hearing, entirely unable to either read or write." This situation (a scam) was particularly insidious because two attorneys, one black and one white, had called upon Mary Wade in August 1905. They told her that they had been appointed by the governor "to prepare the last will and testament of all old colored people." After they had helped Wade draft her last will and testament and read it to her in front of a witness, they asked for a drink of water. The young girl who had witnessed the reading went to the pump for water and Wade stepped out of the room. The attorneys then switched notes and mortgages for the will. A notary was called for the signature. He asked Wade whether she acknowledged the papers, but the notary did not read them to her. The court ruled that Wade had taken every precaution and was not guilty of negligence. There was obvious misrepresentation. Interestingly, the court cited approvingly a statement from *Green v. Wilkee*, an Iowa case, that the "note never had an existence in the sense of the minds of the parties meeting to give it validity."[154]

Courts, as we have seen, were often faced with the problem of deciding under what conditions the principle of duty to read would take precedence over other possible, but conflicting principles. Fraud and misrepresentation were obvious circumstances under which contracts were unenforceable. Lack of knowledge and good business sense were usually not considered prohibitive of carrying out a contract. Oral agreements made prior to written ones also carried little weight. Thus in *Katirina Wilkisius and another v. Elizabeth Sheehan and others* (1926) the court's ruling was unfavorable to the illiterate person largely because of the primacy of the written contract.

The issue in *Wilkisius v. Sheehan* was one of an oral agreement said to be at odds with a written one. The plaintiffs, a husband and wife who were Lithuanians and unable to read or write English, asked that a six thousand dollar note and a mortgage to secure it be cancelled on the grounds that the written agreement was not in accord with a previous oral agreement. Their signatures, said the plaintiffs, had been obtained "by false and fraudulent representations of the defendants. . . ." The court, as it turned out, refused to cancel the agreement and cited the precedent of *Atlas Shoe Co. v. Bloom* in which the defense of "limited intelligence" and "inability to read" was defeated: "mere ignorance of the contents of an instrument which a party voluntarily executes is not sufficient ground for setting it aside if ultimately the paper is found to be different from what [it is] supposed . . . to be."[155]

The principle of duty to read was a crucial one in the two cases cited later. *Ford v. National Life and Accident Insurance Co.* (1945) was heard before the Supreme Court of Tennessee. It was not a case, however, to "reform a contract, on the ground of mutual mistake or other equitable grounds." No charge of fraud was made, except in the sense that the agent of the insurance company sought to bind the company, "with the knowledge of the insured, to a contractual liability which he knew was beyond his authority. . . ." The factual issue was one of misrepresenting the condition of the insured's health. The court made it clear that illiterary "creates no presumption" of ignorance "of the contents of the contract." The plaintiff Ford relied upon the agent's statements about the policy's protection, but, said the court, "it was his duty to read the policy and to discover the application which had been copied into and made a part of the policy contract." It concluded that the company was not bound by the policy.[156]

Robertson v. Panlos, et al. (1951) presented a different set of circumstances and did not involve the kind of standard contract found in insurance. As was often the case, it was claimed that the signed instrument was not properly identified. The plaintiffs in this case were Hungarian and "unable to read English." This case rested on a demurrer. The allegation of fraud was not well substantiated and rested simply on the assertion that the papers were signed "without reading it to her, causing it to be read to her, or making known the contents to her." The defendent Ida Mae Echols was unable to read English and did not know of a provision in the contract to sell one property (her home) to reduce the loan on another piece of property.[157]

In *Robertson v. Panlos, et al.* the court acknowledged that inability to read English could be a factor in determining whether or not fraud had taken place. In and of itself, however, inability to read English "is not itself sufficient to authorize the recisson of a contract." The court concluded that she had willingly signed the papers and was diligent in "ascertaining the nature of the contract she was signing." Thus equity could not provide relief to the consequences of the signing.[158]

It has been mentioned that fraud was the most common allegation in proceedings involving illiterate persons seeking relief in the courts. Issues of fraud were not substantially different in the twentieth century from those in the nineteenth. It was a basic principle that fraud was never presumed and "must be affirmatively alleged and proved by the party who relies upon it for the purpose of either attack or defense."[159] A sequence of cases will illustrate the reasoning of the courts in matters of fraud.

Barnett v. Gross (1923) was heard in the Supreme Court of Oklahoma. The defendant, a Creek Indian unable to read English, was inexperienced in business matters. The issue arose over a one-year contract for twelve hundred dollars in which the plaintiff agreed to handle all legal matters for the defendant. The court dismissed the argument that claimed inexperience and the superior intelligence of the plaintiff. The contract contained two provisions that allowed for approval by the "Indian Department" and for using restricted moneys held in trust by the Indian Department. Barnett alleged that an oral agreement that included the two provisions had been made, but that the written contract omitted these. The written contract was not that agreed upon orally and was misrepresented to the defendant. Thus she was not bound by it. The ruling of the court did not actually rest on the question of parol proof versus the written contract. Rather the key issue was misrepresentation, and the court recommended reversal and further proceedings.[160]

Furst and Thomas v. A. D. Merritt, et al. (1925) was a considerably more complex case than the previous, since it involved not only the two parties to the original contract but an innocent third party as surety. Both fraud in the factum and fraud in the treaty were claimed on the part of one J. A. Fowler, an illiterate guarantor of a contract worth $604.87. The particular circumstances of Fowler's signing as guarantor of A. D. Merritt's debts will not be recounted here, but, as the court recognized, there was "sharp conflict in the evidence as to the representations and circumstances under which J. A. Fowler's name was affixed to said instrument.[161]

The opinion of the court in *Furst v. Merritt* included a rather substantial review of the rules governing fraud in contracts. Most of this was devoted to the distinction between fraud in the factum and fraud in the treaty. Of the many precedents cited in the court's review those dealing with the social foundations of contract are most important for our purposes. The "very foundation of all commercial dealings and the integrity of contracts," said the court, demands adherence to the principle that it is the positive duty of the contracting party to have read the instrument or had it read to him. The "failure to do so, in the absence of any mistake, fraud or oppression, is a circumstance against which no relief may be had, either at law or in equity."[162] Reasonable diligence and care were to be exercised in the making of contracts, noted the court; this principle, however, was not to be used as an excuse by those attempting fraud. In other words, a party committing fraud could not claim that the victim was negligent and careless; that, had diligence and care been used by the victim, he would have discovered the fraud.

The determination of fraud was a highly subjective matter and depended in each case upon the "relative situation of the parties and their means of information." Where misrepresentation is obvious and a party to a contract accepts the terms "with his eyes open[,] he has no right to complain." Likewise, when the "parties have equal means of information, the rule of *caveat emptor* applies. . . ." When a "false representation is a mere expression of commendation, or is simply a matter of opinion, the parties stand upon equal footing, and the courts will not interfere to correct errors of judgment."[163] Knowing that fear might lead to cynicism and a degree of caution that would make contractual activity extremely difficult, the court cited the following practical advice to those engaged in business transactions of a contractual nature:

> The law does not require a prudent man to deal with everyone as a rascal and demand covenants to guard against the falsehood of every representation which may be made as to facts which constitute material inducements to a contract. There must be a reasonable reliance upon the integrity of men or the transactions of business, trade and commerce could not be conducted with that facility and confidence which are essential to successful enterprise and the advancement of individual and national wealth and prosperity.[164]

The final case involving alleged fraud is that of *Liddell et ux. v. Lee* (1942) heard in the Supreme Court of Missouri. This was a suit involving a husband and wife, the former who could not read and write and the latter who could read and write "just a little." They did business with Lee

Gin Company, and Lee had financed them, expecting payments from the marketing of their cotton crop. To pay their debts to Lee, the Liddells secured promissory notes with the deed to their land. After two years, the Liddells made an agreement with another gin owner to pay their debt to Lee and asked Lee for an itemized bill. Lee refused and told the Liddells he didn't want Brown to pay off anything. Lee told the Liddells that he could no longer "carry" them and would require the deed to their land. Testimony from the plaintiff and defendant differed considerably over the process of the agreement, but it was clear that the signing of the deed was not witnessed even though witnesses' names were part of the record.[165]

When the court made its decision it pointed out that Lee knew the Liddells were ignorant, illiterate, and easily deceived. It was evident also that the Liddells put their confidence in Lee's integrity and that this had created a situation in which Lee could exercise a good deal of influence over them. The court considered the instrument misrepresented. Given the fact that it had not been read to the Liddells and the contents were misrepresented, they were not bound by it.[166]

New Contexts for Contract and Illiteracy

It has been mentioned previously that standardized contracts altered the context for interpreting the meaning of contract. The difficulties in the doctrine of freedom of contract are evident in large-scale business enterprise oriented toward mass markets, where efficiency of operation is crucial. The standardized contract of insurance, banking, and virtually almost any type of trade was seen as a way to stabilize transactions that no longer involved one-to-one, individualized relationships. From the standpoint of litigation, standardization of contract became an "important means of excluding or controlling the 'irrational factor.' " In this sense standardized contracts are the market equivalents of codification and restatements. They are also what is called *contracts of adhesion,* that is, they limit one party to the contract to accepting or rejecting it (rather than bargaining), thus acknowledging the inequality of bargaining power that exists. One does not bargain with insurance companies or issuers of credit cards, for example. Contracts of adhesion are obviously powerful tools to building and maintaining business empires. Yet, they also obviously reinforce inequalities of power.[167]

Both courts and legislatures have taken on regulatory roles to protect the weaker parties in this type of contract. From the viewpoint of the legal system the central question in contracts of adhesion becomes, can the unity of the law of contracts be maintained in the face of the increasing use of contracts of adhesion? Kessler has pointed out that courts that allow recovery in contract and tort (the larger number) have tried to protect the consumer "against the harshness of the common law and against what they think are abuses of freedom of contract." Courts that deny recovery see insurance policies as contracts not substantially different from other contracts. The application for insurance, then, is no different from any other legitimate offer, and acceptance forms a contract.[168]

Kessler argues that courts must squarely face the tensions within the system and assess their own position on freedom of contract. Even recovery in tort, he notes, pays "tribute to the dogma" (of contract) as evidenced by their careful reminders that plaintiffs are not "seeking recovery in contract." Freedom of contract in the nineteenth century was the foundation of a capitalist, free enterprise system. The free market was thought to be a mechanism for guaranteeing social justice; that is, it was a system of deserts that rewarded merit. Justice in this system, notes Kessler, meant "freedom of property and contract, of profit making and of trade." The concentration of power in monopoly and the decline of laissez-faire capitalism altered the meaning of contract. Kessler argued that contracts of adhesion have enabled "powerful industrial and commercial overlords" "to impose a new feudal order of their own making upon a vast host of vassals." The result is a "return back from contract to status."[169]

Kessler's conclusion that contracts of adhesion mark a return to status rather than contract is probably overstated, but it points to the decline in the concept and practice of bargaining as the basic activity in contractual relations. It also resurrects the issue of duty to read as it applies to the highly technical, stylistically convoluted standard contracts drawn for consumers.

Stewart Macauley has treated extensively the problem of duty to read in the context of large-scale business operations that use standard contracts.[170] The standardization of forms in business (contract) dealings has grown throughout the twentieth century. Technical language, confusing to all but experts, abounds in these forms. Duty to read is a principle that has tended to support the values of self-reliance, autonomy, and rationality. The assumption is that people will calculate their risks in market terms before signing a contract and protect their own interests. From the viewpoint of large business organizations, duty to read has supported those able to dictate the terms of an agreement. In dealing with both individuals and business organizations predictability is increased, but, in the case of individuals particularly, dependency is increased.

Macauley's analysis of the credit card "contract" is useful to explore here even though he does not see illiteracy as an "extreme limiting case" to practices of large business organizations to limit their liability.[171] By the 1950s credit cards were widely used in virtually every form. Most litigation involving the duty-to-read principle arose over lost or stolen credit cards and the system whereby the "holder is liable until notice." Common-law approaches to settling this problem were varied:

> Some courts looked for what could be labeled fault, another for a real contractual assumption of risk, another sought a fair allocation of risk in light of business practices by way of a "constructive contract," and still another treated fine print as if a contract had been made—and then qualified its abstract approach to square the case with its feeling about justice.[172]

Recent regulatory action taken on credit cards has insisted that assumptions about liability be made in readable print (usually eight- to eleven-point type). A market orientation has tended to persist, with the efficiency of mass marketing techniques being of great concern to courts.[173]

Macauley points to contexts other than the market in which duty to read also may be considered. These include transactional, social planning, and relief-of-hardship policies. A *transactional policy* toward duty to read is also market-oriented but employs a case-by-case strategy. It is aimed at reforming or construing a written contract "in light of the bargain-in-fact of the parties." A *social planning policy* is not oriented toward the market. The bargain-made-in-fact is not the issue here; rather, the issue is the contract that should have been made. A social planning policy toward duty to read might be aimed, says Macauley, toward certain classes of people who are not bound by contracts they did not read. Illiterate persons might constitute one such class as could minors, or those incapacitated in some way.[174]

A *relief-of-hardship policy* is primarily concerned with equity on an individual basis. Macauley points out that relief of hardship is often dealt with under "innocent misrepresentation and mistake doctrines."[175] In the case of illiterate persons or those of meager education, for example, questions arising from the duty-to-read principle are difficult to resolve. It would be difficult to argue that the illiterate person is duty bound to admit his ignorance, though courts have consistently said that there is an obligation to have a document read. On the other hand, a business organization cannot be expected to know the educational status of all the people with whom its salespeople deal.[176] The principle of duty to read thus cuts across both institutional and individual dimensions.

In the twentieth century, the pressures of mass markets, standardized contracts, and the increasing lack of autonomy in contractual relations moved the legal profession and legislatures toward both a codification and a redefinition of the meaning of contract in American society. In his critique of the Gilmore thesis in *The Death of Contract,* Speidel stresses the contribution that "perceived costs or excesses" of the market system made to the rethinking of general contract theory. These included the "wasteful utilization and inefficient allocation by private parties of increasingly scarce resources, the accumulation and frequent abuse of strategic market power, and a growing disparity in wealth, capacity, and opportunity among those who used or, in some cases, were used by contract." Thus government agencies and courts were "invited . . . to do battle with the 'market gods.'" Speidel points out that, in addition to factors cited by Gilmore, general contract theory was "fragmented by the demands of context, stretched by changes in the character of exchange relationships, and absorbed in part, by the legislative-administrative process."[177]

Speidel stresses that "individual consent is still of dominant importance in law." New relational duties, however, have altered the process of consent. Frequently, technical discourse itself is an obstacle to reading and understanding and hence has the effect of denying both. The degree to which this is true will depend very much on the extent to which the designers of contracts have a duty to emphasize and clarify critical terms that affect liability. Speidel concludes that the critical jurisprudential question of our time is where the "new imperatives should stop and 'freedom *from* and freedom *to'* begin."[178] The answers to this question will help define the place of consent in contractual relations and the balance of fairness and efficiency.

Codification and redefinition have taken various forms, but the *Restatements* (first and second) and the Uniform Commercial Code (UCC) are probably the most widely known. The Uniform Commercial Code was the product of the postrealist period in American law. The code was rooted in the common law but was recast in a "realist mode." It was, Friedman points out, the "realist's version of the *Restatement.*" The *Restatement (second),* he notes, was also marked by a "good deal of the realist revolution and the spirit of the code. . . ."[179]

The Uniform Commercial Code explicitly recognizes freedom of contract as a principle, but stipulates provisions under which contracts are not enforceable.[180] It thus functions as a guideline and gatekeeper to proper contracts. Yet as Quinn points out, individuals are free to alter basic rules of the code.[181] Thus the code reads: "the general and residual rule is that the effect of all provisions of the Act may be varied by agreement."[182]

Restrictions on freedom of contract are defined by standards of "commercial decency." They are, says Quinn, "control mechanisms designed to lessen the danger of possible injury to the unsuspecting."[183] Good faith, diligence, and reasonableness should prevail. "Unconscionable" contracts are not likely to be enforced, or at least courts are likely to exclude the unconscionable clause or clauses when otherwise enforcing a contract. In dealing with fraud and misrepresentation, the code notes that when reasonable opportunity to read and obtain knowledge of the essential features of a contract are thought to be absent, factors such as "age, sex, intelligence, education, experience, [and] literacy [ought] to be considered."[184] In his commentary on the UCC Anderson notes that in the area of negotiable instruments the extension of the concept of fraud is made "in recognition of the reality that the person with little education is likely to sign a paper without knowing its true character." In a commercial setting it is likely to be otherwise when experienced businessmen place their signatures to a transaction. Thus, when a negotiable instrument is clearly titled and a person of "reasonable age, business experience, and education" neglects to read its terms, and relies "on the word of a total stranger" then there is no fraud.[185]

The *Restatement of the Law (second)* on "Contracts," though more comprehensive, is in most respects similar to the code. Of course, its function is different as it attempts to synthesize the prevailing wisdom in the law of contracts. Freedom of contract is preserved but put within the context of codification. A high priority is assigned to mutual understanding and common meaning among parties to a contract. When explicit government regulation is not the issue, the objective of interpretation "is to carry out the understanding of the parties rather than to impose obligations on them contrary to their understanding: 'the courts do not make a contract for the parties.'"[186] In its explanation of interpretation, *Restatement (second)* attaches great importance to the context for meaning:

A word changes meaning when it becomes part of a sentence, the sentence when it becomes part of a paragraph. A longer writing similarly affects the paragraph, other related writings affect the particular writing, and the circumstances affect the whole. Where the whole can be read to give significance to each part, that reading is preferred; if such a reading would be unreasonable, a choice must be made . . . . To fit the immediate verbal context or the more remote total context particular words or punctuation may be disregarded or supplied; clerical or grammatical errors may be corrected; singular may be treated as plural or plural as singular.[187]

Like the code, *Restatement (second)* is explicit about good faith agreements. *The Restatement (second)* notes, however, that the "focus on honesty is appropriate to cases of good faith purchase; it is less so in cases of good faith performance." Among the indicators of bad faith, however, are included "evasion of the spirit of the bargain, lack of diligence and slacking off, willful rendering of imperfect performance, abuse of a power to specify terms, and interference with or failure to cooperate in the other party's performance."[188]

The unconscionable contract is a major concern with illiterate persons and those having little bargaining power. When there is "no meaningful choice, no real alternative, or [no] . . . assent to unfair terms," unconscionability is quite possible. Among the factors likely to contribute to a finding of unconscionability are the unlikelihood that the weaker party will perform the contract, the absence of substantial benefits to the weaker party, and "knowledge of the stronger party that the weaker party is unable reasonably to protect his interests by reason of physical or mental infirmities, ignorance, illiteracy or inability to understand the language of the agreement, or similar factors."[189] *Restatement (second)* gives the following illustration apropos of dealings involving minority language groups:

> 3. A, literate only in Spanish, is visited in his home by a salesman of refrigerator-freezers for B. They negotiate in Spanish; A tells the salesman he cannot afford to buy the appliance because his job will end in one week, and the salesman tells A that A will be paid numerous $25 commissions on sales to his friends. A signs a complex installment contract printed in English. The contract provides for a cash price of $900 plus a finance charge of $250. A defaults after paying $32, and B sues for the balance plus late charges and a 20% attorney's fee authorized by the contract. The appliance cost B $350. The court may determine that the contract was unconscionable when made, and may then limit B's recovery to a reasonable sum.[190]

Mass markets, standard contracts, specialities in law, regulatory statutes, greater emphasis on liability in tort, and merging of common law and equity principles in codification all helped to reshape the meaning of contract and its relationship to illiterate persons. Little change in the sharp edges of common-law contract principles occurred in the first three decades of the twentieth century. Codification, however, helped to bring the dependent status of the illiterate person to the attention of those preparing contracts. Fraud and misrepresentation continued to be the most common claims in litigation involving illiterate persons. Duty to read was commonly cited as an important principle governing individual behavior and the enforceability of a contract. Contributory negligence continued to be a factor that influenced a court's willingness to consider fraud as a reason for nonenforcement.

Conclusion

The issues arising from illiterate persons' entering into contracts in the twentieth century remained essentially the same as they did in the nineteenth. Fraud and misrepresentation were still the predominant reasons for litigation. Duty to read remained an important principle, and ignorance was not an acceptable defense. The impact of duty to read, however, was modified by the increasing amount of business done under standard contracts and the regulation of these contracts under codes, for example, the Uniform Commerical Code. Literate and illiterate persons alike probably struggled with the technical language and complex syntax of these agreements, and both also relied on company representatives to explain the terms. When the essential terms were misrepresented, this was an acceptable reason to defeat or at least modify a contract. Courts continued to consider it prudent for a person to read or have read to him the terms of a contract, but they often found illiteracy, when accompanied by fraud, a legitimate reason to defeat a contract. Unconscionable contracts were ruled unacceptable under the Uniform Commercial Code. This in itself was no doubt a deterrent to writing such contracts.

Racial and ethnic minorities, the poor, ignorant, and elderly were overrepresented in cases involving illiterate persons. This fact, coupled with the usual unequal bargaining power of litigants, continued to create problems of fairness in contractual relations. Codification and regulations governing standard contracts probably helped to stabilize the relations among unequal parties, however. Moreover, codification and regulation probably acted as deterrents to exploitation through unconscionable contracts. Regulations stipulating clear statements of liability also helped to protect literate persons. The illiterate person, of course, still relied upon others for knowledge of this information.

The trend to greater codification, regulation, and standardization of contracts raised some knotty philosophic and practical issues about autonomy, dependency, consent, and freedom of contract. Courts did not subordinate their concern with responsibility and the avoidance of negligence to principles of equity. To do that would have diminished the importance of the stability of contract. Guidelines for writing reasonable, fair, and defensible contracts were more often available, however. The same guidelines also made it easier for courts to interpret liability. With protection came greater security, but also greater dependency. There is no question that freedom of contract was preserved, but the principles of equity embodied in codes and regulations circumscribed the autonomy of individuals entering into contractual agreements. Codification itself was one way of acknowledging the presence of mass markets, and it also brought greater protection, if only by its presence rather than its application, to simple contracts between single parties.

Consent continued to be problematic for the illiterate person. None of the obstacles to understanding had been removed by standardization. Yet standardization of agreements did bring literate and illiterate together on more equal terms. To the extent that bargains between individuals were also made in the mold of codified and acceptable practices, then inequalities in simple contracts were also reduced. Standardization obviously could not overcome the debility of illiteracy. What it could do, however, was limit its effects. Barring fraud, agreement to a standard contract was the same for all individuals. Of course the illiterate person would continue to be disadvantaged with respect to assessing the impact of the agreement on his/her own welfare and resources. For those with very meager resources, a group in which illiteracy rates continued to be high, an uninformed choice about the potentially adverse affects of a contract could be devastating. Thus despite the safeguard of the standard contract, the illiterate person continued to be information-poor. Rational choices, that is, those that presume some calculation of future benefits and potential risk, continued to be more difficult for the illiterate person.

6

The Worth of Liberty

. . . .

The meanings of literacy as they were formed within the broad context of the liberal ideal have been a major focus of this study. In turn, these meanings have been linked to the ideal of contract broadly conceived and the idea of social contract as embodied in the concept of constitutional democracy. These formative ideas, in turn, led to an examination of illiteracy as it related to assumptions made by American liberalism about human reason and progress, property rights, and the nature of justice. It became evident that these several elements of liberal democratic thought and the transcendent importance of the ideal of contract were important determinants of the meanings, purposes, and functions of literacy in American society.

It was seen that a wide range of collective purposes— nationalism, social reform, economic growth, and political stability—assumed that literacy was essential to their fulfillment. Each of these took on a special meaning within the framework of liberal democractic thought and the preeminence of the contractual ideal. The range of individual motivation, likewise, was broad, though upward socioeconomic mobility, greater respect from peers, and a sense of personal liberation were among the more salient motives that prompted adult illiterates to learn to read.

The purposes of educational reform and campaigns against illiteracy have been as diverse as the functions of literacy itself. Most, however, have included both moral and utilitarian dimensions. Most also have seen literacy as both an individual attribute and a social fact necessary to the survival of modern institutions. The meaning of literacy as an individual attribute has been formed by both ideological and functional contexts. In the context of liberal thought this has meant that individual expectations associated with the achievement of reading and writing skills have been part of the meritocratic ideal. Full membership (in a functional sense) in the political community and opportunity for personal economic advancement have been the anticipated payoff for literacy. The social significance of literacy and the outcomes associated with its achievement have been political stability, the development of human resources, and a fair distribution of scarce economic resources. For the illiterate person the meaning of political membership, the exercise of constitutionally protected rights, and the exercise of liberty as an opportunity concept have been diminished though not necessarily denied by lack of access to print.

Within the contexts of liberal democratic thought and the contractual ideal, one of the major problems discussed at the outset of this study was the relationship between literacy and justice, both social and individual. It was pointed out early in the study that problems of justice always arise in situations of limited resources, and that this fact leads us directly to the question of justice as fairness when competing claims are made. For the student of illiteracy the question, in turn, becomes, given a documentary society in which the contractual ideal is politically and economically revered and in which the legal system depends heavily upon the printed word, how does the illiterate person fare in terms of justice? How are the rights and obligations of the illiterate person affected by his/her illiteracy?

The greatest obstacle to giving simple answers to these questions is the absence of a single standard of reference among courts themselves. A single normative standard simply was not present. To decide what was just by deciding what was in conformity with positive law was always a strong tendency for judges, yet decisions were often reasoned with the aid of both natural law precepts and principles of social utility. Making the situation even more complex was the fact that concerns with social utility were often concerns with the way decisions would affect the potential for economic growth in society in general. On the other hand, reasoning founded on principles of natural law often treated the question of justice in more absolute terms and attempted to resolve competing claims by appealing to innate and universal principles of justice.

The frequent participation of illiterate persons in basic economic activities such as mortgaging, deeding, and the willing of property; their involvement in civic responsibilities such as jury duty; and their exercise of voting privileges raised special problems for the legal system and illiterates alike. From a philosophic perspective, most of the economic problems were questions of intent, promise, and the nature of obligation. From a strictly legal perspective the same problems were usually questions of fraud, misrepresentation, or negligence. When illiteracy raised issues about jury duty, testimony, and depositions, they often concerned due process, impartiality, and the judgment of the representative, average person. Questions about the rights of citizenship and due process were usually fundamental to disputes about voting and balloting. Not infrequently, beliefs about the intelligence, reasonableness, and competency of illiterate persons cut across all of these areas—economic, civic, and political—and colored the reasoning and verdicts of judges. For the illiterate person himself, these same legal issues, philosophic questions, and assumptions about the abilities and competency of illiterate persons often were reduced to questions of fairness and legitimate expectations.

The relationship of the illiterate person to major political, economic, and legal institutions was fundamentally different from that of the literate person. The reality of text, the messages of print, and the visual reality associated with print were closed to the illiterate person. Translation and interpretation were the norms. The literal meanings of obligations, responsibilities, rights, benefits, and risks were once removed though they carried the same moral and practical import as for literate persons. Consent, the heart of contractual relations, was often problematic. The link between individual needs and expectations on the one hand and those of primary social institutions on the other was uncertain. The sharing of political and economic expectations (publicity) was undermined by the poverty of information for illiterate persons.

Fairness and legitimacy assume a mutuality of guidelines for conduct and an understanding of information common to the parties involved in a dispute. Yet perceptions of fairness and legitimacy may differ radically, depending upon the accessibility of information. This, of course, is the illiterate person's major problem, and it is the relative scarcity of information for the illiterate that may affect decisions about promising, obligation, testimony, or the exercise of voting privileges, for example. At both the individual and general levels, scarcity of information resulting in differing expectations and different perceptions of fairness affects the degree of liberty under law available to the illiterate person. Varying levels of dependency and understanding of the illiterate person may be found, of course, and this is true of the literate person, as well. Still, the fundamental difficulty persists, namely, that liberties under law are circumscribed by the absence or misinterpretation of relevant information.

The extent of illiteracy in the population has been linked historically to age, sex, race, ethnicity, wealth, and occupation. The poor and racial and ethnic minorities were frequently those experiencing difficulties with contractual arrangements. The structure of literacy itself was one that affected the poor and minority groups far more often than the mainstream of the population. Yet only in special circumstances, such as the use of literacy tests or disqualification from a jury, were illiterate persons excluded from fundamental political and economic activities. This, of course, does not mean that the quality of that participation was the same as it was for the literate person. Thus it is fair to say that their participation was marginal, that it was often dependent on others, and that consent to the terms of participation was doubtful. In short, the worth of participation and the worth of liberty to participate were problematic.

The large number of illiterates participating in important economic and political activities might be expected to put some stress on the legal system. The court cases discussed in this study depict the burdens that illiteracy forced the legal system to carry. Illiteracy was a deviant condition with which courts were obligated to deal. These cases allow us to examine the "worth" of liberty for the illiterate person, but they also allow us to examine the quality of institutional response to illiterate persons.

It was pointed out that restrictions on political participation in the form of literacy tests were one way of helping to guarantee that a "community of interests" would be maintained in support of cherished political beliefs. It was presumed, as well, that proper socialization through literacy would result in at least minimum qualifications for citizenship. Thus it was assumed by some that certain civic responsibilities such as jury duty required literacy. Jury duty, like intelligent voting, fell under the canopy of responsible citizenship. Most of the problems of illiteracy associated with jury duty pertained at least indirectly to citizenship. Judges usually focused on the implications of illiteracy for the defendant or plaintiff or the inefficiency with which illiteracy burdened the court. A juror's facility with language was thus most germane to the "worth" of liberty for the plaintiff or defendant, and it was his/her rights and expectations for justice that were of foremost concern to the courts. The result of this focus led judges to admit or dismiss the problems of illiteracy according to their relevance for a specific case. Functional literacy was the test, and the definition of functionality was the prerogative of the judge(s) hearing the case.

It is quite obvious that the use of educational or literacy qualifications for voting directly affects the "worth" of liberty for the illiterate or uneducated person. It was a well-settled constitutional principle that states had the right to control voting qualifications and procedures, and that citizenship itself did not necessarily confer the right to vote.

Though this principle was challenged in such early cases as *Luther v. Borden, United States v. Miller,* and *Minor v. Happersett,* it was not until the late nineteenth century that literacy tests became a political issue of any importance. The disfranchisement of blacks and recently arrived immigrant peoples from southern and eastern European countries brought numerous cases to court after 1890. During this time the most frequently heard defense of literacy tests was that they helped to guarantee the intelligent voting necessary for a stable, democractic government. With the Voting Rights Act of 1965, problems relating to the discriminatory use of literacy tests were resolved. Yet the principle that educational or literacy qualifications ought to help quarantee at least a minimal level of voter competence was not really successfully challenged. It was, rather, shunted aside in favor of an educational solution to the problem of voter competence.

Whether the situation was one of discriminatory literacy tests, election fraud, or improper assistance to voters, the focus of a court's concern was often on improper procedures and the way they affected the worth of the voters' ballots. This was both a collective and an individual concern. The former often occurred with contested elections in which ballots of illiterate voters would alter the outcome. The latter was usually in situations in which the voter's intent might be jeopardized by improper assistance or the secrecy of the voter's decision went unprotected. The introduction of the Australian ballot in the late nineteenth century put the illiterate voter in a precarious position. This innovation in balloting was instituted, of course, to protect the intent of the voter by securing the secrecy of the ballot. The effect on the illiterate and uneducated voter, however, was to imperil seriously his ability to vote as he wished. In responding to the dilemma of the illiterate person, courts were generally unsympathetic. The disadvantage of the illiterate voter was clearly recognized, but there was little help from the courts. In terms of the "worth" of liberty for illiterate voters, the court in *State ex rel. Weinberger v. Miller* perhaps put it best when it noted that the opportunities are the same for the educated and the uneducated, but the uneducated person "is not in a position to take advantage of these. . . ."

It has been observed that in the evolution of a documentary society based upon contractual ideals, certain assumptions regarding man's freedom and rationality made the "worth" of liberty for the illiterate person increasingly suspect. The ascendance of literalism in contractual agreements made the printed work a standard measure of a person's intent and assent. The written record was the one that counted most, yet just as clearly it was a false measure of intent and assent for the illiterate person. The procedure of offer, acceptance, and consideration helped to ensure the validity of the contract and guarantee that obligations would be met. The rational, self-reliant individual freely negotiating contractual agreements was assumed, quite vigorously by utilitarians, to facilitate progress and economic growth in general. Nowhere was autonomous decision making more revered than in the principle of freedom of contract itself.

Freedom of contract and the principles of laissez-faire capitalism saw the general welfare as the sum of individual prosperities. Under these conditions, fairness was a matter of allotting rewards proportional to merit, a formula that generally put those lacking information and understanding of contractual relations at a disadvantage. The atomistic conception of social welfare was eventually compromised by the findings of twentieth-century social scientists concerned with structural inequalities and institutional constraints on individual behaviors. Collective concerns aside, however, contracts and their effects remained very much matters working to the benefit or detriment of individuals.

Literalness, it has been pointed out, could be a powerful principle in validating unfair bargains, though principles of equity could be invoked to rectify grossly unfair bargains. Yet setting aside an unfair bargain made with an unlettered person was not easy. Illiterate or not, it was and is a fundamental principle of contract that obligations must be met and contracts fulfilled. Stability and continuity in contractual relations were and are highly valued, and the fact of illiteracy cannot, barring special circumstances, be allowed to supersede them. Mutual understanding has remained the essence of contract, and the signing of a contract implies an understanding of its terms. In a documentary society where the contractual ideal predominates and the values of self-reliance and individual initiative are held in high regard, the principle of mutuality of understanding in contract assumes that parties to a contract are literate or at least have access to the correct meaning of the terms of the contract. Where the written document is taken to be a reliable measure of intent and assent, mutuality of understanding as a principle of contract would be largely inoperative without mass literacy.

For the unlettered individual entering into contractual arrangements, the problem of mutual understanding is a practical one. "Freedom of contract" has a hollow ring for one whose lexical skills are insufficient to decipher most contracts. Though some consolation and satisfaction might be gained by asking the aid of a literate acquaintance, the condition of dependency for the illiterate is still very apparent. Unlike many advocates of literacy tests, courts did not assume that the illiterate person lacked sufficient intelligence for contracting. Thus it was generally maintained that the illiterate person could be assumed to know enough to ask for information prior to the signing of the contract, and that he understood the terms of a contract. This advice was heeded by some, though illiterate witnesses to wills had only the testator's word as evidence of the content of the document. Fraud and misrepresentation raised similar though more severe problems.

There is little question that the merging of law and equity principles in the twentieth century helped to mitigate inequalities between bargaining parties. Standard contracts, regulatory statutes, and codification probably helped to deter unfair and unconscionable agreements. Yet it is not likely that they lessened the dependency of the illiterate person nor made the calculus of benefits and risks any easier. Unscrupulous parties to a contract still practiced duplicity with remarkable facility on an unsuspecting illiterate person.

When deliberate misinformation was not the issue, equal access to the information contained in the contract was assumed. For the unlettered person not to avail himself of that knowledge was to be negligent. Thus when ignorance of the true nature of the agreement was clearly in evidence, courts were often asked to determine the *context* for ignorance. Preserving the integrity of the contract was a high priority for courts, and the measure of justice for the parties involved was generally the extent to which the intent of the parties was fulfilled. When the written agreement represented that intent, or, as sometimes happened, was linked with it in an almost metaphysical way, the burden of illiteracy became quite clear. When the written word took on a life of its own, as often happened, the "worth" of liberty was considerably diminished for the unlettered person. The metaphor of incarceration was appropriate when, in the absence of mutual understanding and a clear recognition of obligations incurred, the word became binding. The written word, so often adulated as the architect of imagination and freedom, became the instrument of misunderstanding, conflict, and bondage.

Appendix

. . .

Sampling the Wills, Deeds, and Mortgages from
Kent County, Delaware and Washington County, Ohio,
1790–1900.

Background

A 100 percent sample was taken from the microfilmed wills of Kent County between 1780 and 1900 and from the photographed and originals of Washington County between 1795 and 1900. These two counties differed in the stability of their populations, the evolution of their economies, and their slave and nonslave characteristics. The population enumeration is given in Table A.1, where the differences in population growth are seen to be very substantial.

Table A.1
The Total Populations of Washington County, Ohio, and Kent County, Delaware,
Classified by Year from 1790 to 1900

County	1790	1800	1820	1840	1860	1880	1900
Washington		5,427	10,425	20,823	36,268	43,244	48,245
Kent	18,920	19,554	20,793	19,872	27,804	32,874	32,764

Source: Various U.S. censuses.

Washington County was one of the three largest counties in Ohio in the early nineteenth century and rode the crest of westward expansion as it moved from a frontier region to a well-settled area of stable communities. It experienced large percentage increases in population. The first half of the nineteenth century was characterized by high geographic mobility among its people. The county remained rural for the most part, except for the city of Marietta. Here increased manufacturing activity reflected the economic expansion of the region. Other towns such as Belpre typified small-town America.

Leather goods, whiskey, and brandy were the most important manufactured items in the county according to a special census of manufacturers in 1822. In 1840 agricultural products dominated the economic output of the county. There was some lumbering and coal production also. Among manufactured products, cutlery and hardware were the most extensive. (*Aggregate Value and Produce, and Number of Persons Employed in Mines, Agriculture, Commerce, Manufactures, etc.*, from the *Sixth Census of the United States* [Washington: Blair and Rives, 1841], reprinted as *American Industry and Manufactures in the Nineteenth Century*, Vol. 4 [Elmsford, N.Y., 1970], pp. 340–341)

By 1860 the value of the extensive hardwood forests in the county was evident in the fact that furniture making, cabinetry, and construction of chairs and wooden ware dominated manufacturing activities. The most important agricultural product was tobacco. This was followed in importance by corn, wheat, and potatoes. (*Manufactures of the United States in 1860, Eighth Census* [Washington: G.P.O., 1864], pp. 480–481; *Agriculture of the United States in 1860, Eighth Census* [Washington: G.P.O., 1864], pp. 118–119)

Kent County, Delaware, was a more stable county than Washington. It experienced only modest percentage increases (and sometimes losses) in population during the 110 years from 1790 to 1900. Delaware was a slave state, but the slave population in Kent County decreased steadily from 2,300 to 427 in the years between 1790 and 1840. Like Washington County, it was predominantly agricultural. The 1822 *Census of Manufactures* listed leather goods as the main manufactured product, but there were only three tanneries employing ten men. (*Digest of Accounts of Manufacturing Establishments in the United States* [1823], p. 17) The agricultural characteristics of the economy are also apparent in 1840, when the only evidence of manufacturing was bricks and lime. Livestock production predominated. Oats were first among the grains and corn was a major crop. Dairy products and potatoes were of intermediate importance. (*Aggregate Value and Produce, and Number of Persons Employed in Mines, Agriculture, Commerce, Manufactures, etc.* [1841], pp. 212–213)

Some activity in commerce was also present. This no doubt reflected the county's geographic proximity to Delaware Bay. The economy remained agricultural in nature and what manufacturing did exist by 1860, for example, was geared toward the production of agriculture-related items such as blacksmithing, wagons, and agricultural implements. (*Manufactures of the United States in 1860*, p. 53)

Illiteracy

Relative to levels of illiteracy at the state and county levels, there are some differences in the testator data. If 1850 is taken as a standard of reference (Table A.2) then some differences between Census data and that of testators is important.

Table A.2
The Percent of Illiterate Testators and Witnesses to Wills Compared to Illiteracy
Rates at State and County Levels for the Year 1850

Kent County		Washington County	
Testators	8	Testators	25
Witnesses	2	Witnesses	0
Kent County		Washington County	
Whites	21	Whites	10
Free Blacks	79	Free Blacks	5
Overall	37	Overall	10
State of Delaware		State of Ohio	
Whites	13	Whites	7
Free Blacks	66	Free Blacks	42
Overall	24	Overall	7

Illiteracy among testators and witnesses in Kent County ran considerably below the overall rate for the county of Kent and the state of Delaware. State and county figures from census data show large differences, also, when illiteracy is classified by race. Illiteracy among free blacks exceeded that among whites by a ratio of four/one to five/one. This latter finding was true for the state of Ohio, but not Washington County specifically. In the latter, there were very few illiterates among free blacks, and the rate was a mere 5 percent compared to 42 percent at the state level. Unlike in Kent County, the illiteracy rate among testators in Washington County exceeded that of the county overall. There were no illiterates among witnesses in the sample from Washington County. (For Kent County, Delaware, the figures for 1860 are for 1860–61. The sample size for 1860 only was thought to be too small to be valid. State and county census data are from *The Seventh Census of the United States,* 1850 [Washington: Robert Armstrong, 1853], pp. 208–213, 810, 818, 860, *Population of the United States, The Eighth Census* [Washington, G.P.O., 1864], pp. 44–45, 364–369, and *Statistics of the United States in 1860, The Eighth Census* [Washington, G.P.O., 1866], p. 508.)

The probate court and the recorder's offices provide the records needed to document illiterate participation in the disposition of property by will, deed, and mortgage (mortgage deed). Rules governing the distribution of property at death, administration of estates, criteria for valid probate, conveying and deeding of land, indebtedness by mortgage, and procedures to be followed for filing proper documentation were established by statute in the various colonies, territories, and states.

The point of having a deed or mortgage deed recorded was, of course, to make possible a proof of ownership. Historically, English conveyancing and rules governing the transfer of land moved away from the deed of feoffment to the deed symbol. That is, they moved from a deed that merely served as a witness of a transaction or transfer of possession to the deed as the instrument to which legal title was transferred. (John C. Payne, "The Theory of Conveyances at Law in Alabama," *Alabama Law Review,* 8 [Fall, 1955]) Virginia (1616), Plymouth (1636), Rhode Island (1638), Connecticut (1639), and Massachusetts (1640) all passed legislation dealing with recording in the early colonial period. In Plymouth, says Haskins, "precautions for security were brought into prominence by the social and economic background of the settlers," namely, the enclosure movement of the sixteenth century. In general, the concern was to prevent fraudulent conveyancing. (George L. Haskins, "The Beginnings of the Recording System in Massachusetts," *Boston University Law Review,* 21 [Jan., 1941], pp. 284, 299–300. See also, J. H. Beale, "The Origin of the System of Recording Deeds in America," *Green Bag,* 19 [1907], 335–339, and Mark DeWolfe Howe, "The Recording of Deeds in the Colony of Massachusetts Bay," *Boston University Law Review,* 28 [Jan., 1948], 1–6.)

In the matter of deeds, the Delaware Constitution of 1792 provided for an "office for recording of deeds" and a recorder. This was extended in 1795 and 1797, and all "bargains and sales, deeds, conveyances of land, tenements and hereditaments" within the state were to be filed in said office within one year after execution. The law of 1797 provided for proper witnessing and acknowledgment by the grantor. (*Laws of State of Delaware,* Vol. 1 [Wilmington, 1797], pp. 219–222)

By law in 1795, a recorder's office was established in every county in the territory of Ohio, and the conveyance of land within the territory was to be recorded "within twelve months after the execution of such deed or conveyance. . . ." Various sections of the law dealt with punishments for forgery and also, as in Delaware, with the entering of "satisfied" mortgages into the record. The process for recording deeds was described in detail, but for our purposes the important passage is that which provides that "all deeds and conveyances . . . shall be acknowledged by one of the grantors or bargainors, or proved by one or more of the subscribing witnesses. . . ." ("The Laws of the Northwest Territory, 1788–1800." *Law Series,* Vol. 1, *Collection of the Illinois State Historical Library,* Vol. 17, ed. Theodore Calvin Pease [Springfield, Ill.: Illinois State Historical Library, 1925], p. 199.) With the coming of statehood, provision for the recorder's office was continued in Ohio. As before, documents were recorded in regular succession. Various provisions for the acknowledgment of deeds, mortgages, and leases were made over the course of the nineteenth century, including the signing and sealing of deeds before two witnesses as provided for in an act of 1805.

The deeds and mortgages sampled from the years 1790–1840 represent 100 percent of those documents filed in the Recorder's Office. For the years 1860 (1859 for mortgages) and 1880, the sample includes 30 percent of the available documents. Fifteen percent of the documents were sampled for the year 1900. Reduction in the percentage of documents represented from 1860–1900 was a simple matter of practicality. The number of documents grew so large in the 1860–1900 period that 100 percent representation was prohibitive. Nonetheless, the sample sizes (Ns) are still large. For the years 1860–1900 the method of sampling was systematic and free from personal bias. It was not random, however. For the years 1860 and 1880, 30 percent of the documents were sampled.

The sampling procedure for this 30 percent began with the first page on which a deed or mortgage was recorded for either 1860 or 1880. Thirty pages were then sampled, seventy pages were skipped, and so on. This method was thought to be preferable to sampling every third entry, because the recording of documents often took more than one page. It was far less time-consuming to record entries in the thirty-page range, and there is no reason to believe that any bias was created in the sample by this method. A similar procedure was followed for the 15 percent sample from 1900.

For each deed transaction the following information was recorded: (1) county, (2) year of transaction, (3) residence of grantor(s) (from 1790 to 1840), (4) type of grantor (individual, company or association, or government), (5) name(s) of grantor(s), (6) value of consideration, (7) sex of grantor(s), and (8) literacy or illiteracy of grantor(s). For mortgage transactions, the same information was recorded, except that residence of the mortgagor was not available. The type of indebtedness was also recorded for mortgage transactions. Each grantor or mortgagor was given a number indicating the order in which the name appeared. Thus, in the case of multiple grantors or mortgagors, it was possible to differentiate between the number of transactions and the number of transactors. Sorting alphabetically by name also made it possible to omit repeated names for certain types of analysis.

Separate deed transactions from Kent and Washington counties, respectively, total 844 and 1,924. Some grantors and mortgagors were involved in more than one transaction, and repeated names were omitted for some parts of the analysis. Repeated names were particularly numerous during the early years in Washington County, when large investments in land were made by a few wealthy individuals. The greatest proportion of transactions over the period 1780–1900, however, were carried out by two people, usually husband and wife but sometimes business partners. In the early years of Washington County, most grantors were male. After 1840, the common pattern became husband/wife pairings. A small percentage of the total transactions were conducted by three or more persons. Usually when five or more individuals were involved in a single transaction they were brothers and sisters engaged in the settlement of an estate.

For analysis, deed transactions were classified into four categories according to type of grantor: (1) individual, (2) company or association, (3) state or county government, and (4) federal government. Individual grantors carried out the great majority of transactions between the years 1780 and 1900. In Washington County, 94.5 percent of the grantors were individuals, whereas 99.4 percent were individual grantors in Kent County. The proportions of transactions conducted by individual grantors ranged from 91 to 100 percent. The lowest proportion was in 1840 for Washington County and in 1820 for Kent. Transactions conducted by companies or associations never rose above 3 percent of the total. Government transactors sometimes comprised as much as 9 percent. Most of these transactions were by the federal rather than the state or local government.

Mortgage transactions were carried out overwhelmingly by individuals also. In all years sampled, the proportion of mortgage transactions made by individuals ranged between 98 and 100 percent. Companies or associations carried out only a total of eleven transactions from the entire Kent and Washington county samples.

Most deed transactions in both counties were negotiated by people living in the counties where the deeds were recorded. The lowest percentages of in-county residents were in Washington County in 1790, 1800, and 1820, when the area was undergoing rapid economic expansion and settlement and intercounty mobility rates were high. By 1840, however, the percentage of in-county transactors had risen to 92 in Washington County, and thereafter rose to over 99 percent.

In Kent County, the in-county percentage of grantors never dropped below 79. Many out-of-state grantors whose deeds were recorded in Kent County were from nearby Pennsylvania and New Jersey. For Washington County, most out-of-state grantors were New Englanders, not a surprising finding in view of the Ohio Company's New England origins. Other out-of-state transactors for Washington County deeds were from New York and Pennsylvania. A few were from Virginia. The percentage of out-of-state grantors declined rapidly after 1820 in Washington County and was only 3 percent of the total in 1840. Out-of-state grantors for Kent County remained proportionately higher than for Washington County.

Those who lived in an Ohio or Delaware county other than Washington or Kent but purchased land in these respective counties never constituted a very large proportion of the sample. For Washington County the highest percentage was 12 percent in 1820; for Kent County, the proportion was 8 percent in the same year. In general, then, the population was local in terms of its economic activity, although the rapid growth of Ohio from 1790 to 1820 led many out-of-state transactors to purchase land in Washington County.

Women and Property

One stipulation of interest in the recording of deeds should be included because of its relation to possible fraud and to the sex distribution of deed and mortgage signatures. The issue of the so-called *feme covert* often arose when confronting the problem of verification of title and evidence to that effect. Numerous statutes in both Delaware and Ohio (as well as other states) dealt with the issue, which was simply one of guaranteeing that land conveyed jointly by husband and wife to another grantee should not, after the death of the husband, be recovered as part of the wife's dower. To make such a claim would have the effect of challenging, defeating, or cancelling the transfer of land carried out jointly by husband and wife before the former's death.

Statutes guarding against this situation provided for a separate examination of the wife by the chancellor, a judge of the supreme court, or justices of the court of common pleas. In this manner it could be ascertained whether or not the wife knew the contents of the deed and whether she agreed voluntarily to enter into the transaction. An Ohio (territory) law of 1795 thus read:

> if, upon such separate examination, she shall declare, that she did voluntarily, and of her own free will and accord, seal, and as her act and deed, deliver the said deed, or conveyance, without any coercion or compulsion of her said husband, every such deed or conveyance shall be [good], and the same is hereby declared to be good and valid in law. ("Laws of the Northwest Territory," p. 243)

The act makes clear that coercion was a definite possibility in joint conveyances. In such a situation, when the transfer was not made voluntarily by the wife, both grantee and widow were likely to suffer financial reverses on the death of a husband. In Ohio, the provisions for *feme covert* were not continuous. An act of 1835 brought a significant change in the responsibility for husband-and-wife conveyances. The act removed the provision for assuring that the wife understood the contents of a deed or mortgage. Thus, the magistrate taking the acknowledgment of deeds, mortgages, and other written instruments did not have to certify that "he read or made known the contents of such deed, mortgage or instrument of writing to such wife, before or at the time she acknowledged the execution thereof." (*Acts of a General Nature . . . of the State of Ohio*, Vol. 33, 9 March 1835 p. 49.) The suspicion that a husband might coerce his wife to sign a written instrument against her will, however, was apparently a lingering one, for in 1882 the Sixty-fifth General Assembly of the State of Ohio ordered the following:

> the officer before whom such acknowledgment is made, shall examine the wife separate and apart from her husband, and shall read, or otherwise make known to her the contents of the instrument; and if, upon such separate examination, she declare that she did voluntarily sign and acknowledge the same, and that she is still satisfied therewith, such officer shall certify such examination and declaration of the wife, together with the acknowledgment, on the instrument, and subscribe his name thereof. (State of Ohio, *General and Local Laws, and Joint Resolutions* Vol. 80 [Columbus: C. J. Brand and Co., 1883], p. 80)

The laws of property as they apply to women are the subject of a recent work by Marylynn Salmon, *Women and the Law of Property in Early America* (Chapel Hill: The University of North Carolina Press, 1986). In the American colonies, explains Salmon, courts did not use the English legal fiction of a fine whereby women conveyed property by a fictitious lawsuit. The private examination of a wife, apart from her husband, which was part of the fine, did become part of conveyances in the colonies. The process, says Salmon, was direct and simple. The wife was asked whether she had freely agreed to the conveyance. If the answer was yes, then it was recorded on the deed or an attached certificate. The result was to bar the woman from "establishing claims to the property." (Salmon, pp. 17–18)

There were great variations among the colonies and the states in the early nineteenth century. Procedures for dealing with *feme covert* conveyances in the South tended to be well established. In the North, says Salmon, "colonial Connecticut, Massachusetts, Pennsylvania, and New York exhibited a more casual attitude. . . ." Wives in Connecticut had no property rights until 1723. Northern states were committed to the principle of "unity of person," the effect of which was to reinforce the man's (husband's) prerogatives in the property ownership. Massachusetts, New York, and Pennsylvania did not include provisions for private examinations in their statutes. (Salmon, pp. 20–23, 37–39)

In matters of contract, the situation was similar. Control of property by husbands resulted in "the inability of femes coverts to contract." "According to common law rules," says Salmon, "a woman's services belonged to her husband. They could not be given to another unless he consented." She continues: "Judicial acceptance of coercion as a factor in the relations of husbands and wives made all financial transactions by women suspect, particularly those that directly affected their husbands. According to this reasoning, the law acted for the good of women by removing their contractual capacity." (Salmon, pp. 41–42)

Women could contract jointly with their husbands. If given a letter of attorney by her husband, a woman could contract independently. She thus became a *feme sole* with respect to contract. If married, a woman might also act as an agent of her husband. Thus she might enter into business agreements in her husband's absence, if she had regularly entered into them previously with his consent. This was not a settled affair, however, so that courts in different states did not interpret a woman's independence consistently. Overall, there were "few formal guidelines . . . in the eighteenth and early nineteenth-century law for governing women's contractual rights." Even a so-called *feme sole* trader was controlled by male privileges. There was "scant protection" for the property rights of women.

(Salmon, pp. 42–44, 56–57) Gradually those rights became greater. By the end of the eighteenth century in the area of separate estates a simple contract between husband and wife could "reserve certain property for the sole use of the wife." Married women's property acts followed in the 1840s to protect "women's property from husband's creditors." (Salmon, pp. 117–119, 140)

Notes

. . .

Preface

1. James Willard Hurst, *Law and Social Order in the United States* (Ithaca, N.Y.: Cornell University Press, 1977), p. 134.

2. Ibid., pp. 23–24.

Chapter 1

1. William J. Gilmore, "Elementary Literacy on the Eve of the Industrial Revolution: Trends in Rural New England, 1760–1830," *Proceedings of the American Antiquarian Society,* 92 (1982), 87–178; Carl F. Kaestle and Maris A. Vinovskis, *Education and Social Change in Nineteenth Century Massachusetts* (New York: Cambridge University Press, 1980); Carl F. Kaestle, "The History of Literacy and the History of Readers," in Edmund W. Gordon (ed.) *Review of Research in Education,* 12 (Washington, D.C.: American Educational Research Association, 1985); Kenneth Lockridge, *Literacy in Colonial New England* (New York: W. W. Norton and Co., 1974); Daniel P. Resnick and Lauren B. Resnick, "The Nature of Literacy: An Historical Explanation," *Harvard Educational Review,* 47 (Aug., 1977), 370–385; Lee Soltow and Edward Stevens, *The Rise of Literacy and the Common School in the United States: A Socioeconomic Analysis to 1870* (Chicago: University of Chicago Press, 1981); M. T. Clanchy, *From Memory to Written Record, England, 1066–1307* (Cambridge, Mass.: Harvard University Press, 1979); David Cressy, *Literacy and the Social Order: Reading and Writing in Tudor and Stuart England* (Cambridge: Cambridge University Press, 1980); François Furet and Jacques Ozouf, *Lire et écrire* (Paris: aux Editions De Minuit, 1977); Jack Goody and Ian Watt, "The Consequences of Literacy," *Comparative*

Studies in Society and History, 5 (1962), 304–345; Egil Johannson, *The History of Literacy in Sweden in Comparison with Some Other Countries,* Educational Reports (Umea: Umea University and Umea School of Education, 1977); Mary Jo Maynes, *Schooling in Western Europe, A Social History* (Albany: State University of New York Press, 1985); R. S. Schofield, "Dimensions of Illiteracy, 1750–1850," *Explorations in Economic History* 10 (1973), 437–454; Sylvia Scribner and Michael Cole, *The Psychology of Literacy* (Cambridge, Mass.: Harvard University Press, 1981); Lawrence Stone, "Literacy and Education in England," *Past and Present,* 42 (Feb., 1969), 69–193; E. G. West, "Literacy and the Industrial Revolution," *Economic History Review,* 31 (1978), 369–383; Harvey J. Graff, *The Literacy Myth: Literacy and Social Structure in the Nineteenth-Century City* (New York: Academic Press, 1979); Harvey J. Graff (ed.), *Literacy and Social Development in the West* (Cambridge: Cambridge University Press, 1981); Harvey J. Graff, *The Legacies of Literacy, Continuities and Contradictions in Western Culture and Society* (Bloomington: Indiana University Press, 1987); Lawrence A. Cremin, "Reading, Writing, and Literacy," *Review of Education,* 1 (1975), 517–521; Lawrence A. Cremin, *American Education: The National Experience, 1783–1876* (New York: Harper and Row, 1980).

2. Sylvia Scribner, "Literacy in Three Metaphors" in Nancy L. Stein (ed.), *Literacy in American Schools, Learning to Read and Write* (Chicago: University of Chicago Press, 1986), p. 8.

3. Kaestle, "History of Literacy and History of Readers," p. 13.

4. Geraldine Joncich Clifford, "Buch und Lesen: Historical Perspectives on Literacy and Schooling," *Review of Educational Research,* 54 (Winter, 1984), 474.

5. Scribner, "Literacy in Three Metaphors," p. 8.

6. Ibid., p. 9.

7. David R. Olson, "Review of *Toward a Literate Society,*" *Proceedings of the National Academy of Education,* vol. 2, ed. John B. Carroll and Jeanne Chall (Stanford, Calif.: National Academy of Education, 1975), p. 160.

8. Sylvia Scribner and Michael Cole, *The Psychology of Literacy* (Cambridge, Mass.: Harvard University Press, 1981). See, also, the more recent works of Suzanne de Castell, Allan Luke, and Kieran Eagan (eds.), *Literacy, Society, and Schooling, a Reader* (Cambridge: Cambridge University Press, 1986); Jenny Cook-Gumperz (ed.), *The Social Construction of Literacy,* Studies in International Sociolinguistics 3 (Cambridge: Cambridge University Press, 1986); Kenneth Levine, *The Social Context of Literacy* (London: Routledge and Kegan Paul, 1986).

9. Kenneth S. Goodman, *Language and Literacy: The Selected Writings of Kenneth S. Goodman,* 2 vols., ed. Frederick V. Gollasch (Boston: Routledge and Kegan Paul, 1982); George L. Dillon, *Constructing Texts, Elements of a Theory of Composition and Style* (Bloomington: Indiana University Press, 1981); George R. Klare, *How to Write Readable English* (London: Hutchinson,1985).

10. M. A. K. Halliday and Rugaiya Hasan, *Cohesion in English* (London: Longman, 1976), p. 26.

11. Victoria Seitz, "Literacy and the School Child: Some Perspectives from an Educated Country," *Educational Evaluation and Policy Analysis* 3 (Nov.–Dec., 1981),16.

12. As in Robert L. Hillerich, "Toward an Assessable Definition of Literacy," *English Journal* 65 (Feb., 1976), 52.

13. John R. Bormuth, "Reading Literacy: Its Definition and Assessment," in *Toward a Literate Society,* ed. John B. Carroll and Jeanne S. Chall (New York:

McGraw-Hill, 1975), pp. 6–8.

14. Bernard Asbel, "Illiteracy: The Key to Poverty," in *The Drive Against Illiteracy,* ed. Irwin Isenberg (New York: H. W. Wilson Co., 1964), p. 45.

15. Soltow and Stevens, *The Rise of Literacy,* pp. 8–9.

16. William S. Gray, *The Teaching of Reading and Writing An International Survey* (Paris: UNESCO, 1956), p. 19, quoted in UNESCO, *World Illiteracy at Mid-Century, a Statistical Study* (Paris, 1957), p. 20.

17. As in Hillerich, "Toward an Assessable Definition," p. 53.

18. Ibid.

19. Sylvia Scribner and Michael Cole, "Literacy without Schooling: Testing for Intellectual Effects," Vai Literacy Project, Working Paper No. 2, New York, Rockefeller University, April, 1978, p. 25, as in Carman St. John Hunter and David Harman, *Adult Literacy in the United States, A Report to the Ford Foundation* (New York: McGraw-Hill Co., 1979), pp. 18–19.

20. Irwin Isenberg, *The Drive Against Illiteracy* (New York: H. W. Wilson Co., 1964), p. 11.

21. Malcolm S. Adiseshiah, "Literacy's Functionality to the Fight for Social Justice," *Convergence* 8 (1975), 23.

22. Marshall McLuhan, "The Printed Word: Architect of Nationalism," in *The Future of Literacy,* ed. Robert Disch (Englewood Cliffs, N.J.: Prentice Hall, 1973).

23. As cited in David R. Olson, "Review of *Toward a Literate Society,*" p. 116.

24. Cynthia Brown, "Literacy in 30 Hours: Paulo Freire's Process in Northeast Brazil," *Social Policy* 5 (July-Aug. 1974), 25 as in Soltow and Stevens, *The Rise of Literacy,* p.7

25. UNESCO, *The Experimental World Literacy Programme: A Critical Assessment* (UNDP: The UNESCO Press, 1976), p. 117.

26. John Oxenham, *Literacy, Writing, Reading and Social Organization* (London: Routledge and Kegan Paul,1980), pp. 12, 66.

27. Charles Jeffries, *Illiteracy, A World Problem* (London: Frederick A. Praeger, 1967), p. 65.

28. Ibid., p. 67.

29. Jonathan Kozol, *Illiterate America* (New York: Anchor/Doubleday, 1985), pp. 4–5.

30. Graff, *The Literacy Myth,* p. 240.

31. *Tenth Annual Report,* Eastern State Penitentiary, Pennsylvania (Philadelphia: 1839), p. 9.

32. John C. Greene, "Science, Learning, and Utility" in Oleson, Alexandra and Brown, Sanborn S. (eds.), *The Pursuit of Knowledge in the Early American Republic* (Baltimore: Johns Hopkins University Press, 1976), p. 13.

33. Resnick and Resnick, "The Nature of Literacy," p. 378.

34. Rev. Joseph Cook, "Evil of Illiteracy," *Pennsylvania School Journal* 31 (1883), 433.

35. J. C. Zachos, "An Address to the Friends of Education, Especially among The Illiterate Classes" (New York, Aug. 1, 1891), pp. 12–15.

36. Robert L. Church and Michael Sedlak, *Education in the United States, an Interpretive History* (New York: The Free Press, 1976), pp. 79–80.

37. Michael B. Katz, *The Irony of Early School Reform* (Boston: Beacon Press, 1968), p. 112.

38. Statement of Hon. Philander P. Claxton, commissioner of education, House Committee on Education, *Hearings,* H. R. 6490, Sixty-fifth Congress, Second Session [March 9, 1918] (Washington, D.C.: G.P.O., 1918), p. 7.

39. Memorandum for the Adjutant General of the Army, June 27, 1918, National Archives, Washington, D.C., The Adjutant General's Office Record Group 407, File Box No. 805, 350.5 (7-31-18 to 6-27-18).

40. Statement of Hon. Philander P. Claxton, *Hearings,* H. R. 6490, pp. 8–10.

41. Statement of Hon. John W. Abercrombie of Alabama, *Hearings* on H. R. 6490, p. 21.

42. Additional testimony of Hon. Philander P. Claxton, *Hearings,* H. R. 6490, p. 31.

43. Letter from Van. H. Manning, director, Bureau of Mines, Department of Interior, House Committee on Education, *Hearings,* H. R. 15402, Sixty-fifth Congress, Third Session [Feb. 14, 15, 1919] (Washington, D.C.: G.P.O., 1919), p. 15.

44. Mr. Herbert Kaufman, "Digest in re Smith-Bankhead Americanization Bill," *Hearings,* H. R. 15402, p. 19.

45. Statements of Herbert Kaufman, *Hearings,* H. R. 15402, pp. 23–24.

46. Statement of Hon. Philander P. Claxton, commissioner of education, Bureau of Education, Department of the Interior, *Hearings,* H. R. 15402, p. 32.

47. Eli Ginzberg and Donald W. Bray, *The Uneducated* (New York: Columbia University Press, 1953), pp. 34–35, 37.

48. The extensive United States Army program for the education of illiterate inductees is, from a historical standpoint, an untold story, though a wealth of archival information exists on the subject. The most valuable is that contained in correspondence and memoranda of the Adjutant General's Office, the Information and Education Division (I and E), and studies of illiteracy and education conducted under contract for the U. S. Army and Navy.

49. Memorandum from Ralph C. Holliday, colonel, 367th Infantry, to commanding general, Third Army, Smith-Young Tower, San Antonio, Texas, Camp Claiborne, Louisiana, May 23, 1941, Records of the Adjutant General's Office, RG 407, AG 350.5, Unclassified Decimal File, 1940–45.

50. Memorandum from P. G. Fleetwood, captain, Med. Adm. C., assistant adjutant, Camp Pickett, Virginia, to the adjutant general, U. S. Army, Washington, D.C., Dec. 10, 1942, Records of the Adjutant General's Office, RG 407, 319.1, Unclassified Decimal File, 1940–45.

51. Letter from J. A. Ulio, major general, to Paul A. Nagle, director, Veterans Service Center, May 11, 1945, Records of the Adjutant General's Office, RG 407, 350. 5–1, Unclassified Decimal File, 1940–45.

52. Ginzberg and Bray, *The Uneducated,* pp. 38, 62–63.

53. Ibid., pp. 69–70. The army and navy together accepted 435,000 illiterates or semiliterates, 384,000 of whom were in the army. Approximately 300,000 were assigned to special training units, and 255,000 of these were graduated, though not all had passed the final exam. From the 300,000, Ginzberg and Bray selected a sample of 400 illiterates or semiliterates (200 white and 200 black), the majority of whom came from small-town, rural America. Of the sample 55 percent had never attended school; 228 were illiterate. (Ginzberg and Bray, pp. 73–81)

A report on the Navy's Literacy Program noted that "while illiterates are at a disadvantage in civilian life, they may be a distinct hazard in a military situation." Not only was illiteracy a "national disgrace," said one writer: it was a "grave national problem" "in the face of the Communist threat. . . ." (Wanda Dauksza Cook, *Adult Literacy Education in the United States* [Newark, Del.: International Reading Association, 1977], pp. 67–68)

54. Ibid., pp. 91–92

55. Ibid., p. 98.

56. Ibid., pp. 125, 131.

57. Department of Commerce, Bureau of Census, *Current Population Reports,* "Population Characteristics" (Feb. 4, 1960), Series P. 20, No. 99 (Washington, D.C.: G.P.O., 1960), pp. 2–3.

58. Cook, *Adult Literacy Education,* pp. 81–86, 103.

59. Statement of Albert J. Hayes, president, International Association of Machinists, House General Subcommittee on Labor and Select Subcommittee on Education of the Committee on Education and Labor, *Hearings,* on H. R. 10143 and H. R. 10191, Eighty-seventh Congress, Second Session, Feb. 14, 15, 16, 19 in Washington, D.C., and Feb. 23, 1962, Morehead, Kentucky (Washington, D.C.: G.P.O., 1962), p. 29.

60. Exhibit C from Ambrose Caliver, "Needed: Another Crash Program," *Adult Leadership* (Oct., 1958), *Hearings* on H. R. 10143 and H. R. 10191, p. 35.

61. Exhibit of Harley M. Kilgore, "Literacy and the National Welfare," *School Life* (Mar., 1952), *Hearings,* H. R. 10143 and H. R. 10191, p. 128.

62. Exhibit A, Statement of Richard J. Crohn, *Hearings,* H. R. 10143 and H. R. 10191, p. 29.

63. Exhibit A, Statement of Willard Givens, *Hearings,* H. R. 10143 and H. R. 10191, p. 30.

64. Statement of Glenn Jensen, executive director, Adult Education Association of the United States, *Hearings,* H. R. 10143 and H. R. 10191, p. 137.

65. Cook, *Adult Literacy Education,* p. 105.

66. Jack Mezirow, Gordon G. Darkenwald and Alan B. Knox, *Last Gamble on Education, Dynamics of Adult Basic Education* (Washington, D.C.: Adult Education Association of the United States of America, 1975), p. 6; Carman St. John Hunter and David Harman, *Adult Literacy in the United States, A Report to the Ford Foundation* (New York: McGraw-Hill Co., 1979), p. 100.

67. Hunter and Harman, *Adult Literacy,* p. 103.

68. Mezirow, Darkenwald, and Knox, *Last Gamble on Education,* p. 39.

69. Ibid., p. 41.

70. Hunter and Harman, *Adult Literacy,* p. 105.

71. Ibid., p. 108

72. Scribner, "Literacy in Three Metaphors," p. 9.

73. William McGowan, "Corporations Aim to Wipe Out Illiteracy," *Business and Society Review,* No. 44 (Winter, 1983), p. 37.

74. Ibid., pp. 37, 40.

Chapter 2

1. D. D. Raphael, *Justice and Liberty* (London: The Athlone Press, 1980), p. 174.

2. Ibid., p. 160.

3. Ibid., p. 160

4. Ronald Dworkin, *Taking Rights Seriously* (Cambridge, Mass.: Harvard University Press, 1977), p. 261.

5. Neil MacCormick and Ota Weinberger, *An Institutional Theory of Law* (Dordrecht, Holland: D. Reidel, 1986), p. 212. I do not discuss here the problem of autonomy and rights of organizations. This thorny topic has recently been taken up by Meir Dan-Cohen in *Rights, Persons, and Organizations, A Legal Theory for Bureaucratic Society* (Berkeley: University of California Press, 1986).

Dan-Cohen's analysis points up the weakness of utilitarian theories of business corporations as well as what is called the concession theory, according to which corporations owe their existence to the state and have no rights other than those explicitly granted to them. Dan-Cohen's theory sees organizations as "social entities" that provide a "moral buffer" between concerns of social utility and individual rights.

6. Iredell Jenkins, *Social Order and the Limits of Law, A Theoretical Essay* (Princeton, N.J.: Princeton University Press, 1980), pp. 336–37.

7. H. L. A. Hart, *The Concept of Law* (Oxford: Clarendon Press, 1961), p. 155.

8. Jenkins, *Social Order,* p. 324.

9. John Rawls, "Symposium, Justice as Fairness," *The Journal of Philosophy,* 54 (Oct., 1957), 653.

10. Alf Ross, *On Law and Justice* (Berkeley: University of California Press, 1959), pp. 268–269.

11. Ibid., p. 280.

12. Karl N. Llewellyn, *Jurisprudence: Realism in Theory and Practice* (Chicago: University of Chicago Press, 1962), p. 201.

13. Ibid., p. 203.

14. Ibid., pp. 203–204.

15. Ibid., p. 207.

16. Ibid., p. 209.

17. Ibid.

18. Rawls, "Symposium," p. 657.

19. John Rawls, *A Theory of Justice* (Cambridge, Mass.: Harvard University Press, 1971), p. 59.

20. Ibid.

21. Jenkins, *Social Order,* p. 347

22. Ibid., p. 350.

23. Ibid., p. 351.

24. Ibid., p. 351

25. Judith Shklar, *Legalism* (Cambridge, Mass.: Harvard University Press, 1964), pp. 111–123.

26. Otto A. Bird, *The Idea of Justice* (New York: Frederick A. Praeger), 1967, pp. 55–62.

27. Ibid., pp. 85, 137, 142.

28. Daniel J. Boorstin, "The Perils of Indwelling Law," in Robert Paul Wolff (ed.), *The Rule of Law* (New York: Simon and Schuster, 1971), pp. 88, 90. A very manifest though not extreme case of the spirit of indwelling law is presented by Boorstin in his analysis of law in the antebellum South. Here, he has remarked that southern culture came to "idealize the unwritten law, which was said to be the only proper law for a Christian society, an ennobling influence on all who allowed themselves to be ruled by it." (p. 85) The North was seen, by George Fitzhugh and other "loyal Southerners," as "legalistic, pettifogging, literal-minded, [and] mean-spirited . . . with its eye always on written record and the cash box. . . ." (p. 84) This was to be contrasted to the "indwelling" or "immanent" law of the South: "unwritten, inarticulate, untechnical, and unbending." (p. 86) This is an interesting observation when placed side by side with the high illiteracy rates in the South. What Boorstin is describing here is a society not committed to a formal, contractual way of life, a society where documents do not govern or govern only minimally, where the printed word and statute are not the foundations of progress.

29. Jenkins, *Social Order* p. 316.

30. Ibid., p. 317.

31. John Ladd, "Legal and Moral Obligation," *Political and Legal Obligation, Nomos XII* (New York: Atherton Press, 1970), p. 7.

32. Shklar, *Legalism,* pp. 38, 63.

33. Ladd, "Legal and Moral Obligation," pp. 10–11.

34. Rawls, *Theory of Justice,* p. 128.

35. Hart, *Concept of Law,* pp. 192–193.

36. Rawls, *Theory of Justice,* p. 113.

37. Ibid.

38. Ibid., p. 345.

39. Neil MacCormick, *Legal Right and Social Democracy, Essays in Legal and Political Philosophy* (Oxford: Oxford University Press, 1982), p. 207.

40. Michael J. Sandel, *Liberalism and the Limits of Justice* (Cambridge: Cambridge University Press, 1982), p. 114.

41. Ibid., p. 116.

42. Ibid., pp. 123–134.

43. Rawls, *Theory of Justice,* p. 347.

44. Ibid., pp. 111–112.

45. Sandel, p. 106.

46. Ibid., p. 105.

47. Ibid., p. 106.

48. Ibid., p. 107.

49. MacCormick and Weinberger, *Institutional Theory,* pp. 214–215.

50. John Rawls, "Justice as Fairness," *The Philosophical Review,* 67 (1958), 178.

51. Rawls, *Theory of Justice,* p. 133.

52. Rawls, "Justice as Fairness," pp. 179–180.

53. Ibid., p. 187.

54. Rawls, *Theory of Justice,* p. 240.

55. Ibid., p. 238.

56. Richard E. Flathman, "Obligation, Ideals and Ability," *Political and Legal Obligation, Nomos XII* (New York: Atherton Press, 1970), p. 101.

57. Rawls, *Theory of Justice,* p. 250.

58. Ibid., pp. 197–198.

59. Ronald Dworkin, *Taking Rights Seriously,* p. 273. Dworkin, among others, has taken issue with Rawls's methodology, particularly his use of the hypothetical social compact and a "natural" model that presupposes an objective moral reality. Dworkin proposes an alternative "constructive" model that does not presume fixed, objective principles of justice. Rather, it assumes that "men and women have a responsibility to fit the particular judgments on which they act into a coherent program of action, or, at least, that officials who exercise power over other men have that sort of responsibility." (p. 160) Dworkin sees this model as a "theory of community rather than of particular individuals." (p. 163) In other respects, however, Dworkin is like-minded with Rawls. His sympathies are antiutilitarian. He notes that a "utilitarian argument that assigns critical weight to the external preferences of members of the community will not be egalitarian . . . [and] will not respect the right of everyone to be treated with equal concern and respect." (p. 275) He notes that Rawls's theory of justice as fairness rests on the basic assumption that men "have a right to equal respect and concern in the design of political institutions." (p. 182) MacCormick's

commentary on Dworkin's political philosophy notes that he "gives pride of place to every person's right to equal concern and respect with every other." (MacCormick, *Legal Right,* p. 145) The point, he continues, is "not that people have a right to equality of treatment in every respect, but only that people have a right to treatment as equally deserving an equal measure of concern and respect from the government." (MacCormick, *Legal Right,* p. 146)

60. Rawls, *Theory of Justice* pp. 302–303.

61. Ibid., pp. 302, 204–205.

62. Gerald F. Gaus, "The Convergence of Rights and Utility: The Case of Rawls and Mill" *Ethics* (Oct., 1981), 59.

63. Ibid., p. 65.

64. Ibid., p. 61.

65. Kenneth A. Strike, *Educational Policy and the Just Society* (Urbana: University of Illinois Press, 1982), p. 70.

66. Ibid., p. 70.

67. Ibid., p. 99.

68. Ibid., p. 100.

69. Bruce A. Ackerman, *Social Justice in the Liberal State* (New Haven: Yale University Press, 1980), p. 163.

70. Ibid., p. 164.

71. Ibid., p. 167.

72. Rawls, *Theory of Justice* p. 72.

73. Ibid., p. 73.

74. Ibid.

75. Ibid., p. 74–75.

76. Ibid., p. 75.

77. Ibid., pp. 100–101.

78. Ibid., p. 101.

79. John Oxenham, *Literacy, Writing, Reading and Social Organization* (Boston: Routledge and Kegan Paul, 1980), p. 85.

80. Thomas Childers, *The Information Poor in America* (Metuchen, N.J.: The Scarecrow Press, 1975).

81. Nicholas C. Burbules, Brian T. Lord, and Ann L. Sherman, "Equity, Equal Opportunity and Education," *Educational Evaluation and Policy Analysis* 4 (Summer, 1982), 177–178, 186.

82. Rawls, *Theory of Justice,* p. 302; Allen Buchanan, "A Critical Introduction to Rawls' Theory of Justice" in *John Rawls' Theory of Social Justice, An Introduction,* ed. H. Gene Blocker and Elizabeth H. Smith (Athens: Ohio University Press, 1980), p. 10

83. Rawls, *Theory of Justice,* p. 303.

Chapter 3

1. 3 U.S. 386 at 388.

2. J. G. A. Pocock, *Politics, Language and Time, Essays on Political Thought and History* (New York: Atheneum, 1971), p. 85.

3. Ibid., p. 87.

4. Ibid.

5. Quentin Skinner, "The Idea of Negative Liberty: Philosophical and Historical Perspectives," *Philosophy in History, Essays on the Historiography of Philosophy,* ed. Richard Rorty, J. B. Schneewind, and Quentin Skinner (Cam-

bridge: Cambridge University Press, 1984), p. 214.

6. See Pocock, *Politics, Language and Time,* pp. 91–92.

7. Edmund S. Morgan, *The Challenge of the American Revolution* (New York: W. W. Norton and Co., 1976), p. 78.

8. Ibid., p. 65.

9. Gordon S. Wood, *The Creation of the American Republic, 1776–1787* (New York: W. W. Norton and Co., 1972), p. 108.

10. Ibid., p. 113.

11. Isaiah Berlin, "Two Concepts of Liberty," *Four Essays on Liberty* (New York: Oxford University Press, 1969), p. 123.

12. Skinner, "The Idea of Negative Liberty," p. 194.

13. Ibid., p. 195.

14. Hans Kelsen, *General Theory of Law and State* (Cambridge, Mass.: Harvard University Press, 1946), pp. 414–15.

15. Daniel J. Boorstin, *The Mysterious Science of the Law* (Boston: Beacon Press, 1958), p. 23. The glorification of the common law as the cultural and legal embodiment of man's reason and freedom is still a part of the British legal tradition. See, for example, Richard O'Sullivan, "The Concept of Man in the Common Law," *The Alabama Lawyer,* 16 (July, 1955), 268–284.

16. Boorstin, *Mysterious Science,* p. 91.

17. A. P. d'Entreves, *Natural Law, An Introduction to Legal Philosophy* (London: Hutchinson University Library, 1970), p. 55.

18. Cited in A. Robert Caponigri, *A History of Western Philosophy, Philosophy from the Renaissance to the Romantic Age,* Vol. 3 (Notre Dame, Ind.: Notre Dame University Press, 1963), pp. 98–99.

19. d'Entreves, *Natural Law,* p. 55.

20. Cited in Caponigri, *Renaissance to the Romantic Age,* p. 99.

21. Ernst Bloch, *Natural Law and Human Dignity,* trans. Dennis J. Schmidt (Cambridge, Mass.: The MIT Press, 1986), p. 48.

22. Ibid., p. 49.

23. Caponigri, *Renaissance to the Romantic Age,* p. 99

24. Ibid., pp. 99–100.

25. d'Entreves, *Natural Law,* p. 122.

26. Thomas Hobbes, *Leviathan,* parts I and II, intro. by Herbert W. Schendier (Indianapolis: Bobbs-Merrill, 1958), p. xi.

27. Thomas Hobbes, *De Cive, or the Citizen,* ed. and intro. by Sterling P. Lamprecht (New York: Appleton-Century-Crofts, 1949), pp. 54, 56.

28. J. Kemp, *Ethical Naturalism: Hobbes and Hume* (London: Macmillan, 1970), p. 13.

29. Ibid.

30. Hobbes, *Leviathan,* pp. 109–110.

31. Howard Warrender, *The Political Philosophy of Hobbes, His Theory of Obligation* (Oxford: Oxford University Press, 1957), pp. 58, 102.

32. Hobbes, *Leviathan,* pp. 112, 114–115.

33. Warrender, *Philosophy of Hobbes,* p. 47.

34. Hobbes, *Leviathan,* p. 201.

35. Ibid., p., 216.

36. Hobbes, *De Cive,* pp. 21–22.

37. Hobbes, *Leviathan,* pp. 212–113.

38. Hobbes, *De Cive,* pp. 57, 32.

39. Ibid., pp. 37–38.

40. Hobbes, *Leviathan,* p. 116.

41. John Locke, "First Treatise on Government," in *Two Treatises on Government,* ed. Peter Laslett (Cambridge: Cambridge University Press, 1960), pp. 326–327.

42. Peter Laslett, "Introduction," *Two Treatises on Government,* p. 110.

43. d'Entreves, *Natural Law,* p. 59.

44. P. S. Atiyah, *The Rise and Fall of Freedom of Contract* (Oxford: University of Oxford Press, 1979), p. 50.

45. M. Seliger, *The Liberal Politics of John Locke* (New York: Frederick A. Praeger, 1986), p. 165

46. Locke, *Second Treatise,* §27, p. 305; §26, p. 304; §34, p. 309.

47. James Tully, *A Discourse on Property, John Locke and His Adversaries* (Cambridge: Cambridge University Press, 1980), pp. 9, 37–38.

48. Locke, *Second Treatise,* §35, p. 310; §'s 48–49, p. 320.

49. d'Entreves, *Natural Law,* p. 59.

50. Locke, *Second Treatise,* §193, p. 413.

51. Laslett, "Introduction," *Two Treatises on Government,* p. 111.

52. Locke, *Second Treatise,* §57, pp. 323–324.

53. James McClellan, *Joseph Story and the American Constitution, A Study in Political and Legal Thought* (Norman: University of Oklahoma Press, 1971), pp. 62, 64. "In the decade preceding the *Declaration of Independence* some 2,500 copies of Blackstone's *Commentaries* were purchased and received by the Colonies of the Atlantic seaboard, nearly as many as were sold in England." (O'Sullivan, "The Concept of Man in the Common Law," p. 268)

54. Morton J. Horwitz, *The Transformation of American Law, 1780–1860* (Cambridge, Mass: Harvard University Press, 1977), p. 7.

55. Roscoe Pound, *The Formative Era of American Law* (Boston: Little, Brown and Co., 1928), p. 107.

56. Harold M. Hyman and William M. Wiecek, *Equal Justice Under Law, Constitutional Development, 1835–1875* (New York: Harper and Row, 1982), p. 44.

57. William E. Nelson, "The Eighteenth-Century Background of John Marshall's Constitutional Jurisprudence," *Michigan Law Review,* 76 (May, 1978), p. 926.

58. Ibid., p. 928.

59. 2 Dallas, 304 at 310.

60. Hyman and Wiecek, *Equal Justice,* p. 22.

61. Pound, *Formative Era,* pp. 98, 104, 107. More recently, Antieau has argued that "the identification of natural rights to common law rights by early Americans has been greatly exaggerated." (Chester James Antieau, "Natural Rights and the Founding Fathers—The Virginians," *Washington and Lee Law Review,* 17 [Spring, 1960], 51). Antieau has deemphasized the influence of Locke on the founding fathers, particularly Jefferson, and suggested, instead, that the influences upon Jefferson and his contemporaries were much more diverse. "Burlamaqui exerted a substantial influence upon some of Virginia's Founding Fathers," he notes, and so did Montesquieu, Vattel, Grotius, Filmer, Pufendorf and Aquinas (p. 78).

62. Roscoe Pound, "The End of Law as Developed in Juristic Thought," *Harvard Law Review,* 27 (May, 1914), 626–627.

63. Ibid., p. 628.

64. Wilson Carey McWilliams, "On Equality as the Moral Foundation for Community," *The Moral Foundations of the American Republic,* ed. Robert H.

Horwitz (Charlottesville: University Press of Virginia, 1986), p. 299.

65. Ibid.

66. Ibid.

67. Benjamin R. Barber, "The Compromised Republic: Public Purposelessness in America" in Horwitz, *Moral Foundations,* pp. 47–48.

68. "Records of the Town of Newark, New Jersey" in *Collections of the New Jersey Historical Society,* 6 (Newark: New Jersey Historical Society, 1864), p. 39.

69. Cited in Lee Soltow and Edward Stevens, *The Rise of Literacy and the Common School in the United States: A Socioeconomic Analysis to 1870* (Chicago: University of Chicago Press, 1981), p. 43.

70. Ibid.

71. Ibid.

72. Ibid., p. 46.

73. *Court Records of Kent County, Delaware, 1680–1705,* in *American Legal-Records,* Vol. 8, ed. Leon de Valinger, Jr. (Washington, D.C.: The American Historical Association, 1959), p. 68.

74. Ibid., p. 85.

75. *County Court Records of Accomack-Northampton, Virginia, 1632–1640,* in *American Legal Records,* Vol. 7, ed. Susie M. Ames (Washington, D.C.: The American Historical Association, 1954), p. 108.

76. *Records of the Suffolk County Court, 1671–1680,* Parts I and II, in *Publications of the Colonial Society of Massachusetts,* Vol. 29 (Boston: Colonial Society of Massachusetts, 1933), p. 115.

77. Carl F. Kaestle, *Pillars of the Republic* (New York: Hill and Wang, 1983), pp. 4–5.

78. Ibid., p. 9.

79. Cited in Marchette Chute, *The First Liberty, A History of the Right to Vote in America, 1619–1850* (New York: E. P. Dutton and Co., 1969), p. 297.

80. Lawrence Cremin (ed.) *The Republic and the School, Horace Mann on the Education of Free Men* (New York: Teachers College Press, 1957), p. 63.

81. Chilton Williamson, *American Suffrage, From Property to Democracy, 1760–1860* (Princeton, N.J.: Princeton University Press, 1960), p. 11.

82. Chute, *First Liberty,* pp. 304–313

83. Soltow and Stevens, *The Rise of Literacy,* p. 85. The content of this ideology of literacy is described by Soltow and Stevens as including "an emergent nationalism, a tradition of evangelical Protestantism, and traditional virtues associated with proper child rearing and proper behavior. . . . Literacy had become one of several virtues associated with progress while, at the same time, serving the conservative interests of social and political stability."

84. Ibid., pp. 178–179.

85. Ibid., pp. 52–53, 159–161, 168.

86. George D. Zuckerman, "A Consideration of the History and Present Status of Section 2 of the Fourteenth Amendment," *Fordham Law Review,* 30 (1961), 95.

87. Ibid., pp. 95, 97.

88. Ibid., pp. 108–110.

89. Ibid., pp. 116–117.

90. 34 *Congressional Record* (1900–01), as in Zuckerman, "Consideration of the History," p. 118.

91. Alfred Avins, "The Fifteenth Amendment and Literacy Tests: The Original Intent," *Stanford Law Review,* 18 (Apr., 1966), 821.

92. Zuckerman, "Consideration of the History," p. 95.

93. Avins, "Fifteenth Amendment," p. 811.

94. Ibid., p. 812.

95. Ibid., p. 815.

96. *Martin Luther v. Luther M. Borden, et al.* (1849), 48 U.S. 41 (7 Howard 598).

96. *United States v. Miller, et al.,* 107 F. 913 at 915.

98. 21 Sup. Ct. 163.

99. Ibid., at p. 173. See also, James H. Kettner, *The Development of American Citizenship, 1608–1870* (Chapel Hill: University of North Carolina Press, 1978), pp. 334–351.

100. Ibid., at pp. 177–178.

101. Kirk A. Porter, *A History of Suffrage in the United States* (Chicago: University of Chicago Press, 1981), p. 118.

102. E. Irving Smith, "The Legal Aspect of the Southern Question," *Harvard Law Review,* 2 (Mar., 1889), 374–375.

103. Cited in Wanda Dauksza Cook, *Adult Literacy Education in the United States* (Newark, Del.: International Reading Association, 1977), p. 3.

104. Rev. A. D. Mayo, LL.D., "The Significance of Illiteracy in the United States," *Education* 19 (Sept., 1898), 32, 34, 36.

105. Commissioner of Education, *Illiteracy in the State of New York* (Albany: New York State Education Department, 1906).

106. Ibid., p. 7.

107. Ibid., p. 8.

108. Ibid.

109. 141 N.E. 908.

110. Ibid., at 910.

111. Arthur W. Bromage, "The Political Implications of Illiteracy," Ph.D. thesis, Harvard University, 1928, pp. 229–231. In New York, proof of literacy for new voters could be given in ways other than the literacy test. These included:

a. A certificate or diploma showing completion of work in an approved eighth grade elementary school or of a higher school in which English was the language of instruction.

b. A matriculation card or official letter from a university or college showing attendance at such university or college.

c. A certificate of honorable discharge from any of the Armed Forces of the United States, if the new voter was a resident of the State of New York at the time he became a member of the Armed Forces.

d. An affidavit in lieu of the proof listed in a, b, or c above, executed in the form prescribed by section of 168 of the Election Law.

e. In the case of a military voter, the signature of the voter on the statement accompanying the military ballot.

f. In the case of an inmate or patient in a Veterans' Administration hospital, and certain members of his family, the signature of the voter on an application for registration by a veterans' absentee registration board if the hospital is located in this State, or the signature of the voter on an application for an absentee ballot if the hospital is located outside of this State. (The University of the State of New York, the State Education Department, Division of Educational Testing, *Literacy Testing and the Issuance of Certificates of Literacy* [Albany, 1960], p. 5).

112. As in Julien C. Monnet, "The Latest Phase of Negro Disfranchisement," *Harvard Law Review,* 26 (Nov., 1912), 42.

113. Ibid., p. 51.

114. Cited in *State of South Carolina v. Katzenbach* (1966), 86 S. Ct. 803 at 809.

115. Arthur Bromage, "Political Implications of Illiteracy," p. 87.

116. *Literacy Tests and Voter Requirements in Federal and State Elections.* (1962) Hearings before the Subcommittee on Constitutional Rights of the Committee on the Judiciary, United States Senate, Eighty-seventh Congress, Second Session on Senate Bills 480, 2750, 2979, pp. 4–5.

117. *Stone v. Smith, et al.*, Registrars of Voters, 34 N.E. 521.

118. 81 F. Supp. 872 at 878.

119. Ibid.

120. 238 U.S. 347 at 366.

121. United States Supreme Court, *Records and Briefs*, Vol. 238, p. 29.

122. 168 F. Supp. 183.

123. 83 U.S. 36 at 73, 81.

124. 133 U.S. 587 (1890); 163 U.S. 537 (1896). See also, "'Separate-but-Equal': A Study of the Career of a Constitutional Concept," *Race Relations Law Reporter* (1956), 283.

125. Paul L. Rosen, *The Supreme Court and Social Science* (Champaign: University of Illinois, 1973), pp. 29, 32, 36; 59 Mass. 198 (1849).

126. Ibid., pp. 120–121, 132, 164.

127. Ibid., p. 171.

128. *Brown v. Board of Education of Topeka* (1954), 74 Sup. Ct. Rep., 686 at 691.

129. Ibid., at pp. 691–692.

130. Louise Lassister, Appellant v. Northampton County Board of Elections. No. 584, United States Supreme Court, *Records and Briefs*, Vol. 360, p. 31.

131. 360 U.S. 45 at 53.

132. Ibid., at pp. 51–52.

133. *American Jurisprudence,* Second Edition, Vol. 25 (Rochester, N.Y.: The Lawyers Cooperative Publishing Co., 1966), pp. 749–750.

134. United States Commission on Civil Rights (1961), *Voting,* Book I (Washington, D.C.: G.P.O., 1961), pp. 21–22.

135. Ibid., p. 141; *Congressional Record,* 108, pt. 6, 8060, Eighty-seventh Congress, Second Session. Debate on literacy tests runs from 23 April to 9 May, at which point a motion on cloture was taken in an attempt to stop the southern filibuster.

136. Commission on Civil Rights (1961), *Voting,* Book 1, p. 141.

137. Kathryn M. Werdegar, "The Constitutionality of Federal Legislation to Abolish Literacy Tests: Civil Rights Commission's 1961 Report on Voting," *The George Washington Law Review,* 30 (Apr., 1962), 737.

138. *Congressional Record,* 108, pt. 6, Eighty-seventh Congress, no. 7921.

139. United States Commission on Civil Rights (1963) *Report* (Washington, D.C.: G.P.O., 1963), p. 30; 79 *United States Statutes at Large* (1965) Vol. 79, (Wash.: G.P.O.,1966), p. 439.

140. 86 S. Ct. 803.

141. Ibid., p. 810.

142. United States Code Service, 42, 1973b, p. 180.

143. Paul F. Hancock and Lora L. Tredway, "The Bailout Standard of the Voting Rights Act: An Incentive to End Discrimination," *The Urban Lawyer,* 17 (Summer, 1985), 380–381. See Sam J. Ervin, Jr., "The Truth Respecting the Highly Praised and Constitutionally Devious Voting Rights Act," *The Cumberland Law Review,* 12 (Spring, 1982), 261–281, for his continuing argument against the

constitutionality of the Voting Rights Act.

144. *South Carolina v. Katzenbach,* 383 U.S. at 329, as in Hancock and Tredway, "The Bailout Standard," p. 389.

145. Hancock and Tredway, "The Bailout Standard," pp. 381–382.

146. Ibid., p. 414.

147. Ibid., pp. 417, 421.

148. *The Statutes of Pennsylvania from 1682 to 1801,* Vol. II, compiled by James T. Mitchell and Henry Flanders (Clarence M. Busch, 1896), p. 215.

149. 2 Pa. D. and C. 275.

150. Ibid.

151. 32 S.W. 680.

152. Ibid., at pp. 682–683.

153. 191 So. 484.

154. 42 N.E. 475.

155. 78 P. 626.

156. 273 S.W. 69 at 73.

157. Ibid., at p. 75.

158. Ibid., at p. 74.

159. 55 P. 830 at 834–835.

160. 169 P. 596 at 607.

161. Ibid.

162. Francis W. Treadway, "Needed Reforms in Municipal Charters and Government," *Yale Law Journal,* 2 (Dec., 1892), 61.

163. Herbert Knox Smith, "The Failure of Municipal Government," *Yale Law Journal,* 5 (Oct., 1895), 27.

164. George E. Hill, "The Secret Ballot," *Yale Law Journal,* 1 (Oct., 1891), 27–28.

165. Alexander Hamilton, "Federalist No. 59," *The Federalist Papers,* intro. by Clinton Rossiter (New York: Mentor, 1961), p. 362.

166. 4 Sup. Ct. Rep. 152 at 155.

167. Ibid., at p. 159.

168. Ibid., at p. 155.

169. 87 O.S. 12; as in *State v. Sweeney,* 94 N.E. 2d 785 at 789.

170. 87 O.S. 12 at 35–36.

171. Ibid., at p. 45; as in *State v. Sweeney,* 94 N.E. 2d at 791.

172. 94 N.E. 2d at 789.

173. *Simmonds v. Eyrich, et al.,* 95 N.E. 2d 595 at 597.

174. Ibid., at pp. 597, 599.

175. Ibid., at pp. 600–601.

176. United States Code Service, 28, Procedure, 1865, p. 546. Cumulative Supplement, 1865, p. 291.

177. *United States v. Santos* (1979), 588 F. 2d 1300, cert den 441 US 906, 60 L Ed 2d 374, 99 S. Ct. 1994, cited in 28 USCS, Cumulative Supplement, Juries, 1865, p. 291.

178. *United States v. Gates* (1977), 557 F. 2d 1086, cert den 434 US 1017, 54 L. Ed 2d 783, 98 S. CT. 737, cited in 28 USCS, Cumulative Supplement, Juries, 1865, p. 291.

179. *United States v. Rouco* (1985), 765 F. 2d 983, cited in 28 USCS, Cumulative Supplement, Juries, 1865, p. 291.

180. Proffatt, *A Treatise on Trial by Jury* (San Francisco: Sumner Whitney Co., 1880), pp. 164–165.

181. *State v. Pickett* (1897), 73 N.W. 346.

182. *Redford Mabry v. The State* (1894), 71 Miss. 716 at 721: *Spicer v. The State* (1914), 188 Ala. 9 at 38.

183. 13 Ind. 81 at 101.

184. 23 La. Ann. 16.

185. 25 La. Ann. 472.

186. 2 Brew. 378 at 380.

187. 52 Miss. 216 at 224.

188. 28 La. Ann. 84.

189. 56 Miss. 180 at 194.

190. 41 Tex. 172 at 176.

191. Ibid., at 176–77, 179.

192. 9 Texas Ct. App. 124 at 126.

193. 12 Texas Ct. App. 163 at 164, 168.

194. 5 Colo. 65 at 67.

195. Ibid., at p. 70.

196. Ibid., at p. 71.

197. 22 P. 820 at 822.

198. 21 Texas Ct. App. 368 at 379, citing *Rainey v. The State,* 20 Texas Ct. App. 473.

199. 20 Fla. 981 at 998.

200. Commission on Civil Rights (1961), *Justice,* Book 5 (Wash. D.C.: G.P.O., 1961), p. 99.

201. Hyman and Wiecek, *Equal Justice,* pp. 494–495.

202. Commission on Civil Rights (1961), *Justice,* pp. 90–91.

203. Ibid., pp. 91, 244.

204. 71 *U.S. Statutes at Large,* 638.

205. 298 F. 2d, 522 at 525.

206. Ibid. at 526.

207. 100 N.W. 341.

208. 86 So. 2d 208 at 210, 211.

209. 308 S.W. 2d 815; 25 Cal. App. 3d 776.

210. 308 S.W. 2d 815 at 819.

211. Ibid., at 817.

212. Ibid.

213. 25 Cal. App. 3d 776 at 778, 782.

214. Ibid., at 784.

215. Ibid., at 784–785.

216. Ibid., at 787.

217. Ibid., at 284–285.

Chapter 4

1. Kenneth A. Lockridge, *Literacy in Colonial New England* (New York: W. W. Norton and Co., 1974); Lee Soltow and Edward Stevens, *The Rise of Literacy and the Common School in the United States: A Socioeconomic Analysis to 1870* (Chicago: University of Chicago Press, 1981).

2. Lockridge, *Literacy,* p. 39. For a discussion of difficulties relating to the use of wills see Soltow and Stevens, *The Rise of Literacy,* pp. 34–39.

3. Soltow and Stevens, *The Rise of Literacy,* p. 35.

4. *County Court Records of Accomack-Northhampton, Virginia, 1632–1640,*

in *American Legal Records,* Vol. 7, ed. Susie M. Adams (Washington, D.C.: The American Historican Association, 1954), p. 135.

5. Ibid., p. 155.

6. *Records of the Suffolk County Court, 1671–1680,* Parts I and II, in Publications of the Colonial Society of Massachusetts, Vol. 29 (Boston: Colonial Society of Massachusetts, 1933), pp. 132–133.

7. Excellent discussions of biases in probate data are given in G. B. Nash, "Urban Wealth and Poverty in Pre-Revolutionary America," *Journal of Interdisciplinary History,* 6 (Spring, 1976), 545–584; D. S. Smith, "Underregistration and Bias in Probate Records: An Analysis of Data from Eighteenth-Century Hingham, Massachusetts," *William and Mary Quarterly,* 32 (Jan., 1975), 100–110; and G. L. Main, "The Correction of Biases in Colonial American Probate Records," *Historical Methods Newsletter,* 8 (Dec., 1974), 10–28. The rural poor in particular in Washington County, Ohio, are probably underrepresented in the sample simply because severe problems of transportation and communication would have mitigated against their estates' being probated. (See Edward W. Stevens, Jr., "Books and Wealth on the Frontier: Athens County and Washington County, Ohio, 1790–1859," *Social Science History,* 5 (Fall, 1981), 440.

8. The data for wills in Kent and Washington counties are described in the Appendix.

9. Soltow and Stevens, *The Rise of Literacy,* p. 52.

10. *Records of the Suffolk County Court,* p. 1087.

11. *North Carolina Higher Court Records, 1670–1696,* ed. Nattie Erma Edwards Parker (Raleigh, N.C.: State Department of Archives and History, 1968), p. 205.

12. As in Soltow and Stevens, *The Rise of Literacy,* p. 45.

13. *Court Records of Kent County, Delaware, 1680–1705,* in *American Legal Records,* Vol 8, ed. Leon de Valinger, Jr. (Washington, D.C.: The American Historical Association, 1959), pp. 84–85.

14. See the Appendix for the sample of deeds and mortgages from Kent and Washington counties.

15. The Proportion of Illiterate Grantors of Deeds Classified by Sex and Year for Kent and Washington Counties, 1780–1900

Year	Illiterate			Female/Male Illiterates, Ratio
	M	F	All	(%F/%M)
1780-90				
Kent	.06	.15	.10	2.5
Washington	0.0	0.0	0.0	—
1800				
Kent	.02	.36	.17	18.0
Washington	.02	.13	.04	6.5
1820				
Kent	.04	.19	.11	4.7
Washington	.03	.10	.04	3.3

Year	Illiterate			Female/Male Illiterates, Ratio
	M	F	All	(%F/%M)
1840				
Kent	.11	.24	.17	2.2
Washington	.05	.23	.13	4.6
1860				
Kent	.09	.18	.13	2.0
Washington	.08	.23	.15	2.9
1880				
Kent	.10	.08	.09	0.8
Washington	.07	.15	.11	2.1
1900				
Kent	.07	.10	.08	1.4
Washington	.07	.06	.06	0.85

Source: Subsamples of 1,239 grantors from Kent County, Delaware, and 2,603 grantors from Washington County, Ohio, 1780–1900. Repeated names and institutional grantors are omitted.

16. Soltow and Stevens, *The Rise of Literacy*, p. 178. For wealth estimates in colonial America see Alice Hanson Jones, *American Colonial Wealth, Documents and Methods*, 3 vols. (New York: Arno Press, 1978), and Alice Jones, *Wealth of a Nation to Be by the American Colonies on the Eve of the Revolution* (New York: Columbia University Press, 1980).

17. The sex distribution of grantors overall is 59 percent male and 41 percent female for Washington County and 55 percent male, 45 percent female for Kent County. These proportions, however, altered dramatically in Washington County over the period 1790–1900, and particularly between the years 1820–1860. This, in part, accounts for a rise in county illiteracy rates among grantors during this period. From only 1 female grantor (6 percent) in 1790 in Washington County, female participation grew to 44 percent in 1840 in Washington County. By 1900 female participation was 47 percent. The pattern is linear and the ratio of 17:1 (male/female) in 1790 to 1.13:1 (male/female) in 1900 clearly demonstrates the shift in female participation. The male/female ratio over the 120-year period in Kent County shows much less variation. There is an overall, but slow, trend toward a greater proportion of female grantors. When the two counties are compared for the latter part of the century between the years 1840 to 1900, the male/female ratios are virtually identical.

For individual mortgagors with repeated names eliminated, the sex distribution of the sample is 58 percent male and 42 percent female for Washington County and 54 percent male, 46 percent female for Kent County. As with grantors, the sex distribution for mortgagors changed dramatically in Washington County. Male mortgagors outnumbered female in 1840 by a margin of 2:1. By 1860, this margin had dropped to 1.4:1 and by 1880 to 1.1:1. In Kent County, the male/female ratio remained constant from 1860 to 1900 and was at the same level as it was in Washington County. Thus, for the last forty years of the nineteenth century, the ratio of sexes among grantors and mortgagors in the two counties was approximately the same.

18. The Proportion of Illiterate Mortgagors Classified by Sex and Year for Kent and Washington Counties, 1780–1900

	Illiterate			Female/Male Illiterates, Ratio
Year	M	F	All	(%F/%M)
1840				
Kent	—	—	—	—
Washington	.06	.40	.17	6.7
1860				
Kent	.06	.19	.12	3.2
Washington	.09	.23	.15	2.6
1880				
Kent	.07	.16	.11	2.3
Washington	.10	.16	.13	1.6
1900				
Kent	.07	.08	.07	1.1
Washington	.05	.05	.05	1.0

Source: Subsamples of 806 mortgagors from Kent County, Delaware, and 1,151 mortgagors from Washington County, Ohio, 1840–1900. Repeated names and institutional mortgagors are omitted.

19. Every deed transaction, with the exception of federal land grants, included some "consideration" given in return for land. Generally this consideration represented the value of the transaction. The value of the consideration, however, should not be interpreted as representing the value of the land itself. Even as a measure of the value of the transaction, however, it might be simply a "token" to fulfill legal requirements. Considerations such as "love and affection" or "goodwill" are obvious candidates for omission when calculating the value of transactions. When determining what a token value is, however, the decision is more subjective.

The value chosen for the upper limit of a "token" consideration was $10; values from $1 to $10, then, were interpreted as having only symbolic or technical significance. Most of the values ranging from $1 to $10 were actually $1 considerations, so that there is little question about their significance in a symbolic or technical sense only. Because these values served only a legal function, their inclusion in calculating average values of deed transactions is misleading. Fortunately, token considerations comprise only a small (between 2 and 12 percent) percentage of the total transactions and when omitted still leave us with a sizable sample for analysis.

The deed values for Kent County were considerably higher than for Washington County, though this difference does not seem to have been of any significance in determining the literacy rates of the two counties. Literacy rates were, however, related to wealth at the individual level, as is explained in the following section. On a national level of analysis, also, aggregate wealth has been shown to be related to level of literacy (see note 16). The range of values of deeds in a given year of analysis was very large, and this fact is significant in its relationship to illiteracy.

In Kent County, where the mean values of deeds were higher, the range was also greater than in Washington County. An extreme example occurs in 1880 in Kent County, where the range in values for deed transactions of $10 and above for individual grantors was $15 to $75,000. Even where the range is not so extreme, however, the highest value of a deed in a given year was still between three hundred and nine hundred times the amount of the lowest deed value. In Washington County, the range in deed values was not so great. Even so, the highest values were one hundred to six hundred times as great as the lowest values.

When the general pattern of considerations for deed transactions is analyzed, it is seen that values for Washington County, Ohio, were fairly stable from 1790 to 1840. Thereafter they increased sharply. These patterns persist for both individual and institutional grantors. This is not true for Kent County. Although data for the year 1840 also show a drop in the adjusted values of deeds from the previous years of 1820 and 1800, this drop is considerably larger for Kent County than for Washington County. Following the decrease in Kent County deed values in 1840, there was a steep rise in the next forty years, though by 1900 the adjusted values were at the 1820 level. In Washington County, however, the upward trend in adjusted and unadjusted values is more persistent over the hundred-year period from 1800 to 1900. In 1840, Washington County values also decreased, but not nearly so precipitously, and recovery was steady for the next sixty years.

In percentage terms, the increase in the values of deeds for the period 1880–1900 was in the range of 5.5 percent for all transactions in Kent County. For all individual transactions, as well as those above the $10 token level, there was a decrease in values in 1900 relative to the year 1800 on the order of 3.9 to 6.2 percent. If only the ninety-year period from 1800 to 1890 is examined, there is a large increase in deed values for Kent County, also, regardless of whether the grantors were individual or institutional. This was true for individual transactions over $10 also. Thus, in Kent County, Delaware, the adjusted value of deeds for the three categories varied between $799 and $891 in 1800. By 1890 these adjusted values were in the range of $1,092 to $1,129. Taking the categories separately, then, the range of increase was between 26.7 and 36.6 percent, respectively, for individual transactions above $10 and all transactions, individual as well as institutional.

The increase in deed values for Kent County in the ninety-year period 1800–1890 is comparable to that experienced in Washington County, Ohio, for the hundred-year period, 1800–1900. In the latter county, the greatest percentage increases occurred between 1840 and 1860. During these years percentage increases ranged between 53 percent for individual grantors above the $10 token consideration level and 57 percent for individual grantors overall. Between 1860 and 1880, percent increases were also high, ranging between 37 and 41 percent. In the hundred-year period from 1800 to 1900, adjusted values for deeds in Washington County increased approximately 70 percent for individual grantors and 89.5 percent for institutional grantors.

Certain similarities between deed and mortgage transactions appear when the latter are examined. As with grantors, most mortgagors were individuals.

Most of these individuals were indebted to other individuals from the period 1840 to 1890. The coming of the banking and loan association in the latter part of the nineteenth century, however, changed this pattern radically. This trend was most evident in Washington County, where 56 percent of the mortgage indebtedness was to banking and loan associations in 1900 compared to virtually no indebtedness to such associations prior to that time. The change was not dramatic in Kent County. Nonetheless, the trend away from indebtedness to individuals is apparent in 1900, when 7 percent of the mortgagors were in debt to banking and loan associations and 12 percent to other types of associations.

The values of Kent County mortgages were considerably higher than those in Washington County. This, of course, would be expected, because the values of deeds were higher and would be a major determinant of indebtedness. In Washington County, indebtedness through mortgage increased gradually over the sixty-year period between 1840 and 1900. The average adjusted value of individual mortgage transactions in 1840 in Washington County was $550 compared to $806 in 1900, a 46.5 percent increase. Conversely, in Kent County, the average adjusted value of an individual mortgage dropped from $4,101 in 1860, to $1,710 in 1880, to $1,471 in 1900; overall, this was a 155 percent decrease. The range of indebtedness as determined by mortgage values was very large, as was the case with deed values. It was common to find many mortgages in the $50 to $100 range and a large number in the $400 to $500 range. Some mortgages, however, were thirty times that much. Both the mean and the range of values were strongly related to the literacy of the mortgagors.

20. The Mean Value (*M*) and the Range of Values in Dollars of Deed Transactions Classified by Year and Illiteracy for Kent and Washington Counties, 1780–1900*

Year	Value of Deed Transactions for				Ratio of Mean Values (LI/ILL)
	Literates		Illiterates		
	M	Range	*M*	Range	
1780–90					
Kent	3,362	27–25,515	3,007	270–7,668	1.1
Washington	401	32–1,386	—	—	—
1800					
Kent	922	13–5,940	631	40–2,700	1.5
Washington	396	20–10,300	205	40–800	1.9
1820					
Kent	1,047	30–9,000	673	30–3,250	1.6
Washington	380	12–4,500	369	100–1,000	1.02
1840					
Kent	717	20–6,200	212	16–1,000	3.4
Washington	401	13,4000	294	15–1,500	1.4

Year	Literates		Illiterates		Ratio of Mean Values (LI/ILL)
	M	Range	M	Range	
1860					
Kent	1,417	18–10,500	613	12–8,400	2.3
Washington	652	15–8,000	498	20–2,000	1.3
1880					
Kent	1,495	15–75,000	538	31–2,012	2.8
Washington	863	15–8,500	530	20–2,700	1.6
1900					
Kent	1,179	20–13,000	352	20–1,000	3.3
Washington	932	20–13,000	519	25–3,400	1.8
1780/90–1900					
Kent	1,252	13–75,000	551	12–8,400	2.3
Washington	627	12–13,000	433	15–3,400	1.4

Source: Subsamples of 841 deed transactions from Kent County, Delaware, and 1,060 deed transactions from Washington County, Ohio, 1780–1900. Institutional grantors and "token" considerations of $10 and below are omitted.

*Many transactions had more that one grantor. Many, also, included literates and illiterates within a single transaction .Because the unit of analysis is the transaction, it was necessary in computing the means for literates and illiterates to count a transaction only once. Thus, for example, a transaction having three grantors, two of whom were literate and one of whom was illiterate, was counted once (not twice) for the literate and once for the illiterate. Likewise, a transaction having two illiterate grantors was counted once (not twice) for the illiterate category.

21. The Mean Value (M) and the Range of Values in Dollars of Mortgage Transactions Classified by Year and Illiteracy for Kent and Washington Counties, 1840–1900*

	Value of Mortgages for				
					Ratio of Mean Values (LI/ILL)
Year	Literates		Illiterates		
	M	Range	M	Range	
1840					
Kent	—	—	—	—	—
Washington	581	12–5,200	317	19–2,650	1.8

Continued on next page

Year	Literates		Illiterates		Ratio of Mean Values (LI/ILL)
	M	Range	M	Range	
1860					
Kent	4,189	21–18,000	2,279	21–8,000	1.8
Washington	528	48–5,000	388	50–2,150	1.4
1880					
Kent	1,767	75–18,000	593	70–2,150	3.0
Washington	595	50–3,200	456	31–1,600	1.3
1900					
Kent	1,532	50–12,000	923	100–7,500	1.7
Washington	868	17–12,000	409	60–800	2.1
1840–1900					
Kent	2,056	21–18,000	1,070	21–8,000	1.9
Washington	663	12–12,000	381	19–2,650	1.7

Source: Subsamples of 503 mortgage transactions from Kent County, Delaware and 729 mortgage transactions from Washington County, Ohio, 1840–1900. Institutional grantors and "token" considerations of $10 and under are omitted.

*The same method of computation for grantors is used for mortgagors. (See previous note)

22. Charles Sisson, "Marks as Signatures," *The Library, A Quarterly Review of Bibliography,* 9, 4th ser. (June, 1928), 3–4.

23. As in Sisson, *"Marks as Signatures,"* p. 25.

24. George L. Haskins, "The Beginnings of Partible Inheritance in the American Colonies," in David H. Flaherty (ed.), *Essays in the History of Early American Law* (Chapel Hill: University of North Carolina Press, 1969), p. 214. Thorp L. Wolford, "The Laws and Liberties of 1648," in Flaherty, *Essays,* p. 177.

25. Wolford, "Laws and Liberties," p. 177.

26. Lawrence M. Friedman, *A History of American Law* (New York: Simon and Schuster, 1973), p. 219. Friedman observes that "in a group of Southern and Western states, and states where civil law influence was strong (Texas, Louisiana), holographic wills were also valid. These wills, if entirely handwritten by the testator, required no witnesses." (p. 219n).

27. Ibid., 371.

28. Ohio App. 2d 492 at 495. See also *In the Matter of the Will of Cornelius,* 14 Ark., 75; *Bailey's Heirs v. Bailey's Executor* (1860); 35 Ala. 687, *In re. Kelly's Estate* (1932), 160 A., 454; *Conley v. Coburn et al., Sexton, et al. v. Conley, et al.,* (1944), 297 Ky., 292; and *Bustillos v. State* (1948), 213 S.W. 2d, 837.

29. *Maupin v. Berkely* (1882), *The Kentucky Law Reporter,* 3 (Frankfort, Kentucky, 1882, 617); *Meazels v. Martin* (1892), 93 Ky., 50; *Staples v. Bedford Loan and Deposit Bank* (1895), 33 S.W., 403; *Terry v. Johnson* (1901), 109 Ky., 589.

30. 93 Ky., 50.
31. 32 Engl. Rep., Chancery 12, 324, 450; (8 Ves Jun. 187, 504).
32. 5 John., 144 at 156.
33. 7 N.J.L., 70 at 73.
34. 96 Ga. 1 at 5.
35. Ibid., at 6–13.
36. 13 Eng. Rep. 365 at 369.
37. Ibid., at 372–373.
38. 18 Ga. 397.
39. 59 Ky. (2 Met.), 449.
40. 58 N.H. 7 at 10.
41. 2 Rob. 95 at 96.
42. 49 Eng. Rep. Rolls Court II 710 at 711.
43. 92 N.Y. Sup. Ct. 343 at 355–356.
44. Ibid., at 356.
45. Ibid.
46. 27 Md. 391 at 399, 400.
47. 100 Pa. 434 at 437.
48. 108 Pa. 567 at 568.
49. 80 So. 39 at 40.
50. 10 Paige CH. 85 at 90.
51. 26 N.J. Eq. 337 at 339, 344.
52. 23 Ark. 396 at 404.
53. See *Guthrie, et al. v. Price, et al.,* 23 Ark. at 405. See also, *Lyons v. Riper,* 26 N.J. Eq. 339.
54. 140 P. 340; 31 O.C.A. 463; 101 A. 295; 259 N.W. 894; 185 F. 2d 423; 97 N.E. 2d 260, 259 S.W. 2d 665.
55. *Barlion v. Connor,* 31 O.C.A. 464.
56. 815 F. 2d 423.
57. *Morrow v. Person, et al.* (1953) 259 S.W. 2d 665.
58. 440 P. 340 at 341.
59. 101 A. 295 at 298.
60. 15 D. and C. 261 at 262.
61. 158 A. 2d 548 at 550–551.
62. 143 A. 511 at 512.
63. 71 S.W. 2d 413 at 415.
64. 345 Pa. 447 at 448–50.
65. 259 N.C. 359 at 362.
66. Ibid., at 363, citing *Furst v. Merritt.*
67. 92 Pa. 134 at 137.
68. Ibid., at 137–138.
69. 254 S.W. 126 at 127.
70. Ibid., at 129.
71. 142 Misc. 124 at 125–126.
72. Ibid., at 127, 129.
73. 120 P. 601 at 602.
74. Ibid., at 602.
75. Ibid.
76. Ibid.
77. 44 Kan. 741, P. 221; 27 So. 649; 140 N.C. 100, 52 S.E. 252.
78. 120 P. 601, at 606.

79. 23 A. 307 at 308.
80. Ibid., at 309.
81. Ibid., at 310.
82. 87 Wis. 105; 15 Ohio C.C. 501.
83. 87 Wis. 105 at 109.
84. 15 Ohio C.C. 501 at 502–503.
85. 146 A. 172 at 173.
86. Ibid.
87. Ibid., p. 174.
88. Ibid.
89. Ibid., at 175.
90. 177 So. 399 at 401.
91. Ibid.
92. 265 P. 2d 147.
93. Ibid.
94. 101 A. 24 at 25.
95. Ibid.
96. 51 So. 852 at 853; 223 P. 350 at 851.
97. 166 P. 115 at 1157. The court explained: "The rule is that, where the judgment sought to be vacated is not void for lack of jurisdiction, but is merely voidable because irregularly or fraudulently procured, it will not be vacated until the court has found, not only that the facts alleged in the petition to vacate constitute a defense, but also that there is substantial evidence to support at least prima facie the matter of defense so alleged." (166 P. at 1157)
98. 213 P., 389 at 390.
99. 51 So. 852 at 853.
100. Ibid.
101. 277 N.W. 369.
102. Ibid., pp. 370–371.
103. Grant Gilmore, *The Death of Contract* (Columbus: Ohio State University Press, 1974), pp. 8–13.
104. Cited in Gilmore, *Death of Contract,* p. 10.
105. Ibid., p.16.
106. Ibid., p. 20, citing Holmes.
107. Ibid., p. 21.
108. James William Hurst, *Law and Social Order in the United States* (Ithaca, N.Y.: Cornell University Press, 1977), pp. 62, 232.
109. Gilmore, *Death of Contract,* pp. 63–64, 94.

Chapter 5

1. Lon L. Fuller, *The Principles of Social Order,* intro. by Kenneth I. Winston (Durham, N.C.: Duke University Press, 1981), pp. 174–177.
2. Ibid., pp. 184–185.
3. Fuller citing Bendham, ibid., p. 184.
4. M. T. Clanchy, *From Memory to Written Record, England 1066–1307* (Cambridge, Mass.: Harvard University Press, 1979), p. 245. The imposition of the Norman feudal system on England was accompanied by a centralization of power and administration, which, says Keeton, led to "the steady progress of the royal courts to a position of supremacy over all other courts within the realm." Accompanying this centralization came an increase in numbers of royal documents, a

process, says Clanchy, that itself "tended to enlarge and stratify the bureaucracy which produced them." Blackstone (who characterized the Normans as a "brave but illiterate nation") to the contrary, Clanchy argues that after 1066 there was an "increase in the number of documents made and the gradual extension of literate modes to more people and diverse activities." The pressing need to come to an understanding of and suitable compromise with Anglo-Saxon law and the necessity of collecting revenue undoubtedly contributed to the burgeoning numbers of documents in the late eleventh century. (George W. Keeton, *The Norman Conquest and the Common Law* [London: Ernest Benn Ltd., 1966], pp. 201, 214; Clanchy, *From Memory* pp. 46, 87; Sir William Blackstone, *Commentaries on the Laws of England,* Vol. 1 [Philadelphia: Robert Bell, 1771]. reprint edition by the Layton Press, p. 305)

5. Clanchy, *From Memory,* pp. 56–57. Clanchy has argued that literacy had been extended "to most barons by 1200, to knights by 1250, to peasants by 1300." It would be incorrect to infer, however, that the spread of literacy down the social scale meant that the "majority of people acquired a minimal ability to read and write the language they spoke." "Neither Middle English nor French," observes Clanchy, "was sufficiently standardized, or well enough established as a literary language, to become the basis of elementary instruction in reading and writing until well after 1300." Moreover, an oral tradition was much in evidence particularly in the process of pleading. Still, even here, documentary evidence was forcing a change in thinking: "Narrators survived throughout the Middle Ages, but by the fifteenth century 'counting' was no longer done orally but on paper." Elsewhere, the relative subjugation of the oral tradition and the emergence of the document as authority substantially altered the meaning of witnessing conveyances and wills. (pp. 56–57, 223, 202–203).

6. Compromises with oral tradition were made, as Clanchy observes, yet "writing had the profoundest effects on the nature of proof, as it seemed to be more durable and reliable than the spoken word." (p. 150) Other dimensions of legal procedure exhibited similar tendencies. With the rule under Henry II that "'no one is bound to answer for any freehold of his in his lord's court without a royal writ,' a document (royal writ), instead of a voice, became the basis of legal procedure for all important land transactions in seignorial courts as well as royal ones." Despite the requirement of royal summoners, by the time of Edward I the sheriff was to execute a royal writ "not by instructing summoners orally, as had been the practice in the twelfth century, but by sending a written precept to the appropriate local bailiff ordering him to execute the writ." (p. 220)

That all did not understand such records, nor possess even minimal reading and writing skills, is quite evident. By the seventeenth century illiteracy was still present at all social levels but was particularly prevalent among poor folk of low social standing. Between 1580 and 1700, says Cressy, "some 35 percent of the yeomen giving evidence before the Consistory Court at Norwich . . . could not sign their depositions." (David Cressey, "Levels of Illiteracy in England, 1530–1730," *The Historical Journal* 20 [1977], 7) This illiteracy level, notes Cressey, was above that for the gentry but way below that "of the husbandmen and poorer country folk" (p. 7) Among constables directly responsible for the local execution of legal orders, the level of illiteracy varied enormously. In 1642 only 7 percent of those in Somerset were illiterate; but this may be contrasted with 50 to 53 percent illiterate among the constables of Nottinghamshire, Sussex, Warwickshire, and Buckinghamshire. One hundred percent of the constables in Cheshire and Westmoreland were illiterate. (Keith Wrightson, "Two Concepts of Order; Justices,

Constables and Jurymen in Seventeenth-Century England," in John Brewer and John Styles, *An Ungovernable People, The English and Their Law in the Seventeenth and Eighteenth Centuries* [London: Hutchinson and Co., 1980], p. 28) Suffice it to say that the written records that underlay the extension of the king's justice did not prod all to become literate even when necessary. By the sixteenth century literacy was stratified from highest to lowest by social status: from gentry to yeoman to husbandman to laborer. There is little reason to suspect that a similar stratification was absent in the half-century preceding. Clanchy has observed that it is difficult to speak of minimal literacy levels in the twentieth-century sense in medieval England because of the changing appellations of *clericus* and *literatus.* "By the middle of the fifteenth century London tradesmen [were] being described as literati." (Clanchy, *From Memory,* p. 185)

7. J. R. Gulson, *The Philosophy of Proof in its Relation to the English Law of Judicial Evidence* (London: George Routledge and Sons Limited, 1905), pp. 259, 262.

8. Coke reporting on decision; cited in James Bradley Thayer, *A Preliminary Treatise on Evidence at the Common Law* (Boston: Little, Brown and Co., 1898), p. 401.

9. Ibid., p. 411.

10. Gulson, *Philosophy of Proof,* p. 266.

11. In his work on contract in 1790, Powell offered the following description of the term *contract:* "a contract is a transaction in which each party comes under an obligation to the other, and each, reciprocally, acquires a right to what is promised by the other." Numerous agreements would fall under such a broad definition: feoffment, gift, grant, lease, loan, pledge, bargain, covenant, agreement, and promise. The definition illustrates remarkably well the extent to which the concept of contract had become pervasive in Anglo-American law by the eighteenth century. At the same time, however, it does us little service as an adequate description of either the formalities or nuances of the term as it evolved in early English law. (As in Warren B. Hunting, "The Obligation of Contracts Clause of the United States Constitution," *Johns Hopkins University Studies in Historical and Political Science,* Series 37, No.4 [Baltimore: The Johns Hopkins Press, 1919], p. 34)

12. The attention of medieval man focused upon problems of peace (security) in a "disorderly society largely devoid of public or private records," says Payne; he was not, as in the twentieth century, preoccupied "with how to increase economic mobility" and the ways in which contract could serve that end. (John C. Payne, "The English Theory of Conveyances Prior to the Land Registration Act," *Alabama Law Review,* 7 [Spring, 1955], 235) Payne no doubt greatly underestimates the proliferation of public records by the thirteenth century, yet his remarks do point to the important fact that, relative to the twentieth century in England and America, medieval England was a place where day-to-day uncertainties (particularly in communication and transportation) made it difficult to adopt a "business-as-usual" attitude.

13. Harold C. Havighurst, *The Nature of Private Contract, 1961 Rosenthal Lectures* (Evanston, Ill.: Northwestern University Press, 1961), p. 56. At the risk of oversimplifying the amalgamation of Anglo-Saxon and Norman law, it is quite likely that the evolution of the practice and concept of individual obligation in England was accelerated by the Norman conquest. The personalized relationship that characterized feudal landholding patterns in medieval England was far different from the relationship of individual obligation today.

In a brief synopsis of the historical debate over the existence or nonexistence of Anglo-Saxon contract law, Brody has observed that, although instances of contractual provisions were few by comparison to later medieval times, they constituted an important recognition of the need to resolve private disputes leading to vendettas and to discourage cattle stealing. Over a period of five hundred years prior to the Norman conquest, Anglo-Saxon society developed contractual procedures for dealing with "sales of real estate, cattle and other personal property, testamentary depositions and betrothals." (Burton F. Brody, "Anglo-Saxon Contract Law: A Social Analysis," *De Paul Law Review*, 19 [Autumn, 1969], 295) He notes of written contracts that the Anglo-Saxon will presided over by the church was contractual in nature. Unlike modern wills, which "are the dispositive act of the testator," they "recorded a prior disposition of the property in a legally enforceable exchange" and were thus irrevocable. (Brody,"Anglo-Saxon Contract Law," pp. 287–288) Land contracts, too, were preferably documented: "Within fairly short order the written transfer of land became a ceremony having equal legal stature with the *wed* [symbolic passing of a stick or spear] ceremony" (Brody, "Anglo-Saxon Contract Law," p. 289)

If we extract the concept of personal obligation from the context of status with which it was associated in medieval England, it became centuries later the basis of moral obligation in contractual relationships. Even before the end of the fourteenth century, notes Jenks, courts of common law were regulating "such relationships as innkeeper and guest, lender and borrower, seller and buyer, consigner and carrier, craftsman and customer, master and servant, surety and principal debtor. . . ." Cases involving innkeeper and guest, consigner and carrier, and buyer and seller, he continues, "were probably rather new in the fourteenth century." These relationships, however, were characterized by individual parties to an agreement, and "judges were inclined to lay a good deal of stress on the terms of the 'undertaking,' or *assumpsit* in question." Thus the "law of these subjects proceeded . . . from 'status to contract.'" (Edward Jenks, *The Book of English Law*, Ed. P. B. Fairest, 6th rev. ed. [Athens: The Ohio University Press, 1967], p. 315)

In 1864 the author of *Ancient Law*, Henry Sumner Maine, offered the thesis that "the movement of the progressive societies has hitherto been a movement *from Status to Contract.*" (Henry Sumner Maine, *Ancient Law, its Connection with the Early History of Society and its Relation to Modern Ideas* [New York: Henry Holt and Co., 1888], p. 165) Behind this thesis lay an evolutionary concept of the development of civil law. As Maine would have it:

> The movement of the progressive societies has been uniform in one repect. Through all of its course it has been distinguished by the gradual dissolution of family dependency and the growth of individual obligation in its place. The individual is steadily substituted for the Family, as the unit of which civil laws take account. (Maine, *Ancient Law*, p. 163)

Havighurst has asserted that "Maine is basically correct in his view that when life transcends the family tie, contract becomes more and more the instrument by which relationships are established which set the patterns of living." (Havighurst, *Private Contract*, p. 18)

14. Medieval lawyers thought in terms of particularized transactions rather than a generalized conception of contract. These transactions, which usually had their origin in the numerous arrangements for real property that developed as part of feudal, and later, quasi-feudal arrangements for landholding were, in

turn, translated into a large number of particular actions at common law. (A. W. B. Simpson, *A History of the Common Law of Contract* [Oxford: Clarendon Press, 1975], p. 187)

15. Payne, "Theory of Conveyances," pp. 245, 258.

16. The action of covenant (requiring written terms and usually in the form of a deed or indenture), which was a "remedy for failure to *do* something as agreed, did not lie at common law on a parole agreement." Failure to pay or "hand over a chattel (but not land) as agreed was actionable at common law by writ of debt [seeking restoration of money] or detinue [seeking restoration of a wrongful detention of a chattel]." (Simpson, *Common Law of Contract*, p. 187; Bryce Lyon, *A Constitutional and Legal History of Medieval England* [New York: Harper and Row, 1960], p. 467)

17. S. F. C. Milsom, *Historical Foundations of the Common Law* (London: Butterworths, 1969), pp. 215–216. The distinction between covenant and contract is not a clear one, as Simpson observes. The year-book term for agreement was *covenant*, yet "lawyers of the time," says Simpson, also "were well aware of the fact that the standard debt contracts were the product of the agreement of the parties, at least as a general rule, so that there was a relationship between 'contract' and covenant." Yet contract and covenant were not identical: "the term 'covenant' was most commonly used to refer to agreements which either were actionable by writ of covenant, or would be if only a speciality was available, whilst 'contract' was earmarked for transactions actionable by writ of debt." In the medieval period, the term *contract* did not generally apply in "situations in which debt liability was imposed in the absence of any sort of consensual transaction; the predominant usage limited the term 'contract' to those informal agreements which were actionable by writ of debt." (Simpson, *Common Law of Contract*, pp. 187–190)

18. As in Spencer L. Kimball, *Historical Introduction to the Legal System*, American Casebook Series (St. Paul, Minn.: West Publishing Co., pp. 137–138.

19. W. T. Barbour, "The History of Contract in Early English Equity," *Oxford Studies in Social and Legal History*, IV, ed. Paul Vinogradoff (Oxford: Clarendon Press, 1914), pp. 116–118.

20. Cases brought on the action of assumpsit usually included a plaintiff who had "entrusted his person or property (the property always being a living creature) to the defendant for some particular purpose." The defendant was always one who possessed a skilled craft and who was accused of being negligent in injuring the plaintiff's property. (Simpson, *Common Law of Contract*, pp. 199, 218) The action of trespass and the plea of assumpsit had become well established by the fifteenth century. Milsom has written that "in the fifteenth century common law . . . trespass actions, actions for wrongs, were doing a fair range of work which we should call contractual and which lawyers at the time recognized as having affinities with covenant." (Milsom, *Common Law*, p. 277) According to Simpson, these actions were characterized by the feature "that in them a plaintiff was allowed to claim damages by way of compensation for a wrong which had been done to him." This "legal technique was quite different from the technique of the ancient real actions, in which the claimant demanded seisin of land, and quite different also from the techniques of the ancient contractual actions of debt, detinue, and covenant, where the claimant demanded the specific recovery of the debt, the chattel or charter, or the actual performance of the covenant." (Simpson, *Common Law of Contract*, p. 199)

21. Frederick G. Kempin, Jr., *Legal History, Law and Social Change* (Engle-

wood Cliffs, N.J.: Prentice-Hall, 1963), pp. 82–83.

22. "It was resolved, that every contract executory imports in itself an assumpsit, for when one agrees to pay money, or to deliver anything, he thereby assumes or promises to pay or deliver it, and thus when one sells any goods to another, and agrees to deliver them at a future day, and the other in consideration thereof agrees to pay such a sum at such a day, in that case both parties may have their actions of debt, or actions on the case on an assumpsit, for the mutual executory agreement of both parties imports in itself reciprocal actions upon the case in addition to actions of debt." (As in Kempin, *Legal History*, p. 82)

23. The restrictions of such a concept are very evident, because medieval law generally recognized only *real* contracts, that is, a contract "which only becomes binding when one party has performed his side of the agreement." It is difficult to discern how widespread this particular interpretation of quid pro quo was in medieval law. The concept, says Simpson, seems to have been relevant in cases when the issue was one of whether or not a transaction "ought to be actionable by writ of debt at all." Quid pro quo "served to distinguish bare parole grants of debts, which were not actionable, from parole contracts, which could impose debt liability." The uncertainty with respect to the application of quid pro quo, particularly in the case of third parties, in the long run hampered its usefulness. (Simpson, *Common Law of Contract*, pp.193–194)

24. Ibid., 465–466.

25. Jenks, *Book of English Law*, p. 317.

26. Kempin, *Legal History*, p. 84.

27. According to Havighurst:

In assumpsit, no express subsequent promise to establish, no formal requirements at all, no wager of law or even the defendant's testimony to contend with, no restrictive rules of evidence; if mutual promises were alleged, no necessity for showing a *quid pro quo*. And in covenant, none of these things either, except the formal requirement of the sealed instrument and the delivery. With the recognition of implied assumpsit, moreover, the inability to establish an express promise was not fatal. (Havighurst, *Private Contract*, pp. 57–58)

28. Ibid., p. 58.

29. The Statute of Frauds was amended as follows in 1828:

No action shall be brought whereby to charge any person upon or by reason of any representation or assurance made or given concerning or relating to the character, conduct, credit, ability, trade, or dealings of any other person, to the intent or purpose that such other person may obtain credit, money, or goods upon, unless such representation or assurance be made in writing, signed by the party to be charged therewith. (*Halsbury's Statutes of England*, third edition, vol. 7 [London: Butterworths, 1969], pp. 6–7)

30. P. S. Atiyah, *The Rise and Fall of Freedom of Contract* (Oxford: Clarendon Press, 1979), p. 206.

31. William B. Stoebuck, "Reception of English Common Law in the American Colonies," *William and Mary Law Review*, 10 (Winter, 1968), 393.

32. Ibid., pp. 394–395.

33. Julius Goebel, Jr., "King's Law and Local Custom in Seventeenth Century New England" *Essays in the History of Early American Law*, ed. David H. Flaherty (Chapel Hill: University of North Carolina Press, 1969), p. 117.

34. Leon P. Lewis, "The Development of a Common Law System in Connecticut," *Connecticut Bar Journal,* 27 (June, 1953), 422, 424.

35. Connecticut judges did not reject out of hand the English precedent for some decisions. It was, in in effect, a compromise situation as the case of *Wilford v. Grant* (1786) illustrates:

> The common law of England we are to pay great deference to, as being a general system of improved reason, and a source from whence our principles of jurisprudence have been mostly drawn. The rules, however, which have not been made our own by adoption, we are to examine, and so far vary them as they may appear contrary to reason or unadapted to our local circumstances, the policy of our law, or simplicity of our practice. . . . (Ibid., p. 425)

36. Stoebuck, "Reception of English Common Law," pp. 399, 407.

37. George L. Haskins, "A Problem in the Reception of the Common Law in the Colonial Period," *University of Pennsylvania Law Review,* 97 [1949], 849; Stoebuck, "Reception of English Common Law," p. 399. At times, the administration of English common-law principles was at variance with English common law, such as an act in 1649 that interpreted the widow's share of the husband's estate as including realty as well as personalty. In general, however, and certainly at the appellate level, common-law principles were known and practiced "perhaps from reference to a limited supply of English secondary authorities, such as Coke." (Stoebuck, "Reception of English Common Law," p. 407)

38. Lawrence M. Friedman, *A History of American Law* (New York: Simon and Schuster, 1973), pp. 54–55. For an examination of conveyancing in post-Revolutionary Alabama see John C. Payne, "The Theory of Conveyancing at Law in Alabama," *Alabama Law Review,* 8 (Fall, 1955), 10–36.

39. Friedman, *History of American Law,* p. 55.

40. Stoebuck, "Reception of English Common Law," p. 409.

41. Some of the increasing presence of English common law in the latter half of the eighteenth century was probably due to greater numbers of English-trained lawyers in the colonies. This was true in South Carolina, Virginia, Maryland, Pennsylvania, and New York more than in other colonies. Massachusetts relied little on the inns of court and mostly on reading from local law offices. Rhode Island staffed its bench with laymen uneducated in the law. (Ibid., pp. 411, 413)

42. Nelson points out that "English common law actions, such as trespass, trover, case, debt, covenant, assumpsit, and replevin were also used in Massachusetts." Most cases involving title to land were pleaded under a broad generic plea of land, thus eliminating ancient English actions derived from feudal times. Bringing a suit was expensive, however, first, because of high court costs. Second, there were lawyers fees to be paid though these were not excessive. Finally, the system of pleading (which underwent reform in the late eighteenth century in Massachusetts) helped to raise the cost of litigation because the technical niceties of pleading often produced dismissals. (William E. Nelson, "The Reform of Common Law Pleading in Massachusetts, 1760–1830: Adjudication as a Prelude to Legislation," *University of Pennsylvania Law Review,* 122 [Nov., 1973], 99.

43. Ibid., pp. 108, 113.

44. Nelson explains the antipathy to pleading as follows:

> Opponents of the common law system contended that "the state of pleading in this Commonwealth [had become such] that an honest man . . . [could] not obtain" right and justice "without being obliged to employ a lawyer, at a great

expense." "Artful men in England," they explained, "ha[d] so entangled the mode of managing a cause with the nice distinction of special pleas (and . . . [the courts in Massachusetts had] unfortunately adopted the pernicious practice) that in short justice [could] scarcely be obtained unless it be dearly purchased." "[I]nstead of obtaining justice 'freely,' 'completely,' and 'promptly,'" many litigants saw their "causes . . . carried through every tedious labyrinth" and juries "hindered from coming to a speedy decision of a cause, by the labouring pleadings" of the common law. (Nelson, "Reform of Common Law Pleading," (p.111), citing Austin, *Observations on the Pernicious Practice of the Law* [1794], pp. 3–4)

45. Francis R. Aumann, "The Influence of English and Civil Law Principles upon the American Legal System During the Critical Post-Revolutionary Period." *University of Cincinnati Law Review,* 12 (June, 1938), 290.

46. Ibid., p. 941. The comprehensive reception statute of 1712 in South Carolina that declared 167 statutes of Parliament in force in the colony set the tone for years to come. Legislation in South Carolina remained "keenly property-conscious," and provisions for recording "protected the owners and purchasers of real property." (James W. Ely, Jr., "American Independence and the Law: A Study of Post-Revolutionary South Carolina Legislation," *Vanderbilt Law Review,* 26 [Oct., 1973], 946, 952)

47. (William H. Brantley, Jr., "Law and Courts in Pioneer Alabama," *The Alabama Lawyer,* 6 (1945), 390–400; Elizabeth Gaspar Brown, *British Statutes in American Law, 1776–1836* (Ann Arbor, The University of Michigan Law School, 1964), p. 44. Of the various forms of actions between 1796 and 1805 from which calculations could be made—a total of 1,041—the great bulk (868) were trespass on the case; 496 of these were assumpsit. Thirty-three cases were brought on the action of covenant and sixty-eight in the action of debt.(William W. Blume, "Civil Procedure on the American Frontier, A Study of the Records of a Court of Common Pleas of the Northwest and Indiana Territories (1796–1805)," *Michigan Law Review,* 56 [Dec., 1957], pp. 182–183)

In Texas, British common law relating to juries and evidence was adopted in 1836, although the abolishment of civil law and the substitution of common law in general waited until 1840. The adaptation of the common law generally simplified the process of pleading. The reception of common law (equally as important as its adoption), says Markham, was characterized by "an impatience with the technicalities and formalism of the common law," "a picking and choosing [of the best] attitude," and a "general acceptance of the substantive parts of the common law as contrasted with general rejection of the practice of that system." (Edward Lee Markham, Jr., "The Reception of the Common Law of England in Texas and the Judicial Attitude Toward the Reception, 1840–1859," *Texas Law Review,* 29 [1951], 908–909, 911)

Two midnineteenth-century cases illustrate the attitude in that early period of Texas statehood. (Markham, "Reception of the Common Law," pp. 908, 911):

The rules of the common law have never been considered obligatory, as matter of absolute principle, on questions of practice, but our courts have either adhered to their former practice, or have adopted such rules of their own as seemed dictated by considerations of policy and convenience, rather than pursue the common law practice, where the rule which it afforded was found to be unsuited to our system, or inconvenient of application. (*Grassmeyer v. Beeson* [1855])

Our legislation has not adopted the pleadings and practice, either of courts of law or chancery, as known in the remedial jurisprudence of England and other common law countries; and their rules of practice are not of any obligatory force, as matter of absolute principle, farther [sic] than they have been introduced or recognized by our own statutory provisions. . . . When not in harmony with our remedial system, or inapplicable to it, and inconvenient in practice, they have not been observed. They do not constitute, necessarily, a part of our law of procedure, merely because they obtain, and are deemed of obligatory force, in the courts of common law and chancery in other countries, whose jurisprudence is moulded upon the principles of the common law. (*Sequin v. Maverick* [1850])

48. Grant Gilmore, *The Ages of American Law* (New Haven: Yale University Press, 1977), p. 19.

49. Milsom, *Common Law,* p. 101; Barbour, "Contract in Early English Equity," p. 153.

50. Barbour, "Contract in Early English Equity," p. 153.

51. Milsom, *Common Law,* p. 101.

52. Barbour, "Contract in Early English Equity," pp. 153, 158. Bryant had observed that by the fifteenth century "there had emerged a definite court of equity which had jurisdiction in cases which [fell] outside the common law; in cases where the common law could not be made effective, and in cases which could not be dealt with by the ordinary courts because the law itself was at fault." (James R. Bryant, "The Office of Master in Chancery: Early English Development," *American Bar Association Journal,* 40 [June, 1954], 533)

53. Generally, a complainant before the chancellor avowed that an agreement or bargain had been made. It was also common but not necessary for the complainant to allege that he had suffered some damages such as the payment or part payment of the purchase price or the making of improvements. It should be added that "consideration" was always present in the bargain made. (Barbour, "Contract in Early English Equity," p. 119. Says Barbour, "No action lay at law until Assumpsit was formally recognized in 1504, and at that time the payment of the purchase price was a condition precedent to bringing the action." [pp. 116–117])

54. Stanley N. Katz, "The Politics of Law in Colonial America: Controversies Over Chancery Courts in Equity Law in the Eighteenth Century," in Donald Fleming and Bernard Bailyn (eds.) *Law in American History* [Boston: Little, Brown and Co., 1971], p. 259. To aid in the definition of the difficult concept of equity, Katz offers the following descriptive categories:

(1) *Equity remedies defects in the common law.* It takes notice of fraud, accident, mistake and forgery. It administers relief according to the true intentions of the parties. It gives specific relief in actions for contract and tort, and it gives relief against the penalties assessed by other courts. It has unique powers of examining witnesses, and joining parties to a suit.

(2) *Equity supplies omissions in the jurisdiction of the common law.* It deals with uses and trusts, and, especially, with mortgages and equities of redemption. It disposes of the guardianship of minors and lunatics. It has competence in mercantile law, family settlement, female property, and divorce.

(3) *Courts of equity afford procedures not available at law.* The writ of subpoena, interrogatory process, discovery of evidence, written pleadings, judgment without jury trial, leeway for errors in pleading, specific performance,

injunction, imprisonment for contempt, ability to act *in personam* rather than *ad rem,* powers of account, and administration of estates. (259–260)

To the twentieth-century viewer, unencumbered by the shackles of fifteenth-century common law forms, equity seems commonsensical. Yet the High Court of Chancery had numerous critics. First among these were common lawyers themselves, who, says Katz, "strongly objected to the prerogative character of equity law." Basically, he observes, their complaints were those of Seldon in 1821 that: "For the law we have a measure . . . [but] equity is according to the conscience of him that is Chancellor, and as that is larger or narrower, so is equity." (Katz, "Politics of Law," pp. 260–261) Many of the complaints focused on the administration of the court, observes Katz, not the "character of equity law" itself. (Katz, "Politics of Law," p. 261) The increase in business before chancery and the growing complexities of procedures were managed primarily by the clerks, under-clerks, and attorneys. The lord chancellor had "little control over [the] work habits" of these servants of the court. The increasing importance of precedent in chancery proceedings helped to favor those whose financial resources would allow them to conduct exhaustive researches for cases and records. Common lawyers played a more important role in chancery after 1529, thus leading to a closer harmony of chancery and common-law procedures. Ironically, however, this resulted in a host of procedural complexities that made the quick administration of justice next to impossible. (William J. Jones, "Due Process and Slow Process in the Elizabethan Chancery," *The American Journal of Legal History,* 6 [Apr., 1962], 148–149; Stuart E. Prall, "The Development of Equity in Tudor England," *The American Journal of Legal History,* 8 [1964], 19)

55. Katz, "Politics of Law," p. 246.

56. Pound has noted that the Puritan mind had always opposed equity because it acted "directly upon the person, coerced "individual will," and "means that a magistrate is over us instead of with us. . . ." (Roscoe Pound, *The Formative Era of American Law* [Boston: Little, Brown & Co., 1938], p. 155) The principles of equity, however, were not abandoned. Beginning in 1675 the General Court of Massachusetts authorized county courts and later the superior court to act as courts of equity. The acts, however were negatived. (Katz, "Politics of Law," p. 265) This included, as of 1836, hearing suits for the specific performance of contract. (Friedman, *History of American Law,* p. 130; see also, James R. Bryant, "The Office of Master in Chancery: Colonial Development," *American Bar Association Journal,* 40 [July, 1954], 595–598, and William J. Curran, "The Struggle for Equity in Massachusetts," *Boston University Law Review,* 31 [June, 1951], 287) Finally, in 1857 a statute was passed allowing the General Court to have "'full equity jurisdiction according to the usage and practice of chancery in all cases where there is not a plain, adequate and complete remedy at law.'" (Curran, "Struggle for Equity Jurisdiction," p. 287)

In some colonies, the Crown refused to allow legislation creating equity courts, reasoning that "legislative creations" were a "serious encroachment upon the powers of the Crown." By the early eighteenth century in Great Britain it was apparent that equity needed procedural reform. In the colonies, the sentiment for reform persisted, usually taking the form of giving equity jurisdiction to courts of law. A Virginia act of 1705 establishing and regulating a general court "set forth in detail the oath of a judge of the general court in chancery." And in 1710 an act for establishing county courts "provided that all county courts should have jurisdiction in chancery." According to Bryant, "the chancery practice had become so important in Virginia [by 1745] that the House of Burgesses enacted a law setting aside the first five days of every general court for hearing and determining suits in chancery." (Bryant, "Master in Chancery: Colonial Development," 597–598) In North Carolina, notes Friedman, "an act of 1782 empowered 'each superior court of law' to ' 'be and act as a court of equity for the same district.'" (Friedman, *History of American Law,* p. 130)

The battle between the champions of equity and its opponents in Pennsylvania provides a good illustration of the eventual accommodation of the common law to principles of equity. Attempts to assign the powers of equity to county courts in this colony early met with the same opposition from the Crown as in other colonies. In 1720, however, Pennsylvania did establish a chancery court, which lasted sixteen years and was the "only separate court of chancery Pennsylvania ever had." (Spencer R. Liverant and Walter H. Hitchler, "A History of Equity in Pennsylvania," *Dickinson Law Review,* 37 [1933], 162. The so-called Cosby controversy in New York that resulted in the case of *Attorney General v. Van Dam*(1732) probably influenced the development of chancery jurisdiction in Pennsylvania and, say Smith and Hershkowitz, "contributed to the abolition of the Governor and Council as a court of equity in Pennsylvania. . . ." (Joseph H. Smith and Leo Herschkowitz, "Courts of Equity in the Province of New York: The Cosby Controversy, 1732–1736," *American Journal of Legal History,* 16 [Jan., 1972], 50)

Despite this short-lived success, the principles of equity were part of the heritage of "natural justice" and could not be abandoned. Thus, common-law courts took over the job of equity: "Common law actions [in Pennsylvania] were used to enforce purely equitable claims; purely equitable defenses were permitted in common law actions; and, at rare times, purely equitable reliefs were obtained by means of actions at law. (Liverant and Hitchler, "History of Equity," p. 166)

57. Ibid., pp. 164–174, 178. The predilection of equity courts for written evidence was likewise altered in federal equity cases by the Judiciary Act of 1789, which provided for oral testimony, and in Georgia, for example where trial by jury was allowed in some equity cases. (Friedman, *History of American Law,* p. 131)

Legislative equity also functioned in other states with the granting of equitable relief in response to private petitions for the same. Between 1736 (the date that the chancery court was abolished in Pennsylvania) and 1836 (the date that the Pennsylvania Assembly passed a bill giving the Supreme Court and the common pleas court of Philadelphia equity jurisdiction) the Pennsylvania legislature acted as chancellor in private petitions for equitable relief.

58. Thomas A. Cowan, "Legislative Equity in Pennsylvania," *University of Pittsburgh Law Review,* 4 (Nov., 1937), 2–4. Cowan has collected seven hundred such instances between 1700 and 1837 in Pennsylvania.

59. 169 U.S., 366.

60. Ibid., at p. 392, cited in *Holden v. Hardy,* (1898).

61. Ibid., at p. 391–392.

62. William E. Nelson, "The Eighteenth-Century Background of John Marshall's Constitutional Jurisprudence," *Michigan Law Review* 76 (May, 1978), p. 960.

63. Joseph P. Cotton, Jr., (ed.), *The Constitutional Decisions of John Marshall,* Vol. 2 (New York: G. P. Putman's Sons, 1905), pp. 174–175.

64. John Marshall, *Ogden v. Saunders,* in Cotton, *Decisions of John Marshall,* Vol. 2, p. 180.

65. Ibid., pp. 198, 199, 209. The obligation of the contract "is a necessary conse-

quence of the right to make it," noted Marshall. Obligation and remedy [for non-performance] are not the same, however, for they "originate at different times, and are derived from different sources." Society "prohibits the use of private, individual coercion, and gives in its place a more safe and more certain remedy." Local governments, noted Marshall, are restrained "from impairing the obligation of contracts, but they furnish the remedy to enforce them. . . ." The language of the Constitution "is the language of restraint, not coercion," Marshall observed, and it "prohibits the States from passing any law impairing the obligation of contracts [although] it does not enjoin them to enforce contracts." (*Ogden v. Saunders,* as in Cotton, pp. 204–205) Marshall illustrated the distinction between obligation and remedy with the following example:

> Should a state be sufficiently insane to shut up or abolish its Courts, and thereby withhold all remedy, would this annihilation of remedy annihilate the obligation also of contracts? We know it would not. If the debtor should come within the jurisdiction of any Court of another State, the remedy would be immediately applied, and the inherent obligation of the contract enforced. This cannot be ascribed to a renewal of the obligation; for passing the line of a State cannot recreate an obligation which was extinguished. It must be the original obligation derived from the agreement of the parties, and which exists unimpaired though the remedy was withdrawn. (Ibid., p. 205)

66. Thomas Hobbes, *De Cive, or the Citizen,* p. 157. For a recent analysis of the moral foundation of promise and contract, see Charles Fried, *Contract as Promise, a Theory of Contractual Obligation* (Cambridge: Harvard University Press, 1981).

67. Marshall, *Ogden v. Saunders,* in Cotton, *Decisions of John Marshall,* pp. 209–210.

68. McClellan describes Story's position as follows: he "stands squarely in the classical and Christian natural law tradition [not the tradition of social contract and natural rights] regarding the origin of the state." He adhered to the idea that the state was "the natural expression of man's true self, . . . the organic development of the polity, originating at the rudimentary stage of family life and progressing to the more complex city-state." It was "an instinctive, unconscious expression of man's conformity to Divine plan, satisfying human needs." (McClellan, *Joseph Story and the American Constitution,* pp. 65–66, 74–75; McClellan notes that by 1820 Story "was clearly under Burke's influence." [p. 79])

Gilmore has noted Story's indebtedness to the thought of Lord Mansfield and the more general sympathy with Mansfieldianism:

> In England itself [in 1820] the tide was already beginning to turn against Mansfield: his radical approach to the problem of judicial law-making was in course of being scrapped in favor of a quasi-Blackstonian approach which emphasized adherence to precedent. In this country, however, a pure Mansfieldianism flourished: not only were his cases regularly cited but his light-hearted disregard for precedent, his joyous acceptance of the idea that judges are supposed to make law—the more law the better—became a notable feature of our early jurisprudence. Justice Story, in particular, both in his opinions and in his non-judicial writings, never tired of acknowledging his indebtedness to, and his reverence for, Lord Mansfield. (Gilmore, *Ages of American Law,* p. 24)

69. McClellan, *Joseph Story,* pp. 84–85.

70. As in McClellan, *Joseph Story,* p. 232.

71. Ibid., pp. 215, 233–234.

72. Kent Newmyer, "Justice Joseph Story, the Charles River Bridge Case and the Crisis of Republicanism," *American Journal of Legal History,* 17 (July, 1973), pp. 234–236.

73. As in Newmyer, "Justice Joseph Story," p. 239.

74. Morton J. Horwitz, "The Transformation in the Conception of Property in American Law, 1780–1860," *University of Chicago Law Review,* 40 (Winter, 1973), 248, 270.

75. Atiyah, *Freedom of Contract,* pp. 36, 214.

76. Ibid., pp. 214, 353.

77. Ibid., pp. 103, 212–213, 243.

78. Atiyah describes the free market model as follows:

> parties deal with each other "at arm's length" ... [each relying] on his own skill and judgment ... the parties bargain or negotiate. ... Neither party owes any duty to the other until a deal is struck. ... Neither party owes any duty to volunteer information to the other. ... Each party must study the situation, examine the subject matter of the contract, and the general market situation. ... The only limitation to this market bargaining is that there must be no fraud or misrepresentation, but even these concepts are narrowly construed. ... The content of the contract, the terms and the price and the subject-matter, are entirely for the parties to settle. (Atiyah, pp. 402–403)

79. Atiyah notes that the principle of caveat emptor was never enforced "to the utmost rigor." (*Freedom of Contract,* p. 471) "The reality of the matter was that buyers frequently did not rely on their own judgment, but on the integrity and responsibility of sellers, or on the general course of business. A person who paid a price which was fair for a sound commodity, was, by that fact alone, demonstrating that he expected to get a sound commodity, and if he did not, the contract was simply an unfair exchange. Although the Courts did not revert to the old language of just prices or fair exchanges, the effect of their decisions in the 1860's was to do precisely this." (*Freedom of Contract,* pp. 474–475)

80. Executory contract theory—will theory—"came to swallow the part executed and even the wholly executed contract. ..." The will theory of contract thus came to mean "mere expectations as entitled to the same protection as actual property." (Atiyah, pp. 428–429)

81. Morton J. Horwitz, "The Transformation in the Conception of Property in American Law, 1780–1860," *University of Chicago Law Review,* 40 (Winter, 1973), pp. 248, 270. The Horwitz theory of the rise of executory contracts and a will theory of contractual obligations has been subjected to a detailed analysis and scathing criticism by Simpson. (A. W. B. Simpson, "The Horwitz Thesis and the History of Contracts," *University of Chicago Law Review* 46 [Spring, 1979], pp. 533–601) This debate is not of immediate concern to this study. My purpose in outlining contractual theory is much more modest, viz., to illustrtate the extreme importance of contractual obligations to social and economic theory and behavior and to the day-to-day actions of individuals who have a "stake" in property, real and otherwise.

I am interested in the contractual basis of the nineteenth-century social order, its dependence on a moral and legal norm of obligation, and the importance of a meeting of the minds for the illiterate person. For critiques of Horwitz's general method of analysis see also, R. Randall Bridwell, "Theme v. Reality in American Legal History: A Commentary on Horwitz, *The Transformation of American Law, 1780–1860,* and on the Common Law in America," *Indiana Law Journal,* 53 (Spring, 1978), 449–496; and Charles J. McClain, Jr., "Legal Change and Class Interests: A Review Essay on Morton Horwitz's *The Transformation of American Law,*" *California Law Review,* 68 (Mar., 1980), 382–397.

82. James Willard Hurst, *Law and Social Order in the United States* (Ithaca, N.Y.: Cornell University Press, 1977), p. 89. Legal historians are agreed that from approximately 1810 to 1890 the great efforts of American common law were in the areas of contract, property, torts, mortgages, and commercial instruments. Just as land had become a major commodity in trade through the fee simple title so freedom of incorporation created "tradeable goods in the shape of stocks and bonds." State judges especially were hard pressed to deal with an expanding market economy characterized by new forms of exchange. Statute law was designed primarily to allow initiative and enable action. (Ibid., pp. 32, 106, 231)

83. Ibid., p. 43.

84. Ibid., p. 57.

85. *Robinson v. Eldridge,* 10 S. and R. 142.

86. Under circumstances in which land was a commodity in a mass market, old English common-law forms for conveyancing were obstructionist. Moreover, land transactions were increasingly treated as contracts and "were subjected to many general doctrines of contract law." Land law, as with other parts of the law, was "greedily swallowed up" by contract. (Friedman, *History of American Law,* pp. 174, 244)

87. Friedman, *History of American Law,* p. 244.

88. Hurst, *Law and Social Order,* p. 58.

89. Ibid., p. 204.

90. Ibid., p. 237.

91. Horwitz has argued that eighteenth-century contract was "still dominated by a title theory of exchange and damages were set under equitable doctrines that ultimately were to be rejected by modern contract law." (Morton J. Horwitz, *The Transformation of American Law, 1780–1860* [Cambridge: Harvard University Press, [1977], p. 162.) The theory of equitable limitations on contractual obligation had as its purpose the assurance that a fair exchange had taken place. This was common in the eighteenth century, according to Horwitz, but was, in the nineteenth century, superseded by a will theory of contract that judged contractual obligation by the "convergence of individual desires." (Morton J. Horwitz, "The Historical Foundations of Modern Contract Law," *Harvard Law Review,* 87 [Mar., 1974], 923)

92. 4 S.C. Eq., 649 at 697. The parallel of *Butler v. Haskell* with British cases in chancery heard only a few years previous is also informative. In one of the common-sailor cases, *Taylour v. Rochfort,* the court remarked that "'if men who are free agents, will with open eyes, ratify unfair agreements, this court will not relieve fools,'" but at the same time "set aside the contract on the ground of the ignorance and poverty of the plaintiff." (Atiyah, *Freedom of Contract,* p. 174) The principle of inadequacy of consideration as evidence of misunderstanding or fraud was also heard in *Heathcote v. Paignton* (1787) a few years later. (Atiyah, p. 174)

93. As in Horwitz, "Historical Foundations," p. 924.

94. Lawrence M. Friedman, *Contract Law in America, A Social and Economic Case Study* (Madison: The University of Wisconsin Press, 1965), p. 21.

95. Horwitz, "Historical Foundations," p. 946.

96. Friedman, *History of American Law*, p. 245. When an expressed agreement existed, when stipulations to a transaction were stated, implied agreements running contrary to or substantially modifying these were not recognized. Implied promises, said Story, "only supply omissions and do not alter express stipulations." (Horwitz, "Historical Foundations," p. 952)

97. Friedman, *History of American Law*, p. 245.

98. Gilmore, *Death of Contract*, citing Holmes pp. 21, 33.

99. Ibid., pp. 44, 47, 56.

100. Gilmore has described the way in which American law under the leadership of Christopher Columbus Langdell, the first dean of the Harvard Law School in 1870, embraced a unitary theory of contract liability after the Civil War. Langdellians, says Gilmore, saw "legal truth" as a "species of scientific truth." By selectively using case law, particularly English precedents, Langdellians sought to reduce the great range of possible bargains to a few basic types. The process was deductive, and law itself came to be viewed as a "closed, logical system." (Gilmore, *Ages of American Law*, pp. 42–46, 62)

The propensity to abstraction, theory building, and a science of the law in the settling of disputes had preceded, by some years, the reform of American legal education. In his study of contract law in Wisconsin, Friedman argues that the period from 1836 to 1861 was the "age of abstraction." "Abstraction," he says, "was not simply a tool of the law; it also reflected the actual state of the economy." Land was often treated as a "colorless commodity" under circumstances in which geographical mobility was high, in which communities were but half-formed, and in which social patterns were uncertain. (Friedman, *Contract Law*, p. 186)

101. Ibid., p. 209.

102. Horwitz, *Transformation of American Law*, pp. 210, 259.

103. Friedman, *Contract Law*, pp. 101–117, 201.

104. Hurst, *Law and Social Order*, pp. 44–45, 67, 137, 197.

105. Friedman, *Contract Law*, pp. 107–117.

106. William W. Story, *A Treatise on the Law of Contracts not under Seal* (Boston: Charles C. Little and James Brown, 1844), p. 13.

107. 15 Mass. 227 at 229.

108. 26 A. 67 at 68.

109. *Craig v. Hobbs*, 44 Ind. 363 at 367.

110. See also *Seeright v. Fletcher* (1843), 6 Ind. (6 Blackf). 380 at 381–382; *May v. Johnson and Another*, 3 Ind. 449 at 450–451; *Rogers v. Place* (1868), 29 Ind. 577; *Craig v. Hobbs*, 44 Ind., 363.

111. 44 Ind. 363 at 366–367.

112. 61 U.S. 506 at 508–510.

113. Ibid., at p. 511.

114. *Suffern and Galloway v. Butler and Butler* (1867) 18 N.J. Eq. 220.

115 *Pennsylvania Railroad Co. v. Shay* (1876), 82 Pa. 198 at 203.

116. 7 Del. Cas. 22 at 26. See also, *Chicago, St. P., M. and O. Ry. Co. v. Belliwith* (1897), 83 F. 437 and *Bates v. Harte* (1899), 124 Ala. 427.

117. *Furst and Thomas v. Merritt* (1925), 190 N. C. 397 at 404. The illiterate person and the literate one are on an "equal footing" with respect to their obligations to read or have read to them the contract to which they are parties. (*Shores-Mueller Co. v. Lonning, et al* (1913), 140 N.W. 147; *Burns v. Spiker, et al.* (1921), 202 P. 370; *Erickson v. Knights of the Maccabees of the World* (1922), 203 P. 674;

Furst and Thomas v. A. D. Merritt, et al. (1925), 190 N.C. 397; *Standard Motor Company v. Samuel Peltzer* (1925), 147 Md. 509; *First National Bank of Sioux Center v. Ten Napel, et al.* (1924), 200 N.W. 405; *Gaetano Pimpinello, Respondent v. Swift and Co., Inc., Appellant* (1930), 253 N.Y. 159; *Sharpless-Hendler Ice Cream Co. v. Davis* (1931), 155 A. 247; *Ikovich v. Silver Bow Motor Car Co.* (1945), 157 P. 2d 785; *Richardson, et al. v. McGee* (1952), 246 N. W. 2d 572).

118. 4 S.C. Eq. 650 at 677.

119. Ibid., pp. 677–681.

120. Ibid., pp. 682–684.

121. Ibid., pp. 686–690.

122. 76 Ga. 322 at 323.

123. Ibid., at pp. 325–326.

124. So. 72, 73.

125. Ibid., p. 73.

126. Story, *Contracts Not Under Seal,* p. 106.

127. 29 Wis. 194 at 199.

128. Ibid.

129. Ibid., at pp. 196, 199.

130. Ibid., at p. 200.

131. 130 Mass. 259 at 260.

132. Ibid., at p. 261.

133. 50 N.Y. Sup. Ct. 241 at 244.

134. Ibid., at p. 245.

135. Ibid.

136. 83 F., at 439–440.

137. 202 P. 370 at 371; 285 S.W. 1015 at 1017.

138. James Willard Hurst, *Law and the Conditions of Freedom in the Nineteenth-Century United States* (Madison: University of Wisconsin Press, 1964), pp. 75–76.

139. Hurst, *Law and Social Order* pp. 238–239.

140. 31 Sup. Ct. Rep. 259 at 262.

141. Hurst, *Law and Social Order* pp. 230–231.

142. Friedman, *Contract Law in America,* pp. 98, 189–191; Lawrence M. Friedman and Stewart Macauley, "Contract Law and Contract Teaching: Past, Present, and Future," *Wisconsin Law Review,* (Fall 1967), 816–817.

143. E. Allen Farnsworth, "The Past of Promise: An Historical Introduction to Contract," *Columbia Law Review,* 69 (Apr., 1969), 598–599.

144. Friedman, *Contract Law,* pp. 189–191, 198.

145. *Wood v. Lucy, Lady Duff Gordon,* 222 N.Y. 88, as in Benjamin N. Cardozo, *The Nature of the Judicial Process* (New York: Yale University Press, 1921), p. 100.

146. *Clarence Rasmus v. A. O. Smith Corporation* 158 F. Supp. 70, at 85–86.

147. 172 A. 2d, 10 at 12.

148. Ibid.

149. Ibid., p. 13.

150. Ibid., p. 14.

151. 144 Ga. 502 at 503–504.

152. 190 N.C. 397 at 403.

153. 65 S.E. 92 at 93.

154. 111 P. 205 at 206–207.

155. 258 Mass., at 240 at 241, 243.

156. 185 S.W. 2d 617 at 622.

157. 65 S.E. 2d 400 at 401, 403.

158. Ibid., at p. 403.

159. *New York Life Insurance Co. v. Kwetkauskas* (1933) 63 F. 2d 890 at 891; *Albert I. Cohen v. Luigi Santoianni and others* (1953) 330 Mass. 187 at 192.

160. 216 P. 153 at 153, 154.

161. 190 N.C. 397 at 399.

162. Ibid., at p. 402.

163. Ibid., at p. 404.

164. Citing *Walsh v. Hall,* ibid., at p. 403

165. 159 S.W. 2d 769 at 770, 771.

166. Ibid., at p. 772.

167. Friedrich Kessler, "Contracts of Adhesion—Some Thoughts about Freedom of Contract," *Columbia Law Review,* 43 (July, 1943), 629–633.

168. Ibid., p. 636.

169. Ibid., pp. 639–641.

170. Stewart Macauley, "Private Legislation and the Duty to Read—Business Run by IBM Machine, the Law of Contracts and Credit Cards," *Vanderbilt Law Review,* 19 (Oct. 1966), 1051–1121.

171. Ibid., p. 1070.

172. Ibid., p. 1076.

173. Ibid., pp. 1076–1083.

174. Ibid., pp. 1061–1062.

175. Ibid., p. 1063.

176. Ibid.

177. Richard E. Speidel, "An Essay on the Reported Death and Continued Vitality of Contract," *Stanford Law Review* 27 (Apr., 1975), 1172–1173, 1176.

178. Ibid., pp. 1178, 1182.

179. Friedman and Macauley, *Contract Law and Contract Teaching,* pp. 808–809.

180. Uniform Laws Annotated, "Uniform Commercial Code" (St. Paul: West Publishing, 1976), pp. 12–13, 252–253.

181. Thomas M. Quinn, *Uniform Commercial Code Commentary and Law Digest* (Boston: Warren, Gorham, and Lamont, 1978), 1–102[A][1] 1–4.

182. *Uniform laws Annotated* "Uniform Commercial Code," p. 13.

183. Quinn, 1–102[A][2] 1–5.

184. *Uniform Laws Annotated* "Uniform Commercial Code," pp. 252–253.

185. Ronald A. Anderson, *Anderson on the Uniform Commercial Code,* third edition, Vol. 1 (Rochester, N.Y.: Lawyers Cooperative, 1981), pp. 39–40.

186. American Law Institute, *Restatement of the Law (Second),* "Contracts," 2d Vol. 2 (St. Paul: American Law Institute, 1981), p. 84.

187. Ibid., pp. 88–89.

188. Ibid., pp. 100–101.

189. Ibid., p. 109.

190. Ibid., pp. 109–110.

Bibliography

· · ·

Books and Journals

Ackerman, Bruce A. *Social Justice and the Liberal State*. New Haven: Yale University Press, 1980.

Adiseshiah, Malcolm S. "Literacy's Functionality to the Fight for Social Justice." *Convergence*, 8 (1975): 23–28.

Aggregate Value and Produce, and Number of Persons Employed in Mines, Agriculture, Commerce, Manufactures, etc., from the *Sixth Census of the United States*. Washington, D.C.: Blair and Rives, 1841. Reprinted as *American Industry and Manufactures in the Nineteenth Century*, Vol. 4. Elmsford, N.Y.: 1970.

American Jurisprudence, Vol. 25, 1966 ed. Rochester, N.Y.: The Lawyers Cooperative Publishing Co., 1966.

American Law Institute, *Restatement of the Law* (Second), "Contracts," 2d. Vol. 2. St. Paul, Minn.: American Law Institute Publishers, 1981.

Anderson, Ronald B. *Anderson on the Uniform Commercial Code*, Third edition, Vol. 1. Rochester, N.Y.: The Lawyers Cooperative Publishing Co., 1981.

Antieau, Chester James. "Natural Rights and the Founding Fathers—The Virginians." *Washington and Lee Law Review*, 17 (Spring, 1960): 43–79.

Atiyah, P. S. *The Rise and Fall of Freedom of Contract*. Oxford: Clarendon Press, 1979.

Aumann, Francis R. "The Influence of English and Civil Law Principles upon the American Legal System during the Critical Post-Revolutionary Period." *University of Cincinnati Law Review*, 12 (June, 1938): 289–317.

Avins, Alfred. "The Fifteenth Amendment and Literacy Tests: The Original

Intent." *Stanford Law Review,* 18 (Apr., 1966): 808–822.

Beale, J. H. "The Origins of the System of Recording Deeds in America." *Green Bag,* 19 (1907): 335–339.

Berlin, Isaiah. *Four Essays on Liberty.* New York: Oxford University Press, 1969.

Bird, Otto A. *The Ideal of Justice.* New York: Frederick A. Praeger, 1967.

Blackstone, William. *Commentaries on the Laws of England,* Vol. 2. Philadelphia: Robert Bell, 1771.

Bloch, Ernst. *Natural Law and Human Dignity.* Trans. Dennis J. Schmidt. Cambridge, Mass.: The MIT Press, 1986.

Blocker, H. Gene, and Elizabeth H. Smith (eds.). *John Rawls's Theory of Social Justice, An Introduction.* Athens: Ohio University Press, 1980.

Blume, William W. "Civil Procedure on the American Frontier, a Study of the Records of a Court of Common Pleas of the Northwest and Indian Territories (1796–1805)." *Michigan Law Review,* 56 (Dec., 1957): 161–224.

Boorstin, Daniel J. *The Mysterious Science of the Law.* Boston: Beacon Press, 1958.

Bormuth, John R. "Reading Literacy: Its Definitions and Assessment." *Toward a Literate Society.* Ed. John B. Carroll and Jeanne S. Chall. New York: McGraw-Hill, 1975.

Brantley, William H. "Law and Courts in Pioneer Alabama." *The Alabama Lawyer,* 6 (1945): 390–400.

Bridwell, R. Randall. "Theme v. Reality in American Legal History: A Commentary on Horwitz, *The Transformation of American Law, 1780–1860,* and on the Common Law in America." *Indiana Law Journal,* 53 (Spring, 1978): 449–496.

Brody, Burton F. "Anglo-Saxon Contract Law: A Social Analysis." *DePaul Law Review,* 19 (Autumn, 1969): 270–297.

Brown, Cynthia: "Literacy in 30 Hours: Paulo Friere's Process in Northeast Brazil." *Social Policy,* 5 (July–Aug., 1974): 25–32.

Brown, Elizabeth Gaspar. *British Statutes in American Law, 1776—1836.* Ann Arbor: The University of Michigan Law School, 1964.

Bryant, James R. "The Office of Master in Chancery: Early English Development." *American Bar Association Journal,* 40 (June, 1954): 498–533.

Burbules, Nicholas C., Brian T. Lord, and Ann L. Sherman. "Equity, Equal Opportunity and Education." *Educational Evaluation and Policy Analysis,* 4 (Summer, 1982): 169–187.

Caponigri, A. Robert. *A History of Western Philosophy, Philosophy from the Renaissance to the Romantic Age,* Vol. 3. Notre Dame, Ind.: Notre Dame University Press, 1963.

Cardoza, Benjamin N. *The Nature of the Judicial Process.* New York: Yale University Press, 1920.

Carroll, John B., and Jeanne S. Chall (eds.). *Toward a Literate Society.* New York: McGraw-Hill Book Co., 1975.

Childers, Thomas. *The Information Poor in America.* Metuchen, N.J.: The Scarecrow Press, 1975.

Church, Robert L., and Michael Sedlak. *Education in the United States, An Interpretive History.* New York: The Free Press, 1976.

Chute, Marchette. *The First Liberty, A History of the Right to Vote in America, 1619–1850.* New York: E. P. Dutton and Co., 1969.

Clanchy, M. T. *From Memory to Written Record, England 1066–1307.* Cambridge, Mass.: Harvard University Press, 1979.

Clifford, Geraldine Joncich. "Buch und Lesen: Historical Perspectives on Literacy and Schooling." *Review of Educational Research,* 54 (Winter, 1984): 472–500.

Cook-Gumperz, Jenny (ed.). *The Social Construction of Literacy,* Studies in International Sociolinguistics 3. Cambridge: Cambridge University Press, 1986.

Cook, Joseph. "Evil of Illiteracy." *Pennsylvania School Journal,* 31(1883): 433–434.

Cook, Wanda Dauksza. *Adult Literacy in Education in the United States.* Newark, Del: International Reading Association, 1977.

Cotton, Joseph P. (ed.). *The Constitutional Decisions of John Marshall,* Vol. 2. New York: G. P. Putnam's Sons, 1905.

County Court Records of Accomack-Northampton, Virginia, 1632–1640 in *American Legal Records,* Vol. 8. Ed. Susie M. Ames, Washington, D.C.: The American Historical Association, 1954.

Court Records of Kent County, Delaware, 1680–1705 in *American Legal Records,* Vol. 8. Ed. Leon de Valinger, Jr. Washington, D.C.: The American Historical Association, 1959.

Cowan, Thomas A. "Legislative Equity in Pennsylvania." *University of Pittsburgh Law Review,* 4 (Nov., 1937): 1–43.

Cremin, Lawrence A. *American Education: The National Experience, 1783–1876.* New York: Harper and Row, 1980.

Cremin, Lawrence A. "Reading, Writing, and Literacy." *Review of Education,* 1 (1975), 517–521.

Cremin, Lawrence (ed.). *The Republic and the School, Horace Mann on the Education of Free Men.* New York: Teachers College Press, 1957.

Cressey, David. "Levels of Illiteracy in England, 1530–1730." *The Historical Journal,* 20 (1977): 1–23.

Cressey, David. *Literacy and the Social Order: Reading and Writing in Tudor and Stuart England.* Cambridge: Cambridge University Press, 1980.

Curran, William J. "The Struggle for Equity in Massachusetts." *Boston University Law Review,* 31 (June, 1951): 269–296.

Dan-Cohen, Meir. *Rights, Persons, and Organizations, A Legal Theory for Bureaucratic Society.* Berkeley: University of California Press, 1986.

de Castell, Suzanne, Allan Luke, and Kieran Egan (eds.). *Literacy, Society, and Schooling, a Reader.* Cambridge: Cambridge University Press, 1986.

Dillon, George S. *Constructing Texts, Elements of a Theory of Composition and Style.* Bloomington: Indiana University Press, 1981.

Disch, Robert (ed.). *The Future of Literacy.* Englewood Cliffs, N.J.: Prentice-Hall, 1973.

Dworkin, Ronald. *Taking Rights Seriously.* Cambridge, Mass.: Harvard University Press, 1977.

Ely, James W. "American Independence and the Law: A Study of Post Revolutionary South Carolina Legislation." *Vanderbilt Law Review,* 26 (Oct., 1973): 939–977.

d'Entreves, A. P. *Natural Law, an Introduction to Legal Philosophy.* London: Hutchinson University Library, 1970.

Ervin, Sam J., Jr. "The Truth Respecting the Highly Praised and Constitutionally Devious Voting Right Act." *The Cumberland Law Review,* 12 (Spring, 1982): 261–281.

Farnsworth, E. Allen. "The Past of Promise: An Historical Introduction to Contract." *Columbia Law Review,* 69 (Apr., 1969): 576–607.

Flaherty, David H. (ed.). *Essays in the History of Early American Law.* Chapel Hill: University of North Carolina Press, 1969.

Flathman, Richard E. "Obligations, Ideals and Ability." *Political and Legal Obligations, Nomos XII.* New York: Atherton Press, 1970.

Fleming, Donald, and Bernard Bailyn (eds.). *Law in American History.* Boston: Little, Brown and Co., 1971.

Fried, Charles. *Contract as Promise, a Theory of Contractual Obligation.* Cambridge, Mass.: Harvard University Press, 1981.

Friedman, Lawrence M. *Contract Law in America, a Social and Economic Case Study.* Madison: The University of Wisconsin Press, 1965.

Friedman, Lawrence M. *A History of American Law.* New York: Simon and Schuster, 1973.

Friedman, Lawrence M., and Stewart Macauley. "Contract Law and Contract Teaching: Past, Present and Future." *Wisconsin Law Review* (Fall, 1967): 805–821.

Fuller, Lon L. *The Principles of Social Order.* Intro. by Kenneth I. Winston. Durham, N.C.: Duke University Press, 1981.

Furet, François, and Jacques Ozouf. *Lire et écrire.* Paris: Aux Editions De Minuit, 1977.

Gaus, Gerald F. "The Convergence of Rights and Utility: The Case of Rawls and Mill." *Ethics,* 92 (Oct., 1981): 57–72.

Gilmore, Grant. *The Ages of American Law.* New Haven: Yale University Press, 1977.

Gilmore, Grant. *The Death of Contract.* Columbus, Ohio: Ohio State University Press, 1974.

Gilmore, William J. "Elementary Literacy on the Eve of the Industrial Revolution: Trends in Rural New England, 1760–1830." *Proceedings of the American Antiquarian Society,* 92 (1982): 87–171.

Ginsberg, Eli, and Donald W. Bray. *The Uneducated.* New York: Columbia University Press, 1953.

Goody, Jack (ed.). *Literacy in Traditional Societies.* Cambridge: Cambridge University Press, 1968.

Goody, Jack, and Ian Watt. "The Consequences of Literacy." *Comparative Studies in Society and History,* 5 (1962): 304–345.

Goodman, Kenneth S. *Language and Literacy: The Selected Writings of Kenneth S. Goodman,* 2 Vols. Ed. Frederick V. Gollasch. Boston: Routledge and Kegan Paul, 1982.

Graff, Harvey J. *The Legacies of Literacy, Continuities and Contradictions in Western Culture and Society.* Bloomington: Indiana University Press, 1987.

Graff, Harvey J. (ed.). *Literacy and Social Development in the West.* Cambridge: Cambridge University Press, 1981.

Graff, Harvey J. *The Literacy Myth: Literacy and Social Structure in the Nineteenth-Century City.* New York: Academic Press, 1979.

Gray, William S. *The Teaching of Reading and Writing, An International Survey.* Paris: UNESCO, 1956.

Gulson, J. R. *The Philosophy of Proof in its Relation to the English Law of Judicial Evidence.* London: George Routledge and Sons Limited, 1905.

Halliday, M. A. K., and Rugaiya Hasan. *Cohesion in English.* London: Longman, 1976.

Hamilton, Alexander. "Federalist No. 59." *The Federalist Papers.* Intro. Clinton

Rossiter. New York: Mentor, 1961.

Hancock, Paul F., and Tredway, Lora L. "The Bailout Standard of the Voting Rights Act: An Incentive to End Discrimination." *The Urban Lawyer,* 17 (Summer, 1985): 379–425.

Hart, H. L. A. *The Concept of Law.* Oxford: Clarendon Press, 1961.

Haskins, George L. "The Beginnings of the Recording System in Massachusetts." *Boston University Law Review,* 21 (Jan., 1941): 281–304.

Haskins, George L. "A Problem in the Reception of the Common Law in the Colonial Period." *University of Pennsylvania Law Review,* 97 (1949): 842–853.

Havighurst, Harold C. *The Nature of Private Contract,* 1961 Rosenthal Lectures, Evanston, Ill.: Northwestern University Press, 1961.

Hill, George. "The Secret Ballot." *Yale Law Journal,* 1 (Oct., 1891): 26–29.

Hillerich, Robert L. "Towards an Assessable Definition of Literacy." *English Journal,* 65 (Feb., 1976): 50–55.

Hobbes, Thomas. *De Cive, or the Citizen.* Ed. and Intro. Sterling P. Lamprecht. New York: Appleton-Century-Crofts, 1949.

Hobbes, Thomas. *Leviathan, Parts I and II.* Intro. Herbert W. Schneider. Indianapolis: Bobbs-Merrill, 1958.

Horwitz, Morton J. "The Transformation in the Conception of Property in American Law, 1780–1860." *University of Chicago Law Review,* 40 (Winter, 1973): 248–290.

Horwitz, Morton J. "The Historical Foundations of Modern Contract Law." *Harvard Law Review,* 87 (Mar., 1974): 917–956.

Horwitz, Morton J. *The Transformation of American Law, 1780–1860.* Cambridge, Mass.: Harvard University Press, 1977.

Horwitz, Robert H. (ed.). *The Moral Foundations of the American Republic.* Charlottesville, Va.: University Press of Virginia, 1986.

Howe, Mark DeWolfe. "The Recording of Deeds in the Colony of Massachusetts Bay." *Boston University Law Review,* 28 (Jan., 1948): 1–6.

Hunter, Carman St. John, and David Harman. *Adult Literacy in the United States, A Report to the Ford Foundation.* New York: McGraw-Hill Co., 1979.

Hunting, Warren B. "The Obligation of Contracts Clause of the United States Constitution." *Johns Hopkins University Studies in Historical and Political Science,* Series 37, No. 4. Baltimore: The Johns Hopkins University Press, 1919.

Hurst, James Willard. *Law and the Conditions of Freedom in the Nineteenth-Century United States.* Madison: University of Wisconsin Press, 1964.

Hurst, James Willard. *Law and Social Order in the United States.* Ithaca, N.Y.: Cornell University Press, 1977.

Hyman, Harold M., and William M. Wiecek. *Equal Justice Under Law, Constitutional Development, 1835–1875.* New York: Harper and Row, 1982.

Isaacs, Nathan. "The Standardization of Contracts." *Yale Law Journal,* 27 (Nov., 1917): 34–48.

Isenberg, Irwin (ed.). *The Drive Against Illiteracy.* New York: H. W. Wilson Co., 1964.

Jeffries, Charles. *Illiteracy, A World Problem.* London: Frederick A. Praeger, 1967.

Jenkins, Iredell. *Social Order and the Limits of Law, A Theoretical Essay.* Princeton, N.J.: Princeton University Press, 1980.

Jenks, Edward. *The Book of English Law.* Ed. P. B. Fairest, 6th rev. ed. Athens:

The Ohio University Press, 1967.

Johansson, Egil. *The History of Literacy in Sweden in Comparison with Some Other Countries*. Educational Reports, Umea, No. 12. Umea: Umea University and Umea School of Education, 1977.

Jones, Alice Hanson. *American Colonial Wealth, Documents and Methods.* 3 vols. New York: Arno Press, 1978.

Jones, Alice Hanson. *Wealth of a Nation to Be by the American Colonies on the Eve of the Revolution*. New York: Columbia University Press, 1980.

Jones, William J. "Due Process and Slow Process in the Elizabethan Chancery." *The American Journal of Legal History,* 6 (Apr., 1962): 123–150.

Kaestle, Carl F. and Maris A. Vinovskis, *Education and Social Change in Nineteenth Century Massachusetts*. New York: Cambridge University Press, 1980.

Kaestle, Carl F. "The History of Literacy and the History of Readers." *Review of Research in Education*. Ed. Edmund S. Gordon, 12. Washington, D.C.: American Educational Research Association, 1985.

Kaestle, Carl F. *Pillars of the Republic*. New York: Hill and Wang, 1983.

Katz, Michael B. *The Irony of Early School Reform*. Boston: Beacon Press, 1968.

Keeton, George W. *The Norman Conquest and the Common Law*. London: Ernest Benn Ltd., 1966.

Kelsen, Hans. *General Theory of Law and State*. Cambridge, Mass.: Harvard University Press, 1946.

Kemp, J. *Ethical Naturalism: Hobbes and Hume*. London: Macmillan, 1970.

Kempin, Frederick G. *Legal History, Law and Social Change*. Englewood Cliffs, N.J.: Prentice-Hall, 1963.

Kessler, Friedrich. "Contracts of Adhesion—Some Thoughts About Freedom of Contract." *Columbia Law Review,* 43 (July, 1943): 629–642.

Kettner, James H. *The Development of American Citizenship, 1608–1870*. Chapel Hill: University of North Carolina Press, 1978.

Kimball, Spencer L. *Historical Introduction to the Legal System*. American Casebook Series. St. Paul: West Publishing Co., 1966.

Klare, George R. *How to Write Readable English*. London: Hutchinson, 1985.

Ladd, John. "Legal and Moral Obligation." *Political and Legal Obligation, Nomos XII*. New York: Atherton Press, 1970.

Lampert, Richard. "Norm-Making in Social Exchange: A Contract Law Model." *Law and Society Review,* 7 (Fall, 1972): 1–32.

Levine, Kenneth. *The Social Context of Literacy*. London: Routledge and Kegan Paul, 1986.

Lewis, Leon P. "The Development of a Common Law System in Connecticut." *Connecticut Bar Journal,* 27 (June, 1953): 419–427.

Liverant, Spencer R., and Walter H. Hitchler. "A History of Equity in Pennsylvania." *Dickenson Law Review,* 37 (1933): 157–183.

Llewellyn, Karl N. *Jurisprudence, Realism in Theory and Practice*. Chicago: University of Chicago Press, 1962.

Locke, John. "First Treatise on Government." In *Two Treatises on Government*. Ed. and Intro. Peter Laslett. Cambridge: Cambridge University Press, 1960.

Lockridge, Kenneth. *Literacy in Colonial New England*. New York: W. W. Norton and Co., 1974.

Lyon, Bryce. *A Constitutional and Legal History of Medieval England*. New York: Harper and Row, 1960.

Maccaulay, Stewart. "Private Legislation and the Duty to Read—Business Run by IBM Machine, the Law of Contracts and Credit Cards." *Vanderbilt Law Review,* 19 (Oct., 1966): 1051–1121.

MacCormick, Neil. *Legal Right and Social Democracy, Essays in Legal and Political Philosophy.* Oxford: Oxford University Press, 1982.

MacCormick, Neil and Ota Weinberger. *An Institutional Theory of Law.* Dordrecht, Holland: D. Reidel, 1986.

Main, G. L. "The Correction of Biases in Colonial American Probate Records." *Historical Methods Newsletter,* 8 (Dec., 1974): 10–28.

Maine, Henry Sumner. *Ancient Law, Its Connection with the Early History of Society and Its Relation to Modern Ideas.* New York: Henry Holt and Company, 1888.

Markham, Edward Lee. "The Reception of the Common Law of England in Texas and the Judicial Attitude Toward the Reception, 1840–1859." *Texas Law Review,* 29 (1951): 904–930.

Maynes, Mary Jo. *Schooling in Western Europe, A Social History.* Albany: State University of New York Press, 1985.

Mayo, A. D. "The Significance of Illiteracy in the United States." *Education* 19 (Sept., 1898): 30–36.

McClain, Charles J. "Legal Change and Class Interest: A Review Essay on Morton Horwitz's *The Transformation of American Law.*" *California Law Review* 68 (Mar., 1980): 382–397.

McClellan, James. *Joseph Story and the American Constitution, A Study in Political and Legal Thought.* Norman: University of Oklahoma Press, 1971.

McGowan, William. "Corporations Aim to Wipe Out Illiteracy." *Business and Society Review,* 44 (Winter, 1983): 37–40.

Mezirow, Jack, Gordon G. Darkenwald and Alan B. Knox. *Last Gamble on Education, Dynamics of Adult Basic Education.* Washington, D.C.: Adult Education Association of the United States of America, 1975.

Milsom, S. F. C. *Historical Foundations of Common Law.* London: Butterworths, 1969.

Monnet, Julien C. "The Latest Phase of Negro Disfranchisement." *Harvard Law Review,* 26 (Nov., 1912): 42–63.

Morgan, Edmund S. *The Challenge of the American Revolution.* New York: W. W. Norton and Co., 1976.

Nash, G. B. "Urban Wealth and Poverty in Pre-Revolutionary America." *Journal of Interdisciplinary History,* 6 (Spring, 1976): 545–584.

Nelson, William E. "The Eighteenth-Century Background of John Marshall's Constitutional Jurisprudence." *Michigan Law Review,* 76 (May, 1978): 893–960.

Nelson, William E. "The Reform of Common Law Pleading in Massachusetts, 1760–1830: Adjudication as a Prelude to Legislation." *University of Pennsylvania Law Review,* 122 (Nov., 1973): 97–136.

New York State Commissioner of Education. *Illiteracy in the State of New York.* Albany: New York State Education Department, 1906.

Newmyer, Kent. "The Charles River Bridge Case and the Crisis of Republicanism." *American Journal of Legal History,* 17 (July, 1973): 232–245.

North Carolina Higher Court Records, 1670–1696. Ed. Nattie Erma Edwards Parker. Raleigh, N.C.: State Department of Archives and History, 1968.

Oleson, Alexandra, and Sanborn S. Brown (eds.). *The Pursuit of Knowledge in the Early American Republic.* Baltimore: Johns Hopkins University Press, 1976.

Olson, David R. *Review of Toward a Literate Society, Proceedings of the National Academy of Education.* Vol. 2. Stanford, Calif.: National Academy of Education, 1975.

O'Sullivan, Richard. "The Concept of Man in the Common Law." *The Alabama Lawyer* 8 (July, 1955): 268–284.

Oxenham, John. *Literacy, Writing, Reading and Social Organization.* London: Routledge and Kegan Paul, 1980.

Payne, John C. "The English Theory of Conveyances Prior to the Land Registration Act." *Alabama Law Review,* 7 (Spring, 1955): 227–270.

Payne, John C. "The Theory of Conveyances of Law in Alabama." *Alabama Law Review,* 8 (Fall, 1955): 10–36.

Pease, Theodore Calvin. "The Laws of the Northwest Territory, 1788–1800." In *Law Series,* Vol. 1, *Collections of the Illinois State Historical Society,* Vol. 17. Springfield: Illinois State Historical Library, 1925.

Pocock, J. G. A. *Politics, Language and Time, Essays on Political Thought and History.* New York: Atheneum, 1977.

Porter, Kirk A. *A History of Suffrage in the United States.* Chicago: University of Chicago Press, 1981.

Pound, Roscoe. "The End of Law as Developed in Juristic Thought." *Harvard Law Review,* 27 (May, 1914): 603—628.

Pound, Roscoe. *The Formative Era of American Law.* Boston: Little, Brown and Co., 1928.

Prall, Stuart E. "The Development of Equity in Tudor England." *The American Journal of Legal History,* 8 (1964): 1–19.

Pulsifer, David (ed.). *Records of the Colony of New Plymouth in New England, Deeds, and Book of Indian Records for Their Lands (1620–1651),* Vol. I. Boston: William White, 1861.

Quinn, Thomas M. *Uniform Commercial Code Commentary and Law Digest.* Boston: Warren, Gorham and Lamont, 1978.

Radin, Max. "Contract Obligation and the Human Will." *Columbia Law Review,* 43 (July, 1943): 575–585.

Raphael, D. D. *Justice and Liberty.* London: The Athlone Press, 1980.

Rawls, John. "Justice as Fairness." *The Philosophical Review,* 67 (1958): 164–194.

Rawls, John. "Symposium, Justice as Fairness." *The Journal of Philosophy,* 54 (Oct., 1957): 653–670.

Rawls, John. *A Theory of Justice.* Cambridge, Mass.: Harvard University Press, 1971.

Reasons, Charles E., and Robert M. Rich (eds.). *The Sociology of Law: A Conflict Perspective.* Toronto: Butterworths, 1978.

Rastatter, Edward H. "Nineteenth Century Public Land Policy: The Case for the Speculator." In David C. Klingaman and Richard K. Vedder (eds.). *Essays in Nineteenth Century Economic History, the Old North West.* Athens: The Ohio University Press, 1975.

Records of the Suffolk County Court, 1671–1680. Parts I and II, in *Publications of the Colonial Society of Massachusetts,* Vols. 29, 30. Boston: Colonial Society of Massachusetts, 1933.

Rehbinder, Manfred. "Status, Contract, and the Welfare State." *Stanford Law Review,* 23 (May, 1971): 941–955.

Resnick, Daniel P., and Lauren B. Resnick. "The Nature of Literacy: An Historical Exploration." *Harvard Educational Review,* 47 (Aug., 1977): 370–385.

Rosen, Paul L. *The Supreme Court and Social Science*. Champaign: University of Illinois, 1973.

Ross, Alf. *On Law and Justice*. Berkeley: University of California Press, 1959.

Salmon, Marylynn. *Women and the Law of Property in Early America*. Chapel Hill: University of North Carolina Press, 1986.

Sandel, Michael J. *Liberalism and the Limits of Justice*. Cambridge: Cambridge University Press, 1982.

Schofield, R. S. "Dimensions of Illiteracy, 1750–1850." *Explorations in Economic History*, 10 (1973): 437–454.

Schultz, Stanley K. *The Culture Factory: Boston Public Schools, 1789–1860*. New York: Oxford University Press, 1973.

Scribner, Sylvia, and Michael Cole. *The Psychology of Literacy*. Cambridge, Mass.: Harvard University Press, 1981.

Seliger, M. *The Liberal Politics of John Locke*. New York: Frederick A. Praeger, 1968.

Seitz, Victoria. "Literacy and the School Child: Some Perspectives from an Educated Country." *Educational Evaluation and Policy Analysis,* 3 (Nov.–Dec., 1981): 15–23.

"Separate-but-Equal: A Study of the Career of a Constitutional Concept." *Race Relations Law Reporter,* 1 (1956): 283—292.

Shklar, Judith N. *Legalism*. Cambridge, Mass.: Harvard University Press, 1964.

Simpson, A. W. B. *A History of the Common Law of Contract*. Oxford: Clarendon Press, 1975.

Simpson, A. W. B. "The Horwitz Thesis and the History of Contracts." *University of Chicago Law Review* 41 (Spring, 1979): 533–601.

Sisson, Charles. "Marks as Signatures." *The Library, a Quarterly Review of Bibliography,* 9, 4th ser. (June, 1928): 1–25.

Skinner, Quentin. "The Idea of Negative Liberty: Philosophical and Historical Perspectives." *Psychology in History, Essays on the Historiography of Philosophy.* Ed. Richard Rorty, J. B. Schneewind, and Quentin Skinner. Cambridge: Cambridge University Press, 1984.

Smith, D. S. "Underregistration and Bias in Probate Records: An Analysis of Data from Eighteenth Century Hingham, Massachusetts." *William and Mary Quarterly,* 32 (Jan., 1975): 100–110.

Smith, E. Irving. "The Legal Aspect of the Southern Question." *Harvard Law Review,* 2 (Mar., 1889): 358–376.

Smith, Herbert Knox. "The Failure of Municipal Government." *Yale Law Journal,* 5 (Oct., 1895): 26–29.

Smith, Joseph H., and Leo Herschkowitz. "Courts of Equity in the Province of New York: The Cosby Controversy, 1732–1736." *American Journal of Legal History,* 16 (Jan., 1972): 1–50.

Soltow, Lee, and Edward Stevens. *The Rise of Literacy and the Common School in the United States, a Socioeconomic Analysis to 1870*. Chicago and London: The University of Chicago Press, 1981.

Speidel, Richard E. "An Essay on the Reported Death and Continued Vitality of Contract." *Stanford Law Review,* 27 (Apr., 1975): 1161–1183.

Stein, Nancy L. (ed.). *Literacy in American Schools, Learning to Read and Write.* Chicago: University of Chicago Press, 1986.

Stevens, Edward. "Books and Wealth on the Frontier: Athens County and

Washington County, Ohio, 1790–1859." *Social Science History,* 5 (Fall, 1981): 417–443.

Stevens, Edward. "Illiterate Americans and Nineteenth-Century Courts: The Meanings of Literacy." In Daniel P. Resnick (ed.), *Literacy in Historical Perspective.* Washington, D.C.: Library of Congress, 1983.

Stoebuck, William B. "Reception of English Common Law in the American Colonies." *William and Mary Law Review,* 10 (Winter, 1968): 393–426.

Stone, Lawrence. "Literacy and Education in England, 1640–1900." *Past and Present,* 41 (Feb., 1969): 69–193.

Story, William W. *A Treatise on the Law of Contracts Not Under Seal.* Boston: Charles C. Little and James Brown, 1844.

Strike, Kenneth A. *Educational Policy and the Just Society.* Champaign: University of Illinois Press, 1982.

Thayer, James Bradley. *A Preliminary Treatise on Evidence at the Common Law.* Boston: Little, Brown and Co., 1898.

Treadway, Francis W. "Needed Reforms in Municipal Charters and Government." *Yale Law Journal,* 2 (Dec., 1892): 60–68.

Tully, James. *A Discourse on Property, John Locke and His Adversaries.* Cambridge: Cambridge University Press, 1980.

UNESCO. *World Illiteracy at Mid-Century, a Statistical Study.* Paris: The UNESCO Press, 1957.

UNESCO. *The Experimental World Literacy Programme: A Critical Assessment.* Paris: UNDP: The UNESCO Press, 1976.

Uniform Laws Annotated. "Uniform Commercial Code." St. Paul, Minn.: West Publishing Co., 1976.

The University of the State of New York, the State Education Department, Division of Educational Testing. *Literacy Testing and the Issuance of Certificates of Literacy.* Albany, 1960.

Vinogradoff, Paul (ed.). *Oxford Studies in Social and Legal History.* Oxford: Clarendon Press, 1914.

Warrender, Howard. *The Political Philosophy of Hobbes, His Theory of Obligation.* Oxford: Clarendon Press, 1957.

Werdegar, Kathryn M. "The Constitutionality of Federal Legislation to Abolish Literacy Tests: Civil Rights Commission's 1961 Report on Voting." *The George Washington Law Review,* 30 (Apr., 1962), 723–743.

West, E. G. "Literacy and the Industrial Revolution." *Economic History Review,* 31 (1978): 369–383.

Williamson, Chilton. *American Suffrage, From Property to Democracy, 1760–1860.* Princeton, N.J.: Princeton University Press, 1960.

Wolff, Robert Paul (ed.). *The Rule of Law.* New York: Simon and Schuster, 1971.

Wood, Gordon S. *The Creation of the American Republic, 1776–1787.* New York: W. W. Norton and Co., 1972.

Wrightson, Keith. "Two Concepts of Order; Justices, Constables and Jurymen in Seventeenth-Century England." In John Brewer and John Styles (eds.). *An Ungovernable People, the English and Their Laws in the Seventeenth and Eighteenth Centuries.* London: Hutchinson and Co., 1980.

Zachos, J. C. "An Address to the Friends of Education, Especially Among the Illiterate Classes." New York, Aug. 1, 1891.

Zuckerman, George D. "A Consideration of the History and Present Status of Section 2 of the Fourteenth Amendment." *Fordham Law Review,* 30 (1961): 93–135.

Documents, Manuscripts, and Unpublished Materials

The Adjutant General's Office, Record Group 407, File Box No. 805, 350.5 (7-31-18 to 6-27-18). *Memorandum for the Adjutant General of the Army, June 27, 1918.* National Archives, Washington, D.C.

Bromage, Arthur W. "The Political Implications of Illiteracy." Ph.D. thesis, Harvard University, 1928.

Civil Rights Act of 1957. 71 *U. S. Statutes at Large,* 638. *Collections of the New Jersey Historical Society,* "Records of the Town of Newark, New Jersey." Vol. 6. Newark: New Jersey Historical Society, 1864.

Commission on Education, House Committee on Education. *Hearings.* H. R. 6490, Sixty-fifth Congress, Second Session, Mar. 9, 1981. Washington, D.C.: G.P.O., 1918.

Committee on Education and Labor. *Hearings* on H. R. 10143 and H. R. 10191, Eighty-seventh Congress, Second Session, Mar. 14, 15, 16, 19 in Washington, D.C., and Feb. 23, 1962, Morehead, Kentucky. Washington, D.C. : G.P.O., 1962.

Committee on the Judiciary: Subcommittee on Constitutional Rights. *Hearings, Literacy Tests and Voter Requirements in Federal and State Elections.* United States Senate, Eighty-seventh Congress, Second Session on Senate Bills 480, 2750, 2979.

Congressional Record, 108, pt. 6, Eighty-seventh Congress, Second Session. April 23–May 9.

Department of Commerce. Bureau of Census. *Thirteenth Census of the United States (1910), Abstract.* Vol. 2. Washington, D.C.: G.P.O., 1933.

Department of Commerce. Bureau of Census. *Current Population Reports, "Population Characteristics."* Feb. 4, 1960. Series P. 20, No. 99. Washington, D.C.: G.P.O., 1960.

Eastern State Penitentiary, Pennsylvania. *Tenth Annual Report.* Philadelphia, 1839.

Halsbury's Statutes of England, Vol. 7, 1969 ed. London: Butterworths, 1969.

House Committee on Education. *Hearings.* H. R. 15402, Sixty-fifth Congress, Third Session, Feb. 14, 15, 1919. Washington, D.C.: G.P.O., 1919.

Kent County, Delaware. *Deeds,* 1780–1900.

Kent County, Delaware. *Mortgages,* 1860–1900.

Kent County, Delaware. *Probate Records,* 1780–1900.

Secretary of State. *Digest of Accounts of Manufacturing Establishments in the United States and of Their Manufactures.* Washington, D.C.: Gales and Seaton, 1823. Reprinted as *American Industry and Manufactures in the Nineteenth Century.* Vol. 3. Elmsford, N.Y.: Maxwell Reprint Co., 1970.

State of Delaware. *Laws of the State of Delaware,* Vols. 1, 4, 5, 7, 16. Wilmington: various printers, 1816–1879.

State of Ohio. *Acts of the State of Ohio,* Vols. 1, 3, 8, 17, 18, 24, 26, 29, 31, 34, 36. Columbus: various printers, 1803–1836.

State of Ohio. *General and Local Laws,* Vol. 80. Columbus: C. J. Brand and Co., 1833.

The Statutes of Pennsylvania from 1682 to 1801, Vol. 2. Compiled by James T. Mitchell and Henry Flanders. Clarence M. Busch, 1896.

United States Census of 1850. *The Seventh Census of the United States.* Washington, D.C.: Robert Armstrong, 1853.

United States Census of 1860. *Manufactures of the United States in 1860;*

Agriculture of the United States in 1860. Washington, D.C.: G.P.O., 1864.

United States Code Service, Vols. 2, 4, No. 1864, 28, No. 1865, 41, No. 1973b.

United States Commission on Civil Rights (1961). *Voting,* Book I. Washington, D.C.: G.P.O., 1961.

United States Commission on Civil Rights (1963). *Report.* Washington, D.C.: G.P.O., 1963.

United States Supreme Court. *Records and Briefs,* Vols. 238, 360.

Washington County, Ohio. *Deeds,* 1790–1900.

Washington County, Ohio. *Mortgages,* 1860–1900.

Washington County, Ohio. *Probate Records,* 1790–1900.

Washington County, Ohio. *The Records of the Court of Common Pleas,* 1793–1860.

Table of Cases Cited

. . .

Guthrie et al. v. Price et al., 23 Ark. 396 (1861)

Harrison v. Harrison, 32 Eng. Rep., Chanc 12, 324 (8 Ves. Jun. 184) [1803]

Thomas Hemphill et al. v. James Hemphill et al., 13 N. C. 251 (1830)

Holden v. Hardy, Nos. 1 and 2, 169 U. S. 366 (1898)

Wiley B. Horton and another v. Alexander Johnson and Wife, 18 Ga. 396 (1855)

Hunt v. Campbell, 169 P. 596 (1918)

Huston v. Anderson, 78 P. 626 (1904)

Ikovich v. Silver Bow Motor Car Co., 157 P. 2d 785 (1945)

In re Allison, 22 P. 820 (1889)

In re Beck's Estate, 140 P. 340 (1914)

In re Cummins' Estate, 259 N. W. 894 (1935)

In re Gluckman's Will, 101 A. 295 (1917)

In re Kelly's Estate, 160 A. 454 (1932)

In the Matter of Adam A. Cross for a Writ of Certiori to James J. Martin and Others as Police Commissioners of the City of New York, 85 N.Y. Sup. Ct. 343 (1895)

In the Matter of Succession of Mary Carroll, Wife of J. M.Shafer, 28 La. Ann. 388 (1876)

In the Matter of the Will of Cornelius, 14 Ark. 675 (1854)

Jackson, ex dem. Van Dusen and Others v. Van Dusen, 5 John 144 (1809)

Albert Johnson v. The State, 21 Texas Ct. App. 368 (1886)

Johnson v. Todd, 5 Beav. 597 (49 Eng. Rep. 710) [1843]

Jones v. Morley, 2 Salk 677 (1696–97)

Kinney et al. v. Ensmenger, 6 So. 72 (1889)

The Lafayette Plankroad Co. v. New Albany and Salem Railroad Co., 13 Ind. 89 (1859)

Languein v. Olson, 227 N. W. 369 (1929)

Lassiter v. Northhampton County Board of Elections, 360 U. S. 45 (1959)

Harris Levy v. Franklin Savings Bank, 117 Mass. 448 (1874)

Lewis v. Mutual Reserve Fund Loan Association, 27 So. 649 (1900)

Liddell et ux. v. Lee, 159 S. W. 2d 769 (1942)

Lord Ex ux v. Lord and Others, 58 N. H. 7 (1876)

Louisville, New Orleans and Texas Ry. Co. v. Mississippi, 133 U.S. 587 (1890)

Gong Gong Lum et al. v. Rice et al., 275 U. S. 78 (1927)

George B. Lyles v. The State 41 Tex. 172 (1874)

Lyons v. Van Riper and Others, 26 N. J. Eq. 337 (1875)

Mann et al., v. Cornish, 185 F. 2d 423 (1950)

Marilla et al., v. Ratterman et al., 273 S. W. 69 (1925)

Martin Luther v. Luther M. Borden and Rachel Luther v. Luther M. Borden et al., 48 U. S. 1 (1849)

May v. Johnson and Another, 3 Ind. Rev. Ed. 450 (1852)

Mayon v. Jahncke Service Inc. et al., 177 So. 399 (1937)

J. McCampbell v. The State, 9 Texas Ct. of App. 124 (1880)

McLaurin v. Oklahoma State Regents for Higher Education et al., 339 U. S. 637 (1950)

McNac v. Chapman, 223 P. 350 (1924)

McNac v. Kinch, 238 P. 424 (1925)

Meazels v. Martin, 93 Ky. 50 (1892)

M'Millan v. M'Neill, 17 U. S. 209 (1819)

Miller v. Cline, 25 Ohio App. 2d 492 (1916)
John Lloyd Mills and Wife, Rosella Mills v. W. H. Lynch, 259 N. C. 359 (1963)
Minor v. Happersett, 88 U. S. 162 (1874)
Missouri ex rel. Gaines v. Canada, Registrar of the University of Missouri et al., 305 U. S. 337 (1938); Petition for writ of certiori granted, 580; rehearing denied, 676
Modern Security Co. v. Lockett et al., 143 A. 511 (1928)
Montgomery v. Oldham, 42 N. E. 474 (1895)
Montgomery v. Perkins, 59 Ky. 448 (1859)
William E. Montoya v. People of the State of Colorado, 345 P. 2d 1062 (1959)
Morrow v. Person et al., 259 S. W. 2d 665 (1953)
The National Exchange Bank of Auburn v. John Veneman, 50 N. Y. Sup. Ct. 241 (1887)
Navar v. First National Bank of Breckenridge, 254 S. W. 126 (1923)
New Jersey v. Wilson, 11 U. S. 164 (1812)
New York Life Ins. Co. v. Kwetkauskas, 63 F. 2d 890 (1933)
Norris v. Alabama, 294 U. S. 579 (1935)
Peter Elias Nusz v. Mary Grove, 27 Md. 391 (1867)
Ogden v. Saunders, 25 U. S. 213 (1827)
Olson v. Goetz, 15 Pa. D and C 261 (1930)
Palto v. Gavenas, 166 P. 1156 (1917)
The People of the State of California v. Ronald Dale Jones, 25 C. A. 3d 776 (1972)
The People of the State of New York ex rel. William M. Chadbourne v. John R. Voorhis et al., Constituting the Board of Elections of the City of New York, 141 N. E. 907 (1923)
Pennsylvania Railroad Co. v. Shay, 82 Pa. 198 (1876)
Pepe et al. v. Caputo 97 N. E. 2d 260 (1951)
Louis Pilié v. Henry B. Kenner, 2 Rob. 95 (1842)
Gaetano Pimpinello v. Swift and Co., Inc., 253 N. Y. 159 (1930)
Plessy v. Ferguson, 163 U. S. 537 (1896)
The Proprietors of the Charles River Bridge v. The Proprietors of the Warren Bridge Co., 26 U. S. 420 (1837)
Clarence Rasmus v. A. O. Smith Corporation, 158 F. Supp. 70 (1958)
Richardson v. McGee, 246 N. W. 2d 572 (1952)
Sarah C. Roberts v. The City of Boston, 59 Mass. 198 (1849)
Roberts v. City of Boston, 59 Mass. 198 (1849)
Robertson v. Panlos et al., 65 S. E. 2d 400 (1951)
Robinson v. Eldridge, 10 S and R 140 (1823)
Rogers v. Place, 29 Ind. 577 (1868)
Elizabeth Rutgers v. Joshua Waddington, Aug. 27, 1784, Mayor's Court of New York City; in *Select Cases of the Mayor's Court of New York City, 1674–1784*, ed. Richard B. Morris, *American Legal Records* II (Wash.: American Historical Assoc., 1935), 302–327
A. D. Scifres v. State of Arkansas, 308 S. W. 2d 815 (1958)
Seeright v. Fletcher, 6 Blackf. 381 (1843)
Gertrudes Flores y Seguin v. Samuel A. Maverick, 24 Tex. 526 (1859)
Francis Seldon V. Lawrence Myers, Philip Pike, Walter Lenox and James C. McGuire, 61 U. S. 506 (1857)
Sharpless-Hendler Ice Cream Co. v. Davis, 155 A. 247 (1931)
Shaw v. Burnham, 191 So. 484 (1939)

Shores-Mueller Co. v. Lonning et al., 140 N. W. 147 (1913)
Shulter's Case, 12 Co. Rep. 90 (77 Eng. Rep. 1366) [1655]
Simmonds v. Eyrich et al., 95 N. E. 2d 595 (1950)
Sioux City and Pacific Railway Co. v. Stout, 84 U. S. 657 (1873)
Slaughterhouse Cases, 16 U. S. 36 (1873)
Spicer v. The State, 65 So. 972 (1914)
Spitze v. Baltimore and Ohio Railroad Co., 23 A. 307 (1892)
Standard Motor Company v. Samuel Peltzer, 147 Md. 509 (1925)
Staples v. Bedford Loan and Deposit Bank, 33 S. W. 403 (1895)
State v. Fowler, 87 P. 731 (1907)
State v. Greenland, 100 N. W. 341 (1904)
State v. Pickett, 73 N. W. 346 (1897)
State ex rel. v. Miller, 87 O. S. 12 (1912)
State ex re. Bateman v. Bode, 55 O. St. 224
State ex rel. Melvin v. Sweeney, 94 N. E. 2d 785 (1950)
State ex rel. Weinberger, a Taxpayer v. Daniel T. Miller, et al., 87 O. S. 12 (1912)
State Insurance Co. v. Gray, 25 P. 197 (1890)
State of Louisiana v. Albert Push, 23 La. Ann. 14 (1871)
State of Louisiana v. Andrew Louis, 28 La. Ann. 84 (1876)
State of Louisiana v. Jasper Brazile, 86 So. 2d 208 (1956)
State of Louisiana v. Jean Gay Fils et al., 25 La. Ann. 472 (1873)
State of South Carolina v. Nicholas de B. Katzenbach, 86 S. Ct. 803 (1966)
Stone v. Smith et al., Registrars of Voters, 34 N. E. 521 (1893)
Sturgis v. Crowninshield, 17 S. Ct. 122 (1819)
Suffern and Galloway v. Butler and Bulter, 18 N. J. Eq. 220 (1867)
Summers v. Alexander, 120 P. 601 (1911)
Sun Oil Co. v. Rhodes et. ux., 71 S. W. 2d 413 (1934)
Swint v. Carr, 76 Ga. 322 (1885)
Terry v. Johnson, 109 Ky. 589 (1901)
Thoroughgood's Case, 2 Co. Rep. 5b (1581)
The Town of Trinidad v. Simpson, 5 Colo. 65 (1879)
Sigfroid Trambly v. Hubert Ricard and Another, 130 Mass. 259 (1880)
Trevett v. Weeden, Superior Court, County of Newport (1786); in James M.
    Varnum, *The Case, Trevett Against Weeden, On Information and Complaint
    for Refusing Paper Bills in Payment for Butcher's Meat, in Market, at Par for
    Specie* (Providence, 1787)
The Trustees of Dartmouth College v. Woodward, 17 U. S. 518 (1819)
United States v. Anthony T. Santos, Anthony C. Cepeda, Tito Naputi, David
    Lujan, Vincente M. Santos, Pedro Q. Salas, Juan Q. Salas, 588 F. 2d 1300
    (1979)
United States v. Eduardo Jaime Rouco, 765 F. 2d 983 (1985)
United States v. George Daniel Gates, 557 F. 2d 1086 (1977)
United States v. Martin Henderson, 298 F. 2d 522 (1962)
United States v. Miller et al., 107 F. 913 (D. Ind.) [1901]
Vanhorne's Lessee v. Dorrance, 2 U. S. 304 (1795)
John P. VanNess and Marcia, His wife v. Perez Pacard, 27 U. S. 137 (1829)
Vanwinkle v. Crabtree, 55 P. 831 (1899)
Virginia v. Rives, 100 U. S. 313 (1880)
Walker v. Ebert, 29 Wis. 194 (1871)
Louis Weiner v. Chase National Bank of the City of New York, 142 Misc. 124
    (1931)

Henry White v. The State, 52 Miss. 216 (1876)
Wilkey's Appeal, 108 Pa. 567 (1885)
Katirina Wilkisius v. Elizabeth Sheehan and others, 258 Mass. 240 (1926)
Willard and another v. Pinard et ux., 26 A. 67 (1892)
Wood v. Lucy, Lady Duff Gordon, 118 N. E. 214 (1917)
James Wright v. The State, 12 Texas Ct., App. 163 (1882)
Yick Wo v. Hopkins, Sheriff, 118 U. S. 356 (1886)
Zobes v. International Paper Co., 101 A. 24 (1917)

Index

. . .